VISUAL QUICKSTART GUIDE

# NetObjects Fusion 2

FOR WINDOWS AND MACINTOSH

**Gillian Hall**
**Mark Wheeler**

Peachpit Press

Visual QuickStart Guide

**NetObjects Fusion 2 for Windows and Macintosh**

Gillian Hall and Mark Wheeler

**Peachpit Press**
1249 Eighth Street
Berkeley, CA 94710
510/524.2178
510/524.2111

Find us on the World Wide Web at http://www.peachpit.com

Peachpit Press is a division of Addison Wesley Longman



Cover design: The Visual Group
Production: Gillian Hall / Big Tent Media Labs



ISBN 0-201-69658-4

9 8 7 6 5 4 3 2 1

Printed and bound in the United States of America.

# Dedication

To Jordi and Mackenzie — G.R.H.

For Peggy – A spirit tempered with age has never flown with such carefree abandon. 1910-1997 — M.W.

# About the Authors

Gillian Hall lives in Phoenix, Arizona with her husband, baby daughter, two monster dogs, and outnumbered cat. While her passion is page layout and design on the Macintosh (of course), she also teaches programming courses at Arizona State University. This is her eighth book on using computer software.

Mark Wheeler has been developing information systems since 1984 in a variety of industries. After completing graduate school and joining corporate America as a Systems Analyst he has found himself increasingly awed at the creative energy being expended to develop more effective methods for accessing information. Mark has had several books on PC-based operating systems published, and also writes fiction. He teaches Information Theory courses in Portland, Oregon, where he lives with his supportive wife, four brilliant children, and too many animals.

# Table of Contents

# Introduction

## The Web Scene

If we were to take everything that's been printed in the past two or three years about the World Wide Web and stack it all in a pile ... we wouldn't be a lot smarter than we are right now. The Internet, and specifically the World Wide Web, have exploded on the scene like nothing we've ever seen. If you pick up a newspaper, read the label from a can of soup, or watch a TV program, chances are you're hearing references to Web pages and Web sites.

There's an entire subculture being built around this new forum. A language has emerged and is flourishing. An etiquette system has surfaced, and with it a fairly complex set of expected behaviors. It's not a new world, but it's an interesting twist on the old. What will change? How about, for a start, magazine subscriptions, catalog product purchasing, information delivery (librarian on your desk), banking, product distribution, the list is almost endless. And it's all about a page: A Web page.



### Web Pages

A Web page is a special kind of text document that has some specific characteristics. It is created using a special language that allows just about anyone to view it using most any kind of computer that has access to the Internet. Web pages have a beginning (a head), an ending (a foot), and some content in the middle. When Web pages are placed on a computer that is connected to the Internet, they become available for viewing by anyone in the world who has access to the Internet.

## Web Sites

A Web site is basically a collection of related Web pages that are connected together in an organized (hopefully) way. For example, a company may have a home page where you "enter" its Web site. The home page is connected to other Web pages that provide specific information about the company, its products, employees, and so on. All of this company's Web pages together make up its Web site.



## Web Browsers

Web pages are viewed using a software tool called a Web browser. Web browsers understand the special language in which Web pages are written and are able to display Web pages the way the developers of those pages intended. Two common Web browsers (but certainly not the only ones) are Netscape's Navigator and Microsoft's Explorer (**Figure i.1**). Both of these tools allow you to view Web pages and "browse" through Web sites.

**Figure i.1**
*Netscape Navigator and Microsoft Internet Explorer are two popular Web browsers.*

When you start developing Web sites with Fusion, you'll want to install a Web browser on your computer. But if you're reading this book, chances are you've already gotten that far! In this book, we'll use Netscape Navigator when a Web browser is called for.

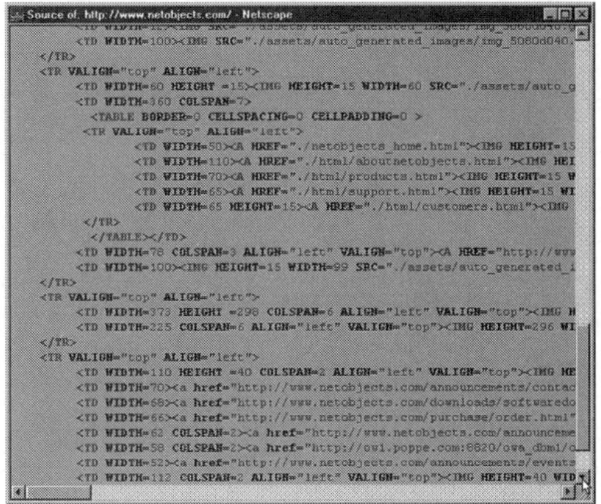


**Figure i.2**
*The HTML source code of a Web page*

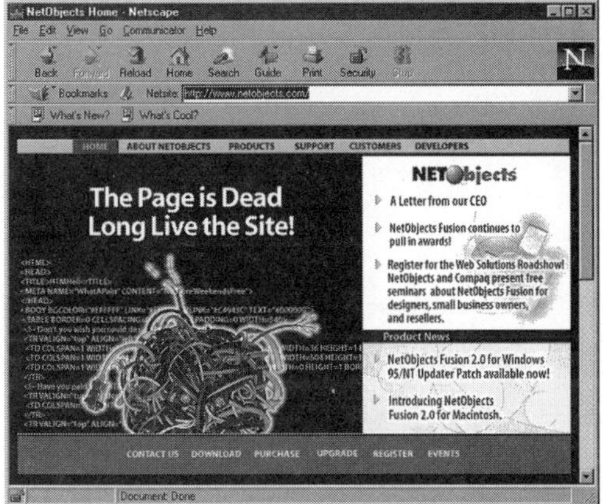


**Figure i.3**
*The Web page described by the HTML in Figure i.2*

# Web Development

Web development refers to creating Web pages and sites. Web authoring has gone through an amazing evolution in just a few short years from the dark ages of basic text editors, to Fusion—the renaissance.

## The Dark Ages

Early Web page development simply assumed you were conversant in hypertext markup language (HTML). You had a text editor of some kind, and you created an HTML text document. Your HTML code would look something like the mess in **Figure i.2**.

HTML is a simple scripting language that uses "tags" and simple syntax to control the appearance of text and images when the document is viewed with a Web browser. The browser reads HTML tags and displays the contents of the document in accordance with those tag commands, as shown in **Figure i.3**.

Creating Web pages by writing HTML using a basic text editor represents the first generation of Web development tools—or "the dark ages."

## The Bronze Age

The next generation of tools began providing a WYSIWYG (What You See Is What You Get) environment for the development of Web pages. Instead of writing your own HTML code, you were now able to "show" (with some notable limitations) the tool what you wanted your Web page to look like. Then the program generated HTML code that would create a Web page matching your specs.

Microsoft's FrontPage and Adobe's PageMill are good examples of these tools. Web pages were constructed in a drag-and-drop environment with a (limited) set of drawing and image manipulation tools. Things were good. It was a real step up from the dark ages. These second generation Web authoring tools brought in the bronze age of Web development.

**Figure i.4**
*NetObjects Fusion*



## Fusion—the Renaissance

The third generation of Web development tools is just starting to emerge and represents the renaissance of Web authoring. NetObjects Fusion (**Figure i.4**) is a prime example of the best that this new generation of tools has to offer.

### Site-Orientation

With NetObjects Fusion, you develop Web sites as a whole, rather than page by page. You can map out the structure of the entire site before you develop the content of a single page. Fusion's site-orientation also allows you to make global changes with the click of a button, apply and modify graphical elements to the entire site, update links automatically, and easily move, delete, and add pages to your site.

### No More HTML

Unlike many Web page development tools on the market today, Fusion shields the user almost entirely from exposure to HTML. This is not to say that Fusion is based on anything other than HTML. Indeed, Fusion is, at its core, an HTML generator. This just means that instead of requiring you to compose line after line of complicated HTML code, Fusion allows you to focus on the finer points of Web site design—issues of content and graphic design.

### Page Layout

Because Web development is an intensely graphical endeavor, Fusion provides a fully graphical, click-and-drag paste-up board interface much like those used by page layout tools such as QuarkXPress or Adobe PageMaker. With Fusion, what you see is what you get (almost), and if you want to preview your work in a Web browser, you can do so with the click of a button.

### Database Publishing

Database publishing is one of the many valuable methods of publishing information on the Web. With Fusion, you can create data objects on your Web pages that display pictures and text from your database.

### Site Management

One of the toughest jobs of the Web site manager is keeping track of all the Web site assets like files, links, and database information. With Fusion, when you make a change to a Web site asset, that change is propagated to all of the pages it affects ... automatically!

## A Note to Mac Users

Throughout this book we use Windows 95 screen shots. We do this because the Mac and Windows 95 versions of Fusion are virtually identical. Where the appearance or functionality of the version or of the operating systems differ, we've inserted *italic instructions* just for Mac users.

# Fusion Basics

## System Requirements

NetObjects Fusion is no wimp. It requires a fast CPU and plenty of RAM, hard drive space, and peripherals. Here are the details.

### Hardware

Fusion will run on a 486/66 PC or an older Power Mac, but will be much happier if you provide a beefier CPU. Fusion requires 16MB of available RAM. But, again, you'll be better off with 24 or more. Be sure to check your disk space before installing—the minimum installation of Fusion takes up 20MB of disk space; the complete installation swallows a whopping 80MB. Because Fusion is distributed on CD, you'll need a CD-ROM drive. As for a monitor nothing too fancy is required (800x600 with 256 colors or higher), but don't forget you're doing graphic design here—a nice big, high res display is definitely a plus.

### Software

Depending on the version of Fusion you're using, you'll need to run Windows 95, Windows NT Workstation 3.51 or later, or Mac OS 7.5 or later. You'll also need a good Web browser such as Netscape Navigator 3.X or later or Microsoft Internet Explorer 3.X or later. Finally, if you plan to do any database publishing, you'll need 32-bit ODBC drivers.

## The Fusion Screen

***Title bar***
The name of the application (Fusion) followed by the currently displayed site appears in the title bar. You can click and drag the title bar to move the Fusion window.

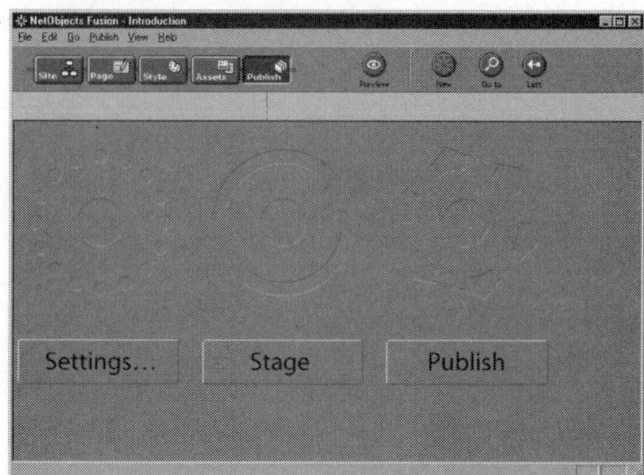


**Publish view**

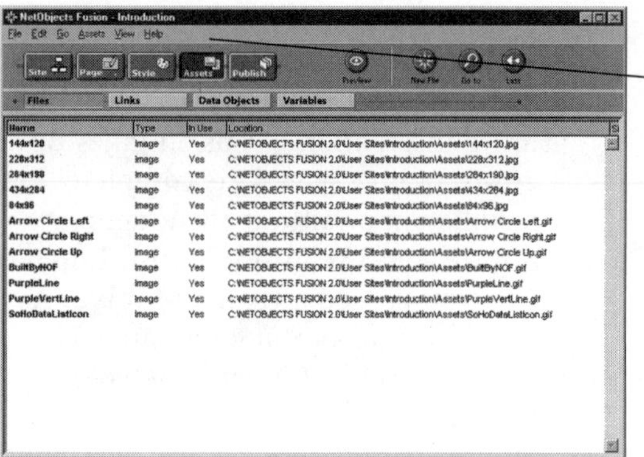


**Asset view**

***Menu bar***
When selected, each heading in the menu bar displays a drop-down list of available Fusion functions.

***Control bar***
The control bar contains view control buttons that allow you to switch between Fusion's five views. The control bar also contains preview, new, and navigational buttons. *The Mac menu bar is located at the top of your screen above the Fusion window.*

**Style view**

**Figure 1.1**
*The Fusion screen*

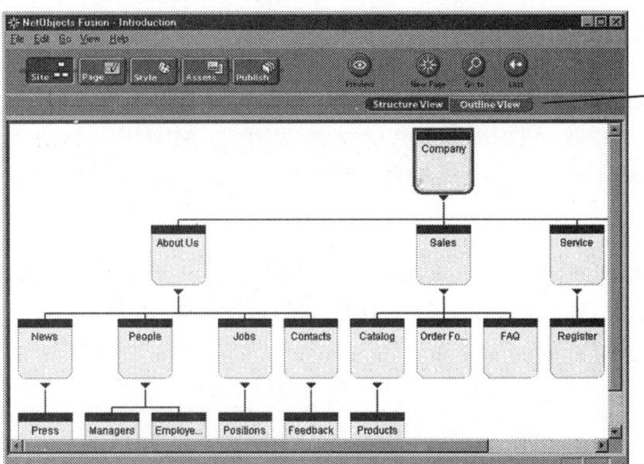


***View display options***
The view options allow you to select different display modes within each view. For example, in structure view, you can select the graphical view shown or an outline version.

**Page view**

***Display area***
The contents of the current view are displayed here. The display area may show the structure of the site, the contents of a page, etc.

**Site view**



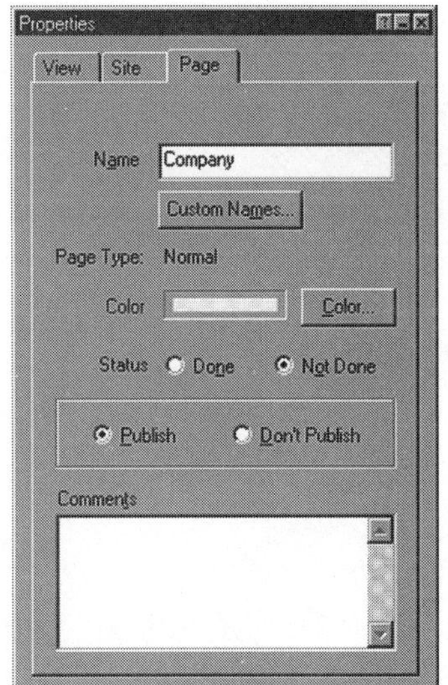


***Properties palette (here, in Site View)***
The properties palette is available only in Site and Page View and contains tabs for Page, Site, and View properties.

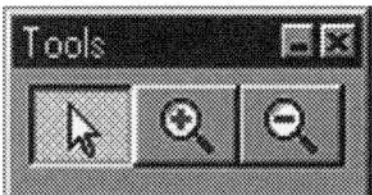


***Tools palette***
The tools palette is available only in Site and Page View and provides tools for viewing and creating page content.

## The Control Bar

Fusion offers five "views" designed to support you in designing, constructing, and managing your Web site: Site View, Page View, Style View, Assets View, and Publish View. The Control Bar contains **view navigation buttons (Figure 1.2)** used to move between these five views.

Site, Style, and Assets Views offer a number of **view display options**. Site View, for example, offers Structure View and Outline View, two different ways in which to view your site. Style View offers Style Gallery and Elements views. Assets View offers view display options for each asset type.

In addition to view navigation buttons, the Control Bar offers a number of **other control buttons**: Preview, New..., Go to, and Last. The Preview button converts your page or site to HTML. It then displays your site in your Web browser, allowing you to ensure that your creation is displayed as you intended. The New button adds a new page, style, or asset file depending on the current view. The Go to button allows you to locate any object within your site by name. The Last button allows you to easily switch back and forth between two views.



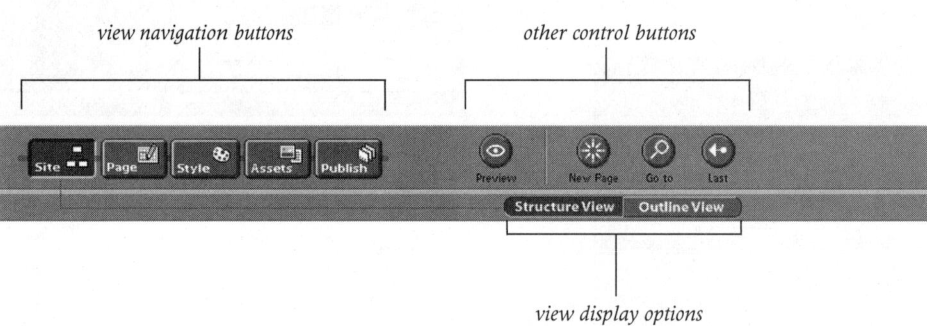


**Figure 1.2**
*The Control Bar*

## Menus

Each menu heading provides access to related commands for building your Web site in Fusion. The five Fusion menus shown in Site View are illustrated in the following pages. The illustrations show the menus in the Windows environment, but the menu headers and contents are the same for Mac users.

To choose from a menu, click the menu header, then click the desired option from the drop-down menu **(Figure 1.3)**. For Mac users, press and drag downward through the menu, and release the mouse when a desired option is highlighted.

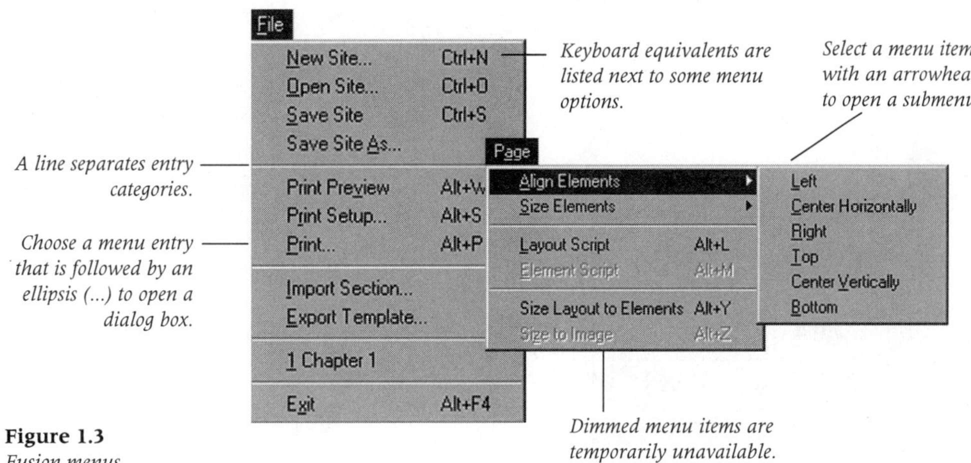


**Figure 1.3**
*Fusion menus*



### The Menu Bars

You will see, when choosing different Fusion views, that Fusion customizes the menu bar for each view by enabling some controls in existing menus, and adding specialized menus for particular views. The menu bar for each view is shown in **Figure 1.4**.

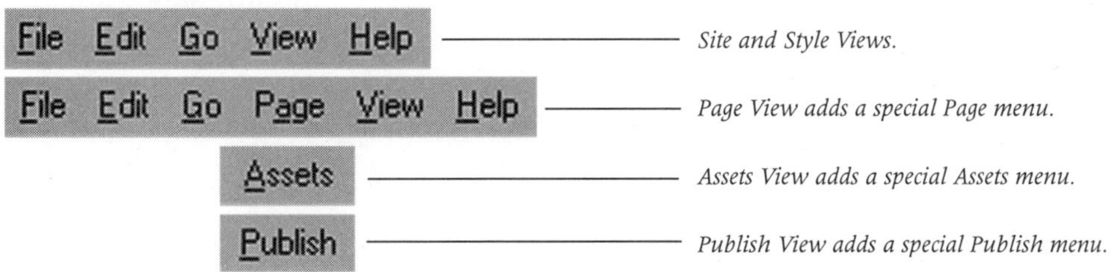


**Figure 1.4**
*The Fusion menu bars*

## The File Menu

The File menu provides access to system activities such as the creation of a new site, or saving your current one. Import options in the File menu differ in the Site, Page, and Style View File menus, as shown in **Figure 1.5**.

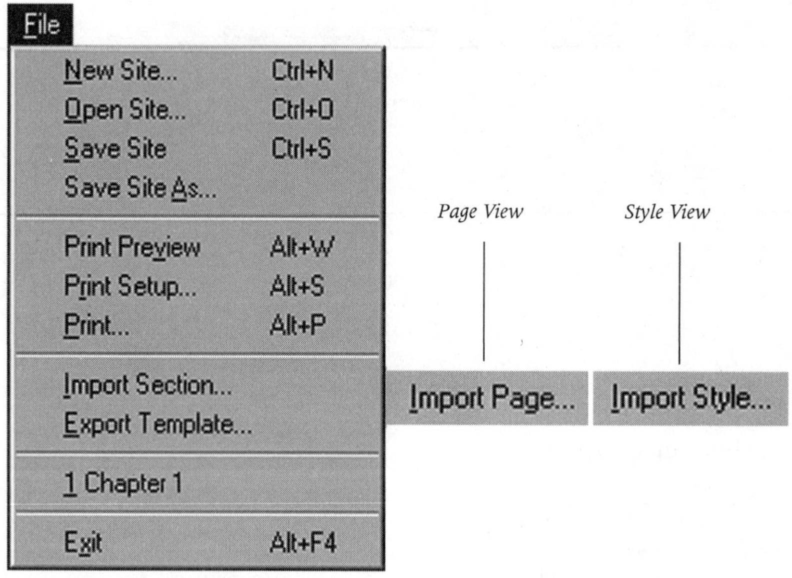


**Figure 1.5**
*The **File** menu (Site View)*

### The Edit Menu

The Edit menu contains the standard cut, copy, and paste commands as well as page insertion and deletion and some other valuable options we'll discuss in more detail later. The five Fusion views each display slightly different New and Delete options in the Edit menu, as shown in **Figure 1.6**.

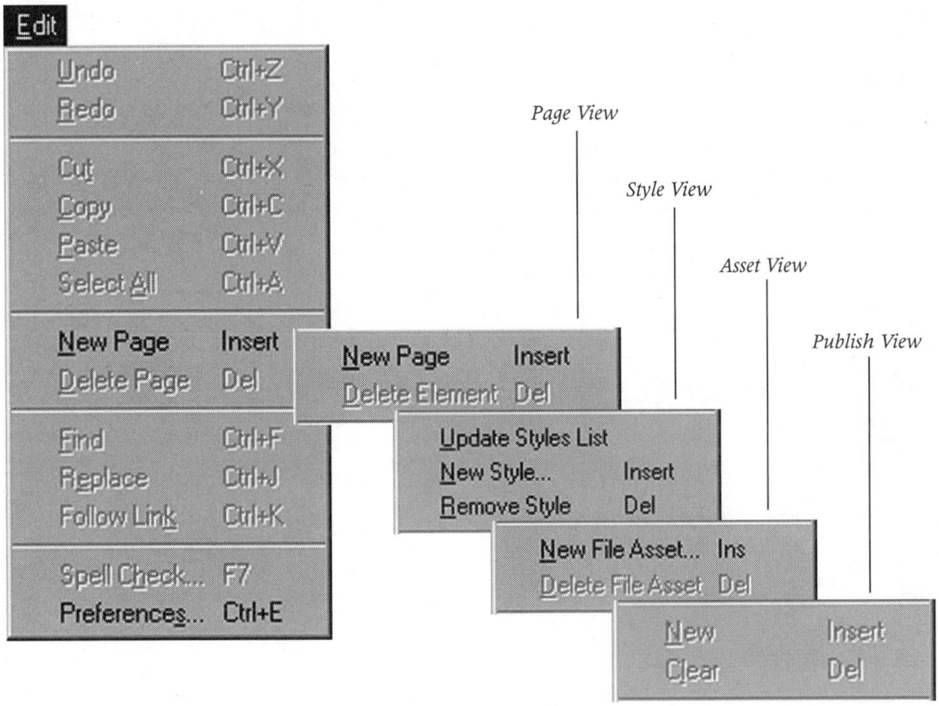


**Figure 1.6**
*The **Edit** menu (Site View)*

Menus

## The Go Menu

The Go menu mirrors the navigation controls on the Primary Control bar, allowing you to switch between Fusion's five views and to navigate within your Web site **(Figure 1.7)**.

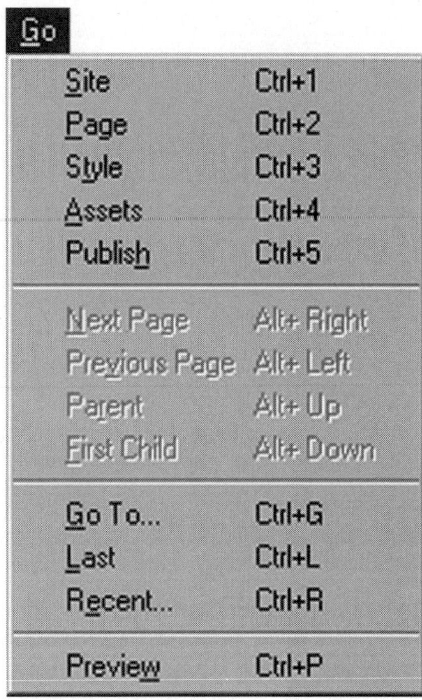


**Figure 1.7**
*The **Go** menu (Site View)*

## The Page Menu

The Page menu appears only when in Page View and contains options for aligning, sizing, and adding scripts to page elements **(Figure 1.8)**. *The Mac Page menu contains two additional options, Select Overlapping Elements and Merge Text blocks.*

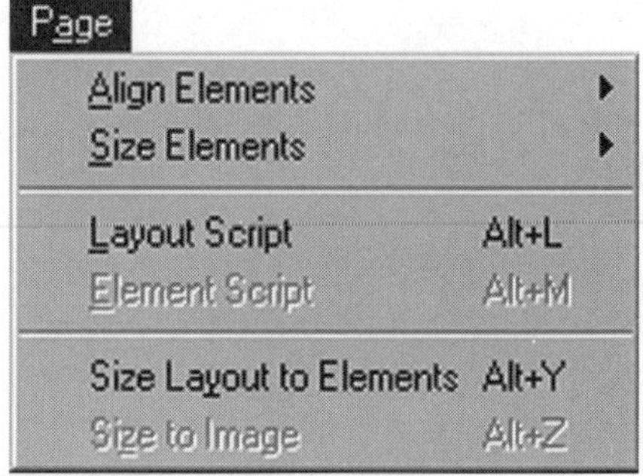


**Figure 1.8**
*The **Page** menu (Page View)*

## The Assets Menu

The Assets menu appears only when in Assets View and contains options for viewing, verifying, and cleaning up various types of assets files **(Figure 1.9).**

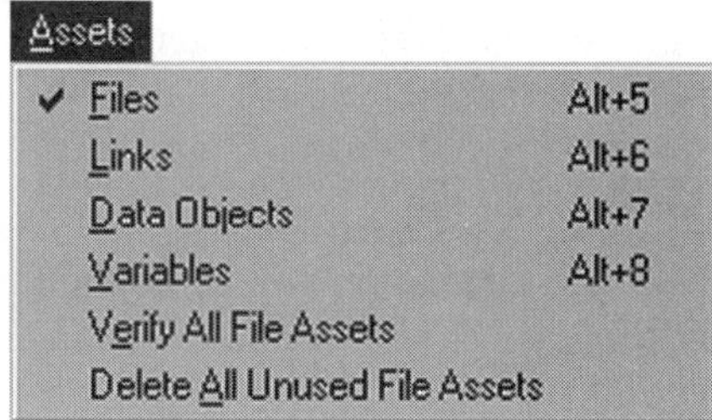


**Figure 1.9**
*The **Assets** menu (Asset View)*

## The Publish Menu

The Publish menu appears only when in Publish View. It contains options for setting up to publish your site, staging, and actually publishing **(Figure 1.10)**.

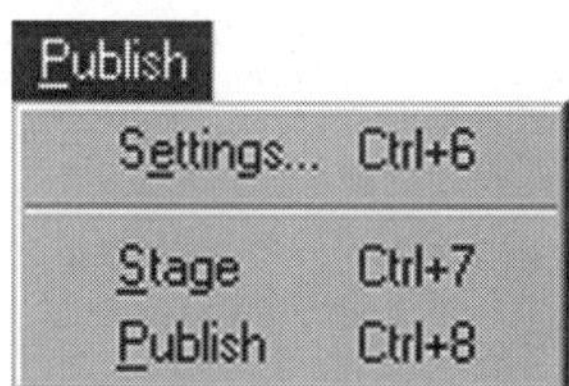


**Figure 1.10**
*The **Publish** menu (Publish View)*

## The View Menu

The View menu **(Figure 1.11)** appears in all views allowing you todisplay or hide the Tools and Properties palettes and element borders and icons (in Page View).

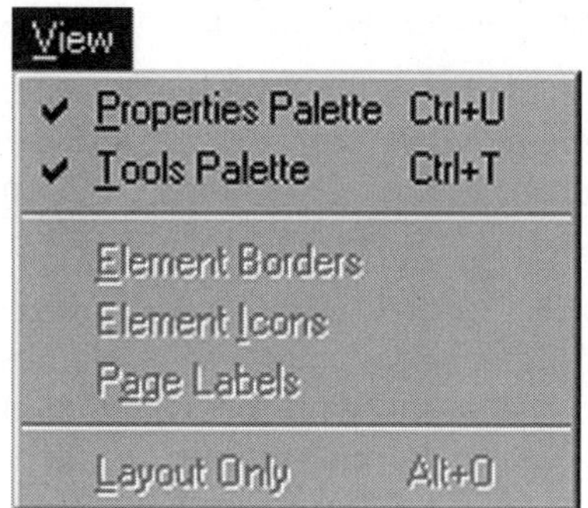


**Figure 1.11**
*The **View** menu (Site View)*

## The Help Menu

The Help menu **(Figure 1.12)** is available in all Fusion views. It provides easy access to NetObjects's online help system for Fusion (located on its company Web site). Choosing the Help Overview option from the Help menu launches your Web browser and displays help documentation.

*On a Mac, the Fusion Help menu is found under the question mark on the upper right corner of your screen and contains the options About Balloon Help...., Show Balloons, and NetObjects Fusion Guide.*

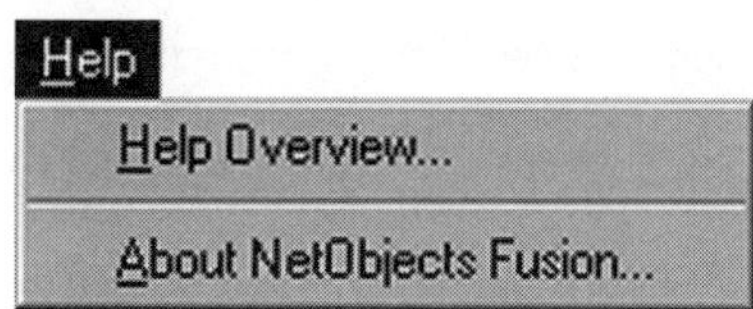


**Figure 1.12**
*The **Help** menu (Site View)*

## Dialog Boxes

You will run into a wide variety of dialog boxes while working with Fusion. Dialog boxes are used for two specific events: to provide you with some needed information (usually a warning of some kind), or to collect information from you.

To open a dialog box of the latter kind, select any menu item followed by an ellipsis (...) or use the corresponding keyboard shortcut.

**Figure 1.13** shows the Preferences dialog box in Windows 95 *(Mac dialog boxes look a little different, but the content is very similar.)* At the bottom of the Preferences dialog box are two common controls labeled OK and Cancel. To leave this dialog box (and most others you'll see), you must choose one of these options.

If you select Cancel, none of the changes you made in the dialog box will be applied to your site or page, and the box will disappear. Clicking on OK, on the other hand, tells the system that you made any changes you need to make, and that the system can now apply the information you provided.

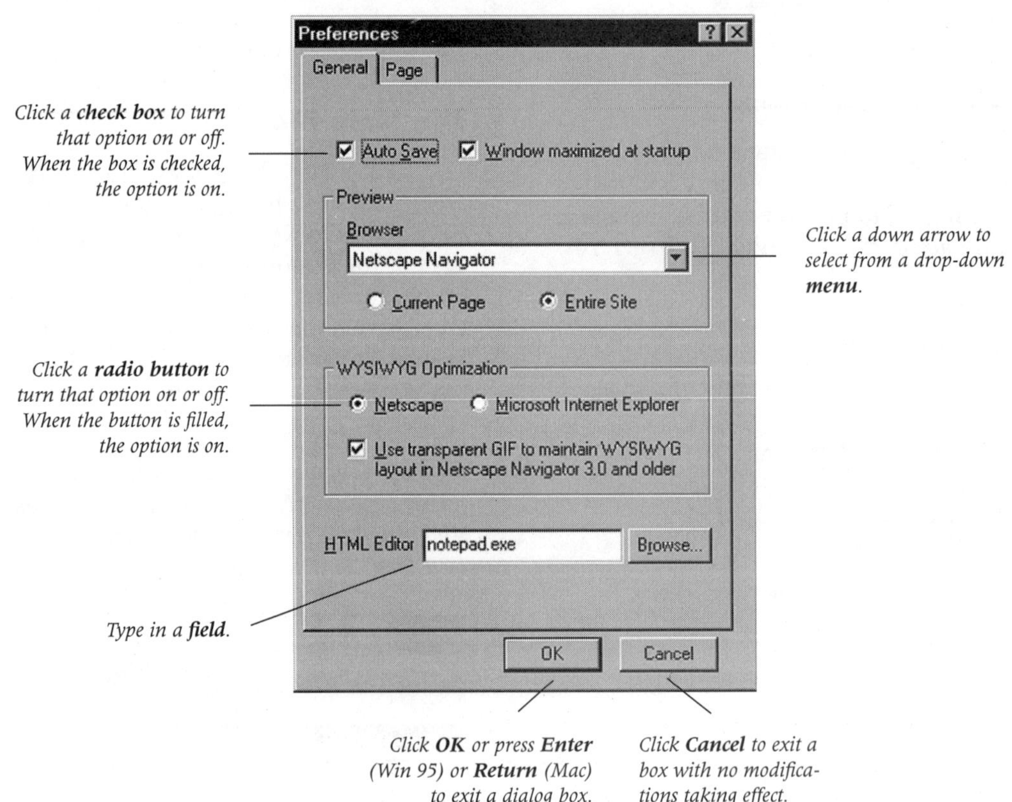
Preferences
General
Page
Auto Save
Window maximized at startup
Preview
Browser
Netscape Navigator
Current Page
Entire Site
WYSIWYG Optimization
Netscape
Microsoft Internet Explorer
Use transparent GIF to maintain WYSIWYG layout in Netscape Navigator 3.0 and older
HTML Editor
notepad.exe
Browse...
OK
Cancel
Click a check box to turn that option on or off. When the box is checked, the option is on.
Click a down arrow to select from a drop-down menu.
Click a radio button to turn that option on or off. When the button is filled, the option is on.
Type in a field.
Click OK or press Enter (Win 95) or Return (Mac) to exit a dialog box.
Click Cancel to exit a box with no modifications taking effect.

**Figure 1.13**
*A sample **dialog box***

## The Tools Palette

The Tools Palette is displayed only in Site and Page Views. It contains tools used to view your page or site and to insert objects on your page that can be sized, shaped, and moved to meet your needs.

As shown in **Figure 1.14**, the Site View Tools Palette contains only three tools: Select, Zoom In, and Zoom Out.

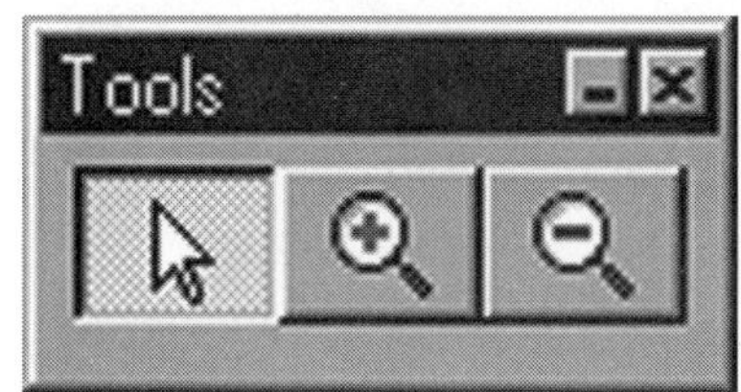


**Figure 1.14**
*Tools palette in Site View*

Click on a tool to select it. In Page view, when some tools are selected, a set of secondary tools is displayed in the bottom portion of the Tools Palette, as shown in **Figure 1.15**. To move the Tools Palette, click and drag its title bar.

A complete set of content tools are provided in Page View as detailed in **Figure 1.16**.

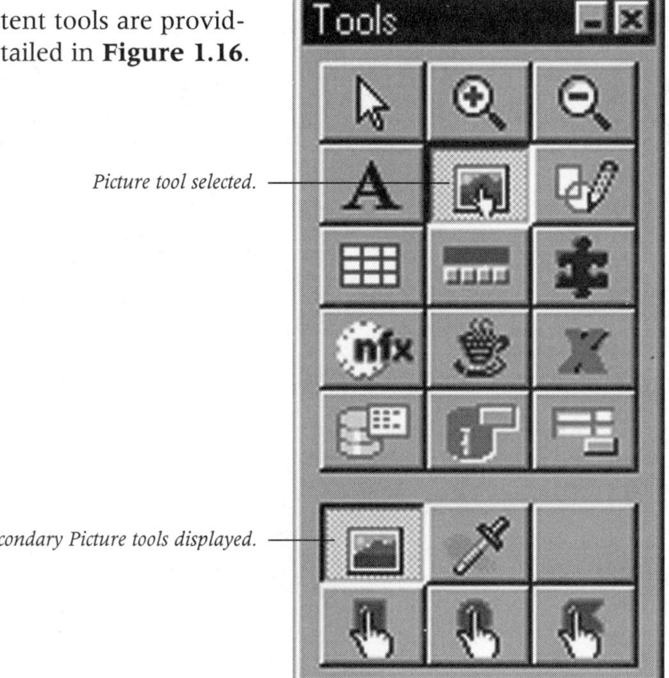


**Figure 1.15**
*Tools palette in Page View*

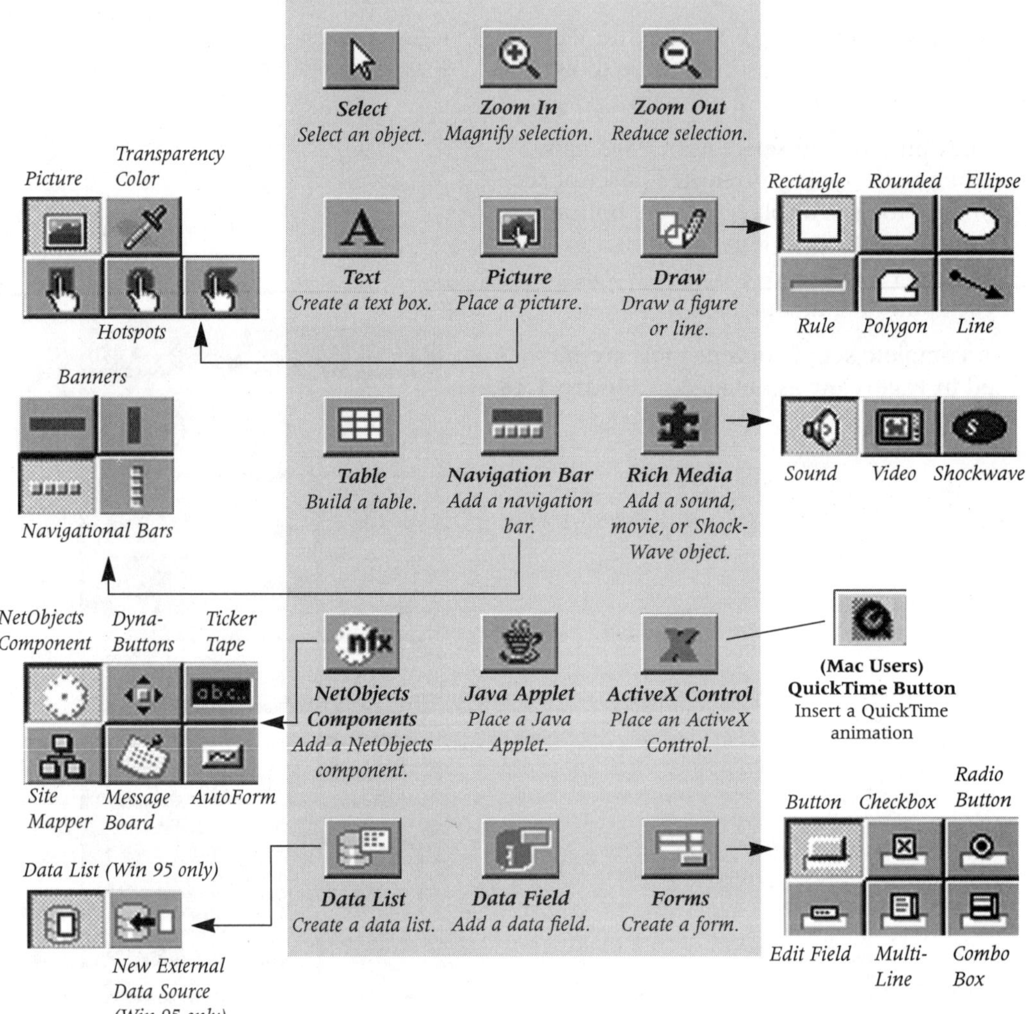


**Figure 1.16**
*Complete set of content tools*

## The Properties Palette

The Properties Palette is displayed only in Site and Page Views. With this palette, you can specify the properties of the site, the desired view, pages, and objects on pages. In Site View, the Properties Palette contains settings that affect your entire site, while in Page View the properties are set for specific content objects on the currently displayed page.

### Site View Properties

The Site View Properties Palette contains three tabs: View, Site, and Page. You can display the properties associated with each tab by clicking on that tab. All of the available Site View properties are shown in **Figure 1.17**.

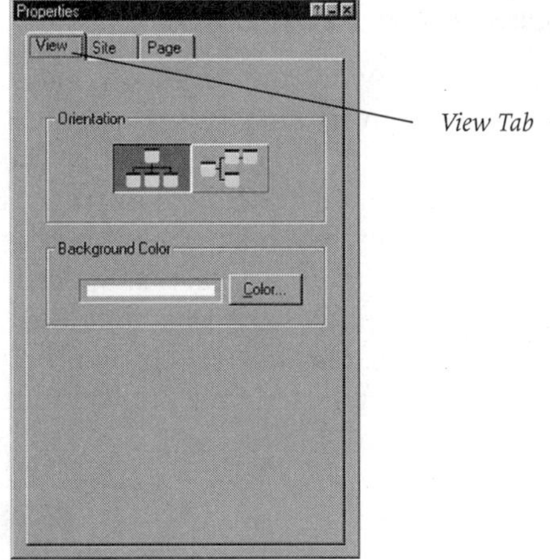


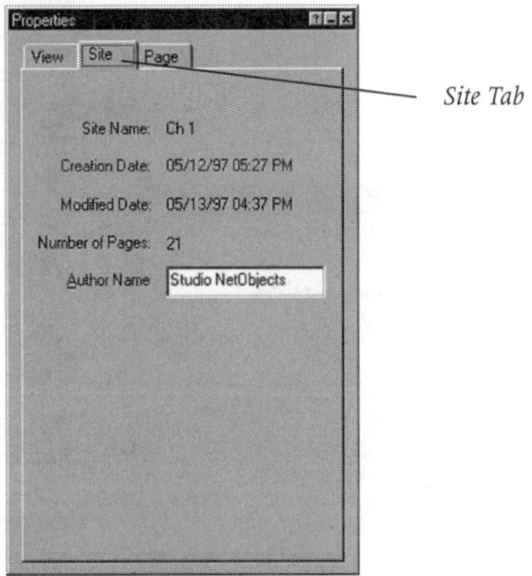


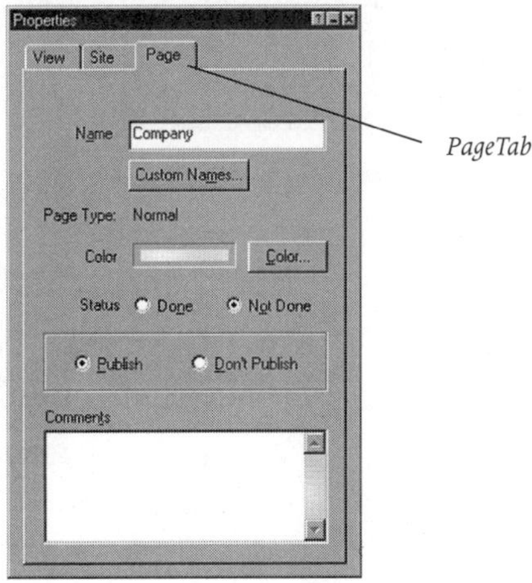


**Figure 1.17**
*The three Properties Palette tabs in Site View*

## Page View Properties

In addition to View and Page tabs, each type of object on a Fusion Web page has a unique tab in the Properties Palette. These special tabs are illustrated in **Figure 1.18** and appear only when an object such as a text box or a picture is selected. Special areas on your page, such as layout and master borders, also have their own Properties tabs when selected (We'll talk about these regions in Chapter 7.)



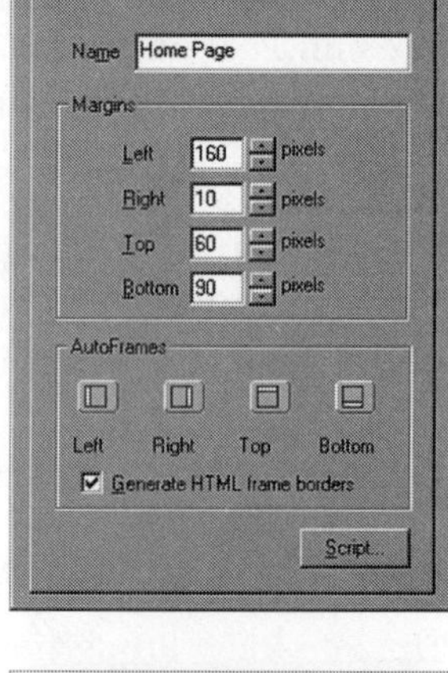

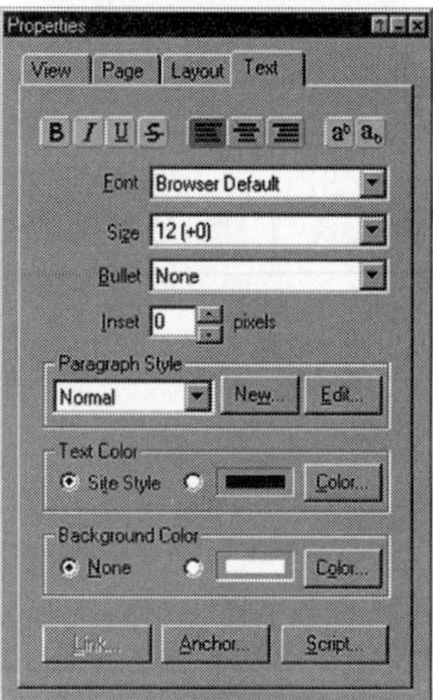


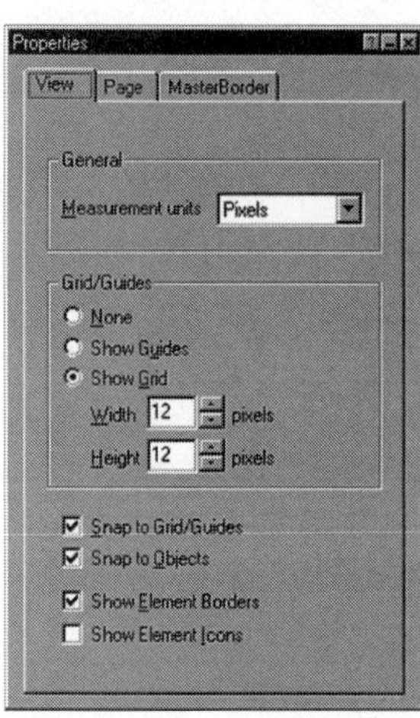


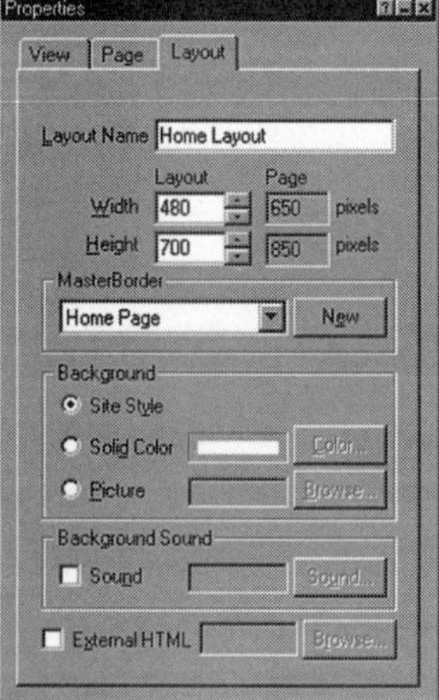


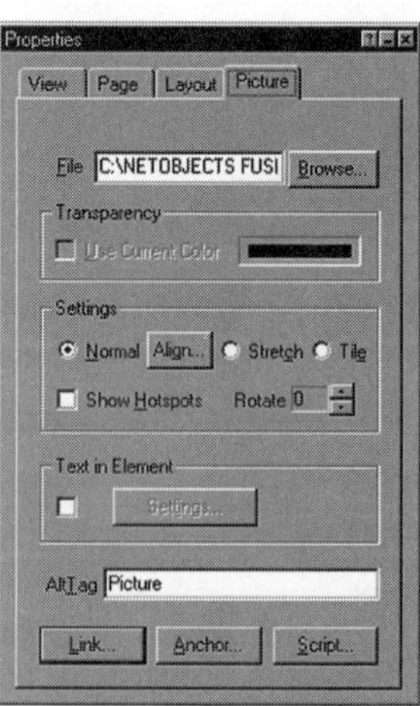


**Figure 1.18**
*Properties Palette tabs in Page View*

## Moving On

Now that you have a handle on the Fusion screen elements and palettes, we'll give you a better look at Fusion's five views and how they are used to support you in your Web development activities.

# The Fusion Way

As you have seen, Fusion employs five views (Site, Page, Style, Assets, and Publish) to support you in your Web development efforts **(Figure 2.1)**. These views are an implementation of "The Fusion Way"—the way in which the folks at NetObjects think Web sites should be born. In this chapter, we'll give you an overview of Web development with NetObjects Fusion.

**Figure 2.1**
*Fusion supports Web development with its five views.*

## Structure First

Decisions regarding what pages to include in your Web site, and how those pages will be organized and linked, are perhaps the most important decisions you will make while developing your Web site. Until very recently, however, issues of structure and organization have not been supported by Web site development tools. This means that planning Web site structure often is relegated to hastily sketched drawings on scratch paper—or worse yet, structure is allowed to "evolve" without any advance planning at all.

As with any software design project, overall structure and organization is extremely important in Web site design. Web site structure should be tackled first, long before you start thinking about logos, color, graphics, and specific content. The structure of your Web site should be considered a skeleton that you "flesh out" through the balance of the design process.

# A Consistent Look and Feel

With Fusion, structure is where the design process begins. Fusion incorporated a graphical facility called **Site View**, shown in **Figure 2.2**, which allows the designer to easily plan and visualize the structure of a Web site. Site View is the starting point in the Web design process in Fusion. Web pages are easily added, deleted, renamed, and moved in Site View.

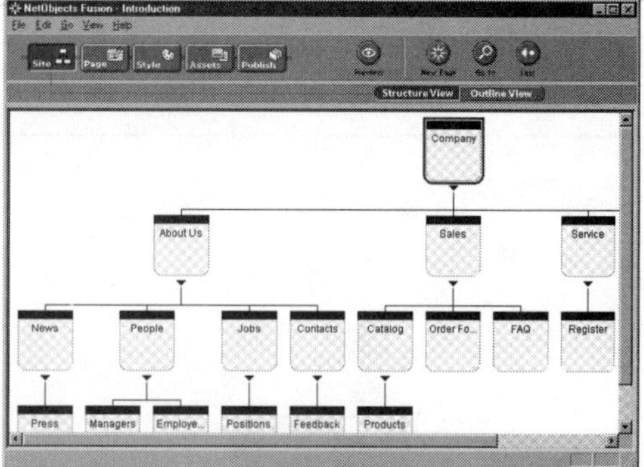


**Figure 2.2**
*Plan the structure of your Web site with Site View.*

After the structure of the Web site has been mapped out, the next critical issue in Web site design is the site's look and feel. One of the dead giveaways of an amateur job is a Web site containing pages with inconsistent basic visual design. Good, professionally designed and prepared sites will always have a consistent look and feel throughout, with consistent, understandable navigational aids.

As shown in **Figure 2.3**, Fusion includes a facility called **Style View** that allows you to specify the look of all standard Web page components. The style you select is automatically applied to all pages in your Web site. You can change the look and feel of your entire Web site simply by selecting a different Web site style. (Fusion provides a variety of prepared styles, but you can also create your own.)

**Figure 2.3**
*Define the look and feel of your site with Style View.*

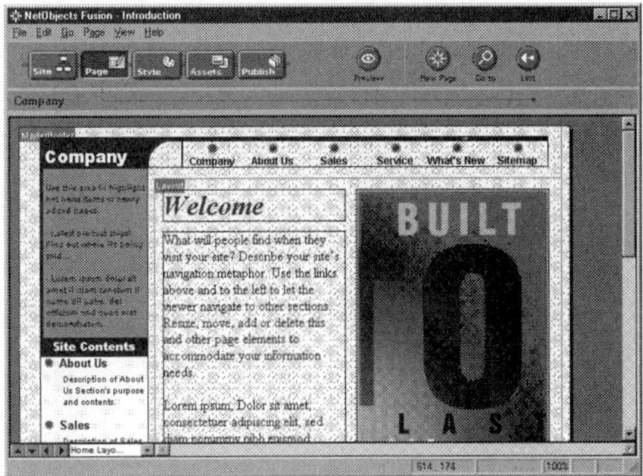


**Figure 2.4**
*Compose the content of each page in your site with Page View.*

## Visual Page Design

Designing the layout and content of each Web page in your site is the natural follow-up to designing the overall structure and look of your Web site. As mentioned, Fusion uses a paste-up board paradigm for its Web page design facility. **Figure 2.4** shows the **Page View** of a Web site home page.

Page View allows you to define the content of each page in a visual environment. You add objects to the page by selecting tools on the Tools Palette and drawing them on the screen. Tools are provided for defining text boxes, pictures, tables, lines and figures, multimedia objects like sounds and movies, ActiveX controls, Java Applets, and more. All of the objects placed on the page are then "clickable" and can be selected, moved, and resized with the mouse.



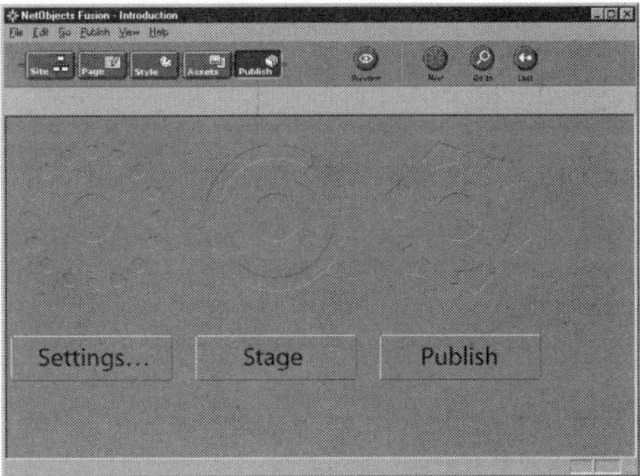


**Figure 2.5**
*Publish your Web site easily with Publish View.*

## Web Publishing

With Fusion, you start by laying out Web pages graphically. Not until you are satisfied with the look, feel, content, and structure of the entire site is the issue of HTML even addressed. It is at this point that you ask Fusion to "publish" your Web site using **Publish View**, as shown in **Figure 2.5**. Fusion then automatically creates a complex set of HTML and auxiliary documents that allow Web servers to host your Web site and Web browsers to display your Web site just as you conceived and designed it using Fusion's graphical design tools. Very slick.

A disadvantage of Fusion's automated HTML generation is that it provides no way for you to view or tweak the HTML code. However, this is only a disadvantage for the more experienced HTML author. For many of us, it is really a blessing. Fusion creates some very complex HTML code, and the most innocent tweaking can result in a garbled mess when viewed by a Web browser. For some of us, staying clear of the HTML is a good thing. But we say to you technoweenies who would rather fine-tune their designs by modifying the HTML source code than by using the nice graphical Fusion paste-up board, there are always text editors! Hack away!

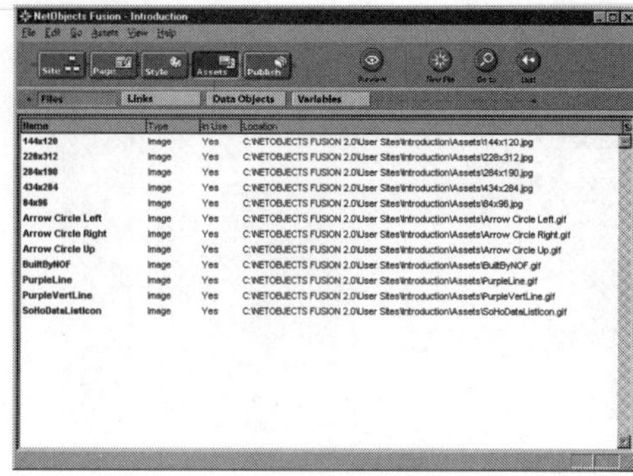

**Figure 2.6**
*Manage Web site assets with Assets View.*



## Web Site Management

Fusion includes some very powerful features for managing your Web site. Examples of Fusion's Web site management features have already been mentioned. These features include Fusion's ability to automatically update HTML tags and links when the structure or look of the Web site is modified.

Fusion's Web site management tools go beyond automatically updating HTML, however, and include valuable site documentation and "asset" organization facilities provided by **Assets View** (**Figure 2.6**). Fusion was designed to provide the Web site developer with complete documentation of the site. If compiled manually, such documentation would be tedious and difficult to maintain, especially as the site changes and evolves over time. The automated generation of site documentation is a critical component both of the development and management of the site.

## Moving On

Now that you are armed with a basic understanding of the Web, Web development tools, Fusion screen components, and "the Fusion way," it's time to get your hands dirty—getting started with Fusion is coming up next!

# The Beginning

**Figure 3.1**
*Launching Fusion from the Windows 95 Start menu.*

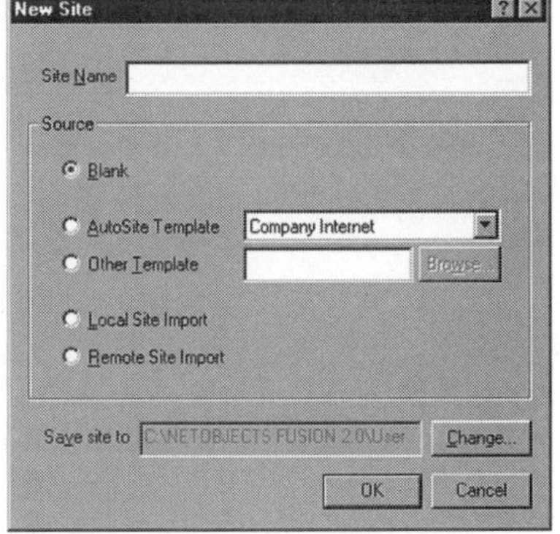


**Figure 3.2**
*The first time you launch Fusion, you will see the New Site dialog box.*

## Launching Fusion

When you installed Fusion 2.0 in Windows 95, a directory was built titled NetObjects Fusion, and the application was installed within it. To launch Fusion you must locate the application and select it. **Figure 3.1** shows what this can look like in Windows 95 Start Menu.

### To Launch NetObjects Fusion:

Locate and select NetObjects Fusion in the Start menu. *For Mac users, locate the NetObjects Fusion icon and double-click it.*

If you have opened a project in Fusion previously, that project will be displayed in the Fusion window.

If you haven't opened a project in Fusion before, the New Site dialog box will appear, as shown in **Figure 3.2**.

The New Site dialog box offers four basic source settings for you to choose from. The Source setting tells Fusion how you want to begin constructing your site. You can create a new blank site, create a site using a template, import a local site, or import a remote site.

## Opening a New Blank Site

Blank is the default source setting in the New Site dialog box (**Figure 3.3**). Choose the Blank Site option when you wish to start your Web site from scratch.

### To create a blank Web site:

1. If the New Site dialog box is not already displayed, select New Site from the File menu.
2. Type a name in the Site Name field.
3. Make sure that **Blank** is selected in the Source option block.
4. Click OK.

   A new blank site is opened, as shown in **Figure 3.4**.

   At this point you can begin adding pages, and you can plan the structure of your new Web site. We'll do that in Chapter 4.

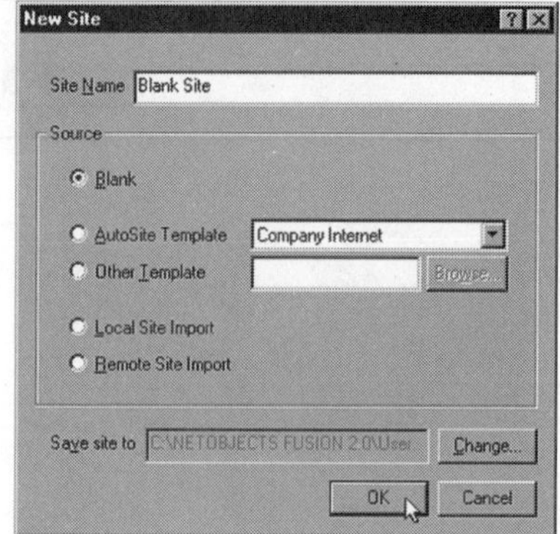


**Figure 3.3**
*Opening a new blank site*

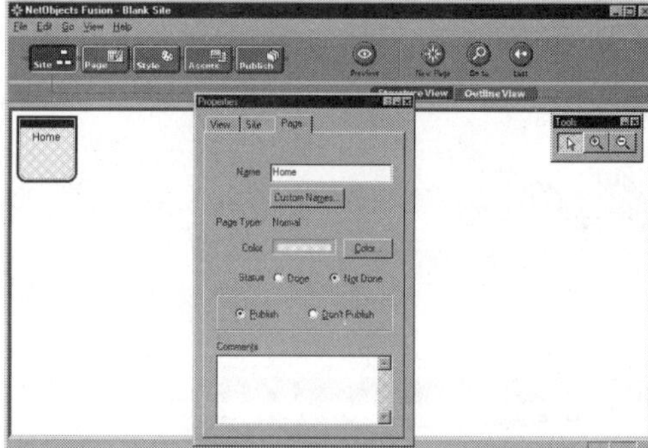


**Figure 3.4**
*A new blank site*

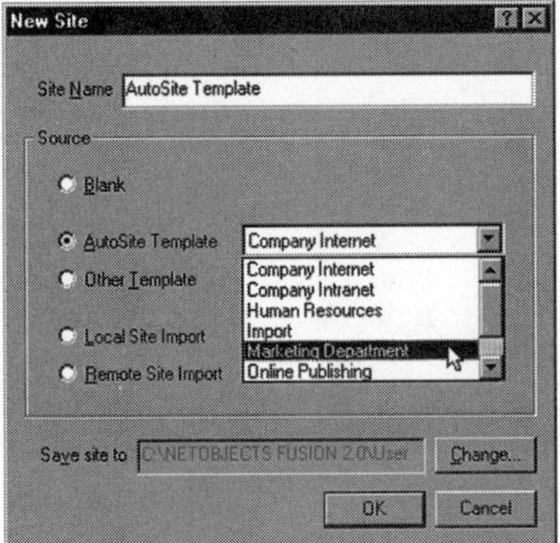


**Figure 3.5**
*Opening a new site using an AutoSite template*

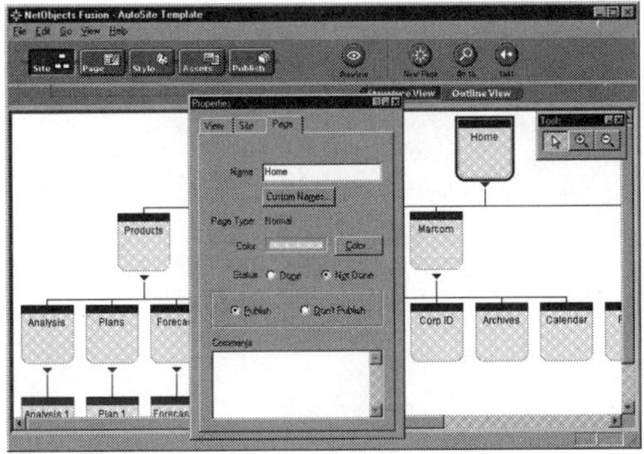


**Figure 3.6**
*A new site using the Marketing Department AutoSite template*

# Opening a New Site from an AutoSite Template

Fusion offers a selection of pre-designed sites to jump-start your development efforts. By choosing AutoSite Template as your source in the New Site dialog box, you can take advantage of a pre-built site designed for a specific purpose. All you have to do is modify the site template to suit your needs.

## To create a Web site using an AutoSite template:

1. Select New Site from the File menu to display the New Site dialog box.
2. Type a name in the Site Name field.
3. Select **AutoSite Template**.
4. Select one of the AutoSite Templates from the drop-down menu **(Figure 3.5)**.
5. Click OK.

   The new site is opened and will look something like the one shown in **Figure 3.6** (depending on the AutoSite template you selected).

### ✔ Tips

- Using an AutoSite template to begin your Web site development is a good strategy to leverage your time.
- The templates will provide you with design ideas, examples of how the Fusion components are used, and some interesting layouts to spark your creativity.

## Creating Your Own Web Site Template

The AutoSite Templates provided by NetObjects give a nice selection of useful Web sites to start from, but you might find that you have a unique need for a site structure that you would like to reuse. You can create your own Web site template by designing a site, and then selecting the Export Template option from the File menu.

### To create your own template:

1. Select New Site from the File menu to display the New Site dialog box.
2. Type a name in the Site Name field.
3. Select one of the Source options.
4. Click OK. A new site is displayed.
5. Select **Export Template** from the File menu, shown in **Figure 3.7**.
6. Select a location in which to save your new template using the Select Folder Dialog box displayed in **Figure 3.8**. *The Mac dialog box is called Select a Folder and looks a little different than the one shown.*
7. Click OK. *Mac users click the Select... button at the bottom of the dialog box.*
8. When it is displayed, click OK in the confirmation alert shown in **Figure 3.9**.

### ✓ Tip

- You can export any Fusion Web site as a template.

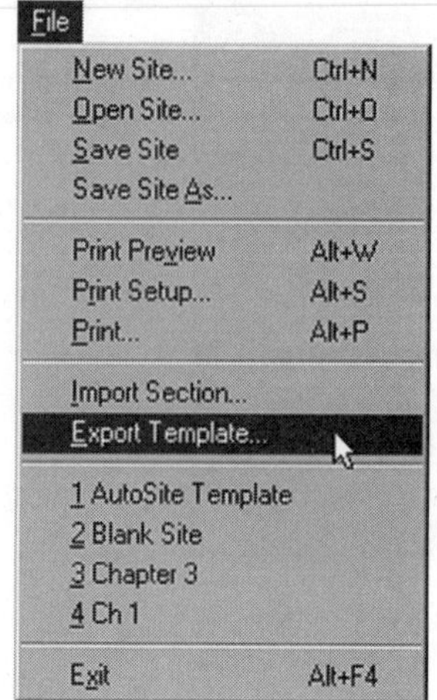


**Figure 3.7**
*Select Export Template from the File menu.*

**Figure 3.8**
*Select a location in which to save your new template.*

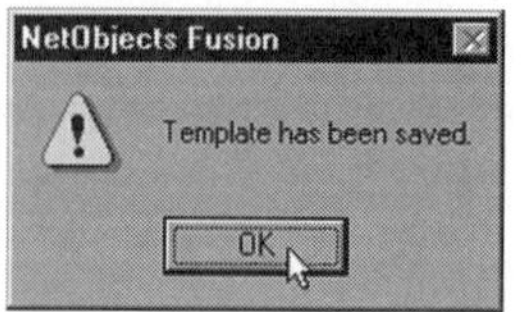


**Figure 3.9**
*Fusion confirms that your template has been saved.*

**Figure 3.10**
*Locate the template you wish to use with the open dialog box.*

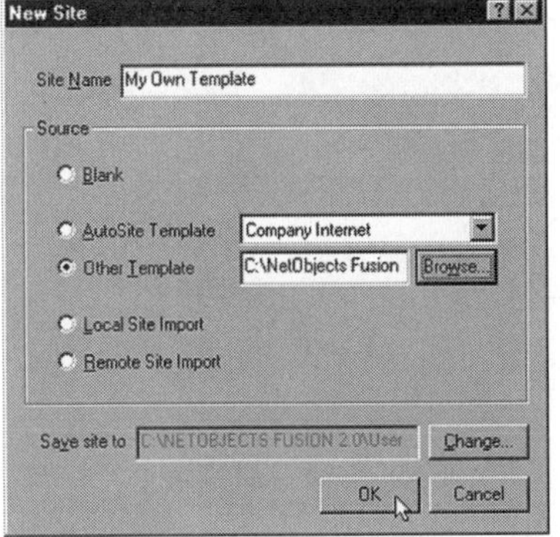


**Figure 3.11**
*The New Site dialog box after selecting an* ***Other Template.***

# Opening a New Site Using a Template

The **Other Template** source option in the New Site dialog box allows you to locate and use a template that you may have already created in Fusion.

The Other Template option in the New Site dialog box allows you the flexibility to access templates from anywhere on your system or network.

### To create a Web site using the Other Template option:

1. Select New Site from the File menu to display the New Site dialog box.
2. Type a name in the Site Name field.
3. Select **Other Template**.
4. Click Browse button next to the Other Template text box. *Click Select... on the Mac.*
5. Locate the template you wish to use with the dialog box displayed (**Figure 3.10**).
6. After locating the template, simply double-click on it (or select it and click the Open button). The name and path information will be returned to the New Site dialog box as shown in **Figure 3.11**.
7. Click OK, and the template is displayed as your new Web site.

# Importing an Existing Web Site

The Local Site Import and Remote Site Import options in the New Site dialog box give you the opportunity to import existing Web sites into Fusion. These Web sites may reside on the same system as your copy of Fusion, or they can be available somewhere else on the Internet.

## To Import a local Web site:

1. Select New Site from the File menu to display the New Site dialog box.
2. Type a name in the Site Name field.
3. Select the Local Site Import option, as shown in **Figure 3.12.**
4. Click OK.
5. In the Set Local Import dialog box, shown in **Figure 3.13**, click Browse. *Mac users click the Select... button at the bottom of the dialog box.*
6. Use the dialog box displayed to locate the home page of the local site you wish to import. (Note: you must have a previously created site on your computer.)
7. Double-click on the name of the home page when located (or select it and click Open), and the name of the selected page is entered in the Home Page field in the Set Local Import dialog box **(Figure 3.14)**.
8. By default, Fusion will convert imported pages to the NetObjects Fusion format. If you do not wish to convert your imported pages, deselect the Convert pages to NetObjects Fusion format option in the Set Local Import dialog. See Tips for more on converting imported pages.

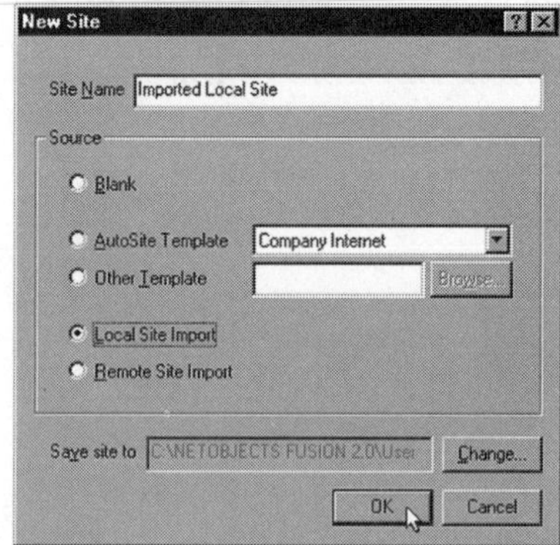


**Figure 3.12**
*Enter a site name and select the Local Site Import option.*

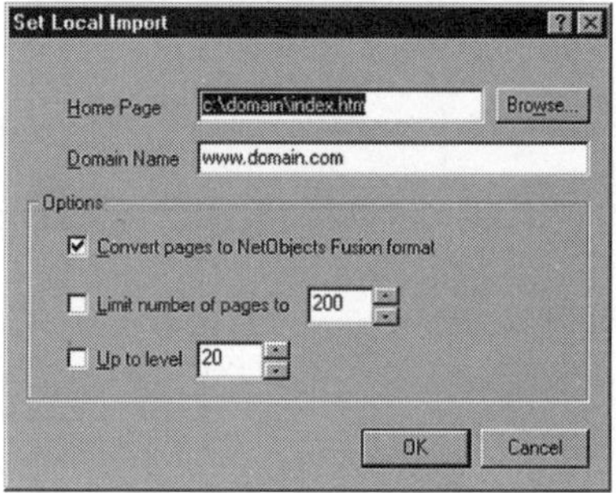


**Figure 3.13**
*Click the Browse button to locate the local site you wish to import and specify the number of pages and levels you wish to import.*

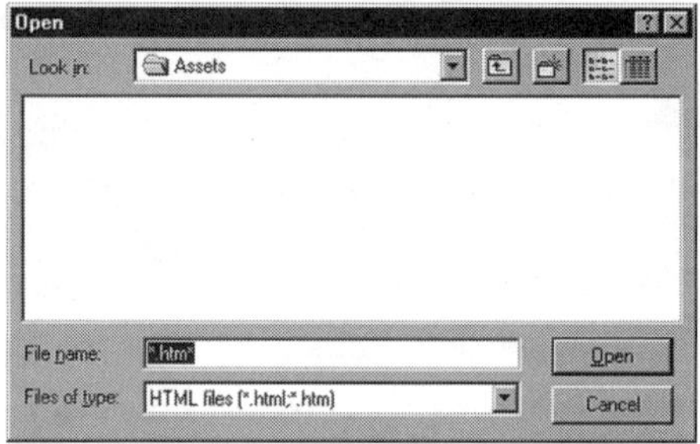


**Figure 3.14**
*Use the open dialog box to select the local site you wish to import.*

9. Type the site's domain name into the Domain Name field using the format provided.
10. Select the number of pages and levels of the Web site that you wish to import.

    These limits are particularly important if you are not familiar with the Web site you are importing. It could be huge.
11. Click OK.

    Fusion will begin converting the Web site into NetObjects Fusion format. When complete, the imported site will appear in Site View.

### ✔ Tips

- When Fusion converts an imported HTML document to the NetObjects Fusion format, it places the content in the Layout area of the new Fusion page (See Chapter 7 for more on layouts). Once converted, imported pages can be edited as desired in Page View.
- If you import pages and do not convert them to NetObjects Fusion format, then you will not be able to modify them in Fusion. In Site View, these pages are displayed with diagonal lines through them. In Page View, such imported pages are displayed as solid gray with an X across the entire page.
- To edit a page which has not been converted to Fusion format, select Edit HTML from the pop-up menu. You can then edit the HTML of the page in the default text editor.

### To Import a remote Web site:

**1.** Make sure your computer is connected to a network through which the Web site can be reached.

**2.** Select New Site from the File menu to display the New Site dialog box.

**3.** Type a name in the Site Name field, as shown in **Figure 3.15**.

**4.** Select the Remote Site Import option.

**5.** Click OK.

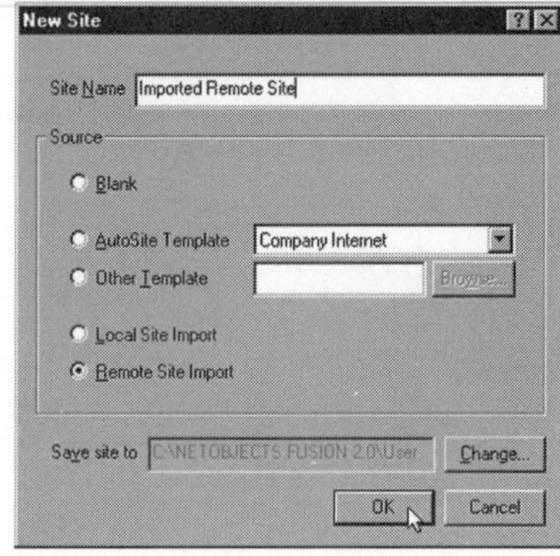


**Figure 3.15**
*Enter a site name and select the Remote Site Import option.*

**6.** In the Set Remote Import dialog box Displayed in **Figure 3.16**, type the URL of the site's home page into the Domain Name field.

**7.** Select the number of pages and levels of the Web site you wish to import.

**8.** Click OK.

Fusion will attempt to locate the Web site at the address you provided. Once located, Fusion will begin converting the Web site into NetObjects Fusion format. When complete, the imported site will appear in Site View.

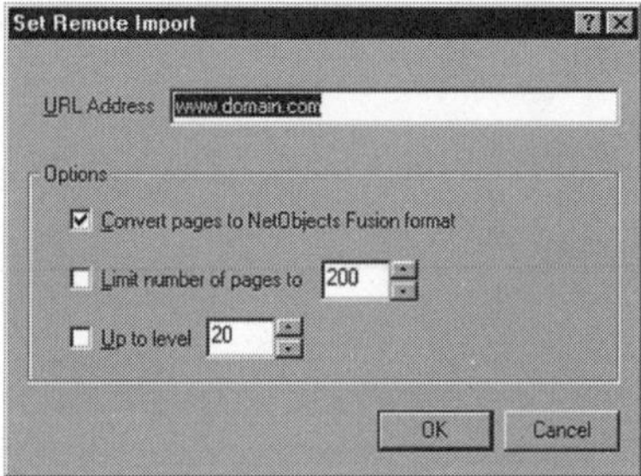


**Figure 3.16**
*Enter the URL of the remote site you wish to import and specify the number of pages and levels you wish to import.*

✔ **Tip**

■ A URL (Universal Resource Locator) is a formatted address that the Internet uses to locate specific resources.

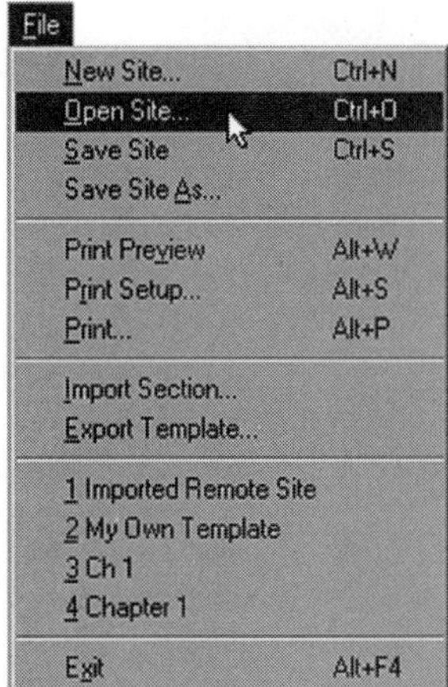


**Figure 3.17**
*Select Open Site from the File menu.*

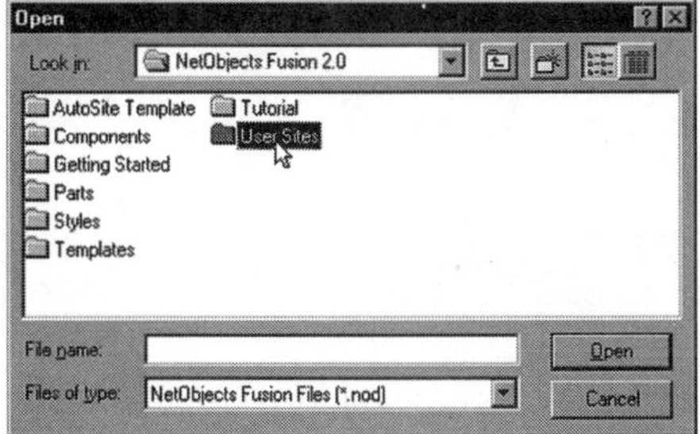


**Figure 3.18**
*Locate the Web site project file you wish to open. Unless you specify otherwise, all of your Web site projects are stored in their own folders inside the User Sites folder.*

# Opening an Existing Fusion Web Site Project

When Fusion is launched, it displays the Web site project that was displayed when the application was last closed. This is a handy feature, allowing you to work on the same Web site project over the course of many sessions by simply launching Fusion. There will be times, however, when you want to open a different Web site project than the one displayed when Fusion is launched.

### To open an existing Fusion Web site project:

1. Select Open Site from the File menu, as shown in **Figure 3.17**.
2. As shown in **Figure 3.18**, use the open dialog box to locate the Fusion project you wish to open.
3. Double-click on the name of the project when located (or select it and click Open), and the selected Fusion project is displayed in the Fusion window.

### ✔ Tips

- You can also open a Fusion Web site project by opening the directory in which it is stored and double-clicking on the file icon.
- In Windows 95, Fusion projects are stored with a file extension of .nod. *Mac Fusion project files have no file extension (of course!).*

## Saving a Fusion Web Site

As you work, it is extremely important to save your work. Save often. Until you save them, changes made to your Web site project will be lost if there is a power outage, your computer hangs, your dog chews through your power cord—you get the idea. If you don't want to redo lost work, then save save save!

### To save a Fusion Web site project:

Select Save Site in the File menu, as shown in **Figure 3.19**.

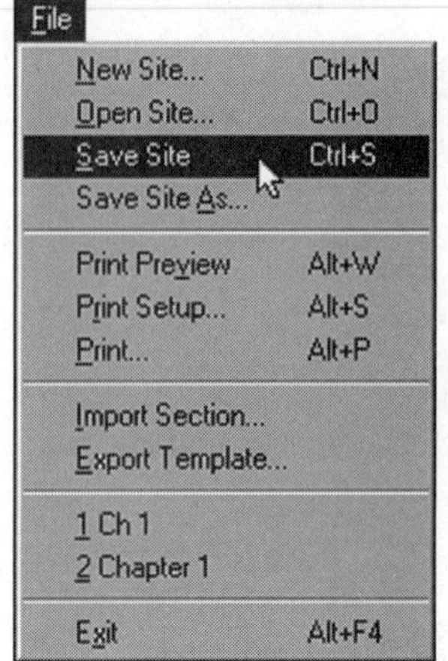


**Figure 3.19**
*Select Save Site from the File menu.*

### To save a Fusion Web site under a new name:

1. Make sure the Site button is selected in the Control Bar.
2. Select Save Site As from the File menu, as shown in **Figure 3.20**.
3. As shown in **Figure 3.21**, use the Choose a File Name... dialog box to enter a new name for the Web site and to select a location where you want it saved.
4. Click Save.

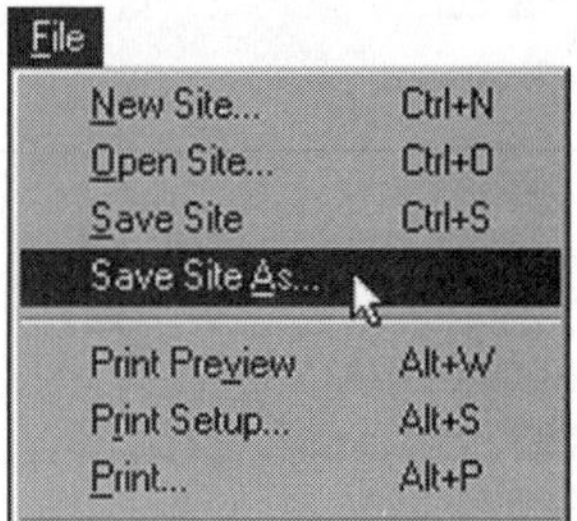


**Figure 3.20**
*Select Save Site As from the File menu.*

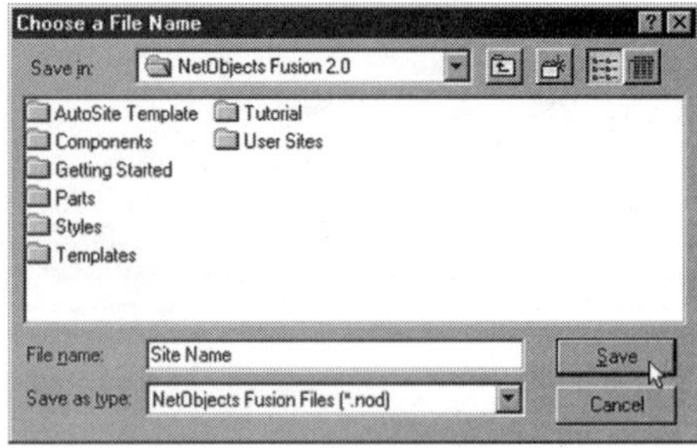


**Figure 3.21**
*Name and save your Web site.*

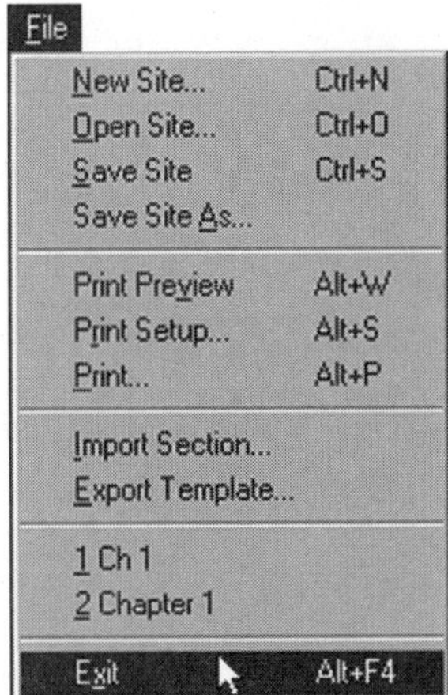


**Figure 3.22**
*Select Exit from the File menu.*

## Quitting Fusion

When you have finished working in Fusion for the time being, you will quit the application. Here's how.

**To quit Fusion:**

Select Exit *or Quit on the Mac* from the File menu, as shown in **Figure 3.22**.

## Moving On

Remember that Fusion is a site-oriented Web development tool. A good place to start is with site structure. In the next chapter, we'll show you how to use Fusion to plan and manage the structure of your Web site.

# Plan Web Site Structure

4

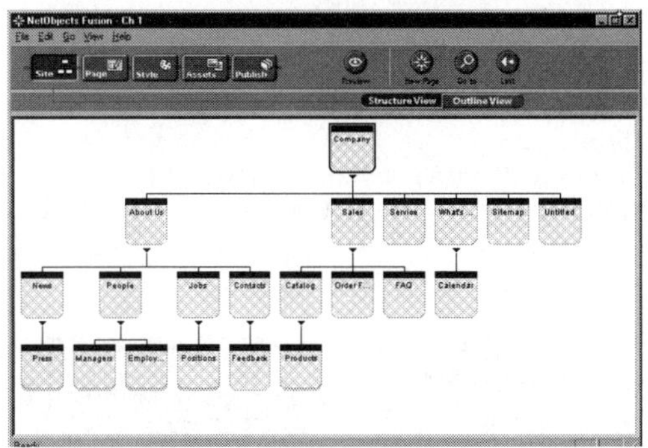


**Figure 4.1**
*The structure of a Web site viewed in Fusion's Site View.*

## Getting Organized

We've shown you the basic building blocks of NetObjects Fusion. The tools to design your Web site and pages are in your grasp. Now what? It's time to start planning the organization and structure of your Web site.

One of the mistakes that we often make in developing Web sites is not spending enough time designing our site structure. What do we want the people accessing our site to be able to do? What information do we want to provide to them? How do we want them to navigate through our structure? What information do we want to collect from them, and how do we want to collect it? **Figure 4.1** shows an example of the structural complexity a development team could experience when designing a moderate to large Web site.

A good way to begin your preliminary design work is to spend some time on the Internet looking at Web sites providing similar services to what you have in mind. Learn from other people's good (and bad) ideas. Another good source of ideas is Fusion's AutoSite templates, which provide many examples of well-designed sites and pages.

You are probably already familiar with Fusion's development environment. (If not, it would be a good idea for you to review Chapter 2.) In this chapter we'll show you how to use Fusion's Site View to plan, layout, and modify the structure of your Web site.

## Getting to Site View

When Fusion is launched, its default is Site View. It's easy to determine which view you are in by looking at the Control Bar: the view navigation button for the current view is selected **(Figure 4.2)**.

### To get to Site View:

If the navigation buttons in the Control Bar indicate you are not in Site View, select the Site button.

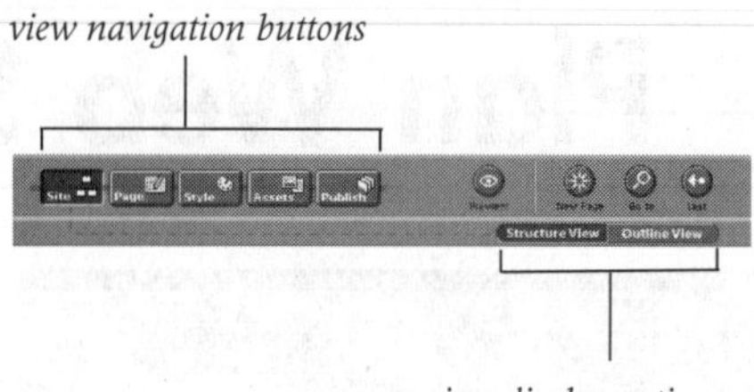


**Figure 4.2**
*The Control Bar with the Site view navigation button selected and the Structure View display option selected.*

## Site View Display Options

Site View offers two view display options, Structure View and Outline View. When in Structure View, your Web site is displayed as shown in **Figure 4.3** with the pages laid out in a tree structure. Outline View displays your site with pages arranged in an outline format along the left side of the display area **(Figure 4.4)**. The display option currently selected is indicated by the display option buttons.

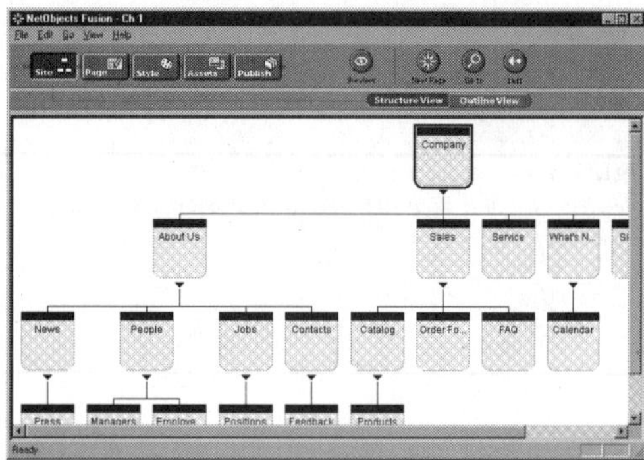


**Figure 4.3**
*Using the Structure View display option in Site View.*

Although the two Site View display options look quite different, you can perform most of the same functions in Outline View as you can in Structure View. You are able to add, move, and delete pages, rename pages, change their colors, and manipulate the other properties available on the Properties palette.

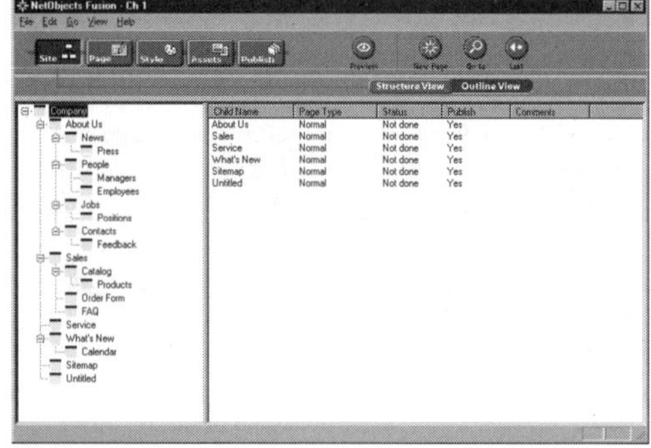


**Figure 4.4**
*Using the Outline View display option in Site View.*

### To select Site View display options:

While in Site View, use the Control Bar to select the view display option you prefer.

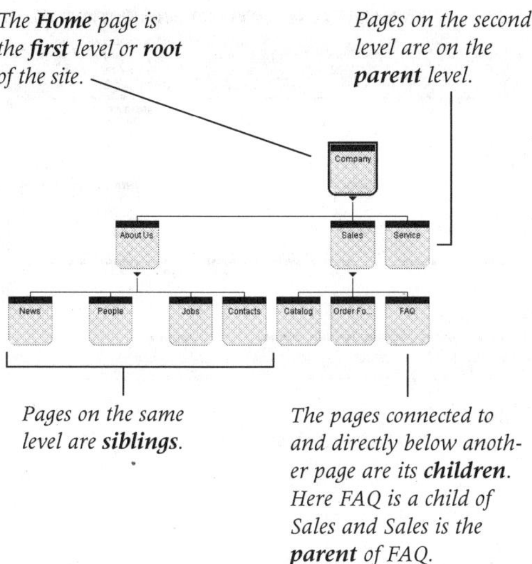
The **Home** page is the ***first*** level or **root** of the site.
Pages on the second level are on the **parent** level.
Company
About Us
Sales
Service
News
People
Jobs
Contacts
Catalog
Order Fo...
FAQ
Pages on the same level are **siblings**.
The pages connected to and directly below another page are its **children**. Here FAQ is a child of Sales and Sales is the **parent** of FAQ.

**Figure 4.5**
*Using the Structure View display option in Site View.*

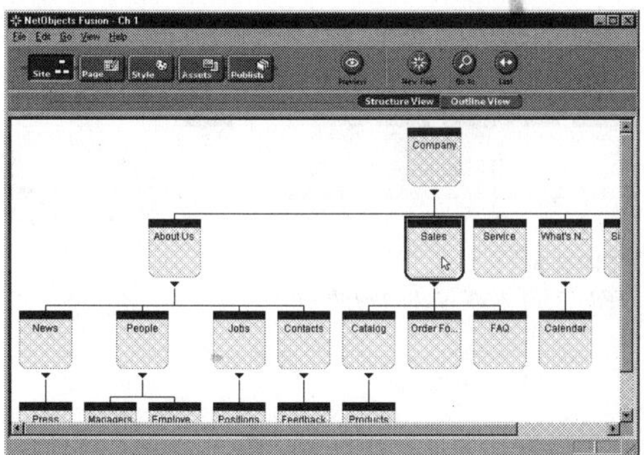
Structure View
Outline View
Company
About Us
Sales
Service
What's N...
News
People
Jobs
Contacts
Catalog
Order Fo...
FAQ
Calendar

**Figure 4.6**
*A page selected (Sales) in Site View.*

## Structural Lingo

To make it easier to discuss the structure of a Web site (or any other tree-like structure), there is some terminology that you'll need.

The Home page is the first page in the Web site hierarchy. It is the first level or the *root*. Pages directly below it are said to be on the *parent* level. If there are multiple pages at the same level of a site they are known as *siblings*.

Pages below the parent level are *child* pages. The terms *child* and *parent* can also be used to describe pages on a specific level of the site. For example, in **Figure 4.5,** Catalog, Order Form, and FAQ can be referred to as the children of Sales. Conversely, Sales is the parent of Catalog, Order Form, and FAQ. You can use this parent/child relationship to describe pages at any level of your Web site. For example, FAQ is the parent of any pages directly below and connected to FAQ (its children).

This nomenclature becomes more important in Page View, but we will utilize it here as well.

## Selecting a Page

Before you can perform any actions on a page in Site View, you must select that page.

### To select a page in Site View:

Click on the desired page. The selected page is displayed with a think (blue) border **(Figure 4.6)**.

## Adding a Page

When you wish to add a page to your site, you must first decide where you want the page inserted. In Fusion's Site View, new pages are always inserted as children of the currently selected page.

### To add a new page:

1. Select the parent of the page you wish to add.
2. Click on the New Page button in the Control Bar.

   A new "untitled" page is added as a child of the selected page **(Figure 4.7)**.

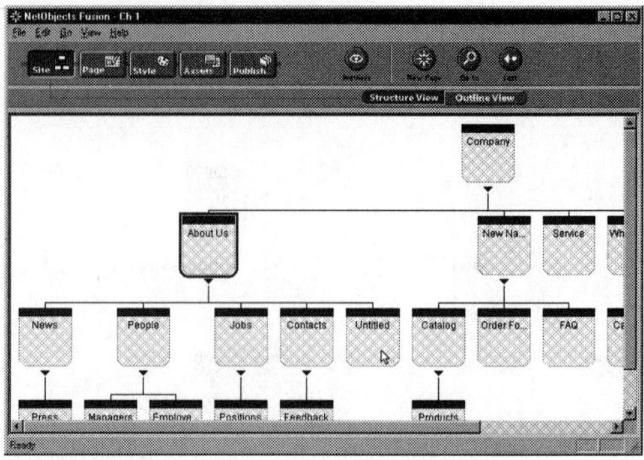


**Figure 4.7**
*A new untitled child page added below the page About Us.*

### ✔ Tip

- Another way to insert a new page as a child of the selected page is to select New Page from the Edit menu. You can also use the Insert key. *Mac users type Command + N.*

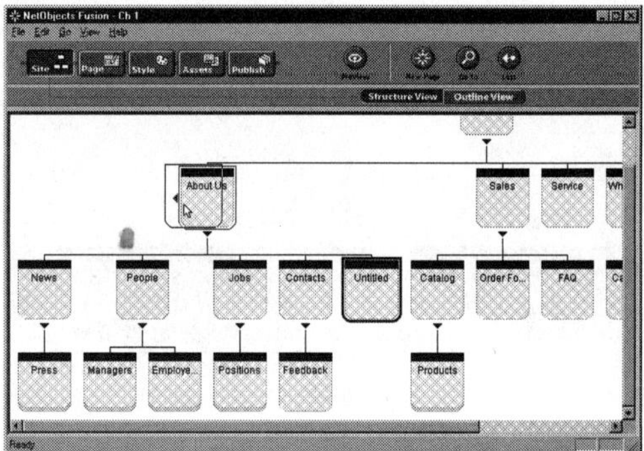


**Figure 4.8**
*Dragging a page to the parent level.*

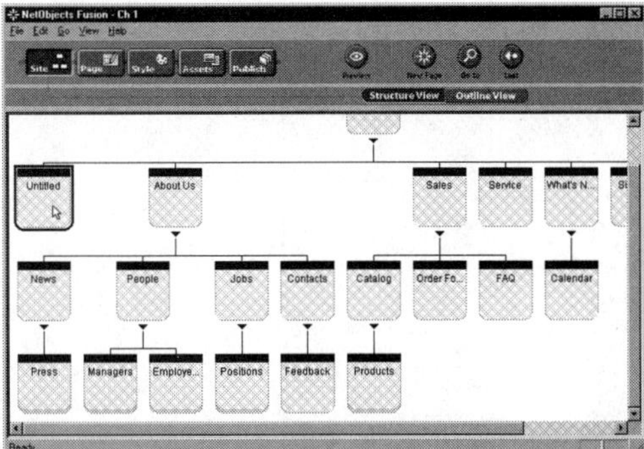


**Figure 4.9**
*The page in Figure 4.8 has been dropped in a new location.*

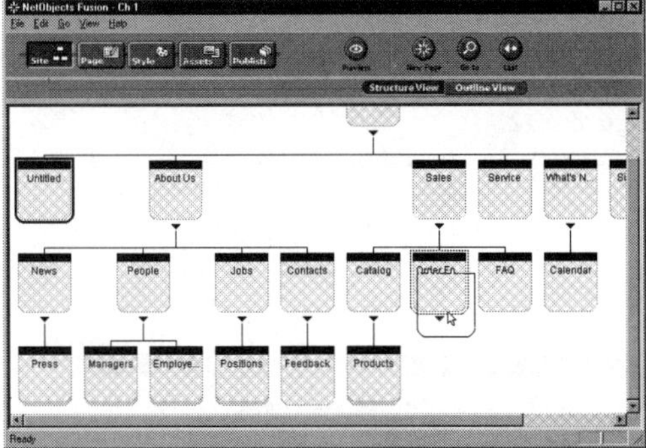


**Figure 4.10**
*Dragging a page to become a child of Order Form.*

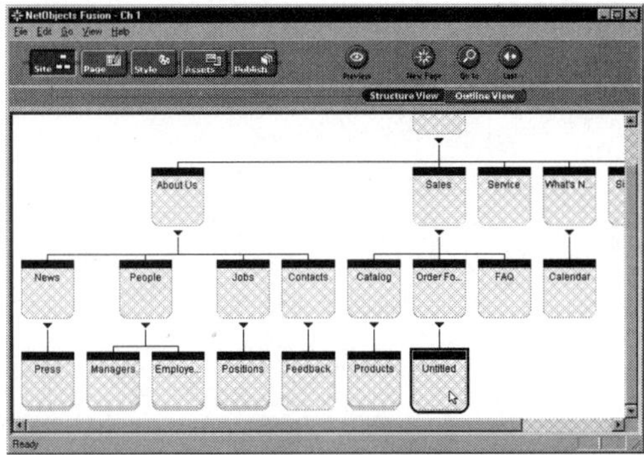


**Figure 4.11**
*The page in Figure 4.10 has been dropped in its new location.*

# Moving a Page

Moving a page is as simple as dragging it to a new location. Keep in mind that the children of the page you move will move right along with it.

### To move a page:

1. Select the page that you wish to move.
2. Drag the selected page to a page with which the selected page will have a sibling or child relationship. This is the target page.

   When you drag the selected page in this way, a red border with an arrow will appear around the target page. The arrow indicates the relationship that the selected page will have with the target page.

   An arrow pointing to the side of the target page indicates the selected page will become the target page's sibling **(Figures 4.8 and 4.9)**.

   When the arrow on the target page is pointing down, this indicates that the selected page will become the child of the target page **(Figures 4.10 and 4.11)**.
3. When the arrow on the target page indicates that the selected page will be moved to your desired location, let go of the mouse to drop the page.

   The selected page will be moved to its new location.

## Removing a Page

When planning your Web site's structure, you may find that you wish to remove a page you have created.

### To remove a page:

1. Select the page you wish to delete.
2. Select the Delete Page option from the Edit menu **(Figure 4.12)**.

   Fusion will display the Warning dialog box **(Figure 4.13)**.
3. Click OK in the Warning dialog box. *Mac users click Yes to delete the page.*

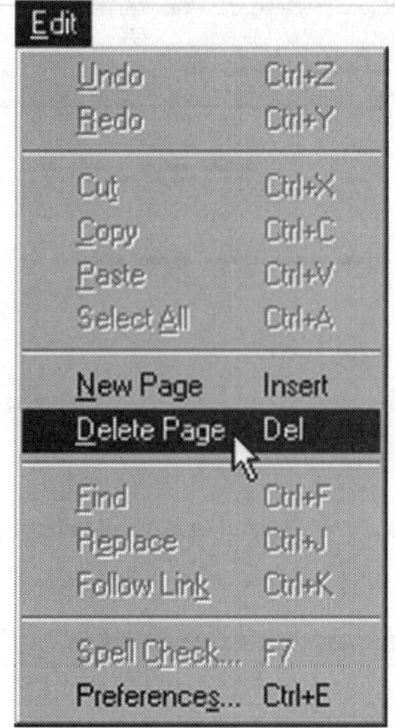


**Figure 4.12**
*Select Delete Page from the Edit menu.*

### ✓ Tips

- When you delete a page in Fusion, all of its children are deleted with it. And when multiple pages are deleted together, the deletion cannot be undone. So take care!
- You can also delete the selected page by using the Delete key.

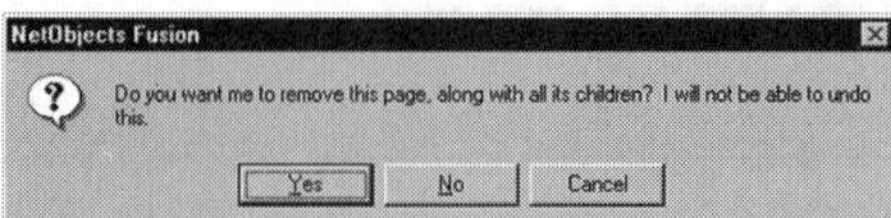


**Figure 4.13**
*Fusion provides a warning before deleting a page.*

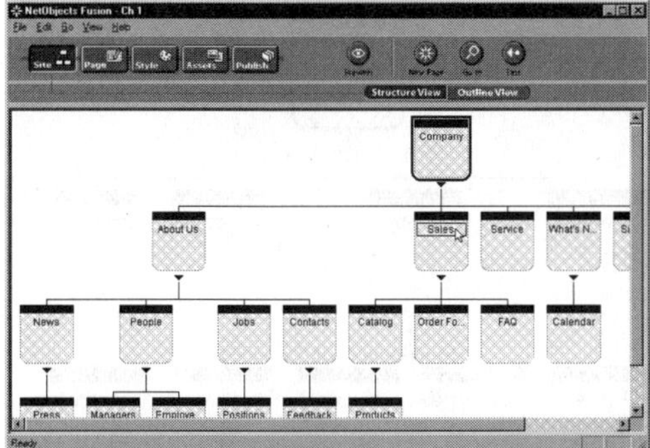


**Figure 4.14**
*Move the mouse pointer over the name of the page name.*

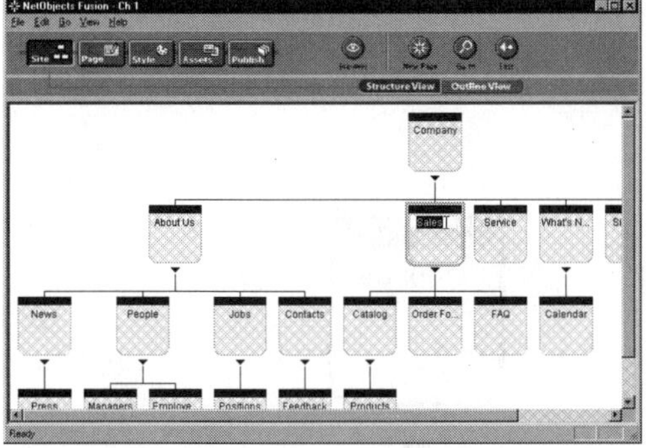


**Figure 4.15**
*Click on the page name to select the name.*

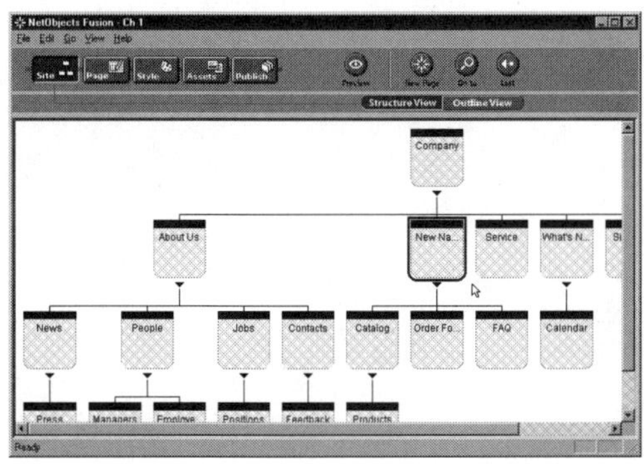


**Figure 4.16**
*Click somewhere off of the page to view your changes.*

# Editing a Page Name

When you create a new page, Fusion automatically names it "Untitled." In Site View, you can easily change the names of new pages or of any existing pages in your Web site.

### To edit a page name:

1. Place the mouse pointer on the name of the desired page.

   A box will appear around the name to show that you are in position to make a change **(Figure 4.14)**.
2. Click on the name, and it is selected **(Figure 4.15)**.
3. Type a new name.
4. Click anywhere else on the page or background to view the change.

### ✔ Tips

- You can also use the Page tab in the Properties Palette to edit a page name. With this method the desired page must be selected.
- When a page name is too long to be fully displayed, it is truncated with an ellipsis (...) **(Figure 4.16)**.

# Expanding and Collapsing the Site Structure

In Site View, you may wish to display only a few levels of your site. To hide site levels you can hide the children of any page.

In Site View, triangles appear at the base of pages with children **(Figure 4.17)**. You can choose to hide the children of any page in Site View by clicking this triangle.

### To hide a page's children:

Click the triangle at the base of the page whose children you wish to hide **(Figure 4.17)**.

All of that page's children are hidden, and a button with a plus sign appears below the parent page **(Figure 4.18)**.

### To show a page's children:

When the children of a page are hidden as in **Figure 4.18**, click the plus sign below the parent page.

All of that page's children are displayed.

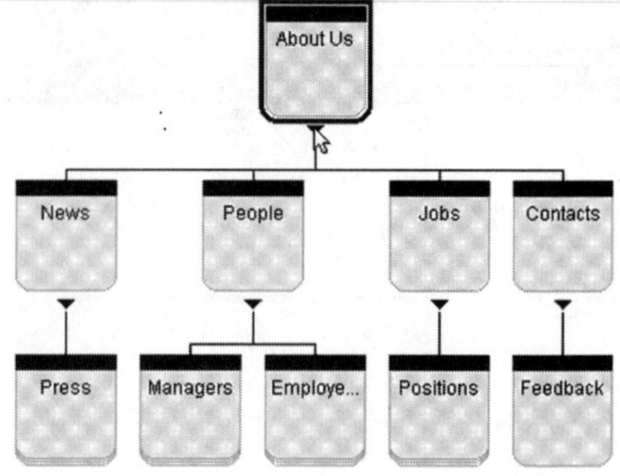


**Figure 4.17**
*Triangles displayed at the base of pages with children can be clicked to hide children.*

**Figure 4.18**
*When a page's children are hidden, a circular button with a plus sign is displayed below the page.*

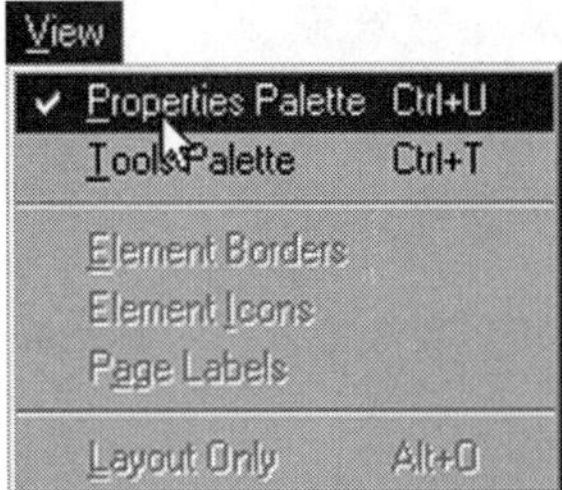


**Figure 4.19**
*To display the Properties Palette, select Properties Palette from the View menu.*

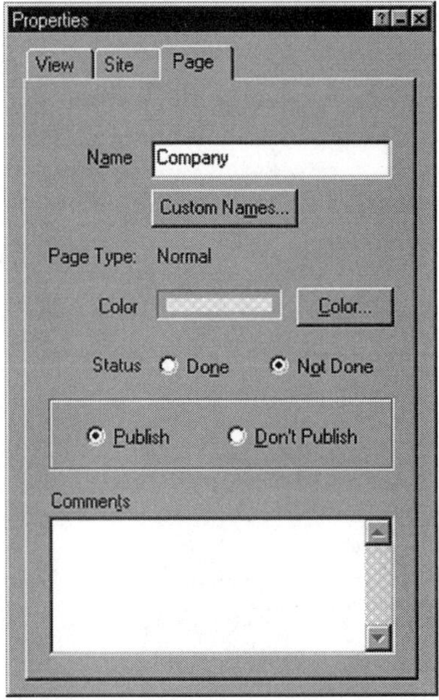


**Figure 4.20**
*The Page properties tab in the Properties Palette.*

# Accessing the Site View Properties Palette

The Site View Properties Palette contains tabs for View, Site, and Page properties.

The Page properties tab includes settings for page name, custom names, page type, color, status, your publishing preference, and comments.

### To access page properties:

1. Select the page whose properties you wish to view or edit.
2. If it is not already displayed, open the Properties Palette by selecting Properties Palette from the View menu **(Figure 4.19)**.

### ✔ Tips

- Because you have a page selected, the Properties Palette is automatically opened displaying the Page properties tab **(Figure 4.20)**.
- You can also access the Properties Palette by typing Ctrl + U.
  *Mac users press Command + U.*

## Using Page Properties to Specify Page Names

The Page properties tab in the Properties Palette contains a number of page naming facilities. First, the Name field allows you to edit the page name. Second, the Custom Names button allows you to specify special names for automatically generated buttons that create links to the selected page, the title banner that is displayed on the selected page, the page's HTML document, and even the file extension for the HTML document.

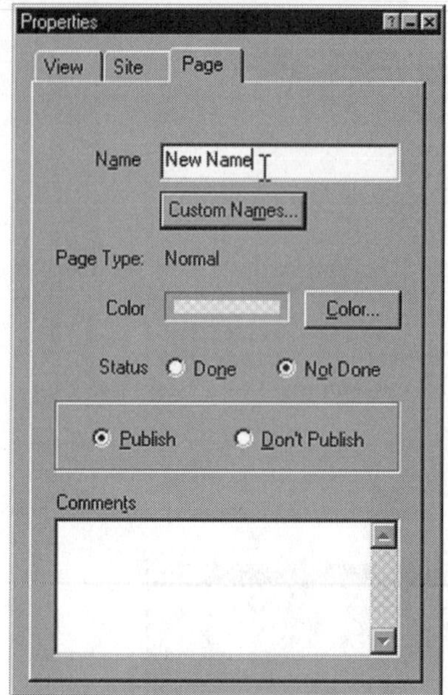


**Figure 4.21**
*Type a new name in the Name field in the Page tab of the Properties Palette.*

### To edit a page name using the Properties Palette:

1. On the Page properties tab in the Properties Palette, type the desired page name in the Name field **(Figure 4.21)**.
2. Click off of the Properties Palette to view your changes.

### To specify custom names for pages:

1. Select the page for which you want to specify custom names.
2. Select the Page tab in the Properties Palette.
3. Select the Custom Names button.
4. Type the desired names in the fields provided **(Figure 4.22)** on the Custom Names dialog box.

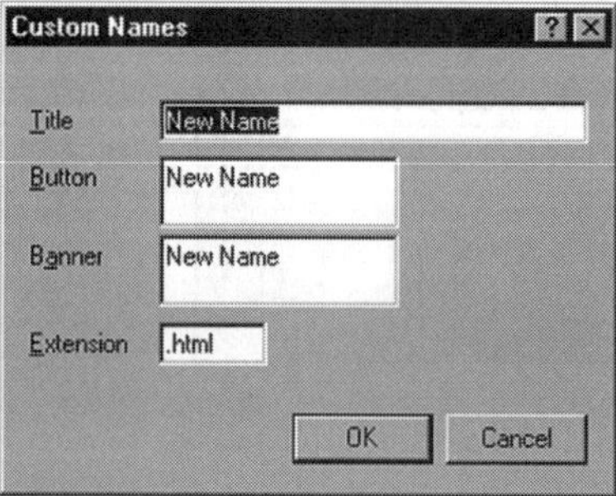


**Figure 4.22**
*The Custom Names dialog box.*

### ✔ Tip

- Custom names allow you to specify different names for a page banner, navigation bar button, and title. See Chapter 7 for more on banners and Chapter 9 for more on navigation bars.

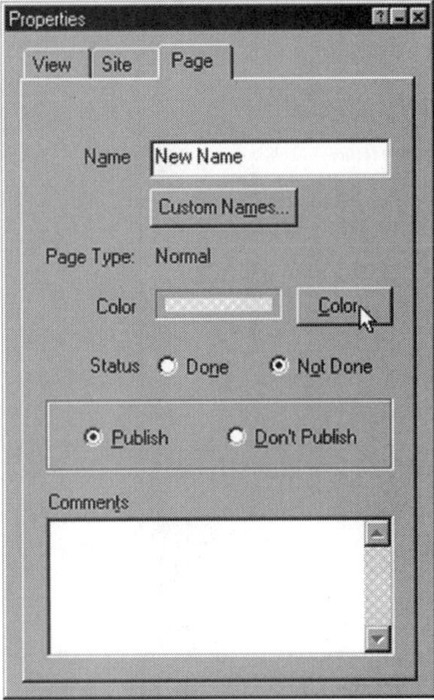


**Figure 4.23**
*Click the Color button to access the Color palette.*

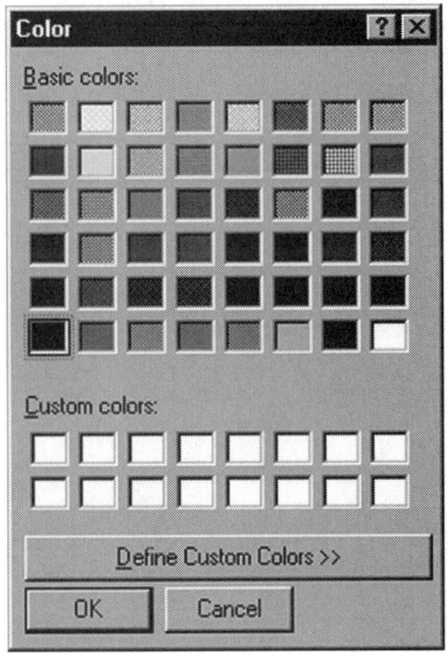


**Figure 4.24**
*Click on the desired color, and then click the OK button.*

## Using Page Properties to Specify Page Color

When working on a site, particularly a large, complex site, it can be very useful to apply a color-coding scheme to your pages in Site View to demarcate site functions or groups of related pages. For example, you might want to apply the same color to all pages related to your company's employees, products, or news announcements.

### To specify page color:

1. Select a page you wish to color.
2. Click on the Color button on the Page tab of the Properties palette **(Figure 4.23)**.
3. Click on a color in the color palette **(Figure 4.24)** to apply it to the selected page.
4. Click OK.

   The page you selected is displayed using the new color selection.

## Using Page Properties to Specify Page Status

The Page Status option in the Page properties tab in the Properties Palette allows you to indicate in Site View which pages are completed and which are still under construction. When the Done radio button is selected **(Figure 4.25)**, the selected page is displayed with a check mark **(Figure 4.26)** indicating it is completed.

**Figure 4.25**
*Click the Done radio button to specify the page is completed.*

### To specify page status:

1. Select the page whose status you wish to specify.
2. Click the Done radio button on the Page tab of the Properties palette.

   The selected page is displayed with a check mark **(Figure 4.26)**.

**Figure 4.26**
*Page in Site View with a done check mark.*

### ✔ Tips

- To specify that a page is not completed, select it and click the Not Done radio button.
- This is a handy feature, especially in Site View, where you can glance and see which pages need work and which are completed.

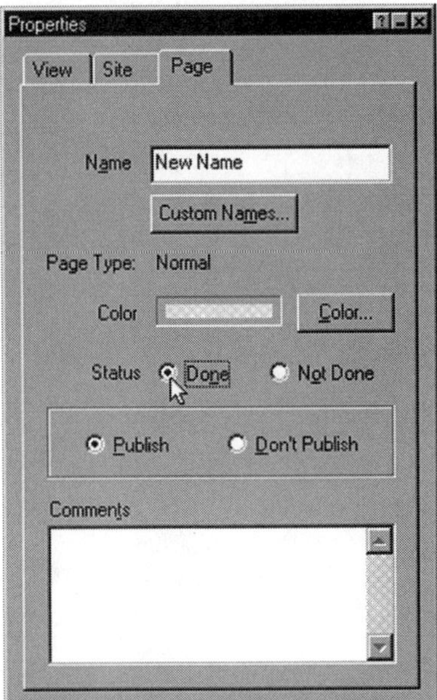


**Figure 4.27**
*Click the Don't Publish radio button to specify a page you don't want published with your site.*

**Figure 4.28**
*Page in Site View with a bullet indicating it will not be published with the site.*

## Using Page Properties to Indicate Pages to Publish

As you create a new site, or modify an existing one, you may create pages that you don't intend to publish immediately. Reasons not to publish a page might be that the page is not completed or you have not yet received the go-ahead from management to publish a new page for your site.

When selected, the Don't Publish option in the Page properties tab in the Properties Palette **(Figure 4.27)** displays a bullet on the selected page indicating a non-publishable page.

### To specify a page not to publish:

1. Select the page you wish to prevent from publishing with the site.
2. Click the Don't Publish radio button on the Page tab of the Properties palette **(Figure 4.27)**.

   The selected page is displayed with a red bullet **(Figure 4.28)**.

✔ **Tips**

- The children of an unpublished page also will not be published with the site.
- When the Web site is published, no HTML is generated for unpublished pages.

# Using Page Properties to Add Comments to a Page

The Comments text box available on the Page tab of the Properties Palette is a convenient way to store information about a specific page. This can be particularly useful when you are working with other people in developing your site.

### To enter comments for a page:

1. Select the page you wish to comment.
2. Click in the Comments text box in the Page properties tab of the Properties Palette.
3. Type your comments in the Comments text box **(Figure 4.29)**.

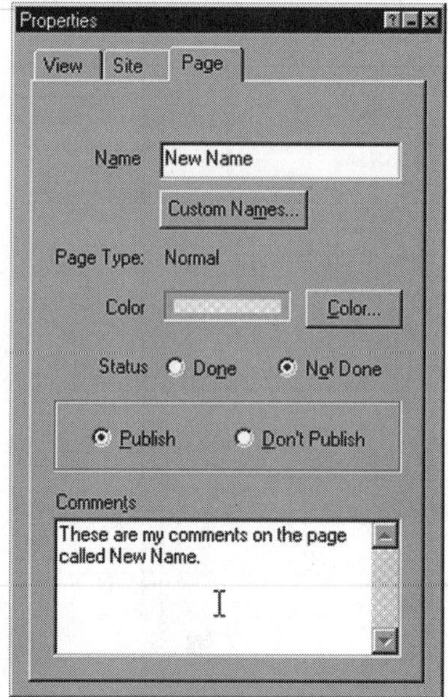


**Figure 4.29**
*Type your page comments in the Comments text box.*

### ✔ Tips

- You can use the comments text box to exchange information or to describe the planned contents for a page.
- When looking at a page in Structure View, there is no indication that comments have been entered for that page. However, you can use Outline View to see page comments at a glance **(Figure 4.30)**.

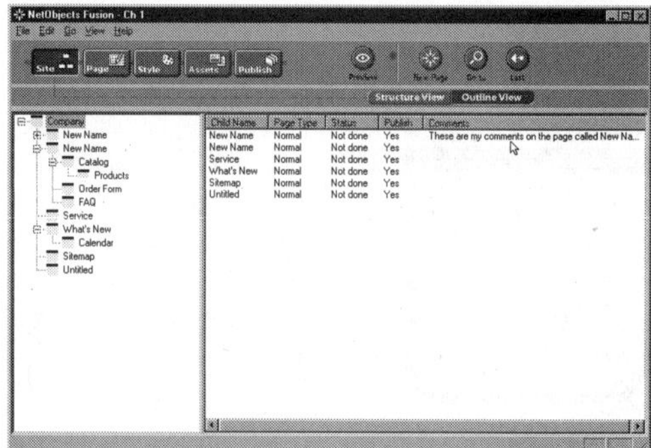

**Figure 4.30**
*You can view commented pages at a glance in Outline View.*

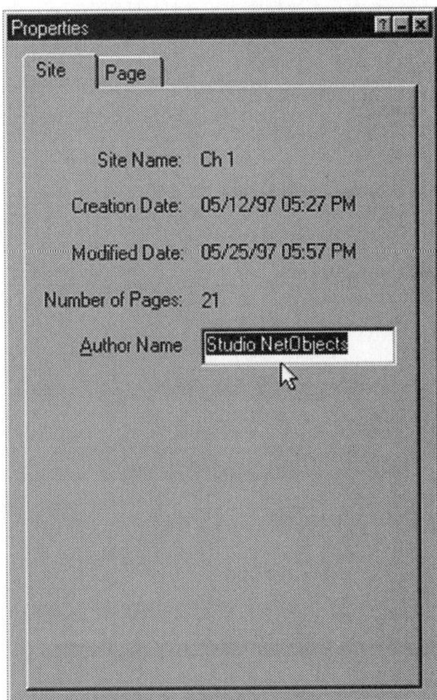


**Figure 4.31**
*You can edit the page author name in the Author Name field on the Site tab of the Properties Palette.*

## Using Site Properties to Specify the Author of a Page

The Site tab in the Properties Palette contains information about the name of your site, its size, the date it was created, and the last date it was modified. In addition, you are provided a text box for entering your name as the site author.

### To edit the author of a page:

1. Select the Site tab in the Properties Palette.
2. Click in the Author Name field **(Figure 4.31)**, and edit its contents as desired.

### ✔ Tip

■ The default author name for sites you create is the name that was entered when Fusion was installed. So if your copy of Fusion is registered in your name, then your name will automatically appear in the Author Name field for pages you create.

## Using View Properties to Select the Site Orientation

Some Web site structures don't lend themselves to being viewed in a vertical orientation. You can change the orientation of your site with options provided on the View tab of the Properties palette.

### To change the orientation of your site:

1. Select the View tab in the Properties Palette.
2. Select the vertical orientation option **(Figure 4.32)** to display your site in a vertical orientation.
3. Select the horizontal orientation option **(Figure 4.33)** to display your site in a horizontal orientation.

✓ **Tips**

- The default orientation is vertical.
- The Properties Palette View tab is available only in Structure View.

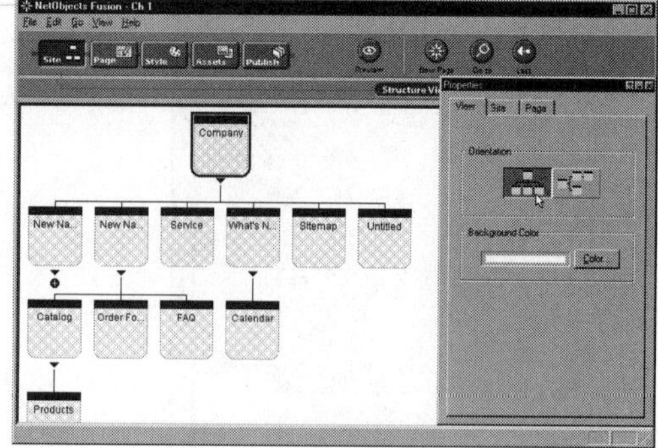


**Figure 4.32**
*The vertical orientation option is selected.*

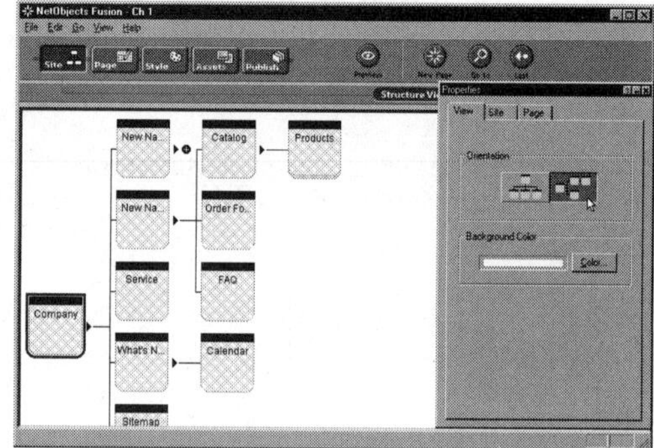


**Figure 4.33**
*The horizontal orientation option is selected.*

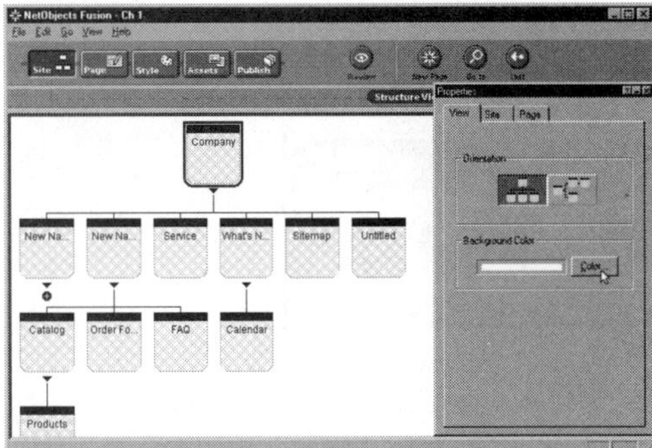


**Figure 4.34**
*Select Color button on the View tab in the Properties Palette.*

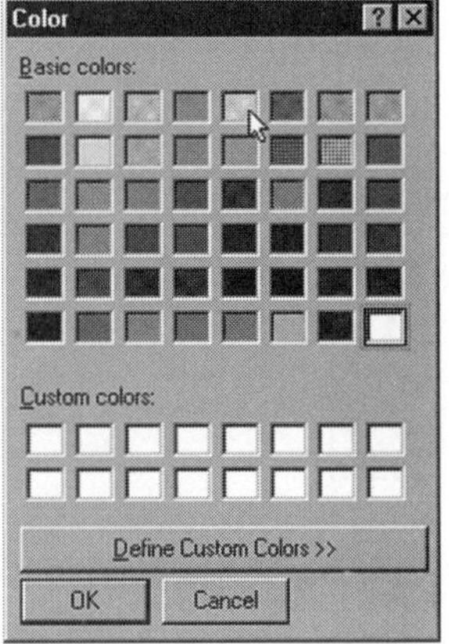


**Figure 4.35**
*The background Color palette.*

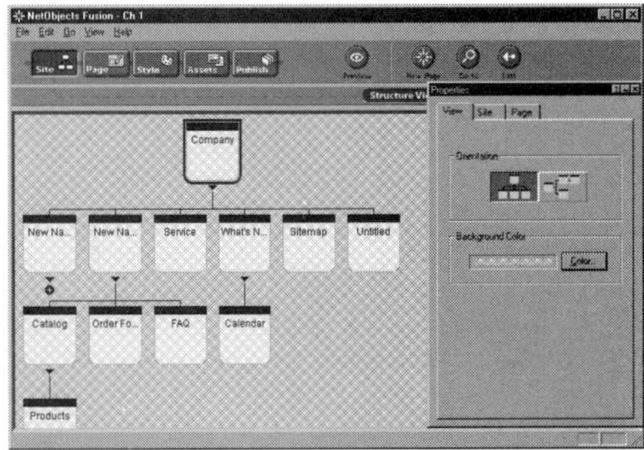


**Figure 4.36**
*A new background color is applied.*

# Using View Properties to Select a Background Color

Depending on your tastes, and the colors chosen for displaying your pages in Site View, you may want to modify the color of your Site View background.

### To change the Site View background color:

1. Select the View tab in the Properties Palette.

   The current site background color is displayed in the Background Color bar.

2. Click the Color button **(Figure 4.34)**.

   The Color dialog box appears **(Figure 4.35)**, and the current background color has a heavy border around it.

3. In the color palette, click on the color you wish to use as your background.

4. Click OK.

   Voila, the new background color is applied **(Figure 4.36)**.

### ✔ Tips

- The background color you select in Site View is for display only. It has no effect on the color or content of your Web pages.
- The default background color is white.
- The Properties Palette View tab is available only in Structure View.

## Accessing the Site View Tools Palette

The Site View Tools Palette **(Figure 4.37)** contains a pointer tool, a zoom in tool, and a zoom out tool. The pointer tool is used for selecting and dragging items in Site View. The zoom tools are used for magnifying or reducing the view of the site displayed in Site View.

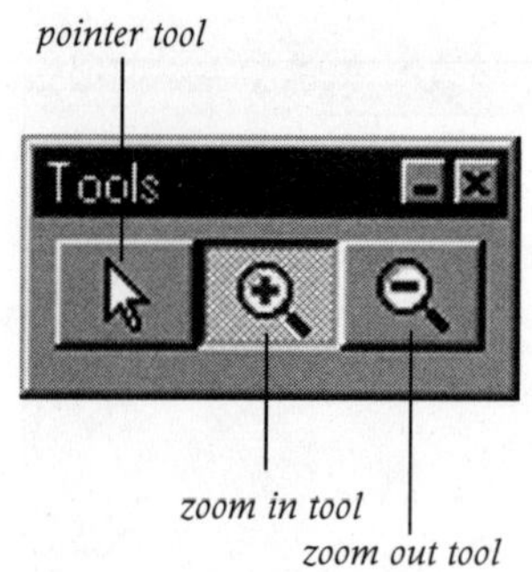


**Figure 4.37**
*The Site View Tools Palette.*

### To access the Tools Palette:

If the Tools Palette is not already displayed, choose Tools Palette from the View menu **(Figure 4.38)**.

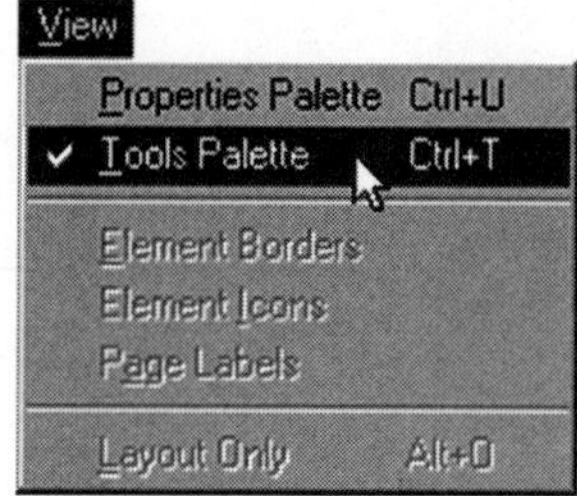


**Figure 4.38**
*To display the Tools Palette, select Tools Palette from the View menu.*

### ✓ Tips

- You can also access the Tools Palette by typing Ctrl + T. *Mac users press Command + T.*
- The Site View Tools Palette can be displayed in Structure View only.

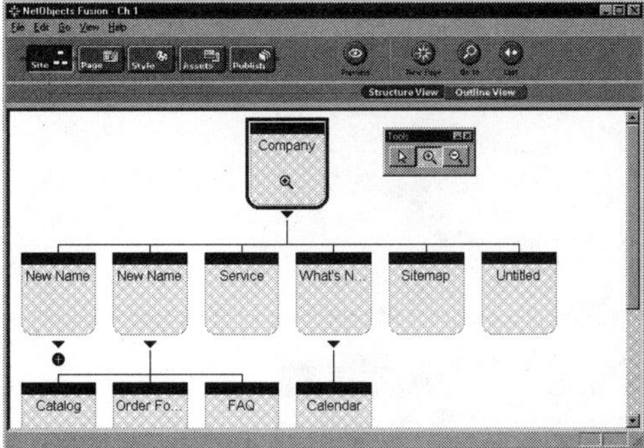


**Figure 4.39**
*Magnify the site displayed in Structure View using the Zoom In tool.*

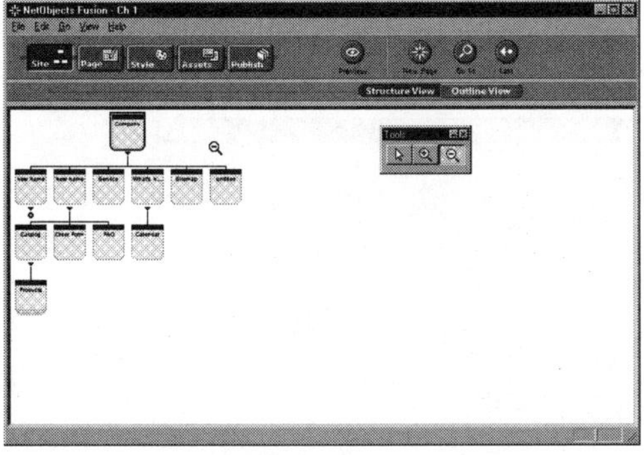

**Figure 4.40**
*Reduce the site displayed in Structure View using the Zoom Out tool.*

# Using the Zoom Tools

The zoom tools on the Site View Tools Palette are used to magnify or reduce the view of your site.

### To zoom in:

1. Select the Zoom In tool from the Tools palette.
2. Click on the area of the site you wish to magnify.

   The site is magnified more each time you click using the Zoom In tool **(Figure 4.39)**.

### To zoom out:

1. Select the Zoom Out tool from the Tools palette.
2. Click on the area of the site you wish to reduce.

   The site is reduced more each time you click using the Zoom In tool **(Figure 4.40)**.

## Importing a Section or Page

In Chapter 3 we introduced you to using templates to speed up your development time. In addition to beginning a site with a template, you can also import existing templates or pages into a Web site you are developing.

You can import pages from another Fusion Web site, AutoSite templates, other templates you or someone else may have created, or pages created in earlier versions of Fusion.

### To import a Fusion site or template as a section:

1. Use the pointer tool to select the page in your site that will be the parent of the imported template.
2. Select Import Section from the File menu **(Figure 4.41)**.
3. Select the Other option from NetObjects Fusion Sites.
4. Click the Browse button **(Figure 4.42)**. *(Mac users click the Select... button.)*
5. Locate and select the template or Fusion site you wish to import using the dialog box displayed.
6. Click Open.
7. Click OK in the Import Section dialog box.

   The selected template or site is imported as a section of the currently displayed site **(Figure 4.43)**.

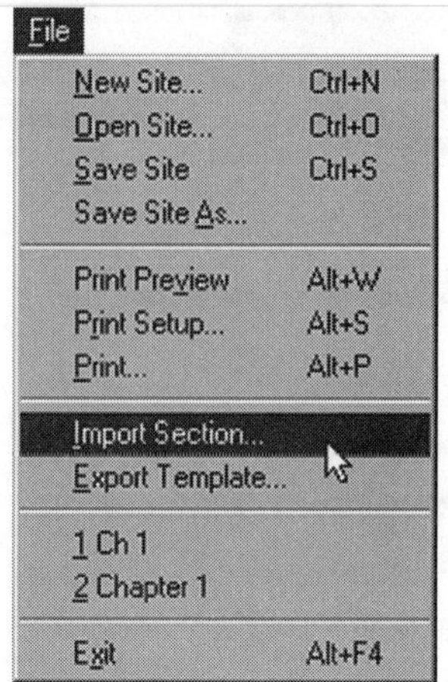


**Figure 4.41**
*Select Import Section from the File menu.*

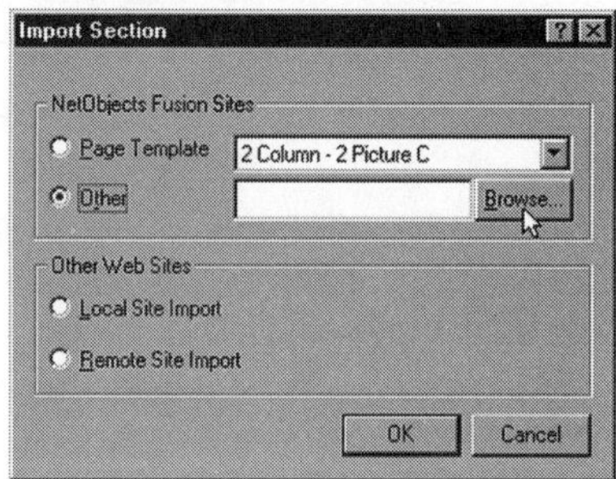


**Figure 4.42**
*Select the Other option, then click the Browse button to select the site or template to import.*

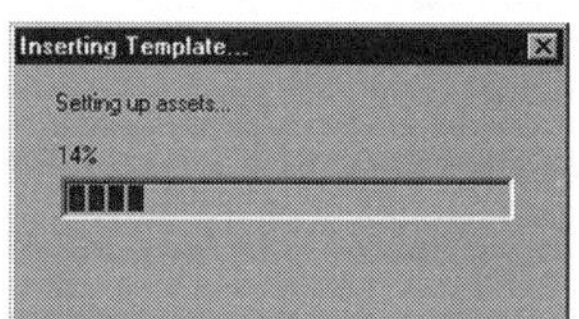


**Figure 4.43**
*The Importing Template dialog box illustrates Fusion's progress on importing the selected site or template.*

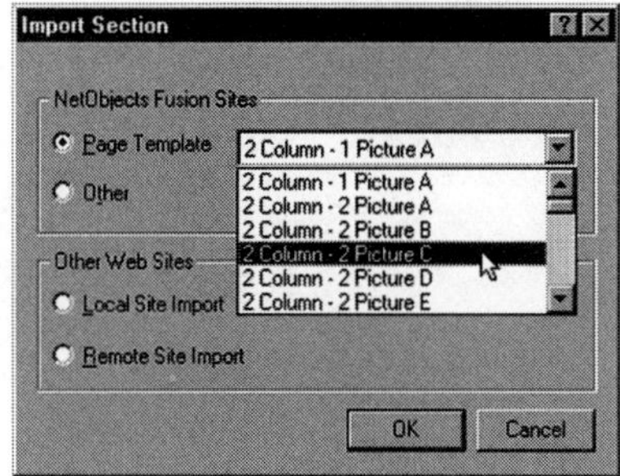


**Figure 4.44**
*Select the desired page template from the drop-down menu.*

## To import a Fusion Page Template:

1. Select the page in your site that will be the parent of the imported page.
2. Select Import Section from the File menu.
3. Select the Page Template option from NetObjects Fusion Sites.
4. Select the desired page template from the drop-down menu **(Figure 4.44)**.
5. Click OK in the Import Section dialog box.

   The selected page template is imported as a child of the selected page.

### ✔ Tips

- Page templates are stored in NetObjects Fusion/Templates/...
- You can add your own page templates by placing a page and its assets in a directory within the Pages directory.
- To view the page template, apply it to a page in Site View, then select Page View to view the selected page's layout.

## To import a local or remote site as a section:

1. Select the page in your site that will be the parent of the imported site.
2. Select Import Section from the File menu.
3. Select the Local or Remote Site Import option in Other Web Sites **(Figure 4.45)**, depending on whether the site you're importing is located on the local machine or on another machine accessible from yours.
4. Click OK, and the Set Local or Set Remote Import dialog box appears.
5. If you are importing a local site, use the Browse button (*Mac users click the Select... button*) and open dialog box to select the home page of the site. Or type the path and file name of the site's home page in the Home Page field **(Figure 4.46)**.

   If you are importing a remote site, enter the URL of that site in the URL Address field **(Figure 4.47)**.
6. Make Options selections as desired.
7. Click OK in the Set Local or Set Remote Import dialog box.

   The imported site is added, and its home page becomes the child of the selected page.

### ✔ Tip

- If you want to modify imported pages in Fusion, you must select the Convert to NetObjects Fusion format option when importing (**Figure 4.47**).

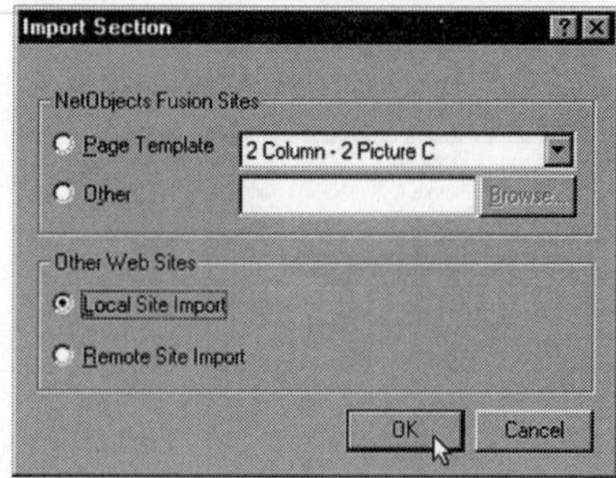


**Figure 4.45**
*Select the Local or Remote Site Import option.*

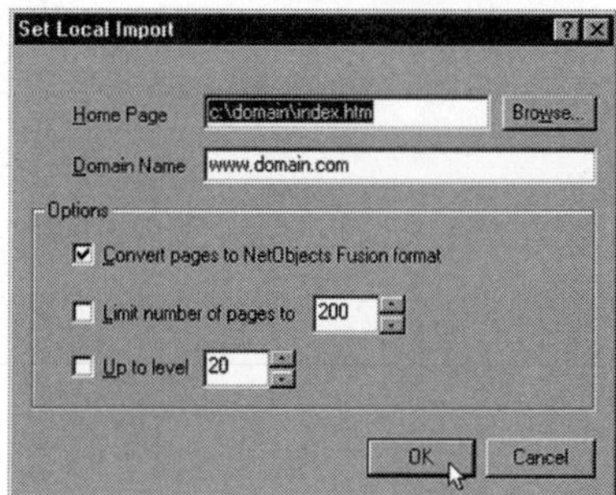


**Figure 4.46**
*Set Local Import.*

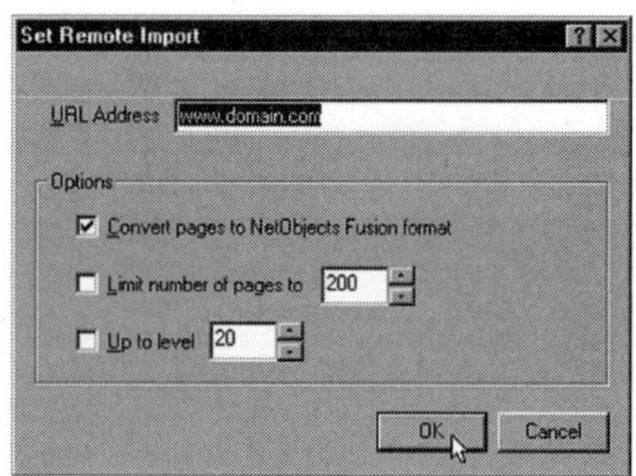


**Figure 4.47**
*Set Remote Import.*

Importing a Section

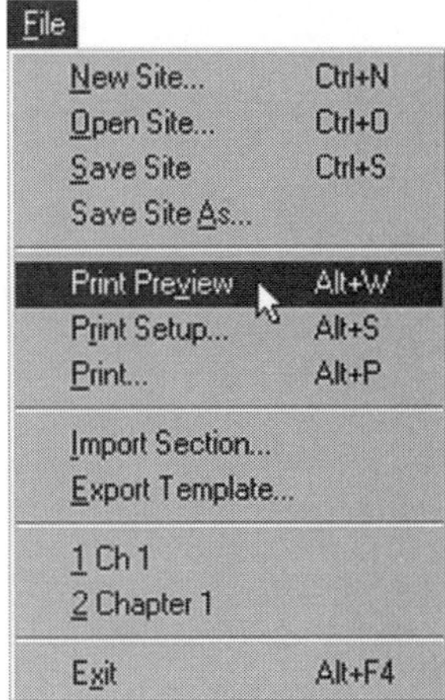


**Figure 4.48**
*Select Print Preview from the File mew.*

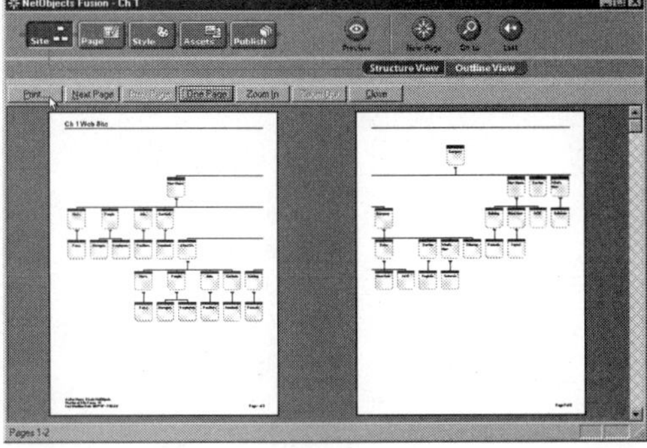


**Figure 4.49**
*Previewing a site before printing.*

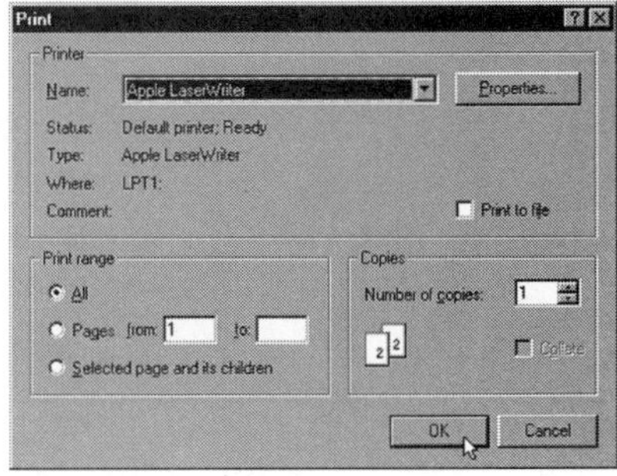


**Figure 4.50**
*The Print dialog box.*

## Printing the Site Structure

While developing your Web site, you will probably want to print your site structure. Fusion provides familiar printing options. However, you can print your site structure only from Structure View. In Outline View, all printing options are disabled.

### To perform a print preview:

1. In Structure View, select Print Preview from the File menu **(Figure 4.48)**.

   Fusion displays your site structure as it will print **(Figure 4.49)**.

2. Select Done to exit the Preview, or select Print to print the site structure. *Mac users select the Close button.*

### To print the site structure:

1. Select Print from the File menu.
2. Select the OK button in the Print dialog box that appears **(Figure 4.50)**. *Mac users select the Print button.*

   Your site is printed on the printer indicated in the Print dialog box.

### ✔ Tips

- You can preview and print any portion of your site structure. Simply select the topmost page of the section you want to print before selecting Print or Print Preview form the File menu.
- You can also select Alt + P to print your site structure.
- You can use the Print Setup option in the File menu to scale the structure or change the print orientation.

# Design the Look and Feel

**Figure 5.1**
*Select the look and feel of your site in Style View.*

## Making Web Pages Look Like a Web Site

In Site View you've experienced Fusion's facility for setting up the organization of your Web site—how each page in your site will be linked to the others. In laying out the structure of your Web pages in Site View, you are truly designing a Web site. But what makes a Web site a "site," other than the fact that a number of related pages are linked together? Fusion's answer to this question is that, together, the pages *look* like a cohesive site.

To help you establish the consistent look and feel of all the pages in your Web site, Fusion provides Style View **(Figure 5.1)** and a collection of SiteStyles. These features are yet another manifestation of Fusion's focus on the *site* rather than the *page*. By applying a SiteStyle, you take an important step in designing the look of all the pages in your site at once.

SiteStyles include the page background, banner, primary buttons, secondary buttons, data list icons, the color and style of text, and the style of horizontal lines. In Style View, you can apply any one of Fusion's prepared SiteStyles to your site, edit existing SiteStyles, or create your own. You can then apply the desired SiteStyle to all the pages in your site with a single mouse click rather than modifying the look of your pages one page at a time.

## Getting to Style View

Again, when Fusion is launched, its default is Site View. It's easy to determine which view you are in by looking at the Control Bar: the view navigation button for the currently displayed view is selected.

### To get to Style View:

If the navigation buttons in the Control Bar indicate you are not in Style View, select the Style button **(Figure 5.2)**.

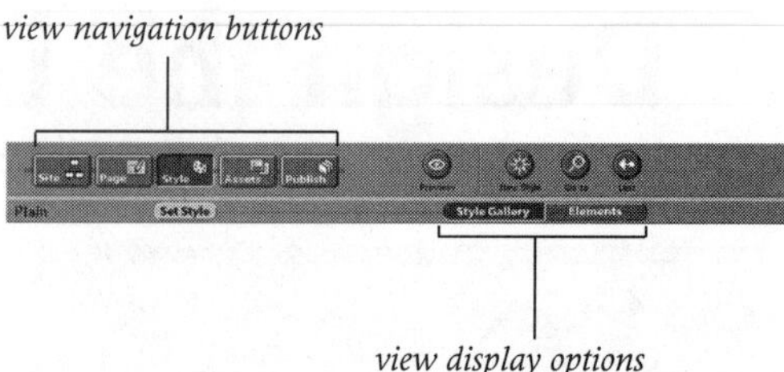


**Figure 5.2**
*The Control Bar with the Style View navigation button selected and the Style Gallery display option selected.*

## Style View Display Options

Style View offers two display options: Style Gallery and Elements.

The **Style Gallery** option displays all of the SiteStyles currently available in the frame on the left, while a preview of the currently selected style is displayed in the frame on the right **(Figure 5.3)**. Style Gallery is used to browse through, preview, and select an existing SiteStyle.

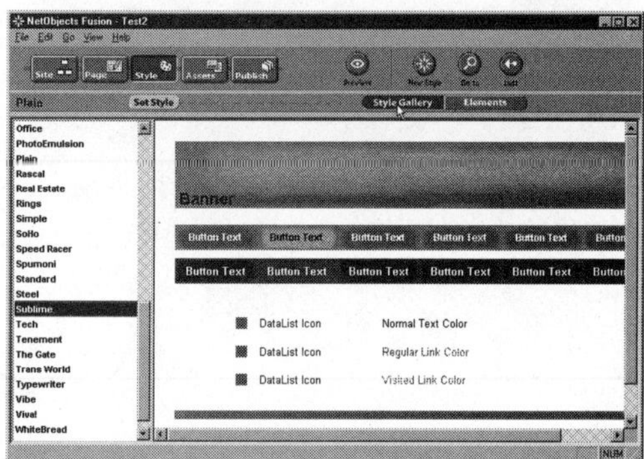

**Figure 5.3**
*Using the Style Gallery display option in Style View*

Rather than listing all of the available SiteStyles, the **Elements** display option displays the names of the different SiteStyle elements in the frame on the left **(Figure 5.4)**. The Elements display option is used to modify a SiteStyle or to create a new SiteStyle. Using the Elements display option, you can select any SiteStyle element and modify it.

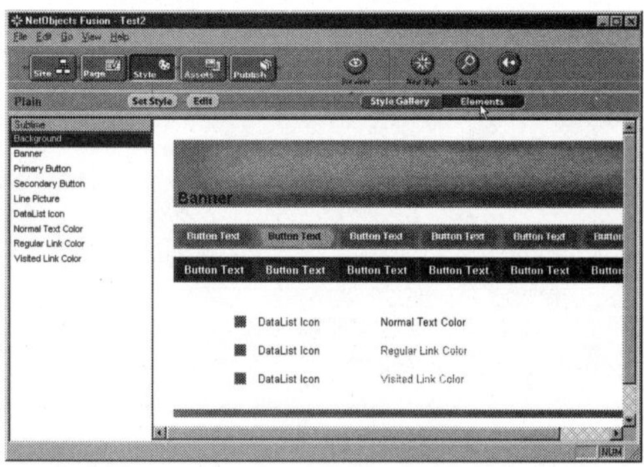

**Figure 5.4**
*Using the Elements display option in Style View*

### ✔ Tip

- The display option currently displayed is indicated by the selected display option button **(Figure 5.2)**.

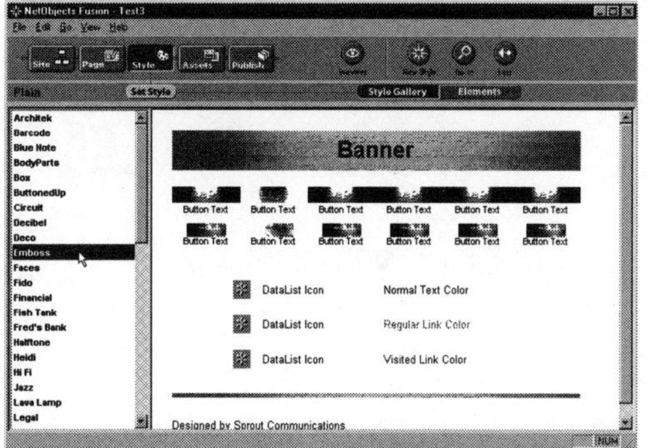


**Figure 5.5**
*Selecting a SiteStyle in the Style Gallery*

### To select Style View display options:

While in Style View, use the Control Bar to select the desired view display option **(Figure 5.2)**.

## Browsing the Style Gallery

Using the Style Gallery display option in Style View, you can browse through the available SiteStyles and view the style elements of each. Styles shown include the SiteStyles provided with your Fusion software and any additional SiteStyles that you have created and added.

### To browse the Style Gallery:

1. With the Style Gallery displayed in Style View, scroll through and select SiteStyles from the list displayed on the left.
2. View the elements of each selected SiteStyle on the right **(Figure 5.5)**.

### ✔ Tip

- As additional prepared SiteStyles become available, NetObjects will make them available for download from its Web site located at: **www.netobjects.com**.

## Understanding Style Elements

The SiteStyle elements displayed in the frame on the right in the Style Gallery include the page background, the banner, primary buttons, secondary buttons, DataList icons, a horizontal line picture, and text styles including text styles for buttons and links **(Figure 5.6)**.

The **banner** is used at the top of each page in your Web site with the name of the page placed on top of the banner image.

The page **background**, if defined, is an image that will be used for the background of your site. This image will appear behind all other elements on each page in your site.

**Primary** and **secondary buttons** are buttons that link the pages of your site together, often in the form of navigation bars. Each SiteStyle even includes special elements for *selected* primary and secondary buttons **(Figure 5.6)**—a touch that can add a particularly professional flair to your Web site.

**DataList icons** are used for database publishing. When you have placed records from a database on a page, this icon appears beside each record.

**Text colors** are specified for normal text, regular links, and visited links—those that have been previously selected by the particular user.

Finally, the **line picture** is used to specify a rule line when you place one on your pages.

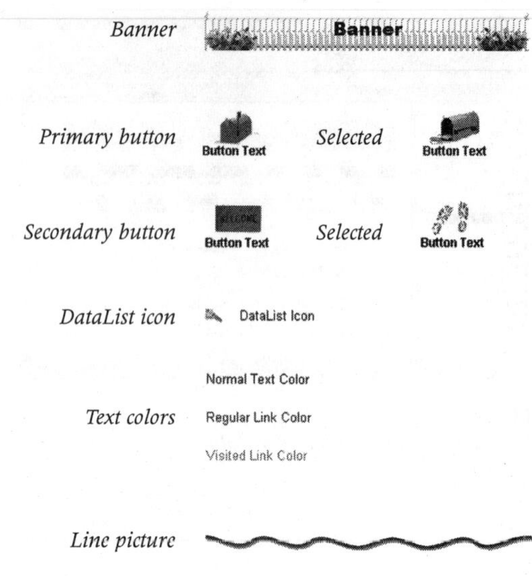


**Figure 5.6**
*SiteStyle Elements.*

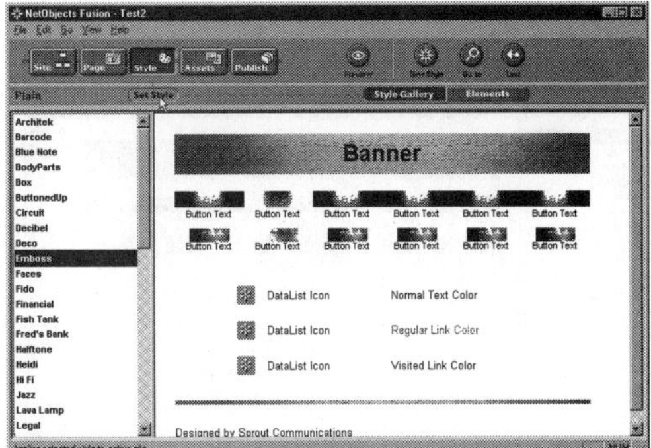

**Figure 5.7**
*Select a SiteStyle, and click the Set Style button.*

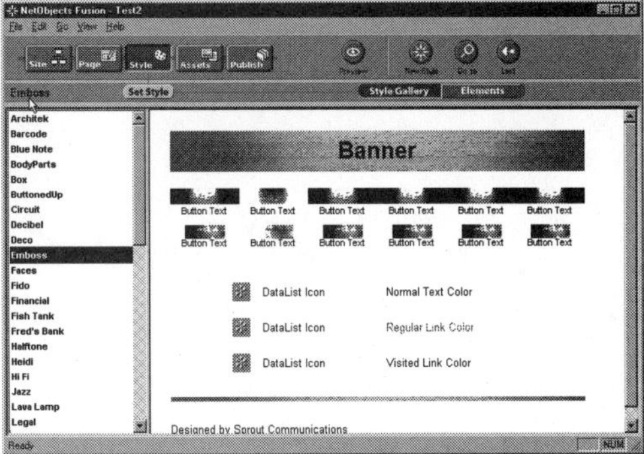

**Figure 5.8**
*The name of the applied style is displayed in the Control Bar.*

# Applying a SiteStyle

When the SiteStyle is applied to a site, the style elements are applied consistently on each page throughout the site. Even when you change the site's structure, add pages, or import sections, the selected SiteStyle will be applied to all of the pages in your site.

### To apply a SiteStyle:

1. With the Style Gallery displayed in Style View, select a SiteStyle from the list on the left.
2. Click the Set Style button in the Control Bar **(Figure 5.7)**.

   The style is applied to the site named in the Fusion title bar. The name of the applied style is displayed above the Style Gallery list in the Control Bar **(Figure 5.8)**.

   That's all there is to it. The next time you view your Web site pages in Page View, you will see these style elements on each page.

# Modifying a SiteStyle

You can also customize any of the SiteStyles listed in the Style Gallery. In customizing a SiteStyle, you can specify different graphics for use as style elements and change the various text color settings.

### To modify a SiteStyle:

1. In Style View, select a style from the Style Gallery.
2. Click the Elements button in the Control Bar to display the elements of the selected style.

   The Elements list appears on the left, displaying the list of standard elements you can modify in the SiteStyle.

   In addition, the Edit button appears in the Control Bar **(Figure 5.9)**.

   You are now ready to edit any element in the SiteStyle.

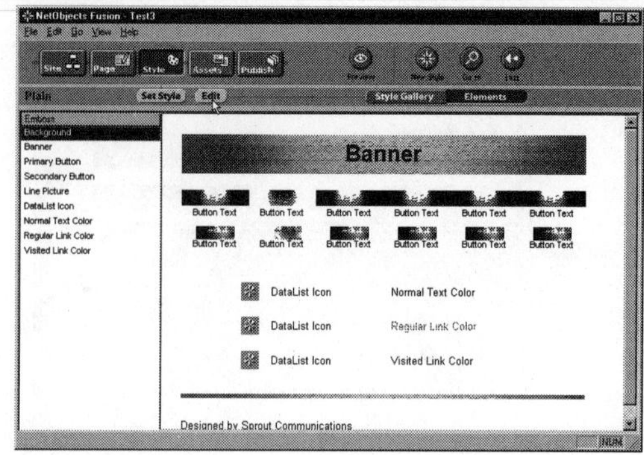


**Figure 5.9**
*The Edit button appears in the Control Bar.*

### ✔ Tips

- Another way to display the elements of a selected SiteStyle is to double-click the style's name in the Style Gallery.
- Changes you make to SiteStyles are saved automatically and generally cannot be "undone" using the Undo option in the Edit menu. So use caution when modifying SiteStyle elements.

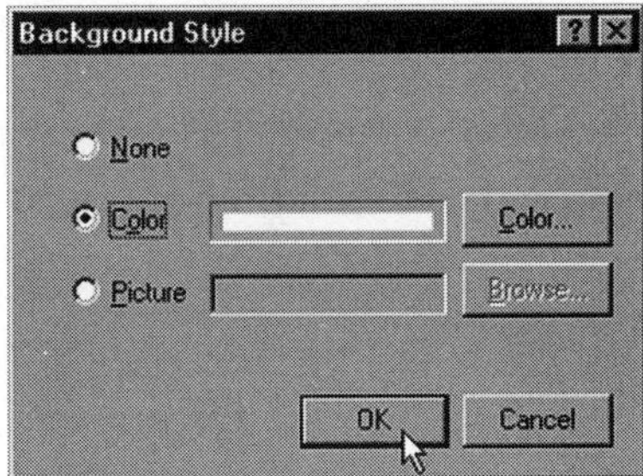


**Figure 5.10**
*The Background Style dialog box.*

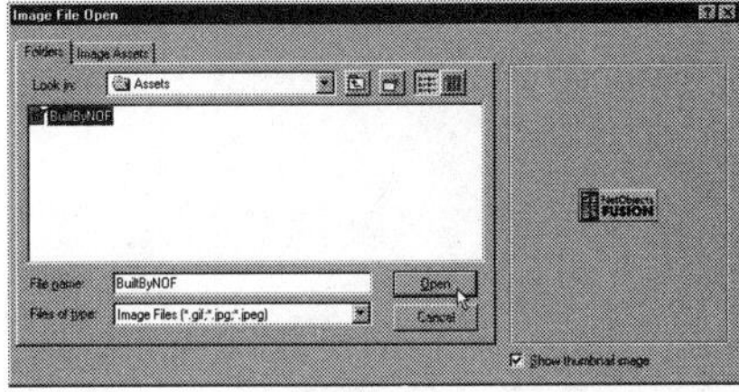

**Figure 5.11**
*Specifying an image file for use as a background.*

## To change the background:

1. In Style View, select Background from the Elements list for the desired SiteStyle.
2. Click the Edit button in the Control Bar to display the Background Style dialog box **(Figure 5.10)**.

   The background options available are:

   **None** displays the browser's default background, usually grey.

   **Color** displays a solid white background or another color selected using the Color... button.

   **Picture** displays a selected image file as a background. Browsers will tile the selected image file across each page in your site. Specify a picture file for a background by using the Browse... button **(Figure 5.11)**. *Mac users click the Select... button.*
3. Select one of the three background options.
4. For the Color and Picture options, select the Color... or Browse... (*Mac, Select..)* buttons respectively, and make color or image file selections.
5. Click OK in the Background Style dialog box.

   Changes you have made to the SiteStyle's background are displayed in Style View.

### ✔ Tip

- Another way to open the Background Style dialog box is by double-clicking Background in the Elements list.

## To edit a banner:

1. In Style View, select Banner from the Elements list for the desired SiteStyle.
2. Click the Edit button in the Control Bar to display the Banner dialog box.
3. Click the Browse… button **(Figure 5.12)** and select an image file for the page banner using the dialog box displayed. *Mac users click the Select... button.*
4. Click Open in the dialog box displayed after selecting the desired image file.
5. Click the Text Settings… button and make desired text style and formatting selections for the page title displayed in the banner **(Figure 5.13)**.

   Available text settings options include relative, vertical, and horizontal alignment within the banner; font, color, and orientation.
6. Click OK in the Text Settings dialog box.
7. Click OK in the Banner dialog box.

   The changes you have made to the banner image and text are displayed in Style View.

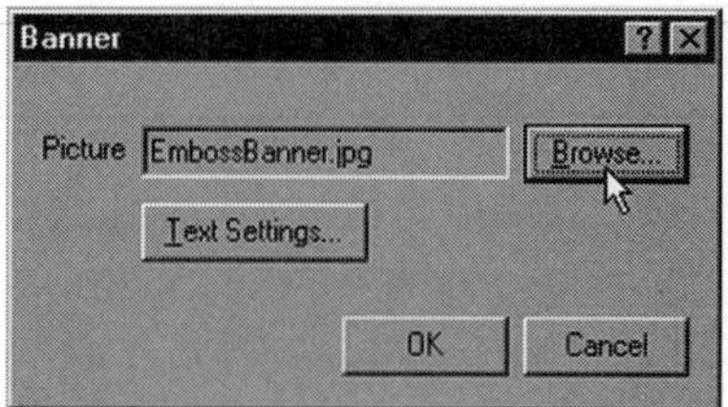


**Figure 5.12**
*The Banner dialog box.*

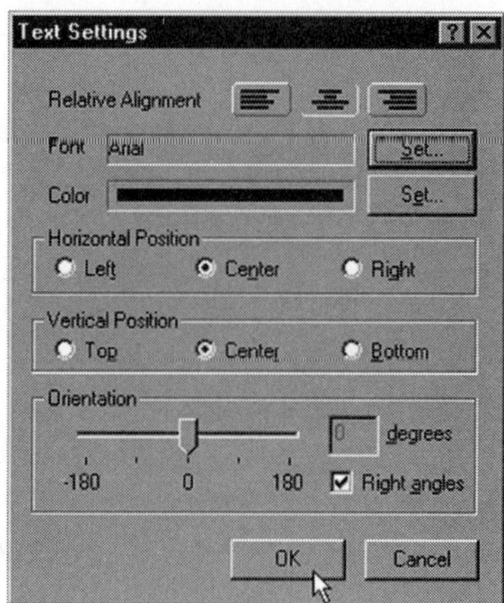


**Figure 5.13**
*Text Settings for the page title displayed on the page banner.*

### ✔ Tip

- You can double-click Banner in the Elements list to display the Banner dialog box.

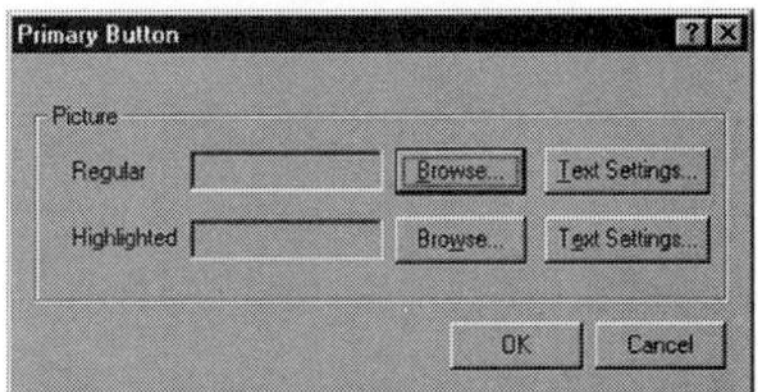


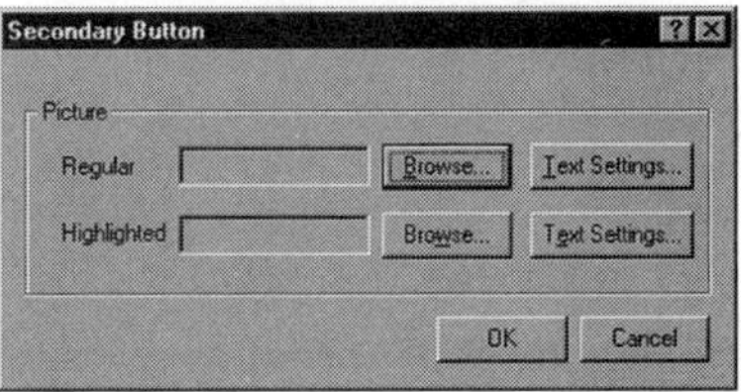


**Figure 5.14**
*The Primary and Secondary Button dialog boxes.*

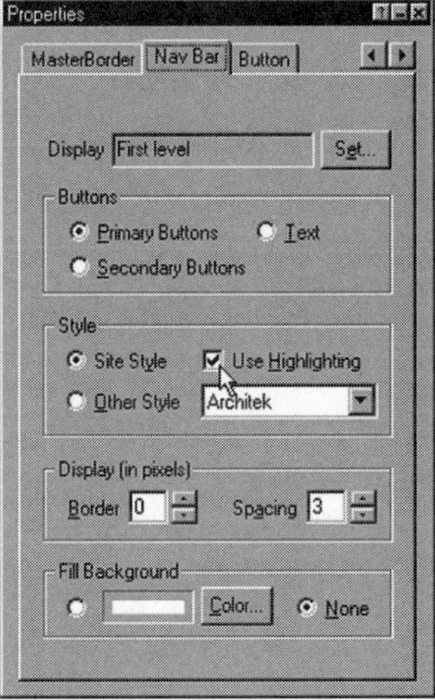


**Figure 5.15**
*Nav Bar properties dialog box (click somewhere off the page to view your changes).*

## To change primary and secondary buttons:

1. In Style View, select Primary Button or Secondary Button from the Elements list for the desired SiteStyle.
2. Click the Edit button in the Control Bar to display the selected button dialog box **(Figure 5.14)**.

   The Primary and Secondary Button dialog boxes allow you to choose a different image file for the regular and highlighted versions of the buttons. By choosing a special image for a highlighted button, visitors to your site will be able to easily determine their current location by glancing at the navigation button bar—the highlighted button indicates the visitor's current location.
3. Click the Browse... button *(Mac users click the Select... button)* for a Regular button, choose an image file to use, and click Open.
4. Click the Browse... button *(Mac users click the Select... button)* for a Highlighted button, choose an image file to use, and click Open.
5. Click the Text Settings... button for both the Regular and Highlighted versions of the button, and make desired text formatting selections **(Figure 5.13)**.
6. Click OK in the Button dialog box.

### ✓ Tip

- You can disable the button highlighting feature for navigation button bars in the Nav Bar properties tab in Page View **(Figure 5.15)**.

Change buttons

## To specify a line picture:

1. In Style View, select Line Picture from the Elements list for the desired SiteStyle.
2. Click the Edit button in the Control Bar to select an image file using the dialog box displayed **(Figure 5.16)**.
3. Select a file to use and click Open.

   Your Line Picture selection is displayed in Style View **(Figure 5.17)**, replacing the Line Picture image previously defined for the selected style.

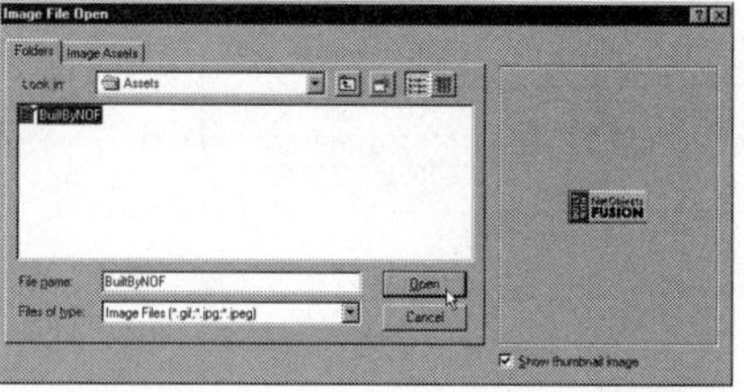

**Figure 5.16**
*Choosing a Line Picture using the Image File Open dialog box.*

### Tip

- You can also display the dialog box displayed for selecting a Line Picture by double-clicking Line Picture in the Elements list.

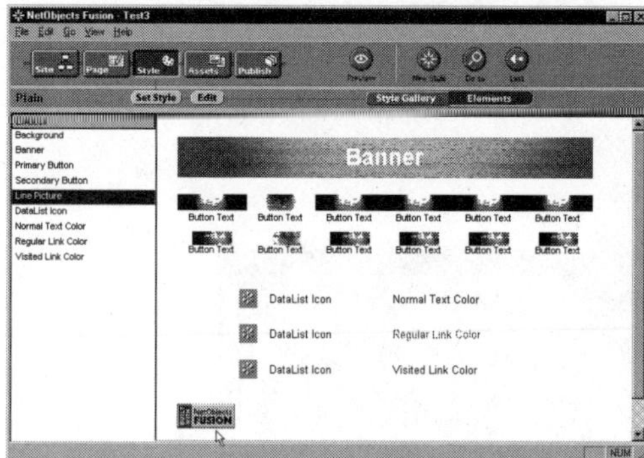


**Figure 5.17**
*The selected Line Picture icon displayed in Style View.*

## To edit the data list icon:

1. In Style View, select DataList Icon from the Elements list for the desired SiteStyle.
2. Click the Edit button in the Control Bar to select an image file using the dialog box displayed **(Figure 5.16)**.
3. Select a file to use and click Open.

   Your new DataList Icon image is displayed in StyleView.

**Figure 5.18**
*Select a color from the color palette.*

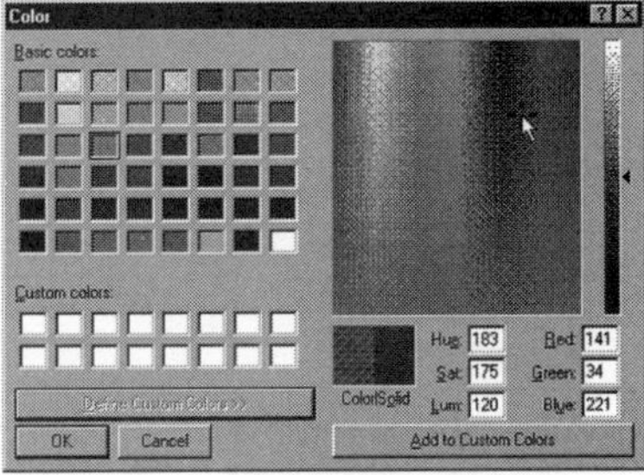


**Figure 5.19**
*Click Define Custom Colors for more color options.*

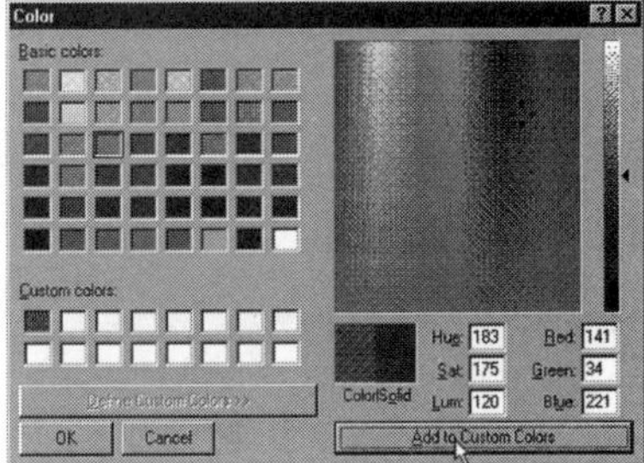


**Figure 5.20**
*Click Add to Custom Colors to include a custom color you define to the standard color palette.*

## To change text colors:

1. In Style View, click the desired text element in the Elements list of the desired SiteStyle.

   **Normal Text Color** controls the color of normal text or content text on your Web pages.

   **Regular Link Color** controls the color in which text links on your Web pages will be displayed.

   **Visited Link Color** controls the color in which you will display links that a visitor to your site has already clicked. Using a special color for visited links helps visitors keep track of where they have been.

2. Click the Edit button in the Control Bar.

   The color palette is displayed **(Figure 5.18)**.

3. Select a text display color from this palette, or click Define Custom Colors for more color options **(Figure 5.19).** *Mac users, define custom colors by clicking a custom color and selecting the Edit... button.*

   If you choose to define a custom color, use the custom color controls to select color values, then click Add to Custom Colors to save your defined color in the color palette **(Figure 5.20)**.

4. Click OK to apply your color selection.

   Your color selections are displayed in Style View.

## Creating a New SiteStyle

Creating a new SiteStyle from scratch is much the same as modifying an existing SiteStyle. It involves specifying images for use as the various SiteStyle elements and making text color selections.

### To create a new SiteStyle:

1. In Style View, select New Style... from the Edit menu **(Figure 5.21)**.

   A Request dialog box appears requesting a name for the new style.

2. Type a SiteStyle name in the field provided, and click OK **(Figure 5.22)**.

   The new SiteStyle is displayed in Style View **(Figure 5.23)**. The background (white, text and link colors elements in your new style have already been defined.

   You can now follow the same procedures presented in the previous section, Modifying a SiteStyle, to make selections for each of the style elements of your new style.

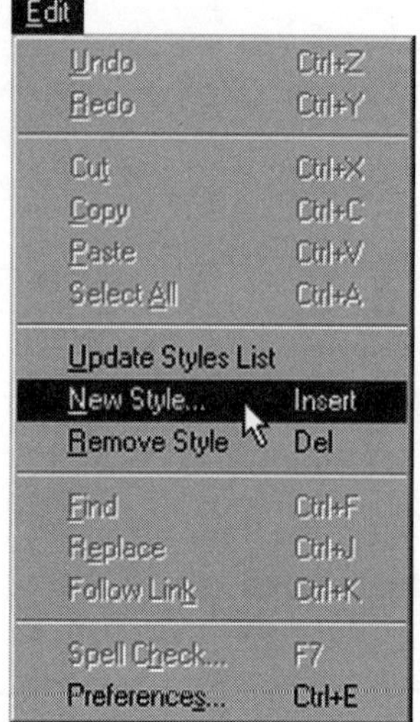


**Figure 5.21**
*Select New Style from the Edit menu.*

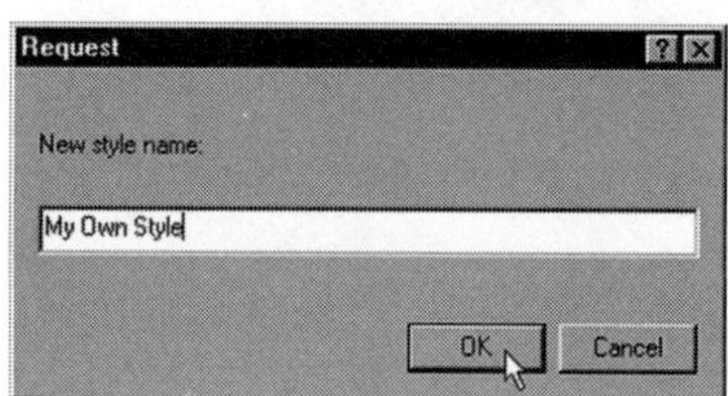


**Figure 5.22**
*Enter a name for the new SiteStyle in the Request dialog box.*

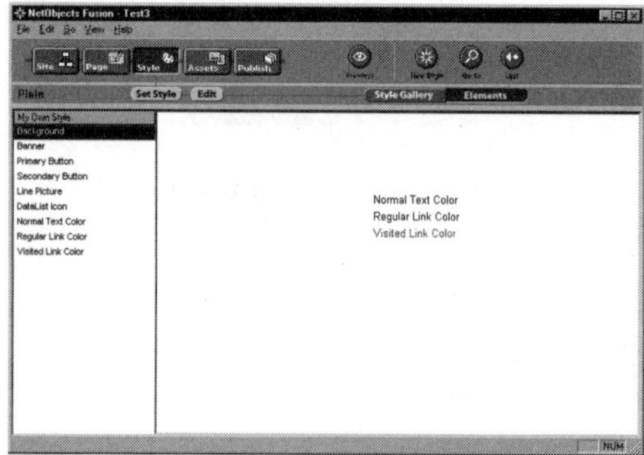


**Figure 5.23**
*The new blank style is displayed in Style View.*

### ✓ Tip

- When Fusion creates a new SiteStyle, it automatically creates a new folder for the style inside the NetObjects Fusion 2.0/Styles folder.

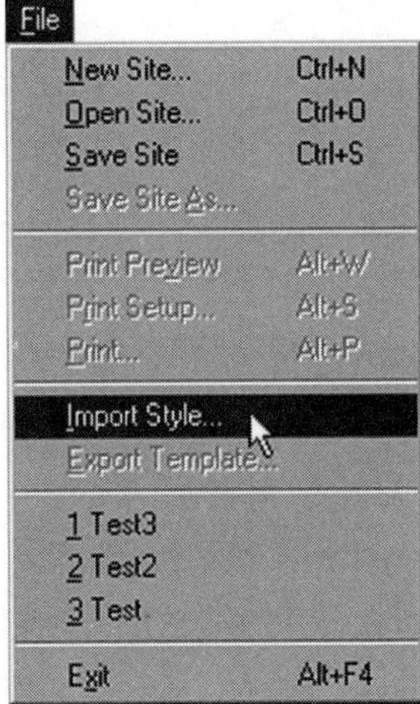


**Figure 5.24**
*In Style View, select Import Style from the File menu.*

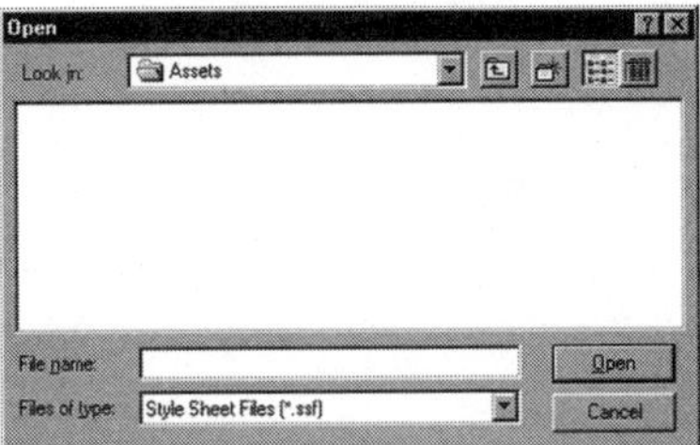


**Figure 5.25**
*Locate and open the SiteStyle to import using the Open dialog box.*

## Importing a SiteStyle

NetObjects will make additional Fusion SiteStyles available for download from its Web site at **www.netobjects.com**. In addition, you may obtain SiteStyles from other Web developers or other sources. In such cases, you will need to import the SiteStyle into the current Web site project before it can be applied to that site.

### To specify custom names for pages:

1. In Style View, select Import Style... from the File menu **(Figure 5.24)**.

   The open dialog box is displayed **(Figure 5.25)**.

2. Use the Open dialog to locate the SiteStyle folder you want to import. Inside this folder, select the style's **.ssf** file.

3. Click Open.

   The imported SiteStyle is displayed in Style View, and its name is added to the Gallery list.

### ✔ Tips

- An imported SiteStyle will be available only in the Style Gallery list for the currently open Fusion site.
- You can update the Gallery list for any given project to include all available SiteStyles (including imported styles) by selecting Update Styles from the Edit menu in Style View.

## Deleting SiteStyles

There may be times when you want to reduce the number of styles displayed in the Style View Style Gallery list.

### To delete a SiteStyle:

1. Select the SiteStyle to be removed in the Style Gallery list.
2. Select Remove Style from the Edit menu **(Figure 5.26)**.

   A warning dialog box will appear.
3. Click Yes to proceed.

   The SiteStyle you selected is removed from the Style Gallery list.

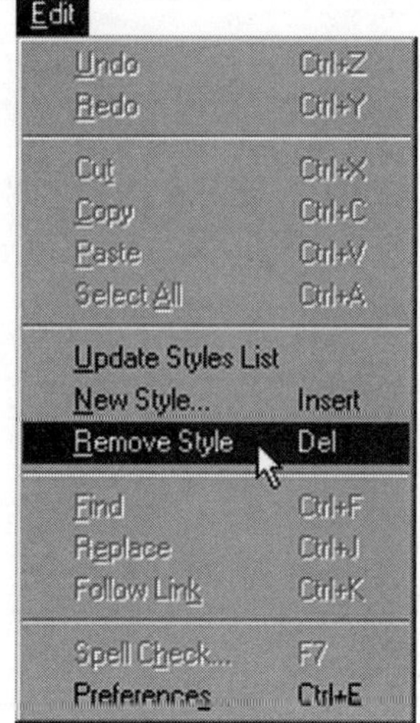


**Figure 5.26**
*Select Remove Style from the Edit menu in Style View.*

### ✔ Tips

- Removing a SiteStyle does not remove its folder or associated files from the Styles folder in the NetObjects Fusion 2.0 folder. To completely remove a SiteStyle, you must manually delete its folder.
- To restore a SiteStyle to the Style Gallery list for a particular site, select Update Styles from the Edit menu.

# Introducing the Fusion Page

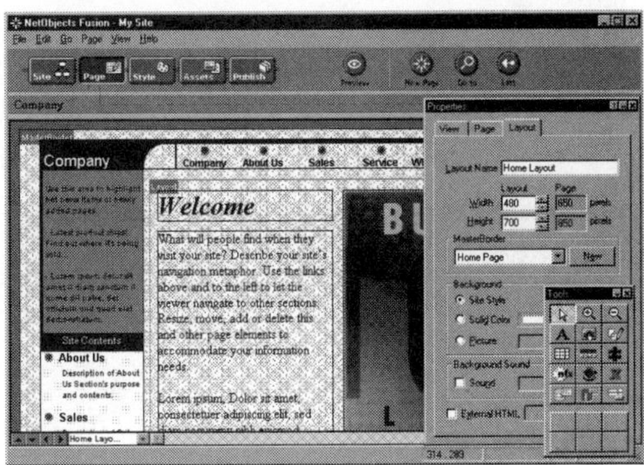


**Figure 6.1**
*Page View and the Page View Properties and Tools palettes.*

## Considering Page Content the Fusion Way

In Style View, you took a first step in creating the look of the Web pages in your site. In Page View, you will flesh out the content of each page, add special links, images, text, tables, frames, and more.

In Page View, you go from affecting changes to the entire site as in Site and Style Views, to working with just one page in your site at a time. And Fusion allows you to consider the content of each page in much the same way graphic artists consider the layout and design of print media.

For designing the layout of your Web pages, Fusion provides a paste-up board complete with a grid and a variety of content-creation tools **(Figure 6.1)**. Rather than focusing your attention on HTML coding, Fusion's completely visual page design environment allows you to concentrate on the look, feel, and texture of each page in your site. In fact, creating Web content with Fusion is much like working with a page layout application like QuarkXPress or PageMaker.

## Getting to Page View

You can get to Page View using the Control Bar or using the pages displayed in Site View.

Remember, when Fusion is launched, its default is Site View. It's easy to determine which view you are in by looking at the Control Bar: the view navigation button for the currently displayed view is selected **(Figure 6.2)**.

### Using the Control Bar:

If the navigation buttons in the Control Bar indicate you are not in Page View, select the Page button **(Figure 6.2)** to go to Page View.

The Page View for the page currently selected in Site View will be displayed.

### Using the Site View:

If you wish to go to the Page View for a particular page displayed in the Site View structure, double-click the desired page **(Figure 6.3)**.

### ✔ Tip

- The Page View displayed is for a specific page in your Fusion Web site. The name of the page currently displayed under the view navigation buttons in Page View is shown in the Control Bar **(Figure 6.4)**.

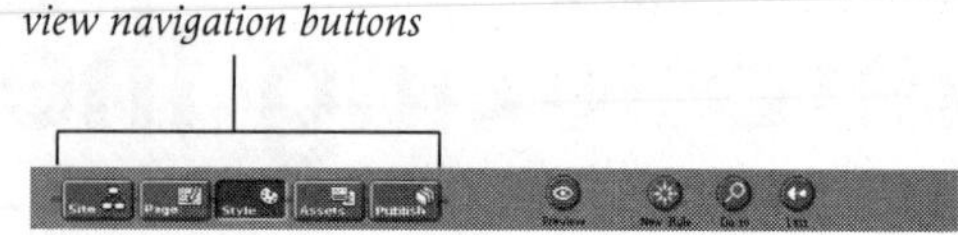


**Figure 6.2**

*The Control Bar with the Page View navigation button selected.*

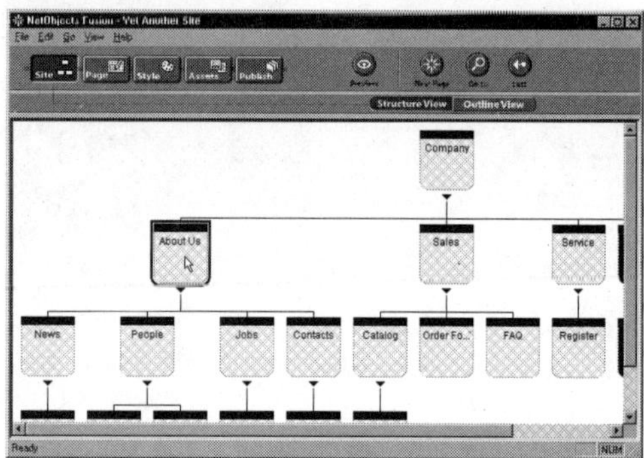

**Figure 6.3**

*Double-click a page in Site View to go to Page View for that page.*

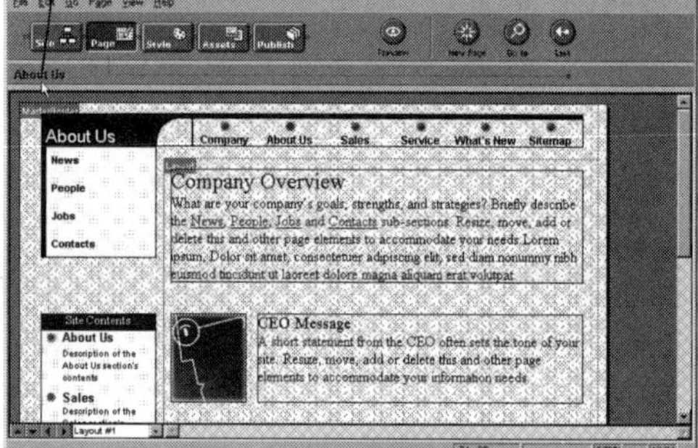


**Figure 6.4**
*The Page View for a page called About Us.*

**Figure 6.5**
*To display the other pages in your site, use the Go to and Last buttons in the Page View Control Bar.*

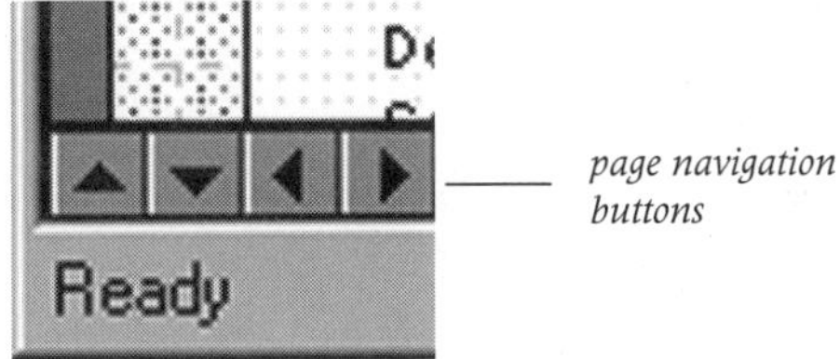


**Figure 6.6**
*Use the page navigation buttons at the bottom left of the Fusion window to display other pages in your site.*

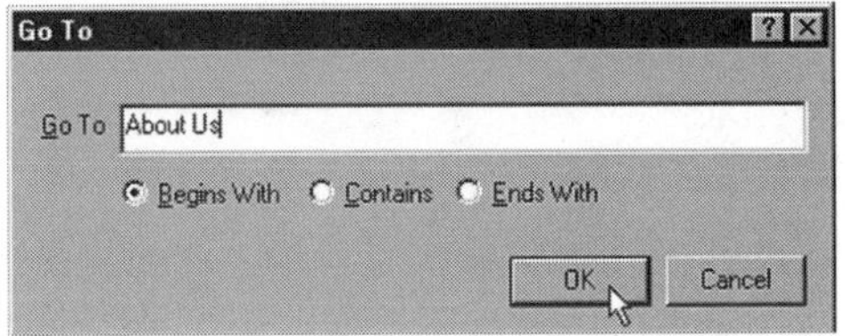


**Figure 6.7**
*Use the Go To dialog box to indicate the page you wish to display.*

## Getting Around Your Site In Page View

Once in Page View of a particular page, you can look at any other page in the site. To navigate from one page to another while in Page View, use the Go To and Last buttons **(Figure 6.5)**, the page navigation buttons **(Figure 6.6)**, or the Go menu.

### To use the Go To button:

1. Select the Go To button in the Control Bar to display the Go To dialog box **(Figure 6.7)**.
2. In the Go To field, type the name of the page you wish to display.
3. If you entered just a partial page name, select the appropriate radio button from those displayed:

   **Begins With** searches for page names beginning with the name you entered.

   **Contains** searches the site for page names containing the name you entered.

   **Ends With** searches the site for page names ending with the name you entered.
4. Click OK, and the desired page (if found) is displayed.

### To use the Last button:

To return to the last page displayed, click the Last button **(Figure 6.5)**.

### ✔ Tip

- You can also use Ctrl + G and Ctrl + R instead of the Go To and Last buttons respectively. *Mac users use Command + G and Command + R.*

### To use the page navigation buttons:

Based upon the structure of your site, select the page navigation button that points in the direction of your destination page **(Figure 6.8)**.

- Displays the **parent** of the currently displayed page.
- Displays the leftmost **child** of the currently displayed page.
- Displays the left **sibling** of the currently displayed page.
- Displays the right **sibling** of the currently displayed page.

With the Sales page displayed in Page View, and given the site structure shown in **Figure 6.9**, ▲ displays the Company page, ▼ displays the Catalog page, ◀ displays the About Us page, and ▶ displays the Service page.

### ✔ Tips

- The Go menu provides menu options equivalent to the four page navigation buttons **(Figure 6.10)**.
- If no page exists in your site at the location indicated by your navigation button or Go menu selection, then the selection has no effect.
- For further explanation of the terms parent, child, and sibling, see Chapter 4.

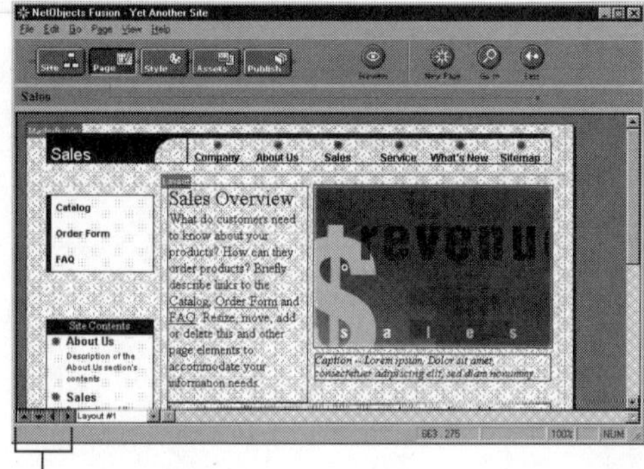


*page navigation buttons*

**Figure 6.8**
*Use the four page navigation buttons to display the parent, child, or siblings of the currently displayed page.*

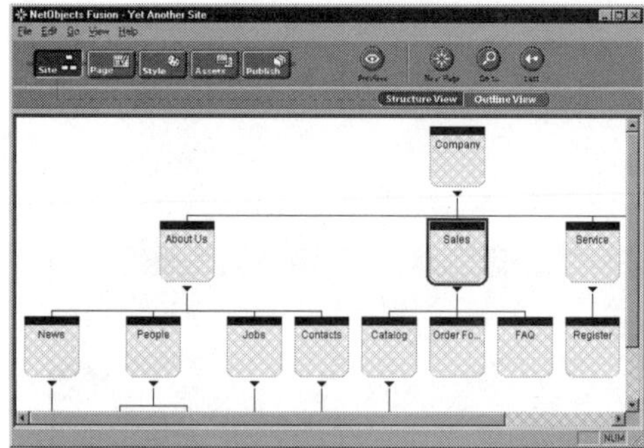


**Figure 6.9**
*The parent of Sales is Company; its children are Catalog, Order Form and FAQ; its siblings are About Us and Service.*

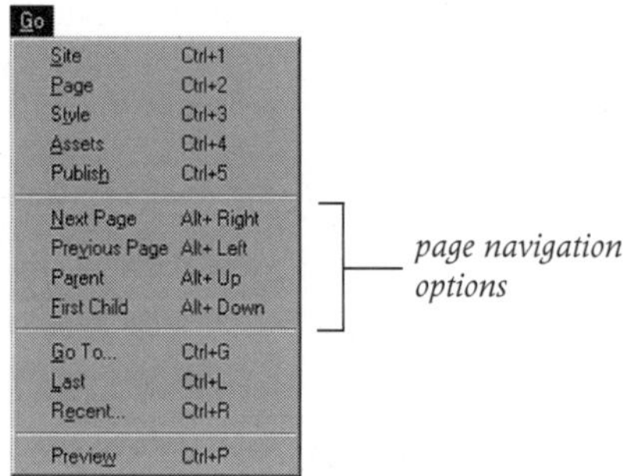


**Figure 6.10**
*The Go menu in Page View.*

**Figure 6.11**
*Use the New Page button in the Control Bar to create a new child page of the currently displayed page.*

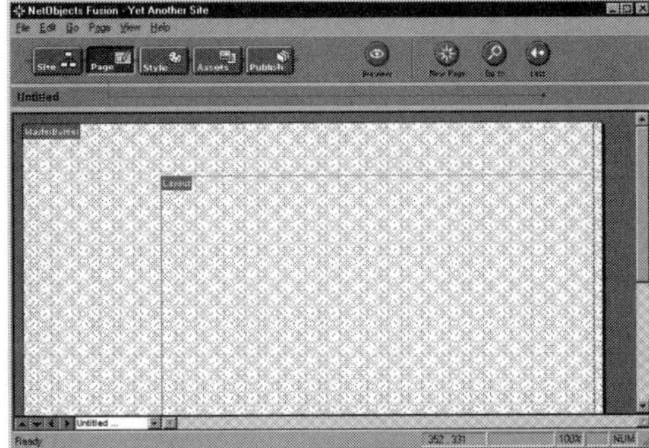

**Figure 6.12**
*A new untitled page.*

## Creating a New Page in Page View

In Page View, you can create a new page using the New Page button in the Control Bar **(Figure 6.11)**. As is the case in Site View, a new page is added as a child of the currently displayed page.

### To use the New Page button:

Select the New Page button in the Control Bar **(Figure 6.11)**.

A new page is displayed **(Figure 6.12)**. The new page is called Untitled by default. It can be renamed either in Site View or using the Page Properties Palette.

✔ **Tip**

- If you create a new page and wish to move it within the structure of the site, go to Site View, and drag the new page to the desired position. See also Chapter 4.

# Accessing the Page View Tools Palette

The Page View Tools Palette **(Figure 6.13)** contains a number of page content tools and several control tools. The control tools are displayed in the first row of the palette and include a select tool, a zoom in tool, and a zoom out tool.

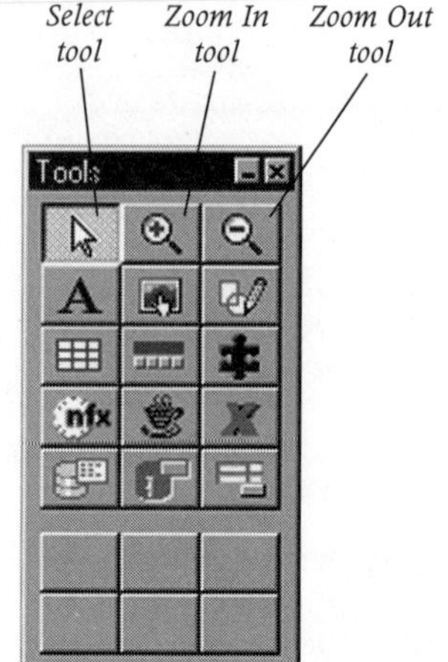


**Figure 6.13**
*To display the Tools Palette, select Tools Palette from the View menu.*

### To access the Tools Palette:

If the Tools Palette is not already displayed, choose Tools Palette from the View menu **(Figure 6.14)**.

**Figure 6.14**
*To display the Tools Palette, select Tools Palette from the View menu.*

### ✔ Tips

- You can also access the Tools Palette by typing Ctrl + T. *Mac users, Command + T.*
- To hide the Tools Palette, you can use the close box in the Tools Palette title bar, select Tools Palette from the View menu, or type Ctrl + T. *Mac users, Command + T.*

**Figure 6.15**
*Magnify the page displayed in Page View using the Zoom In tool.*

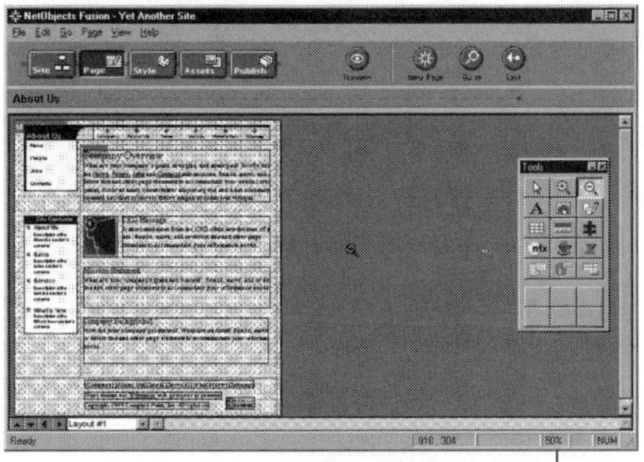


**Figure 6.16**
*Reduce the page displayed in Page View using the Zoom Out tool.*

# Using the Zoom Tools

The zoom tools on the Page View Tools Palette are used to magnify or reduce the view of your page.

### To zoom in:

1. Select the Zoom In tool from the Tools palette.
2. Click on the area of the page you wish to magnify.

   The page is magnified more each time you click when the Zoom In tool is selected **(Figure 6.15)**.

### To zoom out:

1. Select the Zoom Out tool from the Tools palette.
2. Click on the area of the site you wish to reduce.

   The site is reduced more each time you click using the Zoom Out tool **(Figure 6.16)**.

### ✓ Tip

■ The current level of magnification or reduction is displayed in the status bar at the bottom right of the Fusion window as a percent of the actual size **(Figure 6.16)**.

## Using the Select Tool

The select tool is used for selecting, resizing, and dragging content elements on your Web page.

### To select a content element:

1. Click the select tool on the Tools palette.
2. Click an element on the page that you wish to select. (Click and drag or Shift + Click to select multiple elements.)

   The selected element(s) is/are displayed with handles and a heavy border **(Figure 6.17)**.

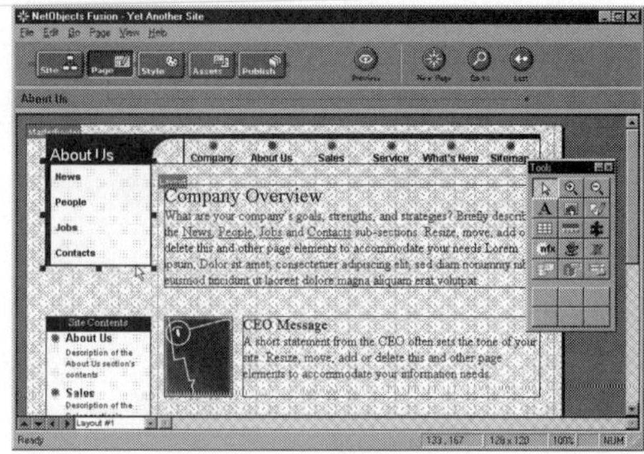

**Figure 6.17**
*Click an element on the page to select it.*

### To move a content element:

1. Click the select tool on the Tools palette.
2. Click and drag the element(s) on the page that you wish to move. As the element(s) is/are dragged, you can see a dotted line representing the new position.

   As the element is dragged, you can see a dotted outline of its new position **(Figure 6.18)**.
3. Drop the element when it is positioned in the desired location.

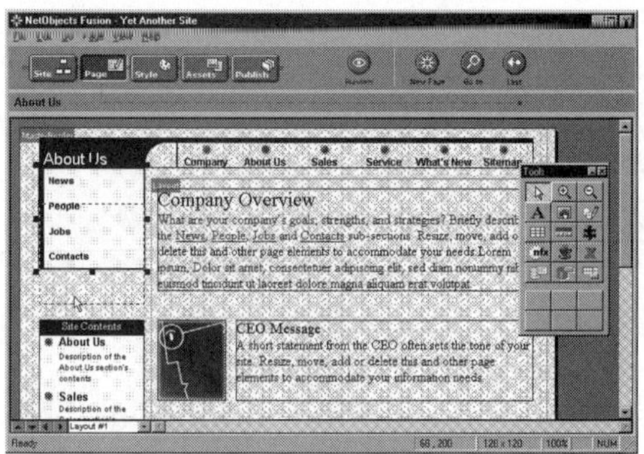

**Figure 6.18**
*Dragging a content element using the select tool.*

### To resize a content element:

1. Click the select tool on the Tools palette, and select the element to be resized.
2. Position the mouse pointer over one of the selected element's handles until a double-ended arrow is displayed.
3. Click and drag the edge of the element to size it **(Figure 6.19)**.

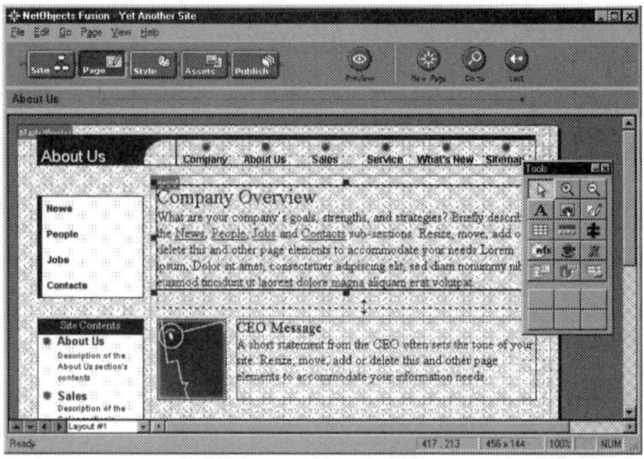

**Figure 6.19**
*Resizing a content element using the select tool.*

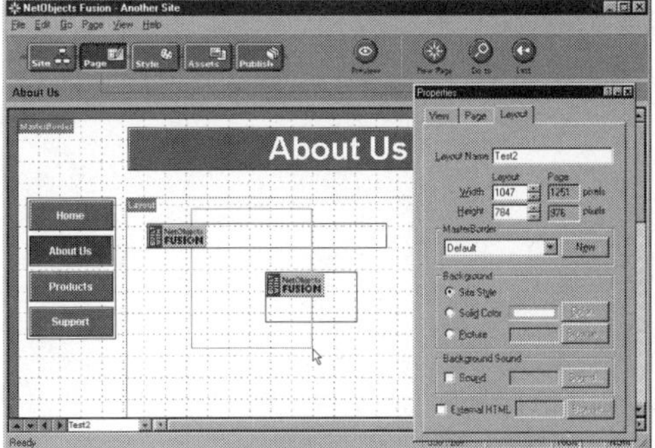


**Figure 6.20**
*Click and drag to select multiple elements.*

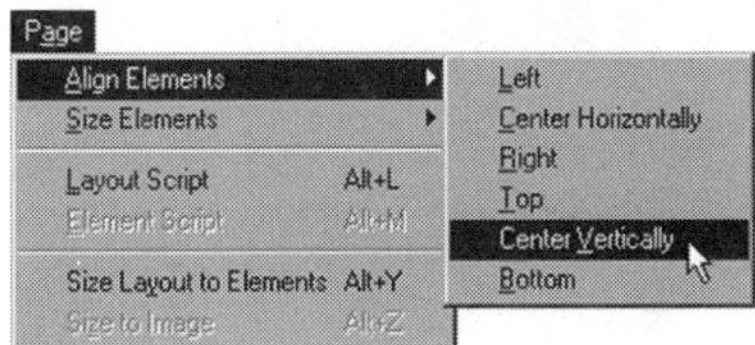


**Figure 6.21**
*Choose the desired Align Elements option from the Page menu.*

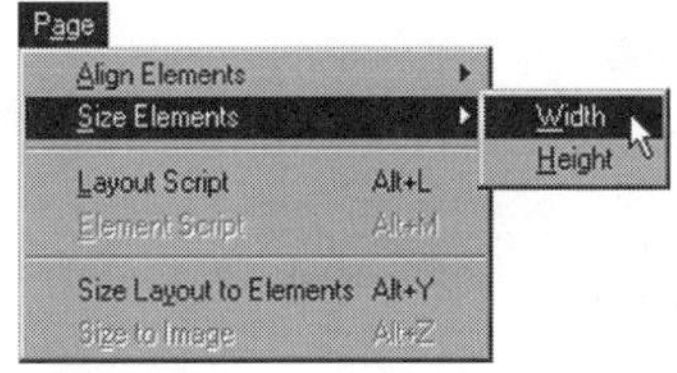


**Figure 6.22**
*Choose the desired Size Elements option from the Page menu.*

**Figure 6.23**
*The selected elements are sized by width or height.*

# Aligning and Sizing Multiple Elements

Fusion allows you to select a number of content elements on a page and align or size all of them using the position or size of the last element selected.

## To align multiple elements:

1. Click and drag to select all the elements you wish to align **(Figure 6.20)**.

   An element is selected when eight handles are displayed in its border.

2. Choose the desired Align Elements option from the Page menu **(Figure 6.21)**.

   Options allow you to align elements along the left, right, top, or bottom border and to center elements horizontally or vertically.

3. The selected elements are aligned based upon the position of the last element selected.

## To size multiple elements:

1. Click and drag to select all the elements you wish to align.
2. Choose the desired Size Elements option from the Page menu **(Figure 6.22)**.
3. The selected elements are sized based on the height or width of the last element selected **(Figure 6.23)**.

### ✓ Tip

- You can undo a size or align elements action by selecting the displayed Undo option in the Edit menu.

# Accessing the Page View Properties Palette

The Page View Properties Palette always displays tabs for View and Page properties **(Figure 6.24)**. (The Page properties tab is the same in Page View and Site View; it is covered in Chapter 4.)

In addition to Page and View tabs, the Page View Properties Palette displays other properties tabs for the currently selected page element.

### To access view properties:

1. If it is not already displayed, open the Properties Palette in Page View by selecting Properties Palette from the View menu **(Figure 6.25)**.
2. Select the View tab in the Properties Palette.

### ✔ Tip

- You can also access the Properties Palette by typing Ctrl + U. *Mac users, Command + U.*

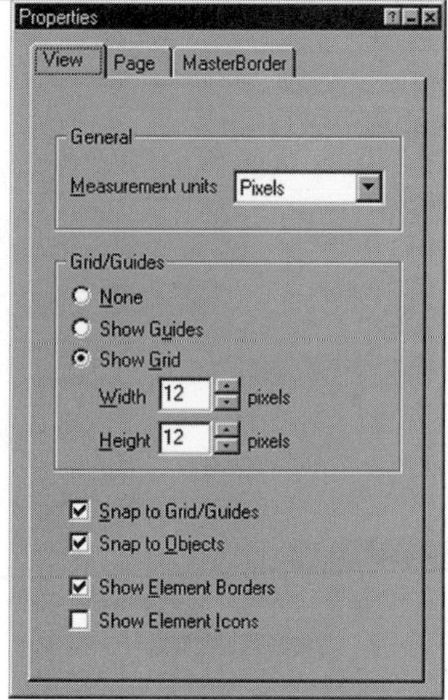


**Figure 6.24**
*The View properties tab in the Page View Properties Palette.*

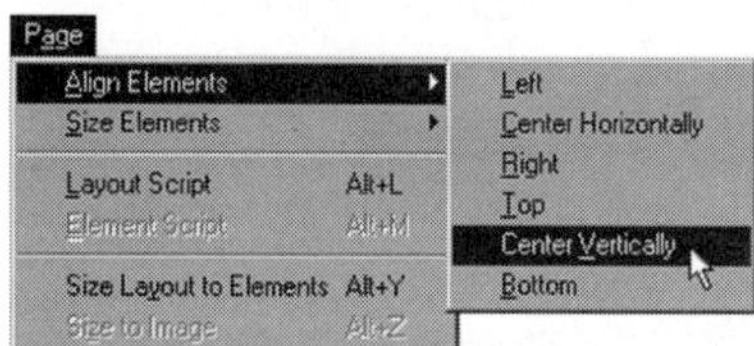


**Figure 6.25**
*To display the Page View Properties Palette, select Properties Palette from the View menu.*

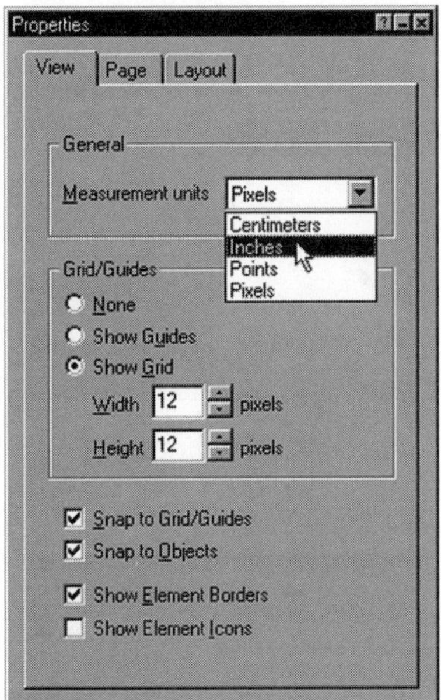


**Figure 6.26**
*Measurement units options in the View tab of the Page View Properties Palette.*

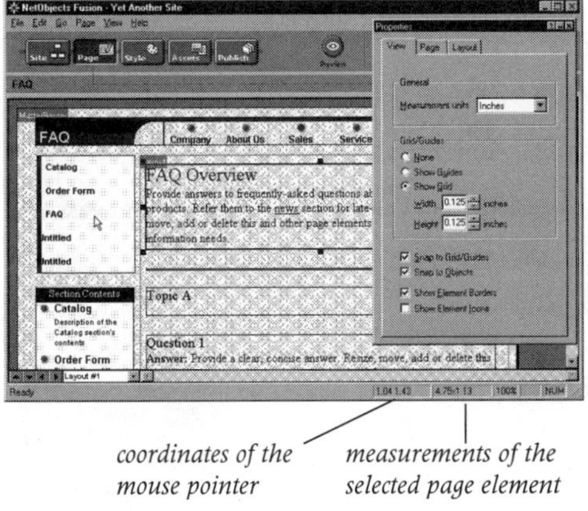


**Figure 6.27**
*Coordinates of the mouse pointer and size of the selected text box shown in inches.*

## Using View Properties to Set Measurement Units

The sizes and positions of objects on your Web pages are expressed by Fusion using the measurement units you select in the View tab of the Page View Properties Palette. Available units of measure are centimeters, inches, points, and pixels.

### To select measurement units:

1. Select the View tab in the Page View Properties Palette.
2. Click the down-arrow in the Measurement units field to display the menu of options **(Figure 6.26)**.
3. Click the desired measurement units option.

### ✔ Tip

- The coordinates of the mouse pointer and size of any selected content elements are shown at the bottom right of the Fusion window using the selected measurement units **(Figure 6.27)**.

## Using View Properties to Set Grid and Guide Options

The Fusion Page View is much like the paste-up board traditionally used in page layout for publishing. Such paste-up boards generally incorporate a grid to assist the artist in lining up elements. Fusion too provides a grid and guides to help you layout your pages efficiently and professionally.

The grid and guide options offered in Fusion's Page View are found in the View properties tab of the Page View Properties Palette.

### To set grid and guide options:

1. Select the View tab in the Page View Properties Palette.
2. Click the desired Grid/Guides radio button option.

   **None** hides both guides and grid **(Figure 6.28)**.

   **Show Guides** displays guides sometimes known as T-squares: horizontal and vertical guides that you can use for aligning objects.

   **Show Grid** displays a grid with cells that are the size specified in the Width and Height fields **(Figure 6.29)**.
3. If desired, adjust the grid size using the Width and Height fields **(Figure 6.30)**.

✔ **Tip**

- If you are using a page background, the grid will not be visible.

**Figure 6.28**
*No grid selected.*

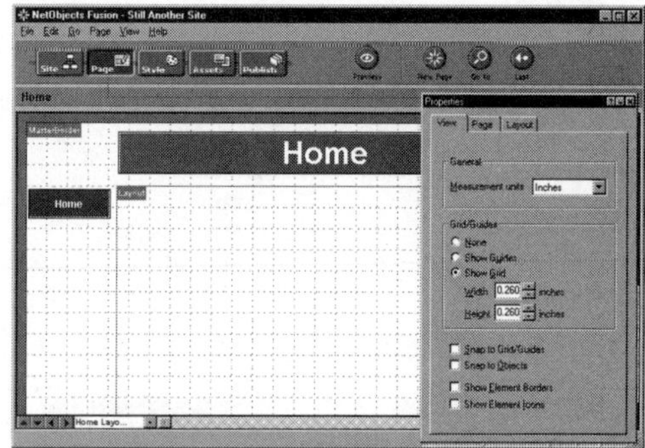

**Figure 6.29**
*Default grid selected.*

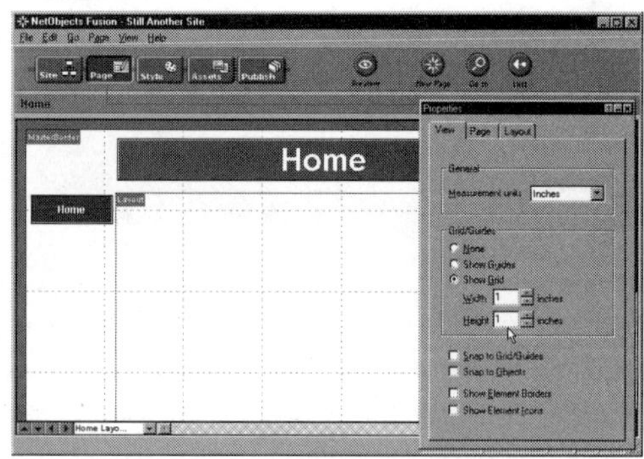

**Figure 6.30**
*Grid size set to one inch by one inch.*

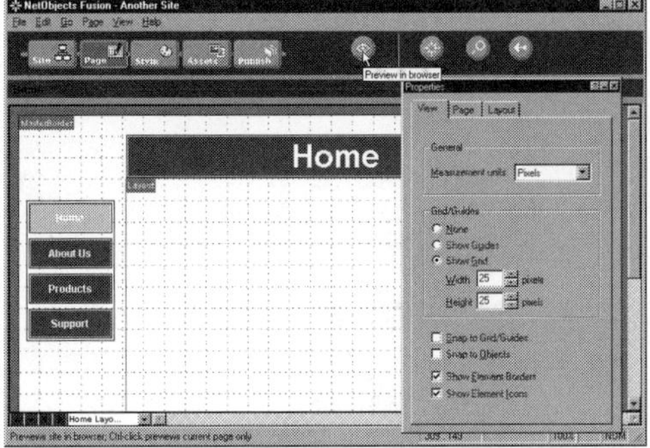


**Figure 6.31**
*Snap to Grid/Guides and Snap to Objects selected. Element borders hidden.*

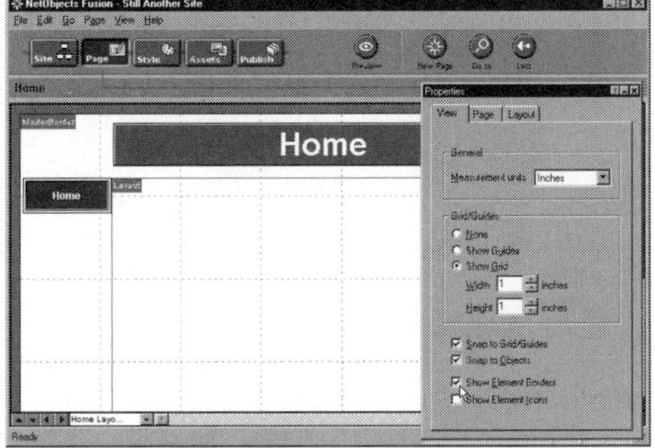


**Figure 6.32**
*Element borders displayed.*

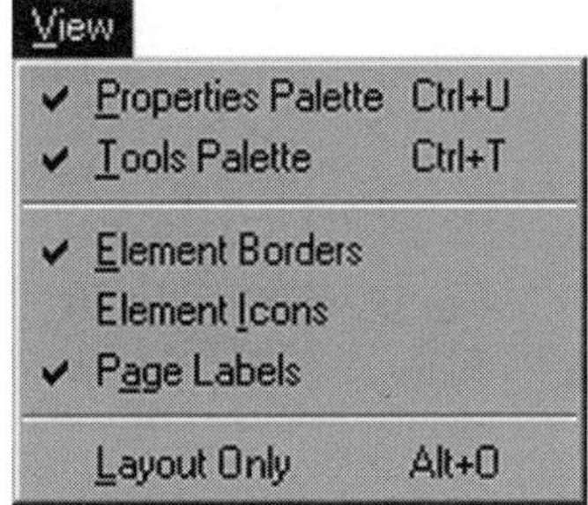


**Figure 6.33**
*The View menu Element Borders and Icons options.*

# Using View Properties to Set Display Options

Fusion offers "Snap to" and display options affecting the behavior and appearance of content elements on your Web pages.

### To set "Snap to" options:

1. Select the View tab in the Page View Properties Palette.
2. Click the check boxes of the desired "Snap to" options **(Figure 6.31)**:

   **Snap to Grid/Guides** causes elements to "snap to" grid lines and guides, allowing you to align elements to grid and guides "by hand

   **Snap to Objects** causes content elements to "snap to" other elements.

### To set border and icon display options:

1. Select the View tab in the Page View Properties Palette.
2. Click the check boxes of the desired "Show" options:

   **Show Element Borders** displays the borders of content elements like navigation bars **(Figure 6.32)**.

   **Show Element Icons** displays link, anchor, and script icons when they appear on the displayed page.

### ✔ Tip

- You can also use the View menu to set border and icon display options (**Figure 6.33**).

## Using the Preview Button

While the Fusion Page View is a graphical interface, you should still check the way your pages look when viewed with a Web browser (like Netscape Communicator or Microsoft Explorer) before finalizing your designs. You can preview a page created with Fusion in a Web browser using the Preview button in the Control Bar.

### To preview a page:

1. In Page View, go to the page you wish to preview in your Web browser.
2. Press and hold the Ctrl key and click the Preview button **(Figure 6.34)**.

   Fusion will build the HTML document for the currently displayed page **(Figure 6.35)**. Fusion then launches your default Web browser and displays the page in the browser window **(Figure 6.36)**.

### ✔ Tips

- To Preview the entire site, just click the Preview button. HTML documents for all of the pages in your site will be built and displayed in your browser window.
- Choose Preferences from the Edit menu, and use Preview options on the General tab of the Preferences dialog to control the effect of the Preview button **(Figure 6.37)**.

**Figure 6.34**
*Hold the Ctrl key and click the Preview button.*

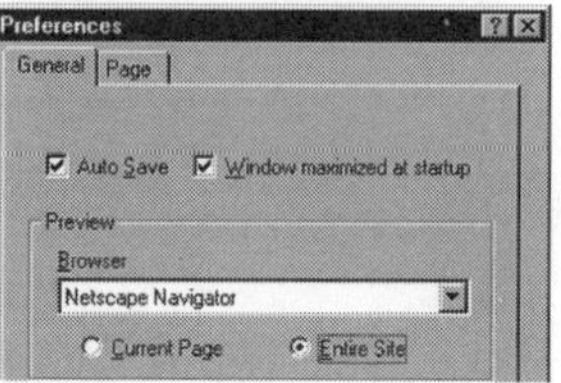


**Figure 6.35**
*Fusion builds the HTML document for the page.*

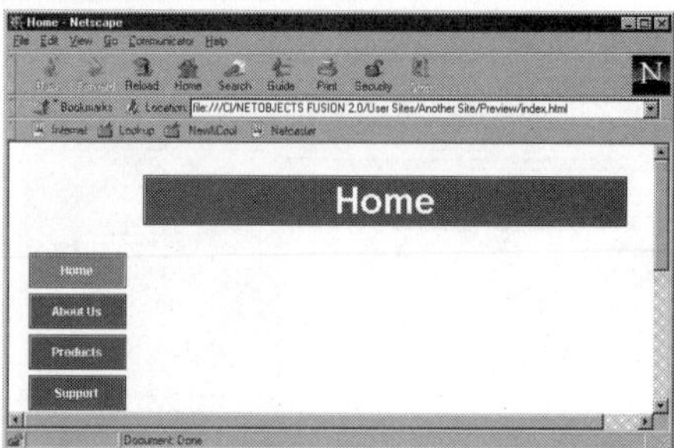


**Figure 6.36**
*The page is displayed in the Web browser window.*

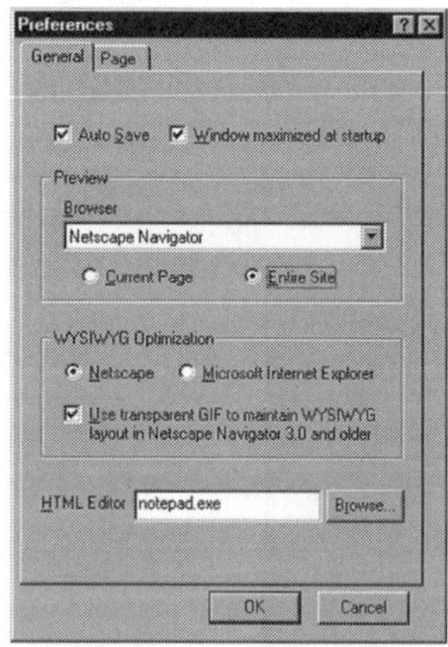


**Figure 6.37**
*Make Preview preferences selections in the General tab of the Preferences dialog box.*

# 7 Page Anatomy

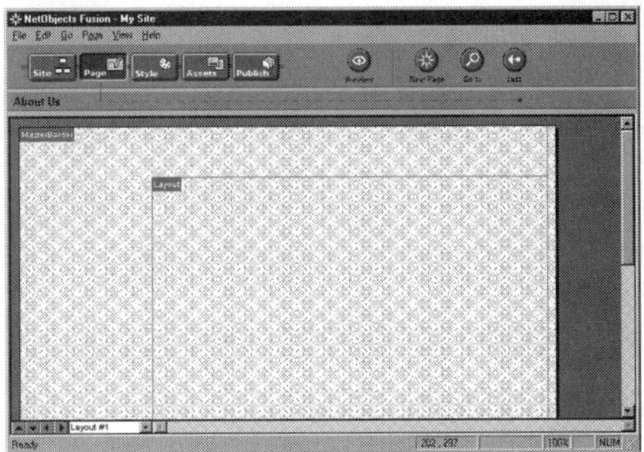

**Figure 7.1**
*The MasterBorder and Layout in Page View.*

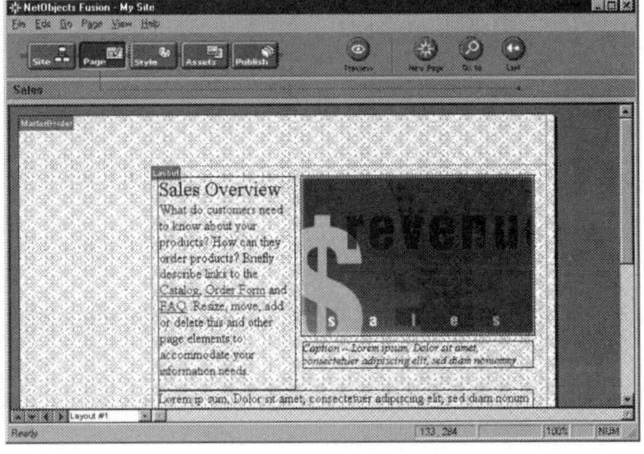

**Figure 7.2**
*Elements placed in the Layout of a page.*

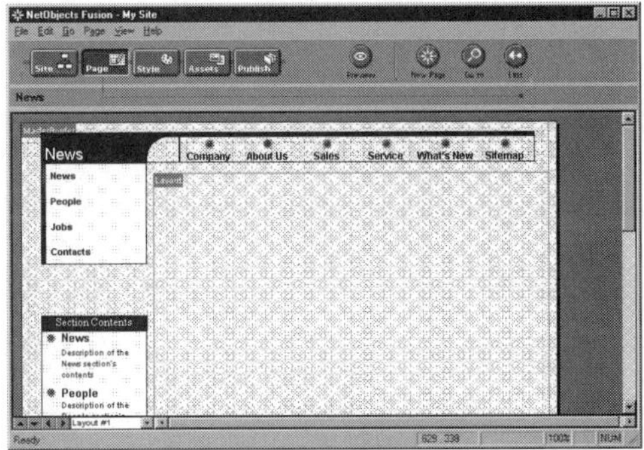

**Figure 7.3**
*Elements placed in the MasterBorders of a page.*

## Layout vs. MasterBorder

Fusion Web pages are composed of two primary components: the **MasterBorder** and the **Layout**. Each area is labeled and enclosed by a box in Page View **(Figure 7.1)**.

The Layout is the area in which you will place objects which are to appear only on the currently displayed page **(Figure 7.2)**.

MasterBorders appear on the top, left, right, and bottom of the page in Page View, and define the margins of your Web page.

MasterBorders provide a place for elements which will appear automatically on pages throughout your site. Elements typically placed in the MasterBorders include a company logo and navigation buttons **(Figure 7.3)**. Like SiteStyles, MasterBorders are another facility which help you create Web sites with a consistent look and feel.

### ✔ Tip

- If you are familiar with Fusion version 1.0, you may be wondering what has become of the page header and footer used in that version. MasterBorders replace the page headers and footers from Fusion version 1.0.

## Getting a Handle on MasterBorders

Fusion automatically creates a default MasterBorder for every page in your site. This default MasterBorder includes a number of components the look of which you can determine by selecting, creating, or modifying a SiteStyle (see Chapter 5).

Components of the default MasterBorder include a banner at the top of the page in which the page name is displayed **(Figure 7.4)**. A navigation button bar along the left side of the page **(Figure 7.4)**, and a text navigation bar at the bottom of the page **(Figure 7.5)** (see Chapter 9 for more on navigation bars).

While these components are the MasterBorders defaults, Fusion allows you to control their look and arrangement. In addition, you can control the margins dictated by MasterBorders.

You can even create multiple MasterBorders for your site, and apply those MasterBorders to specific pages in your site. Then, when you make a change to a MasterBorder on one page, that change is reflected on all pages using that MasterBorder.

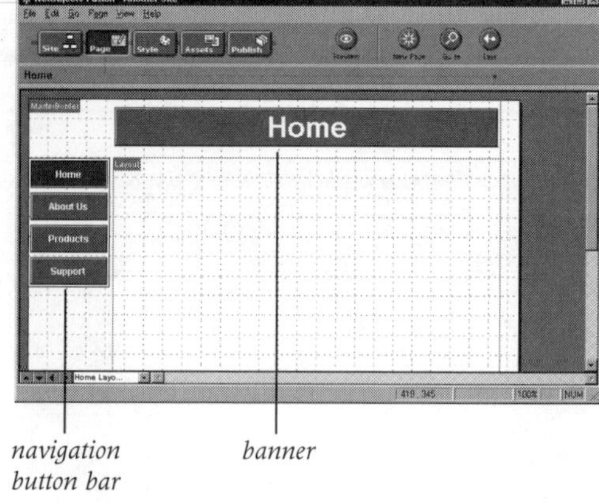


**Figure 7.4**
*MasterBorder with default banner and navigation button bar.*

**Figure 7.5**
*MasterBorder with default text navigation bar.*

## Creating New MasterBorders

Using more than one MasterBorder in your site allows you to create a unique look for pages of different types. For example, you might want some pages in your site to have a large company logo and a navigation bar including links just to the first level of pages in your site, while for other pages you

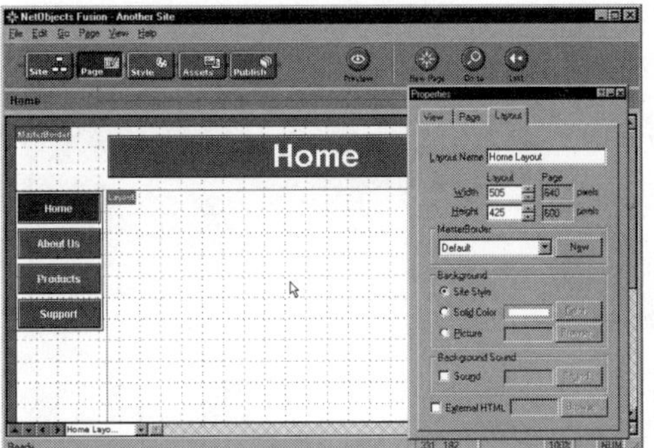


**Figure 7.6**
*Click in the layout area of the page to display the Layout tab of the Properties Palette.*

**Figure 7.7**
*Click New to create a new MasterBorder for the site.*

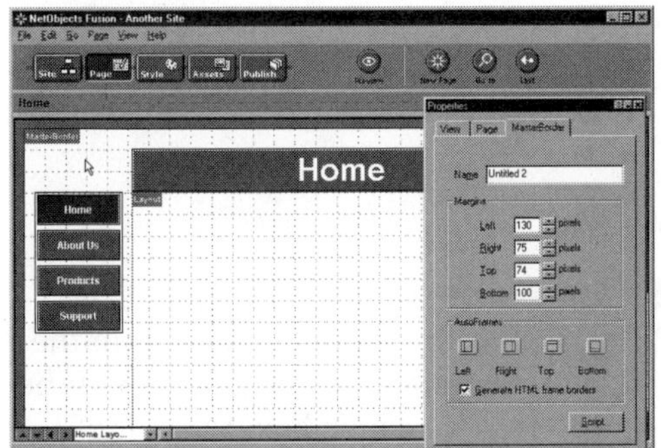


**Figure 7.8**
*Click in the MasterBorder area of the page to display the MasterBorder tab of the Properties Palette.*

might want to use a smaller company logo and a horizontal navigation button bar with buttons creating links to the child pages of the current page. This is a situation in which you should create and customize multiple MasterBorders.

## To create a MasterBorder:

1. Go to Page View.
2. If the Properties Palette is not displayed, select Properties Palette from the View menu.
3. Click in the layout area of the page **(Figure 7.6)** to display the Layout tab of the Properties Palette.

   The MasterBorder field indicates the name of the MasterBorder currently used on the page displayed.
4. Click the New button to create a new MasterBorder for the site **(Figure 7.7)**.

   Fusion automatically names the first new MasterBorder "Untitled 2". Subsequent new MasterBorders are named sequentially.
5. Click in the MasterBorder area of the page to display the MasterBorder tab of the Properties Palette **(Figure 7.8)**.

   The MasterBorder Name field displays the name of the new MasterBorder you just created.
6. In the Name field, type a more descriptive name for your new MasterBorder.

### ✓ Tip

- Once created, MasterBorders cannot be deleted. But you don't have to use MasterBorders you create.

## Modifying MasterBorders

You may decide you want to modify an existing MasterBorder, either the default default MasterBorder for your site or a new MasterBorder you've created. You can customize MasterBorders by modifying the margins and components displayed.

#### To modify a MasterBorder:

1. Go to Page View for a page which uses the MasterBorder you wish to modify.

   You can determine which MasterBorder is used for a page by clicking in the layout area of a page and checking the MasterBorder field, or by clicking in the MasterBorders area of the page and checking the Name field.

2. Click in the MasterBorders area of the page to display the MasterBorder tab of the Properties Palette.

3. In the Margins section, type values for the desired left, right, top, and bottom margins **(Figure 7.9)**.

   You can view the changes to the MasterBorders on the page after you change the values for each margin.

   The MasterBorder will occupy the area between the margins you specify and the edges of the page.

4. Use the Tools Palette to add, delete, modify, and rearrange elements in the MasterBorders.

5. Use StyleView to select or modify images used for buttons and the banner (see Chapter 5).

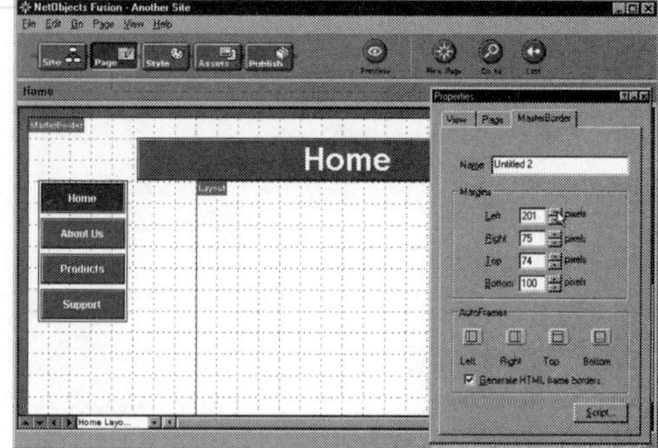


**Figure 7.9**
*Modifying the left margin of the MasterBorder.*

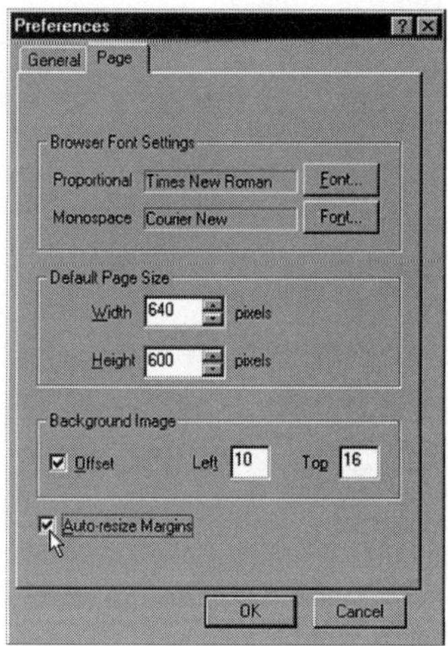


**Figure 7.10**
*Select the Auto-resize Margins option to resize margins by dragging.*

#### ✔ Tip

- To resize MasterBorder margins by dragging, select Preferences from the Edit menu, and in the Page tab of the Preferences dialog box, select the Auto-resize Margins option **(Figure 7.10)**. *Mac users select Drag and Drop Layout Borders.*

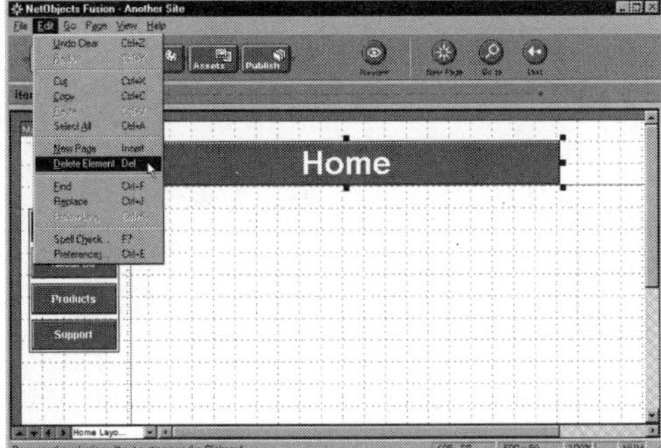


**Figure 7.11**
*Select the banner, and choose Delete Element from the Edit menu.*

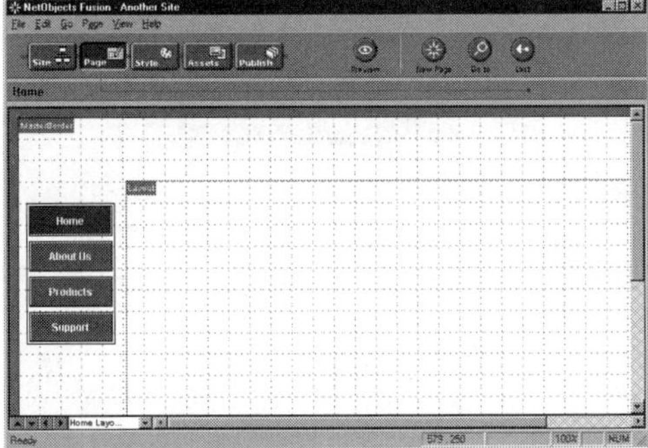


**Figure 7.12**
*The banner disappears.*

# Working with Banners in MasterBorders

While the look of the banners for your site can be determined in Style View (see Chapter 5), you can also modify a banner for a particular MasterBorder in your site. This means that if you choose to use multiple MasterBorders in your site, you can define a different banner for each one. In Page View, you can delete a banner, add a banner, rename a banner, select a different banner image, or use a banner from a different SiteStyle.

## To delete a banner:

1. Go to Page View for the page from which you want to delete the banner.
2. Click the banner to select it.

   The banner is selected when eight handles are displayed around its border.
3. Choose Delete Element from the Edit menu **(Figure 7.11)**.

   The banner disappears **(Figure 7.12)**.

## ✔ Tips

- You can undo the delete by choosing Undo Clear from the Edit menu.
- If you wish to paste the selected banner to another page, you select cut (or copy) from the Edit menu, go to the target page, then choose Paste from the Edit menu.

### To add a banner:

1. Go to Page View and display the page to which you want to add a banner.
2. Select the Navigation Bar/Banner tool in the Tools Palette **(Figure 7.13)**.
3. Select one of the two secondary Banner tools.

   creates a vertical banner.

   creates a horizontal banner.
4. Click and drag in the MasterBorder where you want to place the new banner.

   The new banner appears displaying the name of the current page.
5. Use the Select tool to adjust the size and position of the banner by dragging the banner to a new position or by dragging the banner handles.

### ✓ Tips

- You can add more than one banner to a single page **(Figure 7.14)**.
- You can even place banners in the layout area of the page.

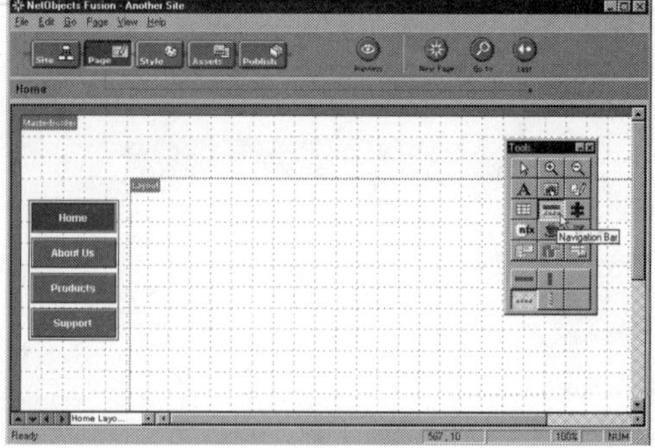


**Figure 7.13**
*Select the Navigation Bar/Banner tool.*

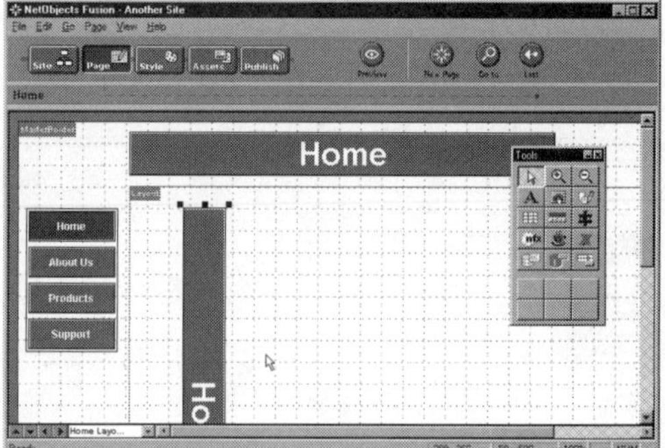


**Figure 7.14**
*You can place multiple banners on a page. You can even place banners in the layout area of the page.*

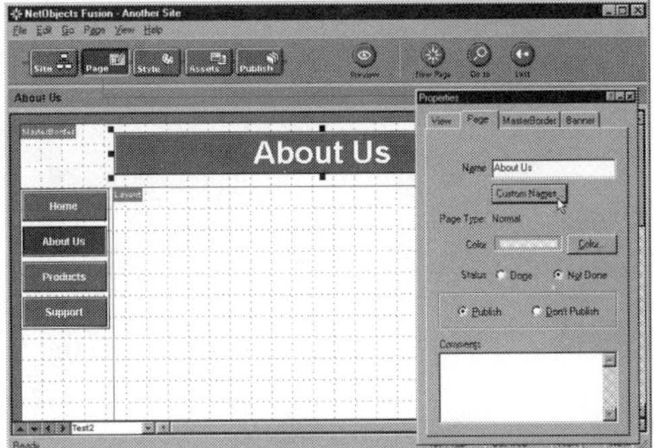


**Figure 7.15**
*Select the Custom Names button on the Page properties tab.*

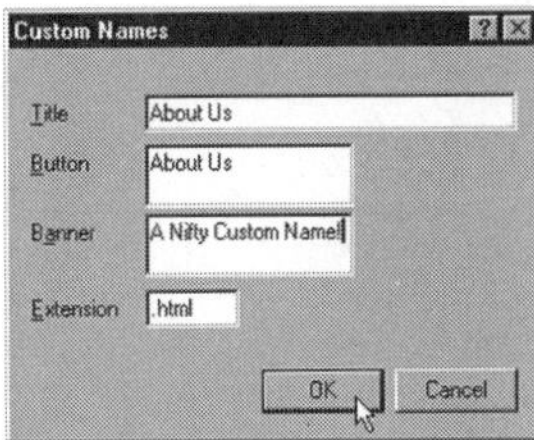


**Figure 7.16**
*Type the new banner name in the Banner field.*

## To rename a banner:

1. Go to Page View and display the page whose banner you wish to rename.

   The banner displays the name of the page on which it is displayed unless you customize it. On servers where a site's home page must be named Index, for example, you might not want the banner on your home page to read "Index."

2. Click the Page tab in the Properties Palette.

3. Click the Custom Names button on the Page Properties tab **(Figure 7.15)**.

   The Custom Names dialog box is displayed **(Figure 17.16)**. Using this dialog box, you can specify different names for the page title, navigation bar button, and banner. By default, the page name appears as the name for all of these elements.

4. In the Banner field, type the name you want to appear in the banner of the current page.

5. Click OK.

### ✓ Tip

- If you change the banner name for a page, you may also want to change the navigation bar button name by typing the same name in the Button field. This way, the name displayed at the top of the page in the banner and the name used for the page in the navigation bars will be consistent.

## To select an image for a banner:

1. Select the banner whose image you want to change.

   The Banner properties tab is displayed in the Properties Palette.

2. Click the Browse button next to the Picture field **(Figure 7.17)**. *Mac users click the Select... button.*

   An open dialog box appears **(Figure 7.18)**.

3. Use the dialog box displayed to locate and select the desired image file.

   You can select from the image assets already defined for this site or from any folder available on your drives. Fusion supports **GIF, JPG, BMP, PCX,** and **PCT** image file formats *(and PICT for Mac users).*

4. Click Open after selecting the desired image file.

   The banner is displayed using the selected image **(Figure 7.19)**.

### ✓ Tips

- If you select an image file which is not a **GIF** or **JPG**, Fusion will offer to convert it for you. This is a handy feature since most browsers can handle **GIF**s and **JPG**s.
- The banner is changed in every page using the current MasterBorder (see applying MasterBorders to a Page).
- If SiteStyle is selected in the Style area of the Banner properties tab, then by selecting another image for a banner, you have effectively modified the selected SiteStyle by adding an additional Banner file.

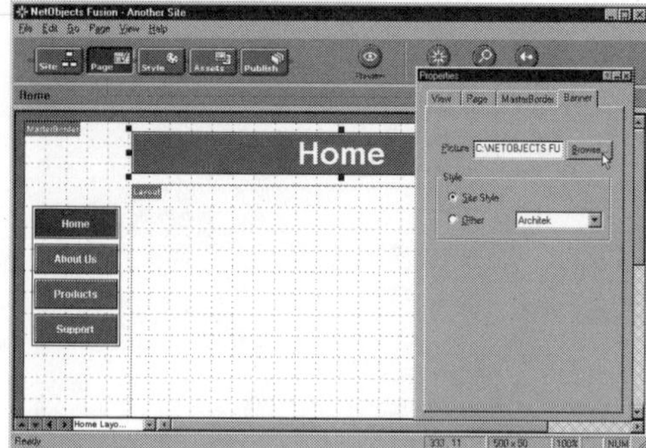


**Figure 7.17**
*Select the banner, then click the Browse button in the Banner properties tab.* Mac users click the Select... button.

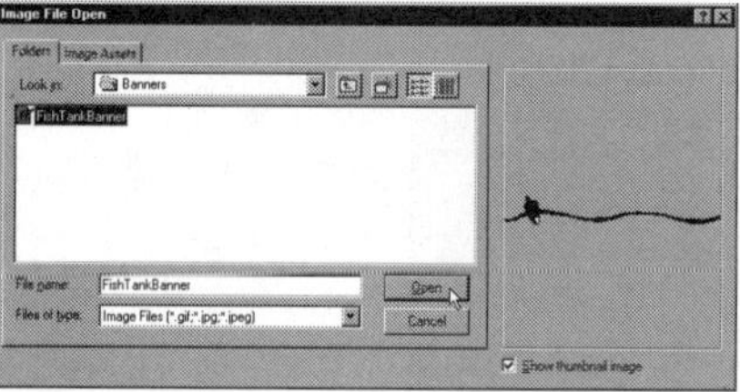


**Figure 7.18**
*Select the desired image file, and click Open.*

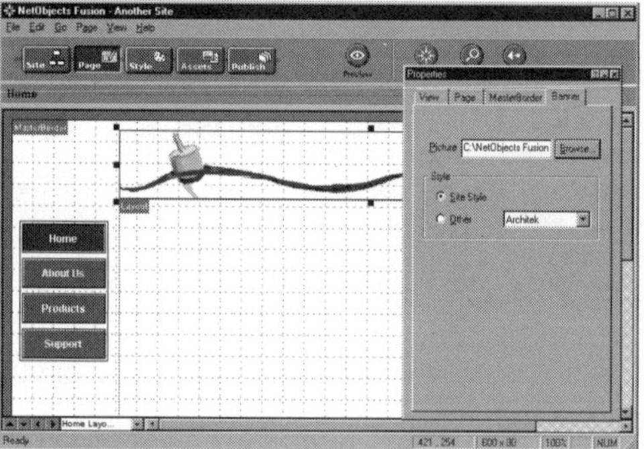


**Figure 7.19**
*The selected banner is displayed using the new image.*

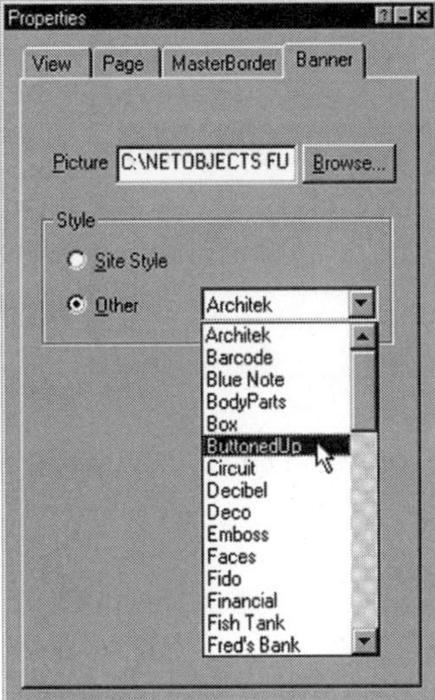


**Figure 7.20**
*Select from the drop-down list of Site Styles.*

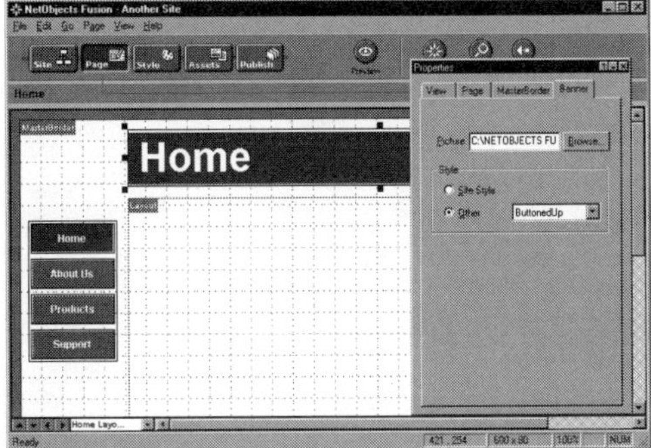


**Figure 7.21**
*The selected banner is displayed with the selected Site Style's banner image.*

## To select another SiteStyle for a banner:

1. Select the banner whose SiteStyle you want to change.

   The Banner properties tab is displayed in the Properties Palette.
2. Click the Other option in the Style area of the Banner properties tab.
3. Select from the drop-down list of SiteStyles **(Figure 7.20)**.

   The banner is displayed using the banner image for the selected SiteStyle **(Figure 7.21)**.

### ✔ Tips

- Changing the image for a banner by selecting another SiteStyle has no effect on the SiteStyle being used in your site.
- You can preview the banner images for all the Fusion SiteStyles in Style View. See Chapter 5.
- To return the banner to the banner image defined for your site's SiteStyle, select the SiteStyle option in the Style area of the Banner properties tab.

## Working with AutoFrames in MasterBorders

A frame is something like a page within a page. It is an area of a Web page defined independently and contains content independent of the rest of the page. This means, that when a frame is scrolled, only the content inside the frame moves. Similarly, when another part of the page is scrolled, the frame content is not affected.

Frames can contain the same content elements as any page, including text, graphics, mulitmedia, buttons, and so on. Frames are often used to display navigation buttons **(Figure 7.22)**, allowing developers to create one set of navigation buttons that is always displayed, regardless of content in other frames. Frames are also sometimes used to create a menu of links to anchors in a long passage of text in another frame.

Generally, defining frames is beyond the skills of the casual Web author. Even for the seasoned pro, defining frames can be time consuming. Thankfully, Fusion offers a feature called **AutoFrames** that allows you to easily add frames to MasterBorders without delving into the HTML behind them.

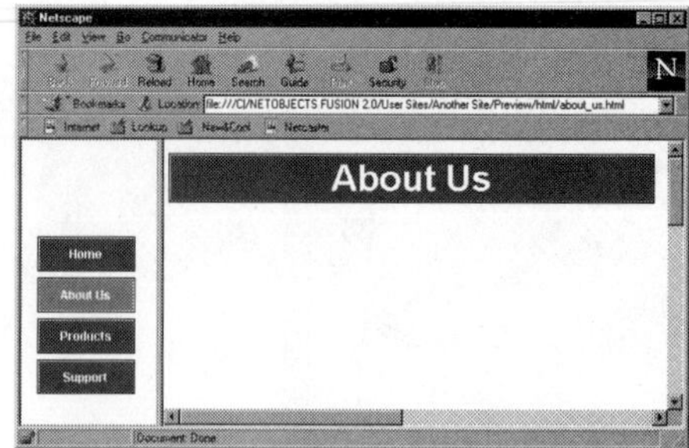


**Figure 7.22**
*Fusion Web page with a banner in the left MasterBorder.*



### ✔ Tips

- You can add your own HTML code to any page in your site. This means you have the option to define your own scripted frames. To add your own HTML code, right click *(Control click for Mac users)* in the layout area, and select Layout Script... from the pop-up menu. You can then use the Script dialog box to add your own HTML code.
- It is important to remember when considering the use of frames in your Web site that not all browsers support frames. If you use frames, it's a good idea to provide a "frame-free" option for visitors. You can do this by defining multiple layouts for pages containing frames, then publishing each version and using a common home page with links to each site version.

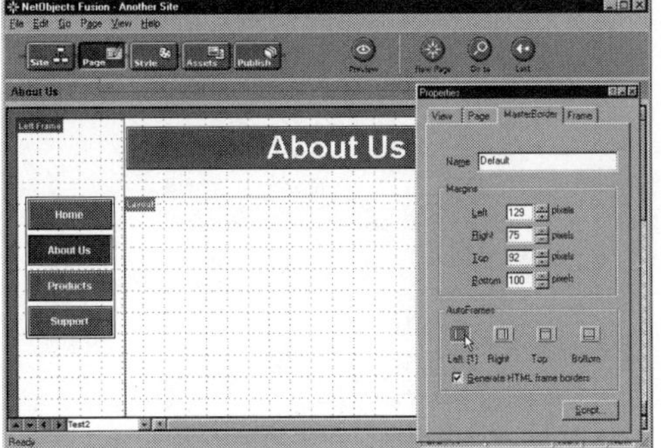


**Figure 7.23**
*Click one of the AutoFrame buttons in the MasterBorder properties tab to create an AutoFrame.*

## To activate an AutoFrame in the MasterBorder:

1. Go to Page View for the page to which you wish to add an AutoFrame.
2. Click in a blank area of the MasterBorder.

   The MasterBorder properties tab is displayed.
3. Click one of the four position buttons in the AutoFrames area of the MasterBorder properties tab **(Figure 7.23)**.

   The AutoFrame occupies the entire selected are of the MasterBorder. A red outline appears in the selected area designating the boundaries of the AutoFrame. If the size of the selected area permits, a red label also appears displaying the frame name **(Figure 7.23)**.

### ✔ Tips

- An AutoFrame can be "deactivated" by clicking the corresponding button in the AutoFrames area of the MasterBorder properties tab. Content elements that were inside the frame are unaffected.
- You can control the way in which AutoFrames overlap using the order in which they are activated. For example, for an AutoFrame to occupy the entire top margin of a page, it must be activated before AutoFrames in the left and right margins.

### To set AutoFrame properties:

1. Click inside the desired AutoFrame.
2. Click the Frame tab in the Properties Palette.

   The Frame tab of the Properties Palette is displayed **(Figure 7.24)**.
3. To change the name of the AutoFrame, edit the **Frame Name** field.
4. To change the name of the AutoFrame, edit the **Frame Name** field.
5. To set the AutoFrame background, select one of the options in the **Background** area.

   **SiteStyle Background** applies the background defined for the selected SiteStyle.

   **Solid Color** allows you to select a color using the Color... button and the color palette.

   **Picture** allows you to select a graphic image using the Browse... button and the dialog box displayed. *Mac users click the Select... button.*
6. Make a selection from the options in the **User Scrollable Frame** area.

   **Yes** causes browsers to display the AutoFrame with vertical and horizontal scroll bars **(Figure 7.25)**.

   **No** causes browsers to display the AutoFrame without scroll bars.

   **Auto** causes browsers to display the AutoFrame with scroll bars only when necessary to view the contents of the frame.

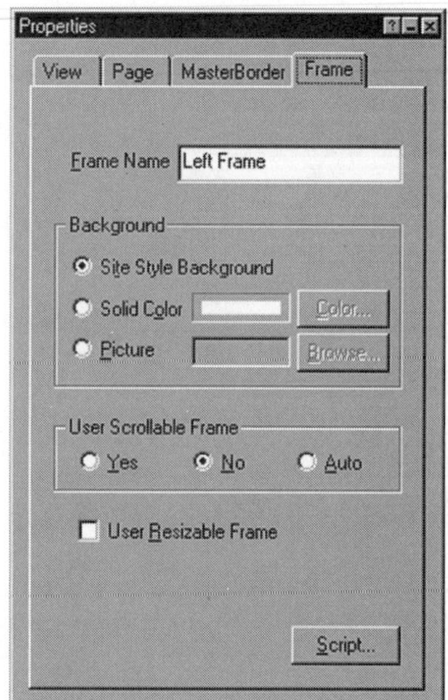


**Figure 7.24**
*The Frame properties tab.*

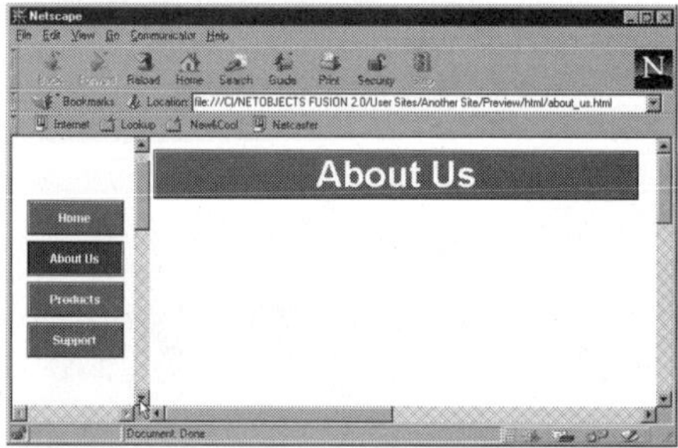


**Figure 7.25**
*Previewing a User Scrollable AutoFrame.*

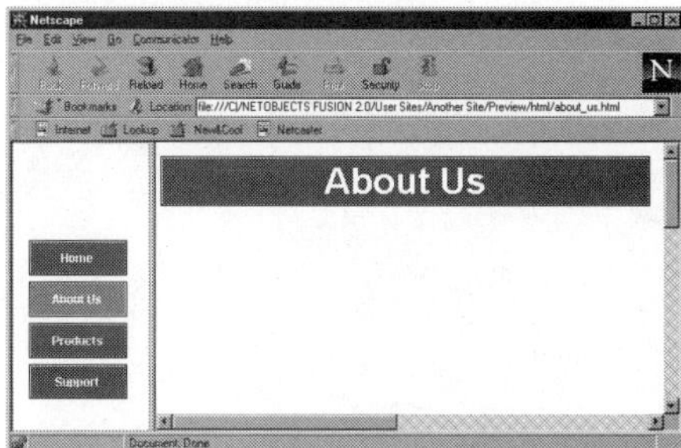


**Figure 7.26**
*Previewing an AutoFrame with frame borders.*

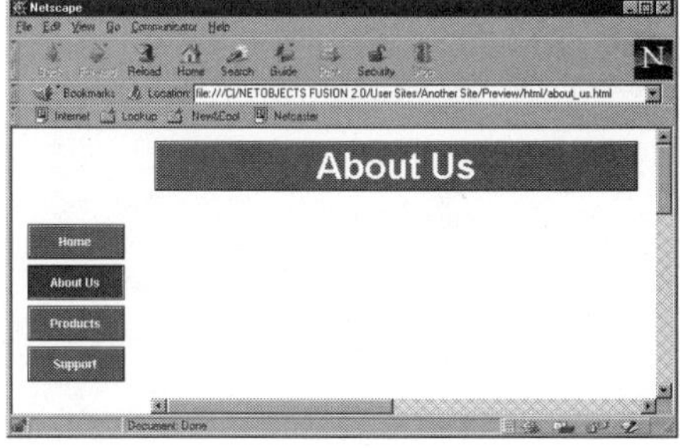


**Figure 7.27**
*Previewing an AutoFrame without frame borders.*

7. To allow browsers to automatically resize frames depending upon the size of the browser window, select **User Resizable Frame**.

## To display an AutoFrame with borders:

1. Click inside the AutoFrame.
2. Click the MasterBorder tab in the Properties Palette.
3. Select the **Generate HTML frame borders** check box in the Auto-Frames area.

   With this option selected Auto-Frames will be displayed by browsers with a rule separating them from other parts of the page **(Figure 7.26)**. Without borders, a frame is displayed as shown in **Figure 7.27**.

### ✓ Tip

- Preview the page to check frame border and scroll bar frame properties. The effect of these options are not displayed in the Page view.

# Applying a MasterBorder to a Page

If your site includes multiple MasterBorders, you must decide which MasterBorder to apply to each page in your site.

### To Select and Apply a MaterBorder:

1. Go to Page View for the page to which you wish to apply a MasterBorder.
2. Click in the layout area of the page to display the Layout tab of the Properties Palette.
3. In the MasterBorders field, select the name of the desired MasterBorder from the drop-down list **(Figure 7.28)**.

   Fusion applies the selected MasterBorder to the current page.

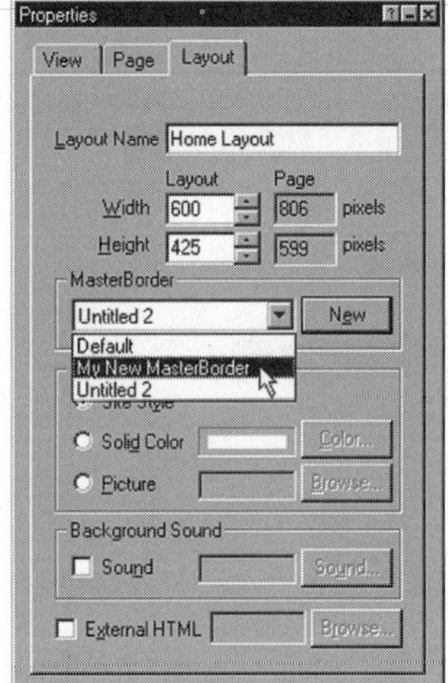


**Figure 7.28**
*Select the desired MasterBorder to apply to the currently displayed page.*

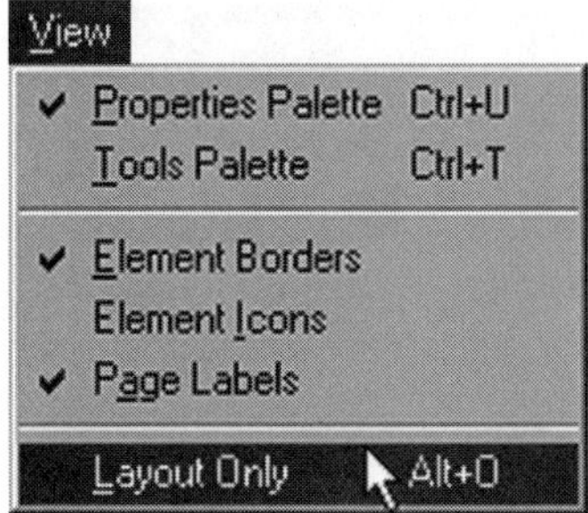


**Figure 7.29**
*Select Layout Only from the View menu to hide or show the the MasterBorders.*

**Figure 7.30**
*Displaying the Layout tab of the Properties Palette.*

# Understanding Layouts

The layout is the part of the page in which you place and arrange content elements that will appear only on that page. Because Fusion creates a default layout for each page you create, each page in your site has at least one layout.

## To display the layout only:

Select Layout Only from the View menu **(Figure 7.29)**.

When MasterBorders are hidden, select Layout Only again to display them.

## To display layout properties:

In Page View, click in the layout area of the displayed page.

The Layout tab of the Properties Palette is displayed **(Figure 7.30)**. The name displayed in the Layout Name field is the name of the layout currently selected for the displayed page.

The Layout tab allows you to specify the size of the layout, size of the page, the selected MasterBorder, the page background, a background sound, and even an external HTML document to use for the page.

## Creating a New Layout

You can rearrange, add, modify, or remove content elements on a page, and then save those changes without losing the original arrangement of the page by saving the changes as a new layout.

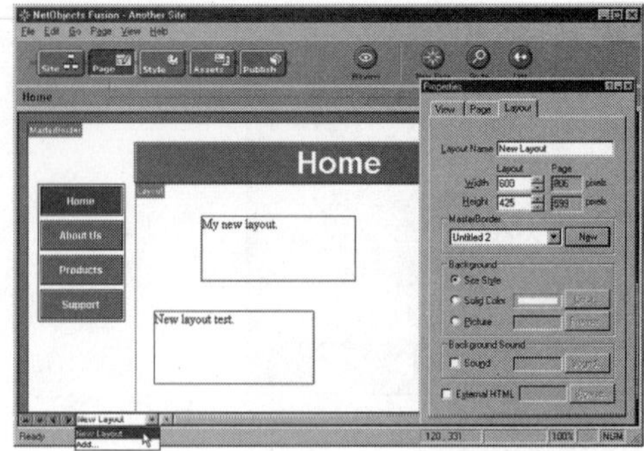

**Figure 7.31**
*New layout created using the Properties Palette, shown in the layout drop-down menu.*

### To create a new layout using the Properties Palette:

1. Arrange content elements as desired in the layout area of a page.
2. In the Layout tab of the Properties Palette, type a new name in the Layout Name field.

   Fusion saves the changes to the page layout as a new layout using the name you provide.

   The layout currently selected for the displayed page is shown in the layout drop-down menu at the bottom left of the Fusion window **(Figure 7.31)**. Notice the the new layout is now displayed as the current layout.

**Figure 7.32**
*Creating a new layout using the Layout drop-down menu.*

### To create a new layout using the Layout drop-down menu:

1. Select Add... from the Layout drop-down menu **(Figure 7.32)**.

   The layout area of the page is cleared.

2. Type the layout name in the Layout Name field in the Layout tab of the Properties Palette.
3. Arrange content elements as desired in the layout area of a page.

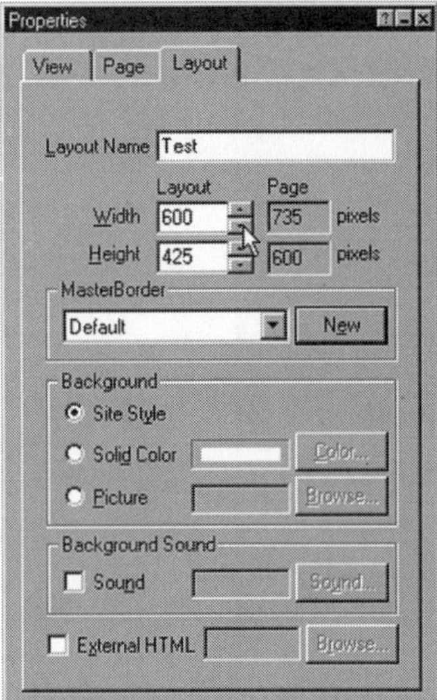


**Figure 7.33**
*Sizing the layout using the Properties Palette.*

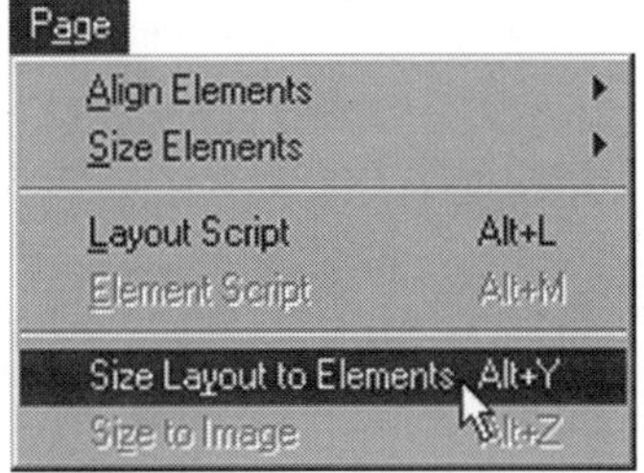


**Figure 7.34**
*Select Size Layout to Elements to automatically resize the layout.*

## Specifying Layout Size

You can set the size of the layout area using the Layout tab of the Properties Palette, the Page menu, or by dragging the margins.

### To use the Properties Palette to size the layout:

1. Click in the layout of the displayed page to display the Layout tab of the Properties Palette.
2. Type or select measurements for the layout width and height in the fields provided **(Figure 7.33)**.

   The size of the layout changes to match your new specifications.

### To automatically size the layout to fit its contents:

Select Size Layout Elements from the Page menu **(Figure 7.34)**.

The layout will adjust its size to accommodate the elements placed there.

### To size the layout by dragging the margins:

1. Select Preferences from the Edit menu.
2. Select the Page tab of the Preferences dialog box.
3. Select Auto-resize Margins, and click OK.
4. Click and drag margins to resize the layout in Page View.

### ✔ Tips

- The units of measure can be selected in the View tab of the Properties Palette. See Page 81.
- You can change the default *page* size in the Page tab of the Preferences dialog box.

## Using Layout Properties to Select the Page Background

On each page in your site, you have the option to accept the background specified by the selected SiteStyle. However, using layouts, you can also override the SiteStyle background, and specify a special background for any layout in your site.

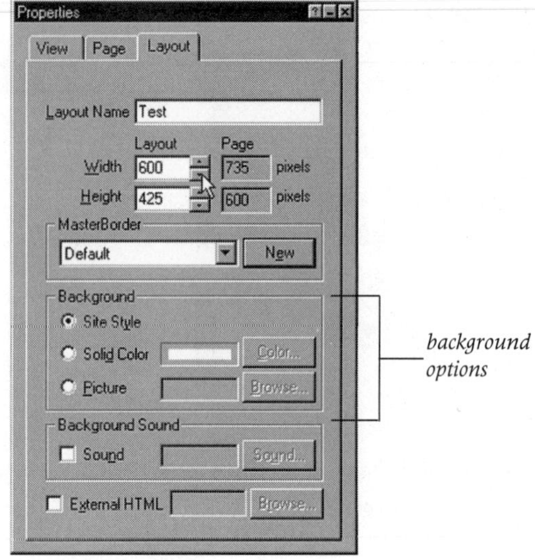


**Figure 7.35**
*Page background options.*

### To select a page background:

1. Click in the layout area of the page to display the Layout tab of the Properties Palette.
2. Select the desired Background option **(Figure 7.35)**:

   **SiteStyle** causes the background image or color for the selected SiteStyle to be used.

   **Solid Color** allows you to select a background color from the standard colors palette.

   **Picture** allows you to select a graphic image file to use as the background for the current page.

   The selected page background is displayed.

### ✔ Tips

- While the Background settings appear on the Layout tab of the Properties Palette, backgrounds are applied to the entire page, not just the Layout area.
- To change the background for every page in the site, go to Style-View and modify the background selected for the site. See Chapter 5.

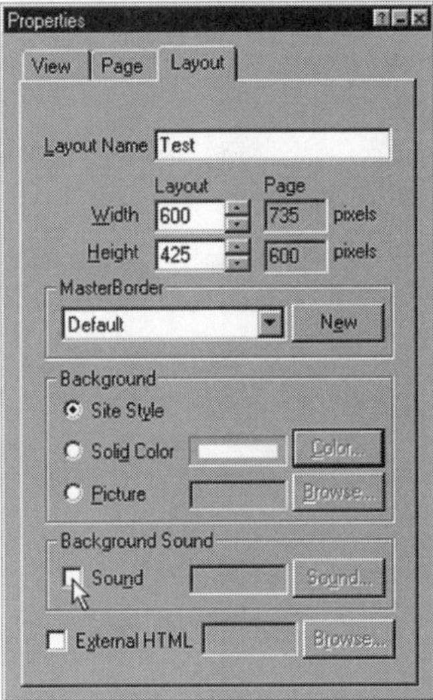


**Figure 7.36**
*Select the Sound box in the Background Sound area.*

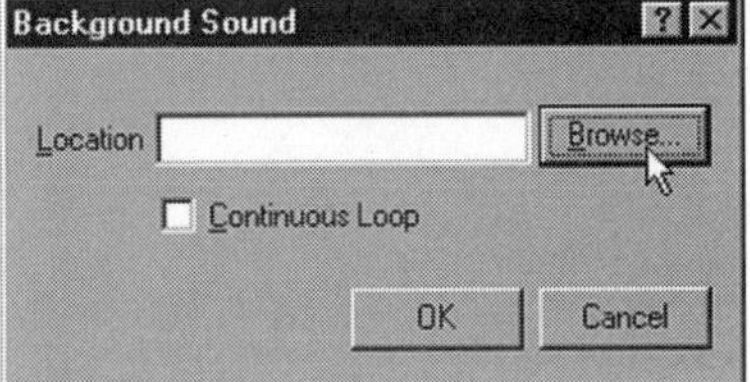


**Figure 7.37**
*Select Browse to choose a sound file to play.* Mac users click the Select... button.

## Using Layout Properties to Select a Background Sound

You may wish to play a background sound when visitors arrive at particular pages in your site. You might want to provide an audio welcome to your site, provide an audio description of special offers, or you may wish to play theme or background music. In any case, Fusion provides a Background Sound facility associated with each layout in your site.

### To select a background sound:

1. Click the layout area of the page to display the Layout tab of the Properties Palette.
2. Click the Sound box in the Background Sound area of the Layout tab **(Figure 7.36)**.

   The Background Sound dialog box appears **(Figure 7.37)**.
3. Select the Browse button (*Mac users click the Select... button)*.to choose an audio file, or type the file path and file name in the Location field.
4. To play the audio file in a continuous loop, select the Continuous Loop box in the Background Sound dialog box.
5. Click OK.

### ✔ Tips

- Compatible audio file formats: **AU, .MID, .MIDI,** and **.WAV**.
- Sounds will be audible only when using browsers capable of playing sound and a computer equipped for sound.

# Using Layout Properties to Designate an External HTML File

There may be occasions when you wish to use an HTML file you created with another tool, that you downloaded from the Web, or that you received from another source as a page in your site. You can use the Layout tab in the Properties Palette to specify use of such an external file.

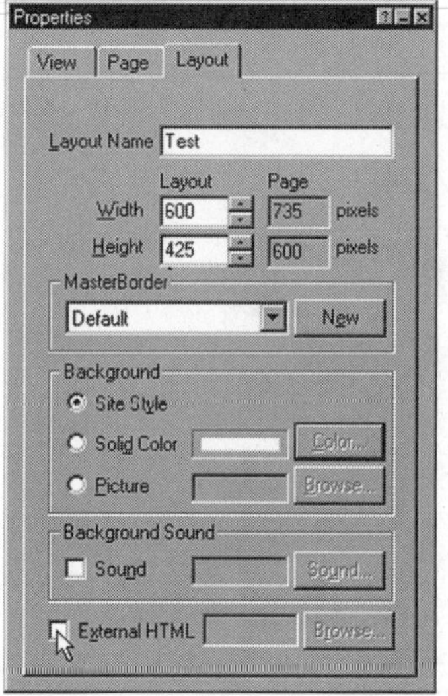


**Figure 7.38**
*Select the External HTML box on the Layout tab.*

### To select an external HTML file:

1. Click in the layout area of the page to display the Layout tab of the Properties Palette.
2. Select the External HTML box in the Layout tab **(Figure 7.38)**.

   The standard open dialog box appears **(Figure 7.39)**.
3. Select the HTML file you wish to use for the current page, then click Open.

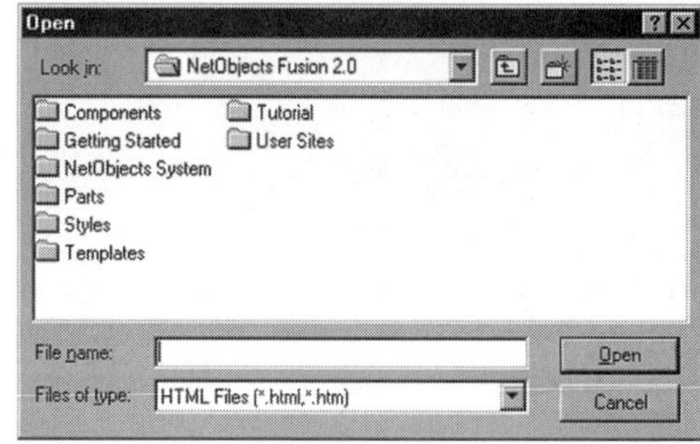


**Figure 7.39**
*Choose the HTML file you wish to use.*

### ✓ Tips

- You cannot combine external HTML files with Fusion elements on the same page.
- See Pages 26 and 52 for more on importing external pages.

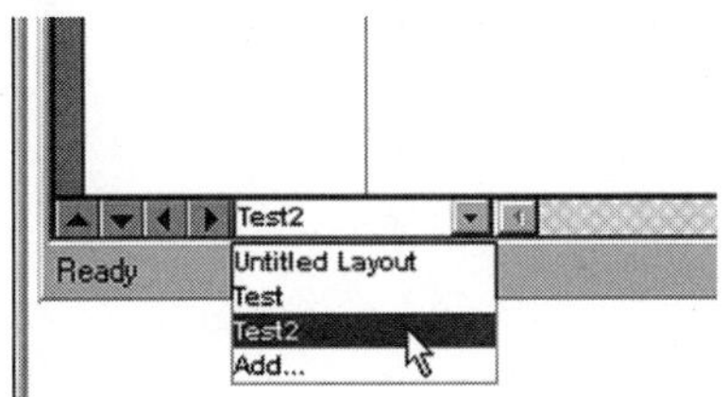


**Figure 7.40**
*Page background options.*

## Using Multiple Layouts

Multiple layouts provide the opportunity to publish your site in several different versions. For example, you might use multiple layouts to publish your site in different languages. Multiple layouts can also be useful for prototyping during site development. For example, a number of page layouts can be developed as options from which a client can choose or request modifications.

When using multiple layouts with a page, you will sometimes want to apply a different layout to a page.

### To apply a layout to a page:

In Page View, select the desired layout from the list displayed in the drop-down Layout menu at the bottom left of the Fusion window **(Figure 7.40)**.

The selected layout will be displayed in the layout area of the current page.

# Working With Text

*text tool*

There are a number of text elements you can add to Fusion Web pages. These include text boxes, tables, and frames. Since working with text in each of these Fusion text elements is the same, the techniques presented in this chapter for selecting, editing, and formatting text are appropriate for use with text contained in any Fusion text element.

## Introducing Text Boxes

As in page layout applications, Fusion utilizes text boxes for adding text to pages. You can place text boxes in both the layout and MasterBorders areas of pages. Text can then be entered and formatted to suit your needs.

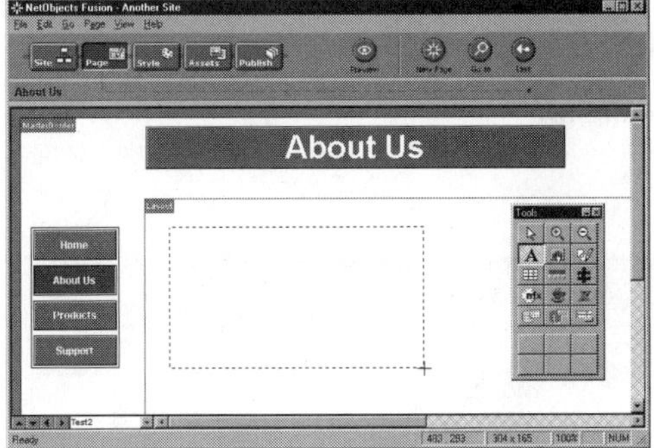


**Figure 8.1**
*Create a text box by selecting the text tool in the Tools Palette and then drawing the text box by clicking and dragging.*

### To draw a text box:

1. In Page View, select the text tool in the tools palette.
2. Position the pointer (now a crosshair) on your page where you want the upper left corner of the new text box to start.
3. Click and drag down diagonally.

   A dotted line indicates the boundary as you draw the text box **(Figure 8.1)**.
4. Release the mouse button when the text box is the desired size.

   The text box appears with eight handles around its edges and a blinking text cursor at the text insertion point **(Figure 8.2)**.

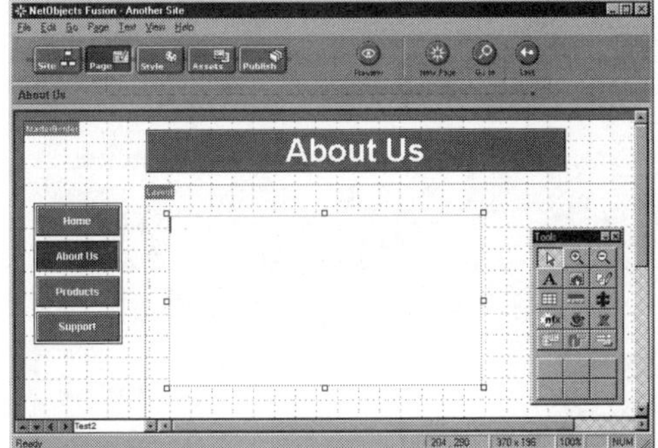


**Figure 8.2**
*The new text box appears with eight handles around its edges and a text cursor.*

## Resizing and Moving Text Boxes

Once you have drawn a text box on your page, you may wish to move or resize it. This is easily accomplished using the mouse and text box handles.

### To resize a text box:

1. Click on the desired text box to select it.

   A text box is selected when its border and handles are displayed.

2. Position the mouse over a text box handle.

   The mouse pointer becomes a double-ended arrow pointing in the directions in which the handle can be dragged.

   You can resize the text box by dragging handles on the ends **(Figure 8.3)**, the top and bottom, or the corners of the text box **(Figure 8.4)**.

3. Click and drag the handle to resize the text box.
4. Release the mouse button to stop resizing the text box.

### To move a text box:

1. Click on the desired text box to select it.
2. Position the mouse pointer over the edge of the text box.
3. When you use the arrow pointer (not a double-ended arrow), click and drag the text box to your desired position **(Figure 8.5)**.

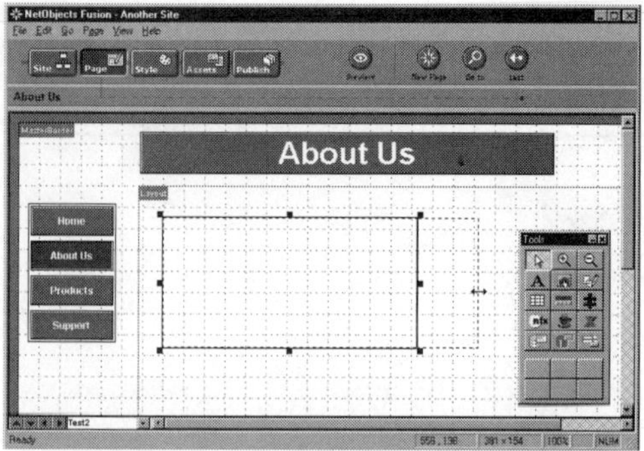


**Figure 8.3**
*Resize a text box by dragging an end handle left or right.*

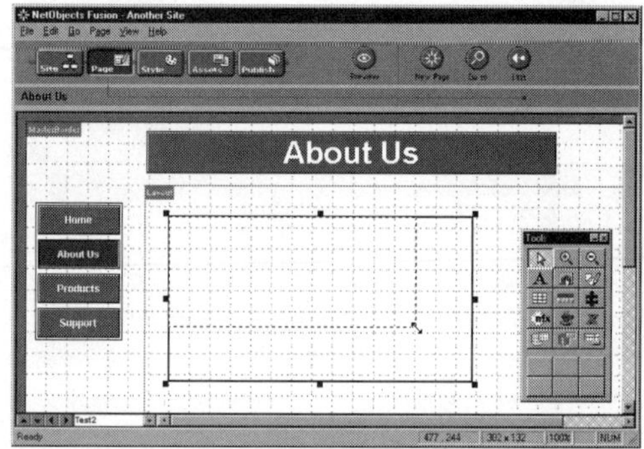


**Figure 8.4**
*Resize a text box by dragging a corner handle diagonally.*

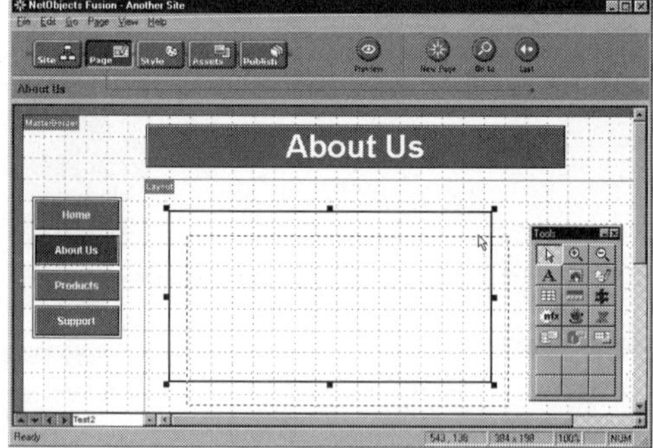


**Figure 8.5**
*Move a text box by dragging with the arrow pointer.*

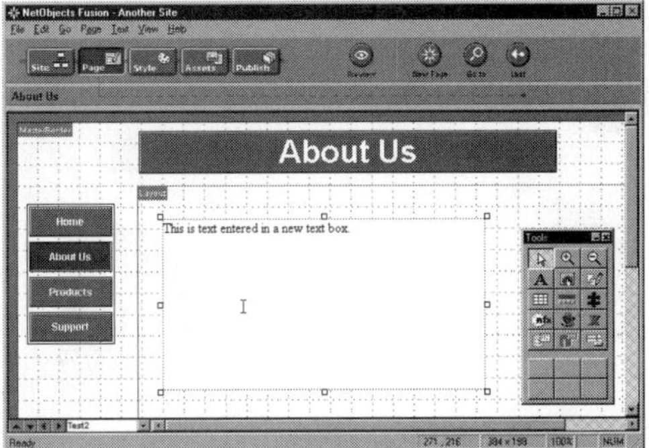


**Figure 8.6**
*Enter text in a text box by typing.*

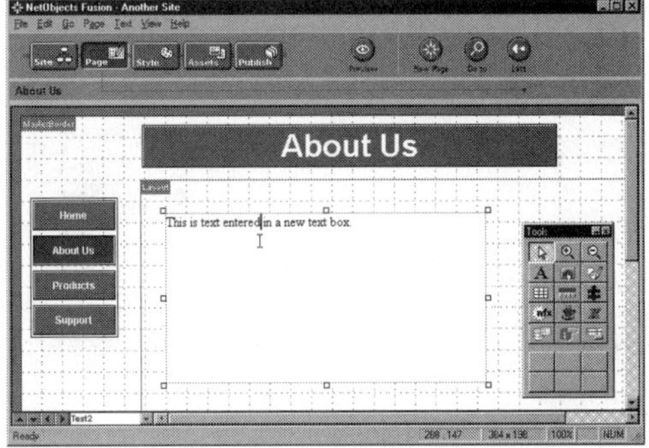


**Figure 8.7**
*Move the text cursor by clicking a location within the existing text.*

## Entering Text

Once a text box or any text element is drawn on your Web page, you can enter text in it simply by typing.

### To enter text in a text box:

1. Click on the desired text element to select it.

   A text element is selected when its border and handles are displayed and a text cursor is blinking inside.

2. Begin typing.

   The text you type appears at the position of the blinking text cursor **(Figure 8.6)**.

   You can type and delete text in a Fusion text box just as in a word processor or page layout program.

### To move the text cursor:

1. Click on the desired text element to select it.

   The blinking text cursor marks the point at which typed text will appear in the text element. You can move the text cursor to any position in the text appearing in the text element.

2. Click the desired position for inserting text **(Figure 8.7)**.

   The blinking text cursor appears in the location you clicked. You can now begin typing at that location.

✔ **Tip**

- To place the text cursor above or below existing text, use the Enter/Return key to move the existing text up or down.

# Selecting Text

An important facet of formatting and editing text in text elements is selecting text. Text must be selected in order to apply styles to text, or to delete, cut, or copy sections of text. Fusion offers a number of methods for selecting text.

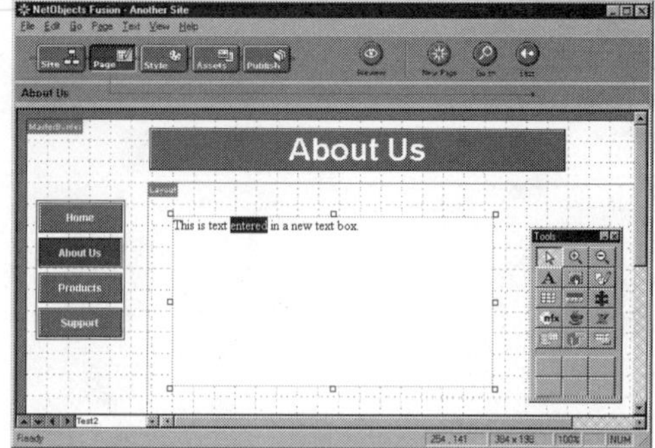


**Figure 8.8**
*Double-click a word in a text box to select it.*

### To select a word:

1. Click on the desired text element to select it.
2. Double-click a word you wish to select.

   You can see that text is selected when it is displayed on a black background **(Figure 8.8)**.

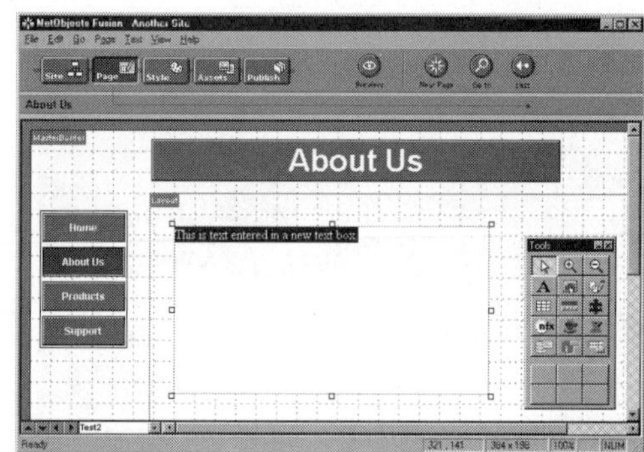


**Figure 8.9**
*Triple-click to select a paragraph.*

### To select a paragraph:

1. Click on the desired text element to select it.
2. Triple-click in the paragraph you wish to select **(Figure 8.9)**.

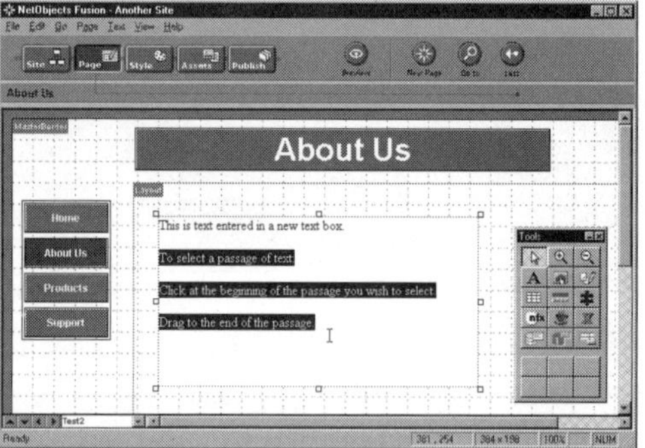


**Figure 8.10**
*Click at the beginning then drag to the end of a paragraph you wish to select.*

### To select a passage of text:

1. Click on the desired text element to select it.
2. Click at the beginning of the passage you wish to select.
3. Drag to the end of the passage you wish to select **(Figure 8.10)**.

### ✔ Tips

- To deselect text, simply click anywhere other than on the selected text.
- You can select all text in a text element by choosing Select All from the Edit menu or by using the keyboard shortcut Ctrl + A *(or Command + A on the Mac)*.

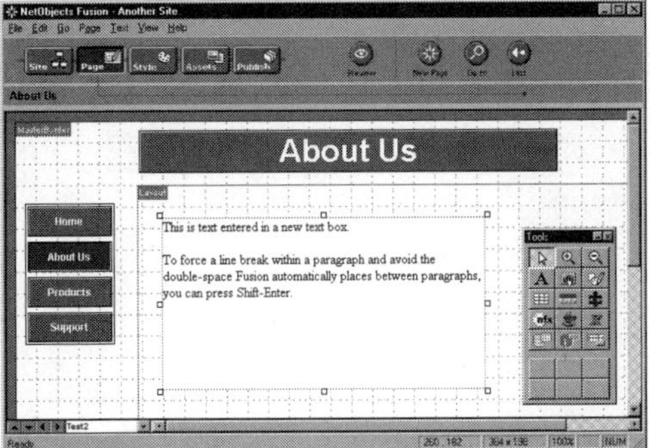


**Figure 8.11**
*To insert a line break, click where you want the line break to occur.*

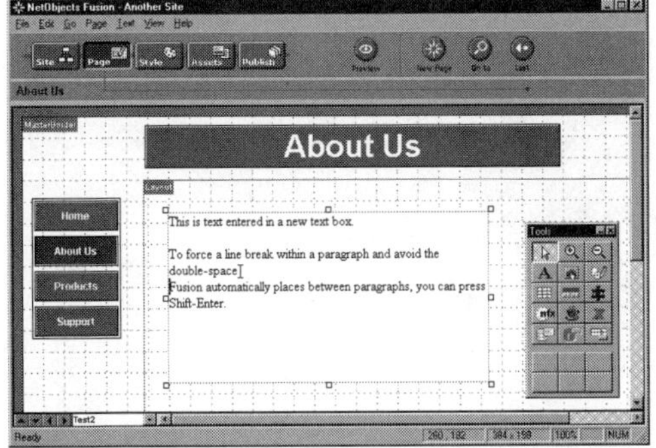


**Figure 8.12**
*Press Shift + Enter to force a line break.*

## Paragraphs vs. Line Breaks

When you press the Enter key *(or Return on the Mac)* in a text element, Fusion ends the paragraph and automatically inserts a double-space. This means that paragraphs will be separated by double-spaces. You can, however, force a line break without ending the current paragraph, thereby avoiding the double-space.

### To force a line break:

With the text cursor positioned where you wish the line to break **(Figure 8.11)**, press Shift-Enter *(or Shift + Return on the Mac)*.

The line break is inserted, and because you have not ended the current paragraph, the lines are single-spaced **(Figure 8.12)**.

## Cutting and Copying Text

You can edit text in Fusion text elements much the same as in word processors or page layout programs. The Edit menu provides the traditional Cut, Copy, and Paste options for text editing.

### To cut text:

1. Click on the desired text element to select it.
2. Select the text you wish to cut (see Page 110 for selecting text).
3. Choose Cut from the Edit menu **(Figure 8.13)**.

   The selected text is removed from the text element and copied to the Clipboard in memory where it will remain until another Cut or Copy operation is performed.

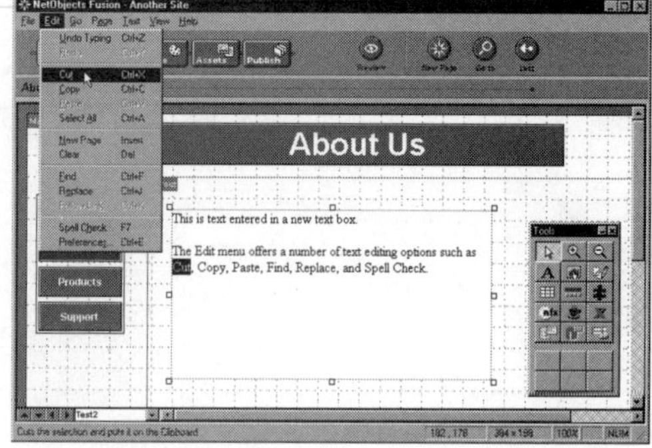


**Figure 8.13**
*Choose Cut from the Edit menu to cut text and copy it to the Clipboard.*

### To copy text:

1. Click on the desired text element to select it.
2. Select the text you wish to copy.
3. Choose Copy from the Edit menu **(Figure 8.14)**.

   The selected text is copied to the Clipboard in memory where it will remain until another Cut or Copy operation is performed.

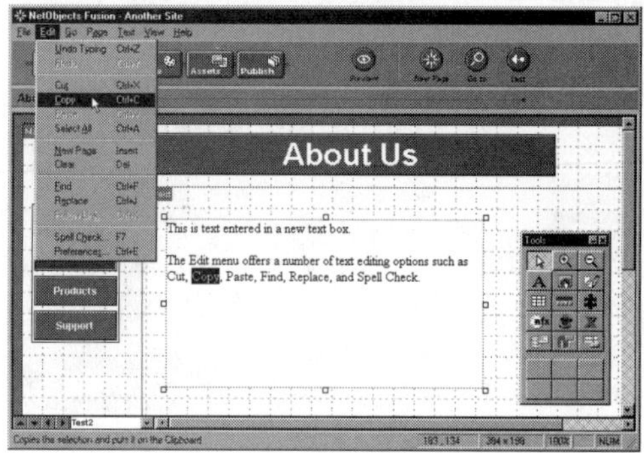


**Figure 8.14**
*Choose Copy from the Edit menu to copy text to the Clipboard.*

✔ **Tip**

■ You can also cut and copy text using the keyboard shortcuts Ctrl + X and Ctrl + C respectively *(or Command + X and Command + C on the Mac)*.

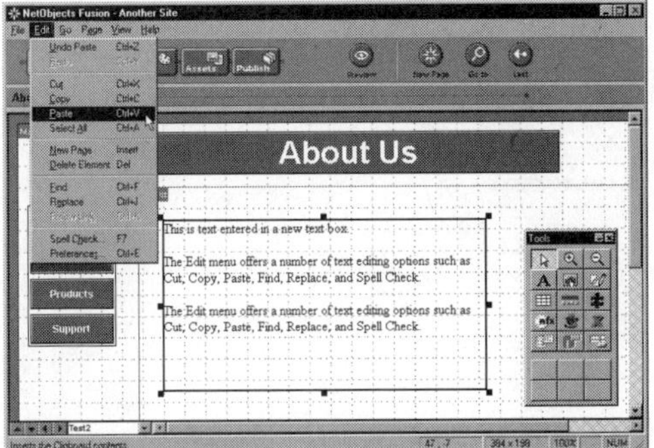

**Figure 8.15**
*Choose Paste from the Edit menu to Paste text in the Clipboard.*

## Pasting Text

After performing a Cut or Copy operation, you can paste the cut or copied text to another location in any text element in any page in your site.

### To paste text:

1. After cutting or copying text, click at the location you wish to paste the text.
2. With the text cursor in the position you wish to paste the text, choose Paste from the Edit menu (**Figure 8.15**).

   The cut or copied text is inserted or pasted to the location you selected.

### ✔ Tips

- You can also paste text using the keyboard shortcut Ctrl + V *(or Command + V on the Mac)*.
- You can paste text into a Fusion text element from other applications by cutting or copying the text in, for example, a word processor, then pasting the text into a Fusion text element.
- You can also replace text using the Paste option by selecting a passage of text you wish to replace with the text in the clipboard, then choosing Paste from the Edit menu. The selected text is replaced by the pasted text.

# Finding Text

Fusion lets you perform find operations like those in word processor and page layout program. Find lets you specify text you wish to locate within a text element so you can edit or format that text.

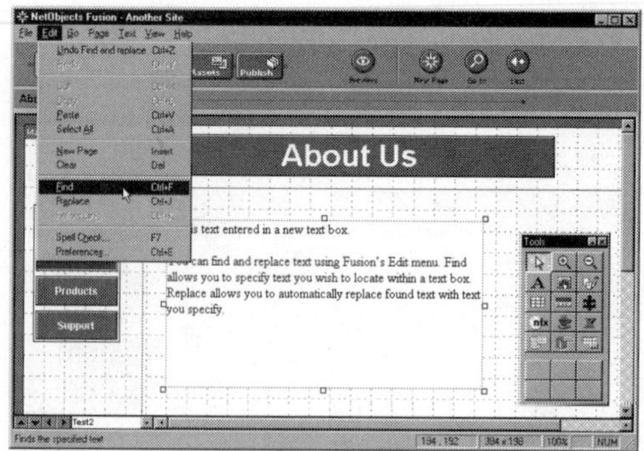


**Figure 8.16**
*Choose Find from the Edit menu.*

### To find text:

1. Click on the desired text element to select it.
2. Click in the text element where you wish to begin searching for the text (typically you will click at the beginning of the text).
3. Choose Find from the Edit menu **(Figure 8.16)**.

   The Find dialog box is displayed.
4. Type the text you wish to find in the Find what field **(Figure 8.17)**.

   If you wish to find the exact text you entered (and not the string of characters you entered embedded in other words), select the **Match whole word only** check box.

   If you wish Fusion to match the case of the characters you enter (for example, initial caps), select the **Match case** check box.
5. Click the Find Next button.

   Fusion searches the selected text element from the point of the text cursor. If matching text is found, Fusion selects it **(Figure 8.18)**. You can then edit the found text, or click the Find Next button again to find the next occurrence of the specified text. You might have to move the find dialog box to see the selected text.

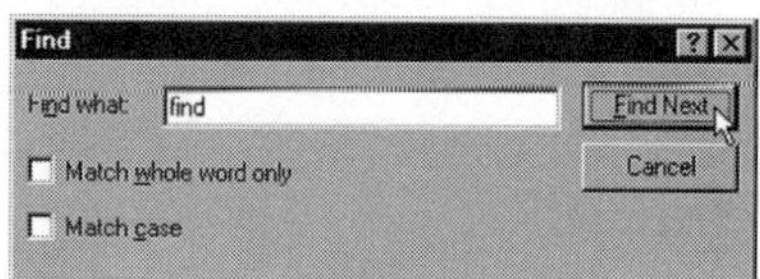


**Figure 8.17**
*Enter the text you wish to find in the Find what field in the Find dialog box.*

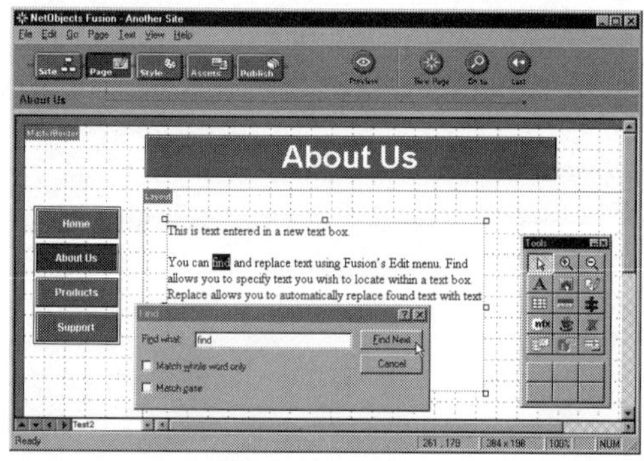


**Figure 8.18**
*Click the Find Next button to search for the specified text. Fusion selects the first occurrence of matching text found.*

 **Tip**

- You can also open the Find dialog box with the keyboard shortcut Ctrl + F *(or Command + F on the Mac)*.

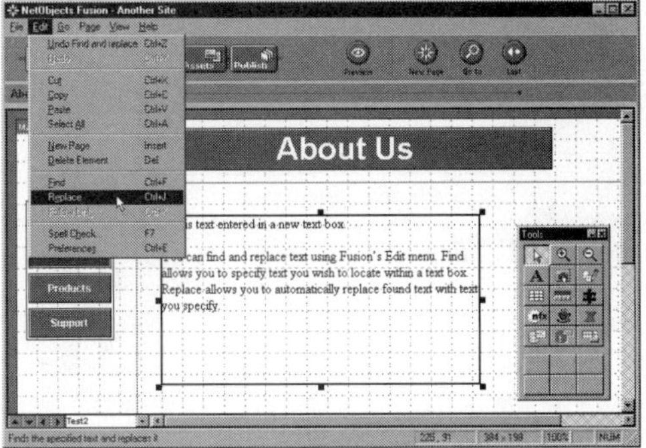


**Figure 8.19**
*Choose Replace from the Edit menu.*

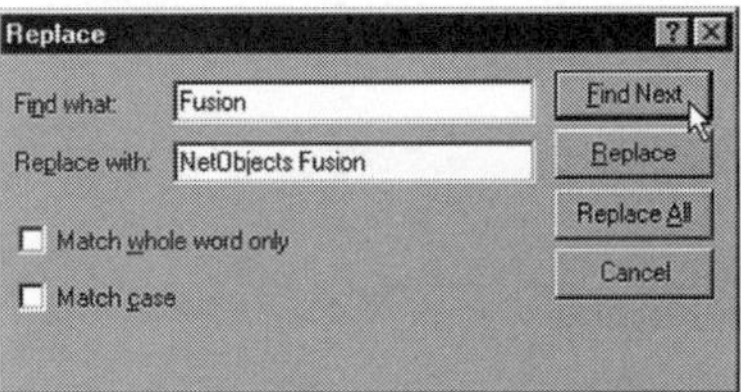


**Figure 8.20**
*Enter the text you wish to find in the Find what field and the text with which you wish to replace found text in the Replace with field.*

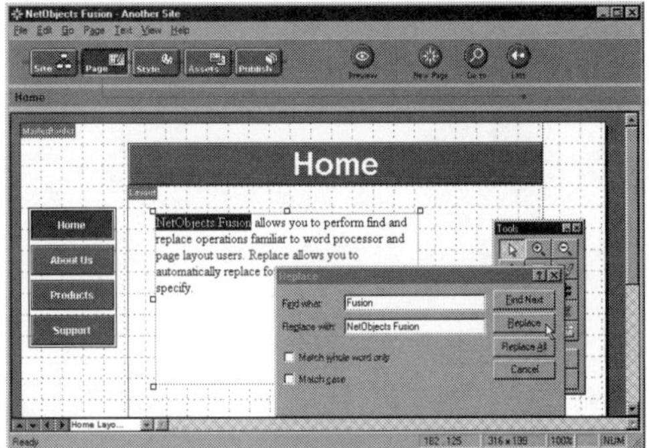


**Figure 8.21**
*Click the Replace button to replace found text.*

## ✔ Tip

- You can open the Replace dialog box with the keyboard shortcut Ctrl + J *(or Command + J on the Mac).*

# Replacing Text

Fusion also allows you to perform replace operations typical to word processor and page layout programs. Replace allows you to specify text to find and then to automatically replace found text with text you specify.

### To replace text:

1. Click on the desired text element to select it.
2. Click in the text element where you wish to begin searching for the text (typically you will click at the beginning of the text).
3. Choose Replace from the Edit menu **(Figure 8.19)**.

   The Replace dialog box is displayed.
4. Type the text you wish to find in the Find what field, and type the text with which you wish to replace found text in the Replace with field **(Figure 8.20)**.

   The **Match whole word only** and **Match case** check boxes behave the same in replacing as in finding on the previous page.
5. Click the Find Next button.

   Fusion searches for the selected text. If matching text is found, Fusion selects it.
6. Click the Replace button to replace the found text **(Figure 8.21)**.

   You can also select **Replace All** to replace all instances of your text or **Find Next** to skip to the next instance of the specified text.

## Checking Spelling

An important editing operation in any document containing text is spell checking. Like most word processors and page layout applications, Fusion offers a spell checking feature to check the text that will appear on your Web pages.

### To check spelling:

1. Click on the desired text element to select it.
2. Choose Spell Check from the Edit menu **(Figure 8.22)**.

   If suspect words are found, the Spelling dialog box appears displaying the suspect word in the **Not found** field **(Figure 8.23)**. Fusion offers suggestions for correcting the spelling of suspect words in the **Suggestions** field.
3. Click the appropriate button in the Spelling dialog box, or type a corrected word in the **Change to** field, and click Change.

   **Ignore** leaves the current instance of the word in question untouched.

   **Ignore All** skips all instances of the current word.

   **Change** changes the current word to the word displayed in the Change to field. **Change all** changes all instances of the word.

   **Add** adds the word in question to the Fusion dictionary. When you add a word to the Fusion dictionary, it will not question the spelling of that word again.

   **Suggest** lists similarly spelled words in the Suggestions field.

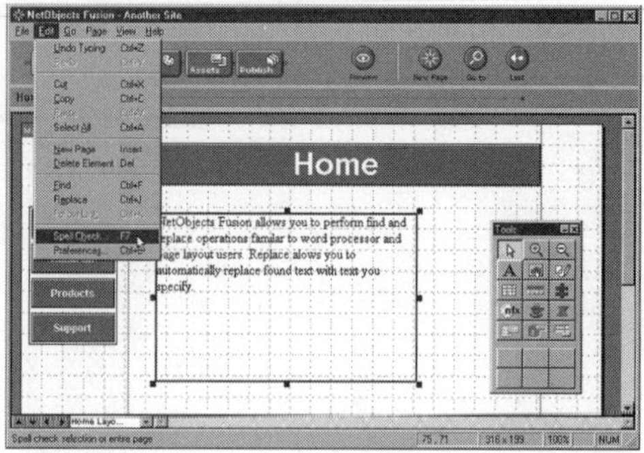


**Figure 8.22**
*Choose Spell Check from the Edit menu.*

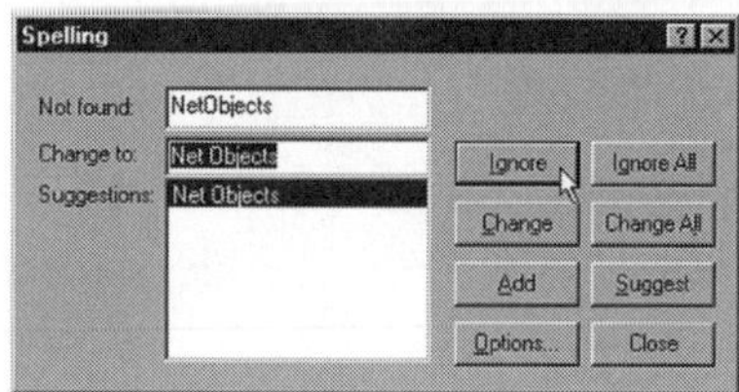


**Figure 8.23**
*Select a buttons in the Spelling dialog box to correct or ignore misspelled words.*

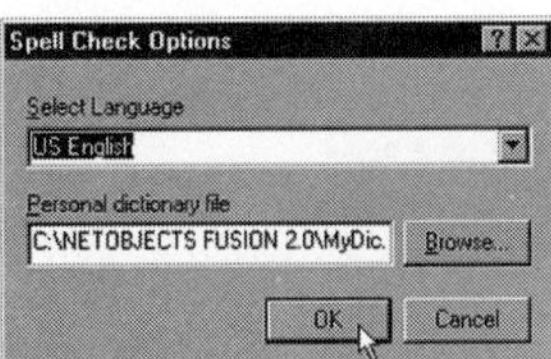


**Figure 8.24**
*Select a button on the Spelling dialog box to correct or ignore misspelled words.*

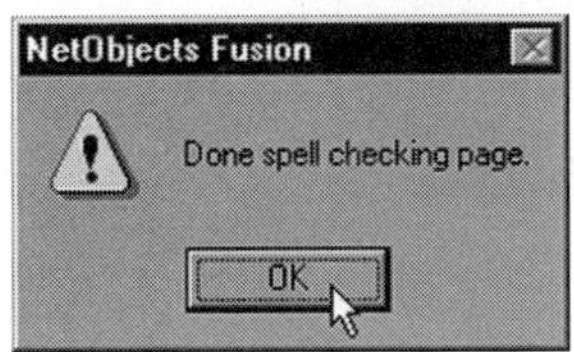


**Figure 8.25**
*When Fusion has finished spell checking , it displays this dialog box.*

**Options** allows you to select the desired Fusion dictionary **(Figure 8.24)**.

**Close** terminates the spell checking session.

4. Repeat Step 3 until you either terminate the spell check by clicking the Close button, or until Fusion finishes the spell check.

   When Fusion has finished spell checking the selected text element, it displays the dialog box shown in **Figure 8.25**.

5. Click OK.

   The Spelling dialog box disappears.

✔ **Tip**

- In Windows 95, you can also open the Spelling dialog box using the keyboard shortcut F7. *There is no keyboard shortcut on the Mac.*

## Formatting Text

The Text tab in the Page View Properties Palette provides a number of options for formatting text in text elements. You can use Text properties to specify text style, alignment, font, font size, paragraph styles, list properties, text color, and even text element background color.

**Figure 8.26**
*Select the desired text style button in the Text properties tab.*

### To access text properties:

1. In Page View, if the Properties Palette is not already displayed, select Properties Palette from the View menu.
2. Click in a text element to select it.

   The Text tab of the Properties Palette is displayed **(Figure 8.26)**.

### To select text styles:

1. Select the text in a text element to which you wish to apply a style.
2. Select the desired text style button:

   **B** displays text in boldface.

   *I* displays text in italics.

   U underlines text.

   S strikes through text.

   $a^b$ makes text superscript.

   $a_b$ makes text subscript.

   The selected text is displayed using the text style chosen **(Figure 8.27)**.

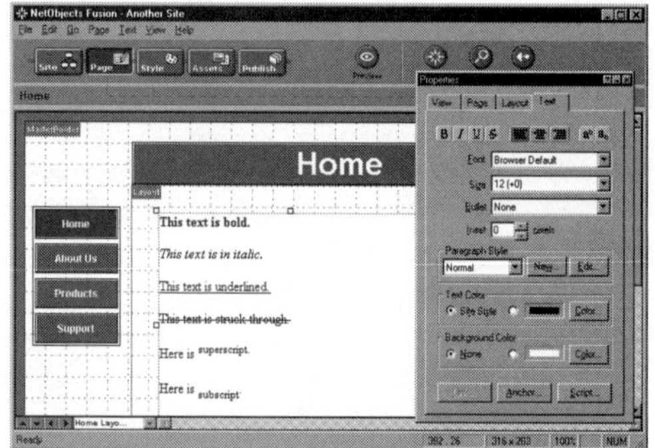


**Figure 8.27**
*The selected text is displayed using the text style chosen.*

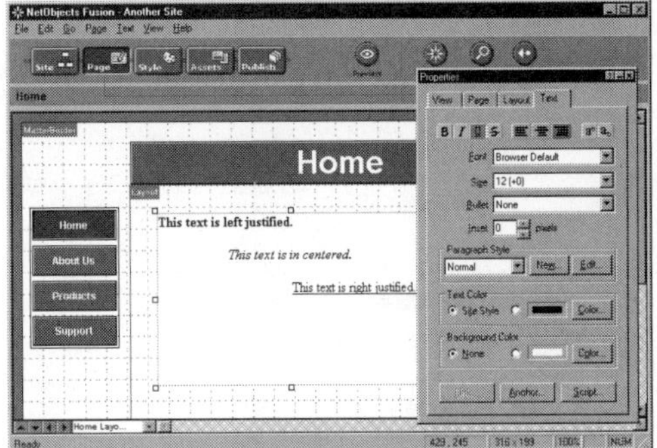


**Figure 8.28**
*Paragraph or selected text aligned as specified.*

### To select text alignment:

1. Click in the paragraph for which you wish to set text alignment, or select multiple paragraphs by clicking and dragging.
2. Select the desired alignment button:

   left-aligns selected text.

   centers selected text.

   right-aligns selected text.

   The paragraph or selected text is aligned as specified **(Figure 8.28)**.

### To indent text:

1. Click in the paragraph you want indented.
2. Choose Indent from the Text menu.

   The entire paragraph is indented. To unindent , choose Unindent from the Text menu. Or, to indent text further, choose Indent again.

**Figure 8.29**
*Select a font from the Font field drop-down menu.*

### To select a font:

1. Select the text to which you wish to apply a different font selection.
2. Click the down-arrow in the Font field of the Text properties tab to display a drop-down menu of available fonts **(Figure 8.29)**.

   The font menu displays all the fonts installed on your system. If the font you use is not available on the system of a visitor to your site, most Web browsers display their default fonts instead.
3. Select the font you wish to use.

   The selected text is displayed in the font you selected.

### To select a font size:

1. Select the text that you wish to resize.
2. Click the down-arrow in the Size field of the Text properties tab to display a drop-down menu of available sizes **(Figure 8.30)**.

   The font sizes displayed are accompanied by the HTML tag equivalent in parentheses.
3. Select the size you wish to use.

   The selected text is displayed in the size you selected.

**Figure 8.30**
*Select the desired font size from the drop-down menu.*

### To select text color:

1. Select the text to which you wish to apply a different color.
2. In the Text Color area of the Text properties tab, select one of the two options:

   **SiteStyle** applies the color defaults for the selected Site Style to the selected text.

   **Color** allows you to specify a color for the selected text using the color palette **(Figure 8.31)**.
3. If using the color palette, click OK after choosing a color.

   The selected text is displayed in the color you selected.

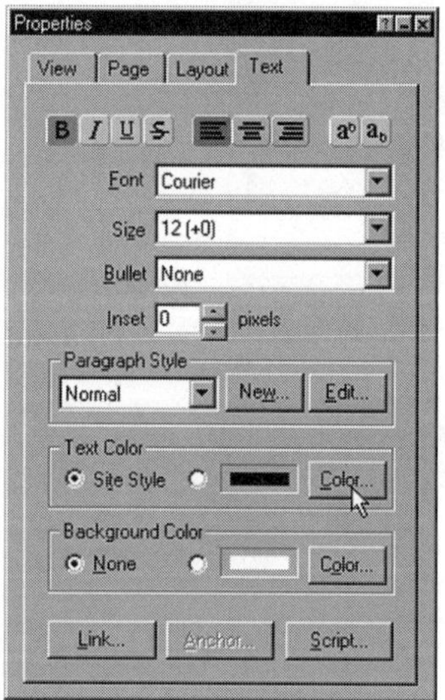


**Figure 8.31**
*Click the Color button to choose a color from the color palette.*

**Figure 8.32**
*Click the down-arrow in the Paragraph Style field to display the available Paragraph Styles.*

**Figure 8.33**
*Select a Paragraph Style, and the selected paragraph is displayed using that style.*

# Using Paragraph Styles

Paragraph styles in Fusion correspond to standard HTML styles including Normal and Headings 1-6. The heading styles are generally used for titles, headings, and subheadings in your Web pages.

### To select an existing paragraph style:

1. Click in the paragraph whose style you wish to change, or click and drag to select multiple paragraphs.
2. Click the down arrow in the Paragraph Style field to display a drop-down menu of available Paragraph Styles **(Figure 8.32)**.
3. Select a Paragraph Style from the menu.

   The selected paragraph is displayed using the paragraph style you selected **(Figure 8.33)**.

### ✔ Tips

- You can edit the currently selected paragraph style by clicking the Edit button in the Paragraph Style area of the Text properties tab. Then make changes in the Paragraph Style dialog box presented.
- You can define your own paragraph style by selecting text that is formatted as you wish, then clicking the New button and naming the new paragraph style. The new paragraph style is defined using the selected text.

## Creating Lists

Fusion lists are a collection of bulleted text items, each of which is its own paragraph. With Fusion you can easily create ordered and unordered lists within text elements. Ordered lists use numbers or letters as the bullets. Unordered lists use bullet symbols.

### To create a list:

1. Type all the items you want in the list. Press the enter key (*Mac users press return)* after typing each item.
2. Select all the items you want in the list **(Figure 8.34)**.
3. Select a bullet style from the Bullet drop-down menu in the Text properties tab **(Figure 8.35)**.

   The Bullet menu offers a variety of bullet styles including symbols, letters, and numbers.

   The selected list items are displayed indented and preceded by the selected bullet **(Figure 8.36)**.

### ✔ Tips

- You can set the beginning value in an ordered list by clicking in the list, then choosing Set List Start Value from the Text menu.
- To change a list bullet style, click in the list, and select another bullet style from the Bullet menu.
- To add an item to a list, click at the end of the list, and press Enter. *Mac users press Return.*

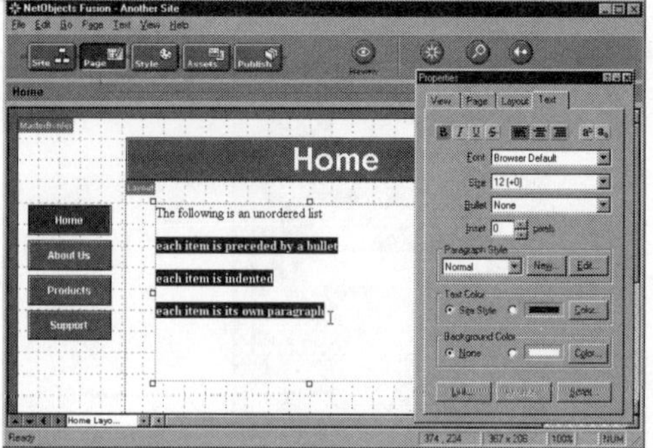


**Figure 8.34**
*Select the paragraphs you wish to make into a list.*

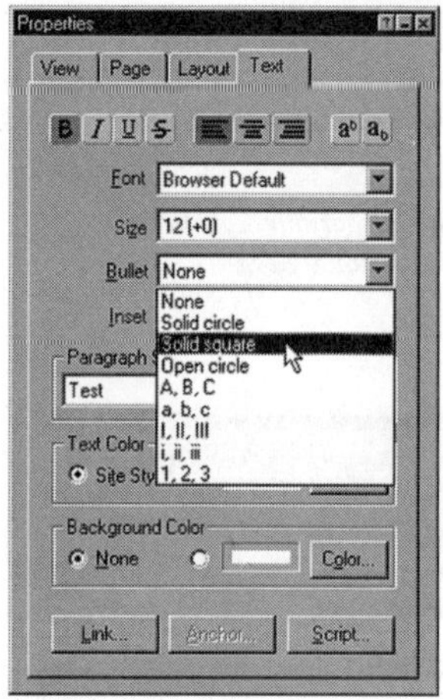


**Figure 8.35**
*Select a bullet style from the Bullet drop-down menu.*

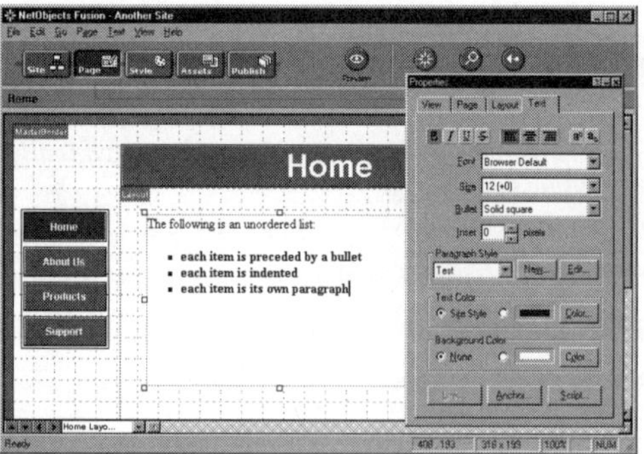


**Figure 8.36**
*The selected paragraphs are displayed as a list using the selected bullet style.*

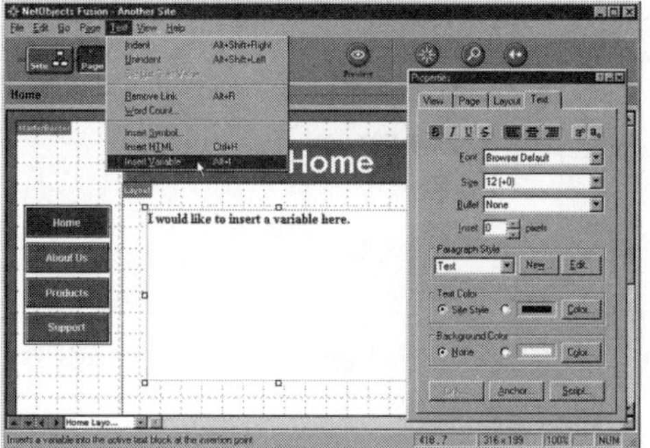


**Figure 8.37**
*Choose Insert Variable from the Text menu.*

**Figure 8.38**
*Choose the Site & General variable type from the Type menu and select the specific variable from those listed.*

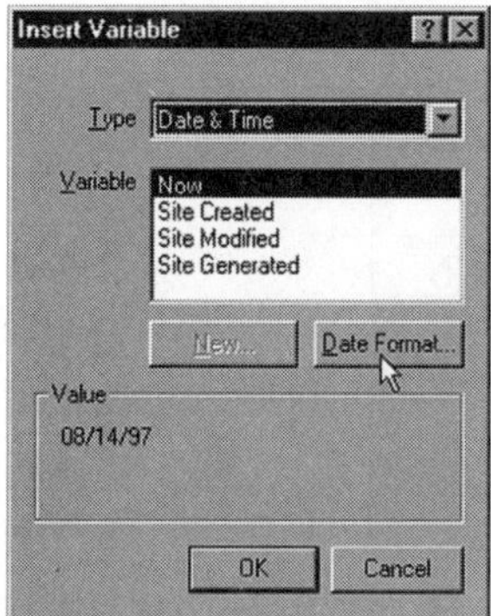


**Figure 8.39**
*Choose the Date & Time variable type from the Type menu and select the specific variable from those listed.*

# Using Variables

Fusion also allows you to use text variables in your site. These are markers for text which may change over time. For example Fusion has defined variables for dates, the site name, and the number of pages in your site. You can also define your own variables in Fusion.

### To insert a variable:

1. Click in the text where you want the variable to appear.
2. Choose Insert Variable from the Text menu **(Figure 8.37)**.

   The Insert Variable dialog box is displayed. Fusion offers three types of predefined variables:

   **Date & Time** includes variables for various key dates and times **(Figure 8.39)**. You can use the Date Format button to choose a date format from a list.

   **Site & General** includes variables for site name, author, number of pages, OS platform, and product used to generate the site **(Figure 8.38)**.

   **User defined** includes any variables that you have defined.
3. Select the variable type from the Type drop-down menu, and the variable you wish to insert from the list of variables displayed.
4. Click OK.

   The selected variable is displayed at the location selected. In Page View, variables are displayed on a gray background to distinguish them from non-variable text.

### To create a new variable:

1. Click in the text where you want the variable to appear.
2. Choose Insert Variable from the Text menu.

   The Insert Variable dialog box is displayed.
3. Choose User defined from the Type drop-down menu **(Figure 8.40)**.
4. Click New.

   The New Variable dialog box is displayed.
5. Type a name for your variable in the Variable name field.
6. Type a value for the variable in the Value field **(Figure 8.41)**.
7. Click OK.

   The New Variable is displayed in the User defined variable list in the Insert Variables dialog box.

   You can now insert the new variable by selecting it and clicking OK **(Figure 8.42)**.

### ✔ Tip

- You can also open the Insert Variable dialog box using the keyboard shortcut Alt + I. *There is no keyboard shortcut on the Mac.*

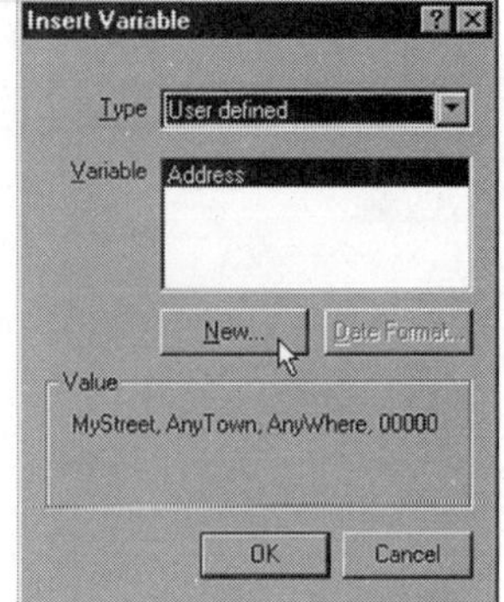


**Figure 8.40**
*Choose User defined from the Type drop-down menu in the Insert Variables dialog box.*

**Figure 8.41**
*Type a name and a value for the new variable, and click OK.*

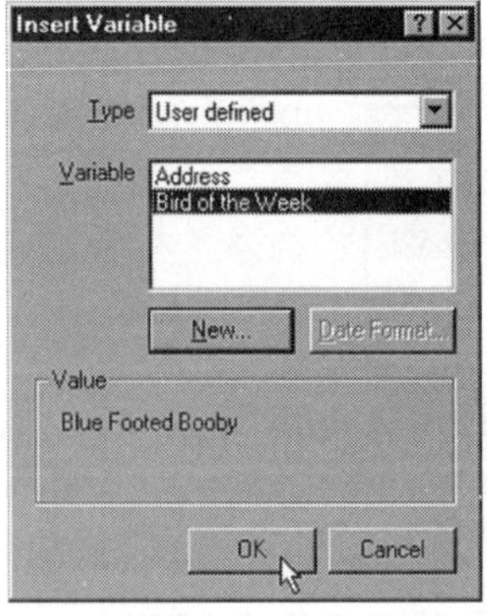


**Figure 8.42**
*To insert the new variable, select it from the Variable list and click OK.*

Create a new variable

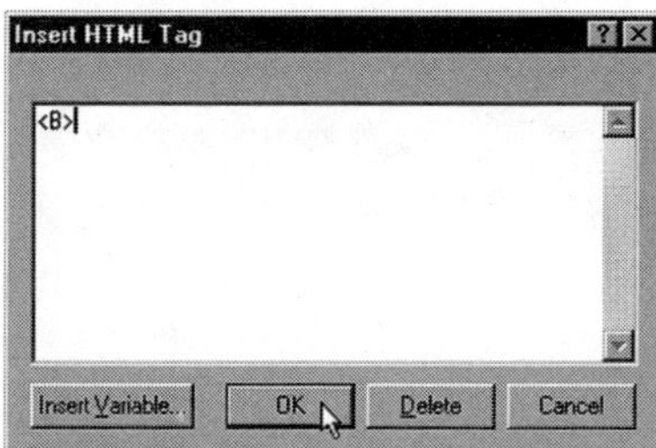


**Figure 8.43**
*Type the desired tag in the Insert HTML Tag dialog box.*

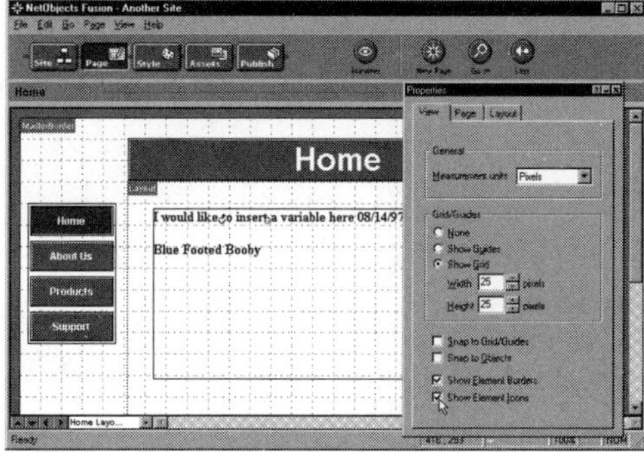


**Figure 8.44**
*The locations of tags are marked with small icons if the Show Element Icons option is selected in View properties.*

## Adding Your Own HTML Tags

Although the idea of the Page View in Fusion is to shield you from HTML tags, there may be instances when you wish to manually insert an HTML tag.

### To insert an HTML tag:

1. Click the location in the text element where you want to insert the tag.
2. Choose Insert HTML from the Text menu.

   The Insert HTML Tag dialog box appears **(Figure 8.43)**.
3. Type the tag in the box provided.
4. Click OK.

   The tag entered is inserted at the location selected. (You won't see the results here.)
5. If the tag you have entered must be closed with another tag, repeat Steps 1–4 for the closing tag.

### ✔ Tips

- You can preview the effects of inserted HTML tags by previewing your page in a Web browser (see Chapter 6).
- If Show Element Icons is selected in the View tab of the Properties Palette, the positions of inserted HTML tags are marked by small icons **(Figure 8.44)**.

# Applying a Background Color

You can use the Text properties tab of the Properties Palette to apply or change a background fill for a text box.

## To apply a background fill:

1. Select the text box whose background you would like to set.
2. If the None radio button is selected **(Figure 8.45)**, click the Color button in the Background Color area of the Text properties tab.

   The color palette is displayed **(Figure 8.46)**. *Mac users click the Color... button to display the color palette.*
3. Click the desired color in the color palette, or use the Define Custom colors button to define a color not displayed on the palette.
4. Click OK on the color palette.

   The selected color is displayed as the background of the selected text box **(Figure 8.47)**.

   *Mac users can define custom colors by clicking a custom color and selecting the Edit... button.*

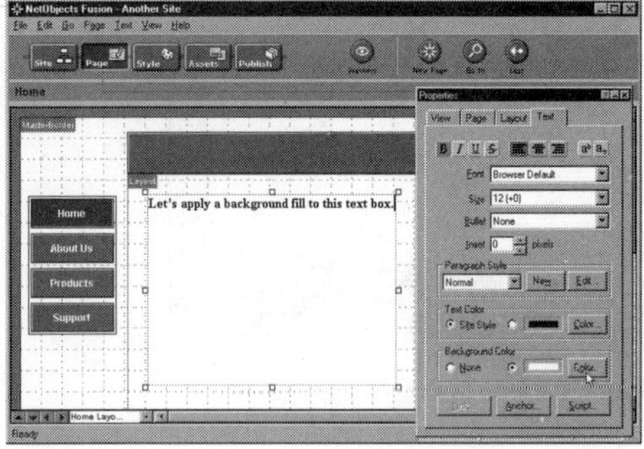

**Figure 8.45**
*Select None in the Background Color area of the Text properties tab to select no background color.*

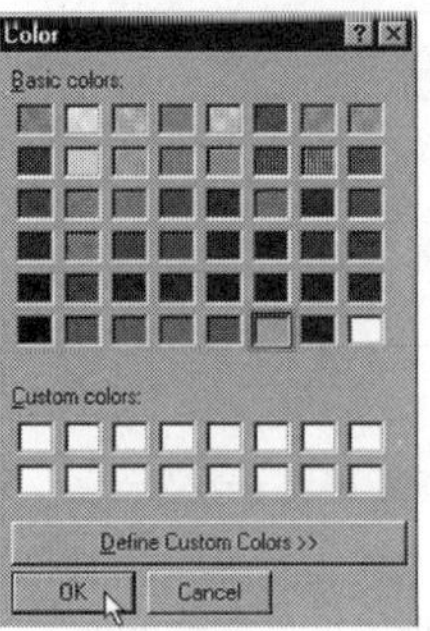


**Figure 8.46**
*To select a background color, select the desired color and click OK.*

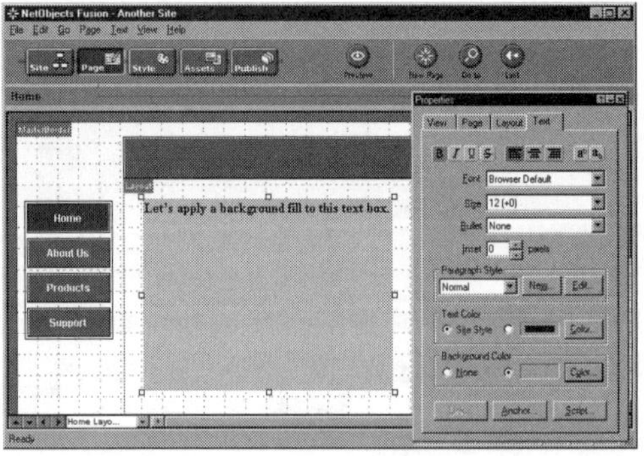

**Figure 8.47**
*The selected color is displayed as the background color for the selected text box.*

# Links and Navigation Bars

## Introducing Links

Links are used to connect text and pictures in your site to other Web pages or even to special anchors within other Web pages. Links can be used to navigate through your own Web site and to connect your Web site to the outside world.

With Fusion, you can use a segment of text, a graphic image, a drawn picture, or a specific part of a picture as a link to another Web document or to a position within the same page. Fusion allows you to create several types of links:

**Internal links** link to pages within your site.

**Smart links** are internal links to page positions within your site structure rather than to specific pages.

**Image maps** allow you to use different ranges of coordinates within a single graphic image to create any number of links to different pages.

**External links** link to pages elsewhere on the Web.

You can also create an **anchor** (sometimes known as a target) within a page. With an anchor you can create a link to a particular point within a page in your site. Such links are helpful in navigating through long text passages.

## Introducing Navigation Bars

**Navigation bars** are a special type of internal link generated automatically by Fusion.

In Site View, you lay out the structure of your site. But without links allowing users to follow the connections you specify between pages, the structure is meaningless. So Fusion creates the "structural" links that connect the pages in your site automatically in the form of navigation bars. These navigation bars are automatically placed within the MasterBorders (see Chapter 7) of each page in your site **(Figure 9.1)**.

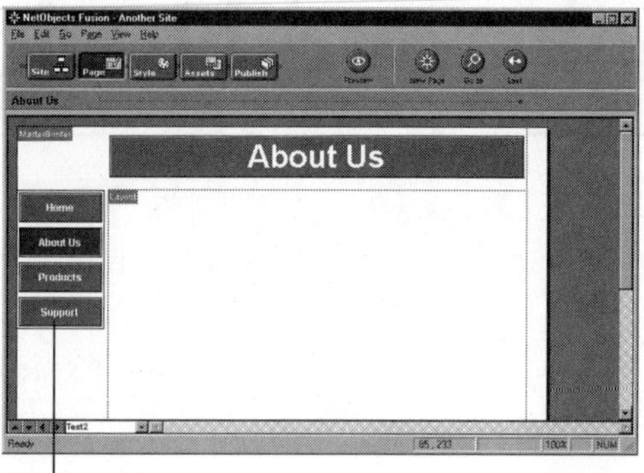


**Figure 9.1**
*Navigation bar created automatically in the MasterBorder of a Fusion Web page*

While navigation bars are generated automatically by Fusion, you do have control over their complexity, orientation, button appearance, button spacing, background color, and position. You can also add additional navigation bars to a page.

To modify most navigation bar attributes, the starting place is the Nav Bar Properties tab in the Page View Properties Palette.

### To access navigation bar properties:

In Page View, select the desired navigation bar to display the Nav Bar tab in the Properties Palette **(Figure 9.2)**.

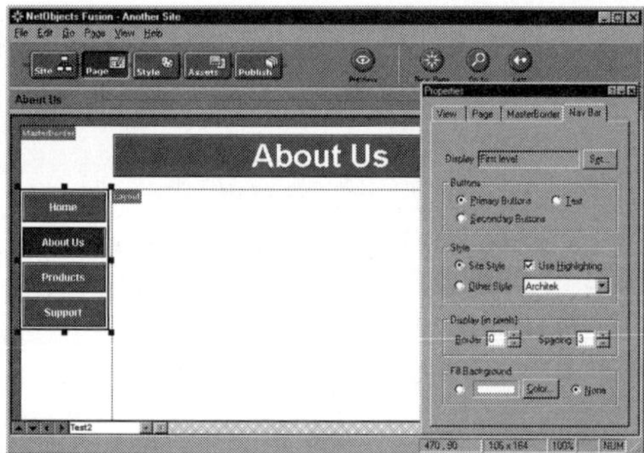


**Figure 9.2**
*Select the desired navigation bar to display the Nav Bar properties tab.*

### ✔ Tip

- If instead of the the Nav Bar Properties tab, the Button tab is displayed when you click the desired navigation bar, click the border of the navigation bar, or click the Nav Bar tab in the Properties Palette.

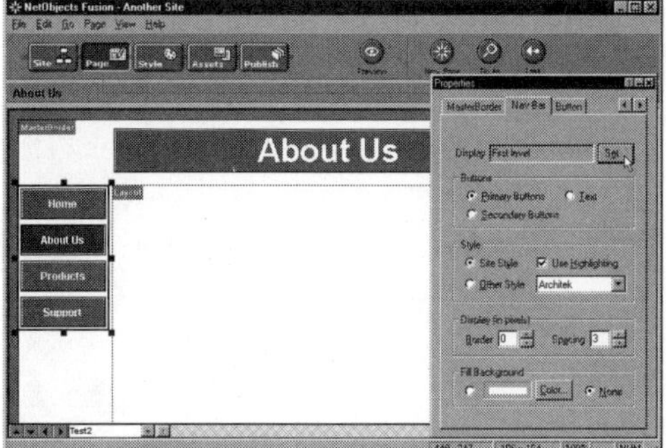

**Figure 9.3**
*Click the Set... button to display the Nav Bar Display dialog box.*

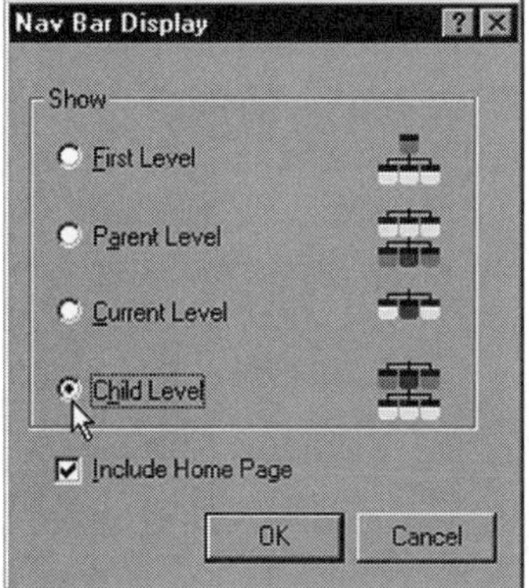


**Figure 9.4**
*The Nav Bar Display dialog box.*

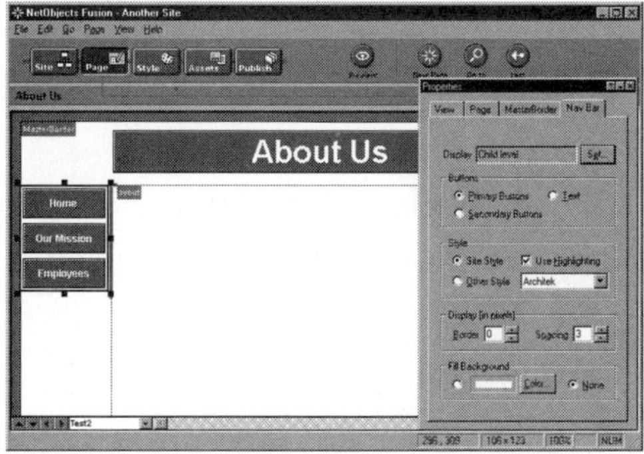

**Figure 9.5**
*The navigation bar display changes to reflect your display level selections.*

## Setting the Display Level for a Navigation Bar

The display level refers to the number of levels in your site structure that will be displayed as buttons in the selected navigation bar. For example, in **Figure 9.3**, the navigation bar shown displays buttons linked to the home page and to pages on the first level of the site.

### To set the display level of a navigation bar:

1. Click a navigation bar in Page View to display the Nav Bar tab in the Properties Palette, select this tab.
2. Click the Set... button next to the Display field **(Figure 9.3)**.

   The Nav Bar Display dialog box appears with a number of Show options **(Figure 9.4)**:

   **First Level** displays buttons for each page in the first level of your site structure.

   **Parent Level** displays buttons for each page in the level containing the parent of the current page.

   **Current Level** displays buttons for each page in the level containing the current page.

   **Child Level** displays buttons for each child of the current page.

   The check box below the Show options allows you to include the home page in the navigation bar.
3. Make your desired Show and Include Home Page selections.
4. Click OK.

   The navigation bar displays your selections **(Figure 9.5)**.

## Specifying Navigation Bar Button Appearance

By default, the buttons in navigation bars are displayed using the Primary Button image for the selected SiteStyle (see Chapter 5). You can use the Nav Bar tab of the Properties Palette to select a different button type or style for a given navigation bar.

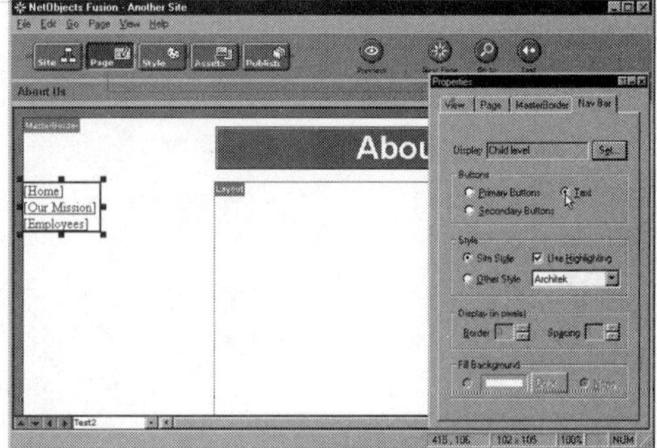

**Figure 9.6**
*A navigation bar displayed using Text buttons.*

### To select the button type for a navigation bar:

1. Click a navigation bar in Page View to display the Nav Bar tab in the Properties Palette.
2. In the Buttons section of the Nav Bar properties, select one of the options displayed:

   **Primary Buttons** displays the navigation bar using the primary button image of the selected .

   **Secondary Buttons** displays the navigation bar using the secondary button image of the selected SiteStyle.

   **Text** displays the navigation bar using the text style specified in the selected SiteStyle.

   (Refer to Page 60 in Chapter 5 for a discussion of these SiteStyle elements.)

   The selected navigation bar will be displayed using the button type specified **(Figure 9.6)**.

Specifying Nav Bar Button Appearance

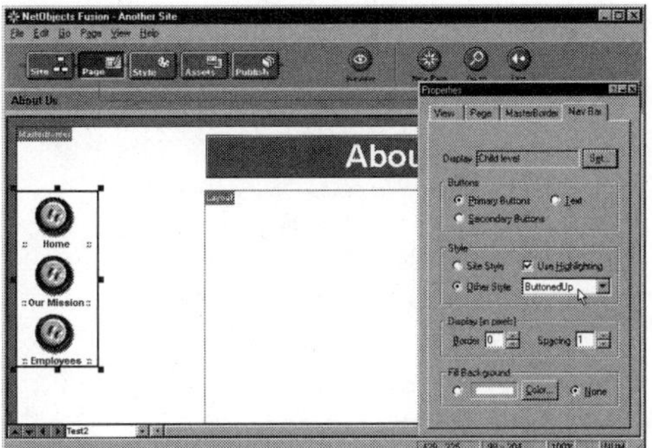

**Figure 9.7**
*Select the button style using the Nav Bar tab of the Properties Palette.*

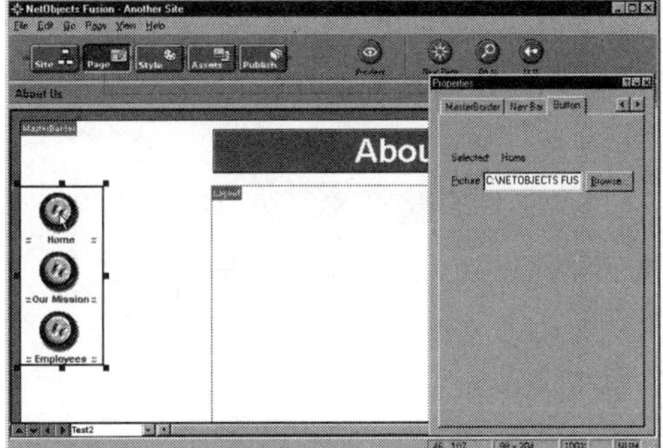

**Figure 9.8**
*Select a button in the navigation bar to display the Button tab of the Properties Palette.*

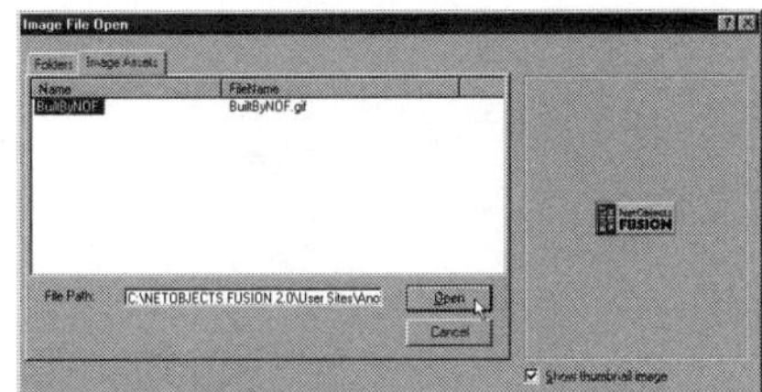

**Figure 9.9**
*Choose an image using the Image File to Open dialog box.*

## To change the button style for a navigation bar:

1. Click a navigation bar in Page View to display the Nav Bar tab in the Properties Palette.
2. In the Style section of the Nav Bar properties, select one of the two options:

   **SiteStyle** uses the button styles defined for the selected SiteStyle.

   **Other Style** uses the button styles for another SiteStyle selected using the menu to the right.

   The **Use Highlighting** option causes the button for the current page to be highlighted.
3. The selected navigation bar will be displayed using the button style specified **(Figure 9.7)**.

## To change the image for a single navigation bar button:

1. Click a button in a navigation bar.

   The entire navigation bar will appear to be selected, but the Button tab instead of the Nav Bar tab will be displayed in the Properties Palette **(Figure 9.8)**.
2. Click the Browse button. *Mac users click the Select... button.*
3. Use the dialog box to locate and open the desired image file for the selected button **(Figure 9.9)**.

### ✔ Tip

- Since Web browsers generally only support **GIF** and **JPG** graphic files, Fusion will offer to convert **BMP**, **PCX**, and **PCT** files to **GIF** or **JPG**.

## Changing Navigation Bar Border and Button Spacing

You can control the amount of space between each button in a navigation bar and the thickness of the border around the navigation bar using options in the Display (in pixels) area of the Nav Bar tab in the Properties Palette.

### To change button spacing in a navigation bar:

1. Click a navigation bar in Page View to display the Nav Bar tab in the Properties Palette.
2. In the Display (in pixels) section of the Nav Bar properties tab, type or select the number of pixels in the Spacing field **(Figure 9.10)**.

   Increasing the number of pixels in the Spacing field increases the amount of space between each button in the navigation bar **(Figure 9.10)**.

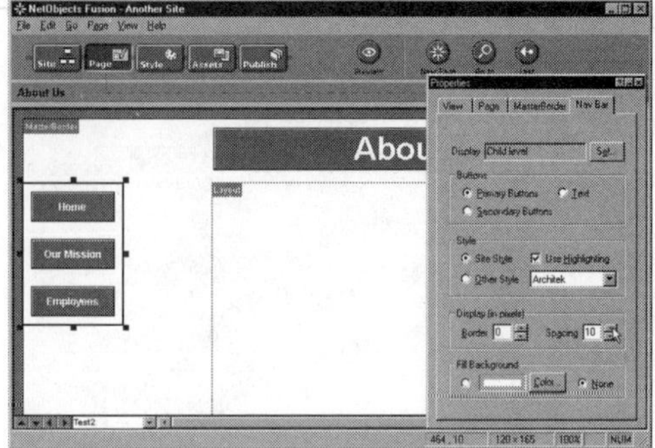

**Figure 9.10**
*Navigation bar button spacing increased to 10 pixels.*

### To change the navigation bar border:

1. Click a navigation bar in Page View to display the Nav Bar tab in the Properties Palette.
2. In the Display (in pixels) section of the Nav Bar properties tab, type or select the number of pixels in the Border field and change as desired.

   Increasing the number of pixels in the Border field increases the thickness of the navigation bar border **(Figure 9.11)**.

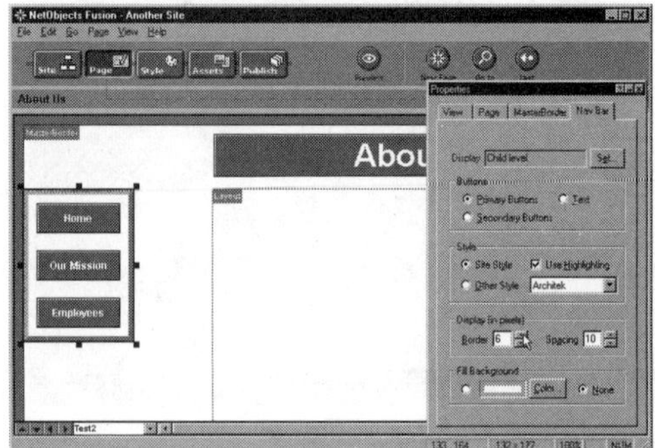

**Figure 9.11**
*Navigation bar border increased to 6 pixels wide.*

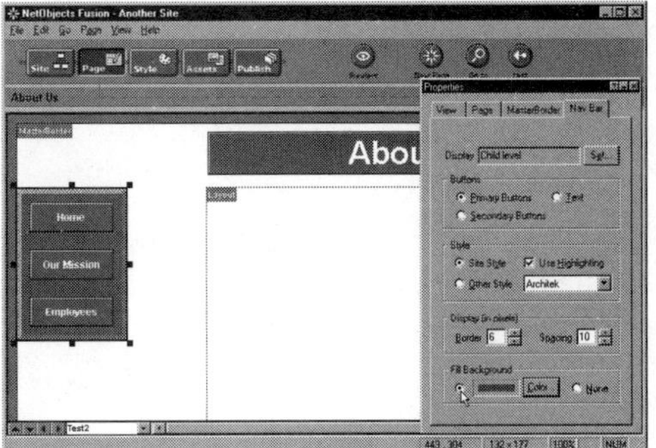


**Figure 9.12**
*Select one of the two options displayed in the Fill Background section of the Nav Bar Properties Tab.*

## Selecting a Background for a Navigation Bar

Fusion allows you to use a background fill for navigation bars. The only fill option is a solid color which you specify in the Fill Background section of the Nav Bar properties tab.

### To change the background in a navigation bar:

1. Click a navigation bar in Page View to display the Nav Bar tab in the Properties Palette.
2. In the Fill Background section of the Nav Bar properties tab, select one of the two options displayed **(Figure 9.12)**:

   **Color** allows you to specify a background fill color using the color palette.

   **None** means that the selected navigation bar will have no background fill.
3. If you selected the Color option, select the Color... button, and choose a color from the palette, then click OK.

   The selected navigation bar will be displayed using the background color you specified **(Figure 9.12)**.

## Creating New Navigation Bars

You may wish to use more than one navigation bar on a page, with each serving distinct purposes. If so, (or if you have accidentally deleted a navigation bar), you'll need to create a new one.

The navigation bar tool in the Page View tools palette is used to create new navigation bars (and banners).

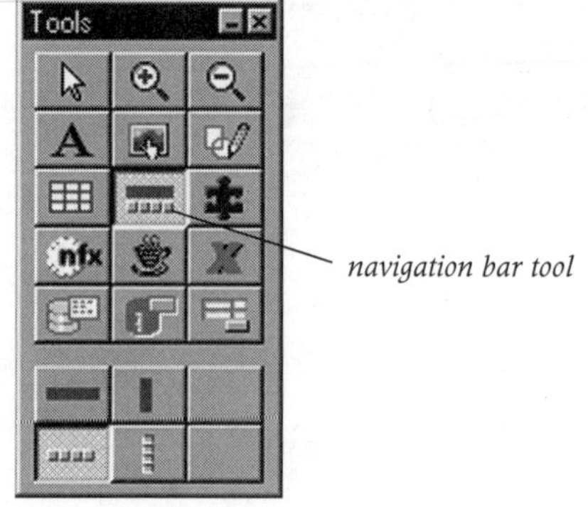


**Figure 9.13**
*The navigation bar (banner) tool selected in the tools palette.*

### To create a new navigation bar:

1. Select View Tools Palette if the Tools Palette is not already displayed.
2. Click the navigation bar tool **(Figure 9.13)**.

   Several secondary buttons appear in the lower portion of the Tools Palette. The two at the bottom displaying segmented icons are used for creating new horizontal and vertical navigation bars, respectively.
3. Select the desired navigation bar button at the bottom of the Tools Palette.

   The mouse pointer changes to a cross-hairs when you move it over your Web page.
4. Click in the MasterBorder area of the page where you want to position the upper left corner of the new navigation bar.

   The new navigation bar will be displayed using default display characteristics **(Figure 9.14)**. To modify its appearance, see the first part of this chapter.

**Figure 9.14**
*A new horizontal navigation bar added to a page.*

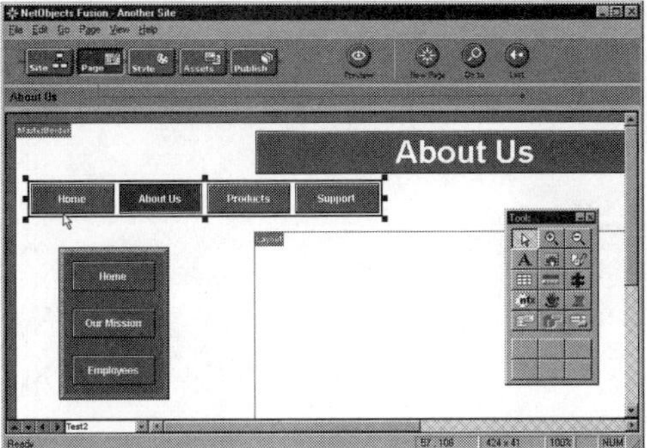


**Figure 9.15**
*You can move a navigation bar by dragging it within the MasterBorders of a page.*

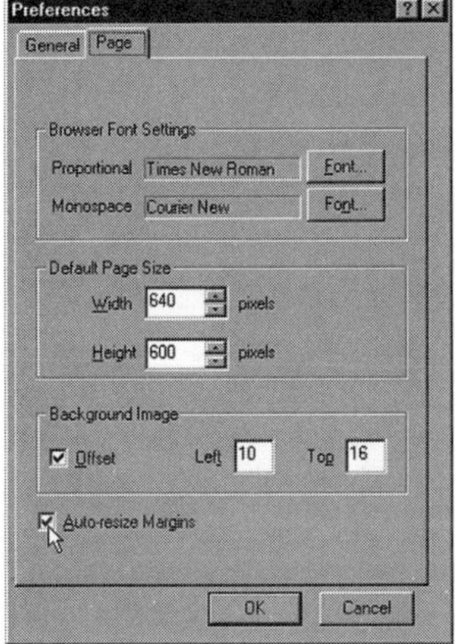


**Figure 9.16**
*The MasterBorders/Layout is resized automatically.*

# Positioning and Deleting Navigation Bars

You can change a navigation bar's position, or delete one you have created, within the MasterBorders.

### To move a navigation bar:

1. Click the select tool in the Tools Palette.
2. Click the navigation bar and drag it to another position within the MasterBorders **(Figure 9.15)**.

### To delete a navigation bar:

1. With the select tool, click the navigation bar you wish to delete.
2. Press the Delete key, or select Delete Element from the Edit menu.

✔ **Tip**

- If the Auto-resize Margins option (*Drag and Drop Layout Borders option on the Mac)* is selected in the Preferences dialog box **(Figure 9.16)**, the MasterBorders will automatically adjust as needed to fit the navigation bars as you reposition them.

## Creating an Internal Link

In addition to the automated links created by Fusion in navigation bars, you can also create links manually. With internal links you create links between pages within your Web site, and with external links, you link pages in your site to Internet documents elsewhere on the Web. With Fusion you can create an internal link using virtually any content element, from segments of text, to images, to drawn shapes (see Chapter 11 for using multimedia in Web pages).

### To create an internal link:

1. Select the content element you wish to use as the "clickable" link on your Web page. If you want to use text as the link, select the desired segment of text (see Chapter 8 for selecting text).

   The properties tab for the selected element will be displayed in the Properties Palette. A Link button is displayed at the bottom of the properties tab for all "linkable" content elements. Notice the Link button at the bottom of the Text tab in the example in **Figure 9.17.**

2. Click the Link button.

   The Link dialog box is displayed. The Link dialog box contains three tabs: Internal Link, Smart Link, and External Link. The Internal link tab is displayed as the default. All of the pages in your site are listed in the Page area of the Internal Link tab.

3. Select the page in your site to which you wish to create a link.

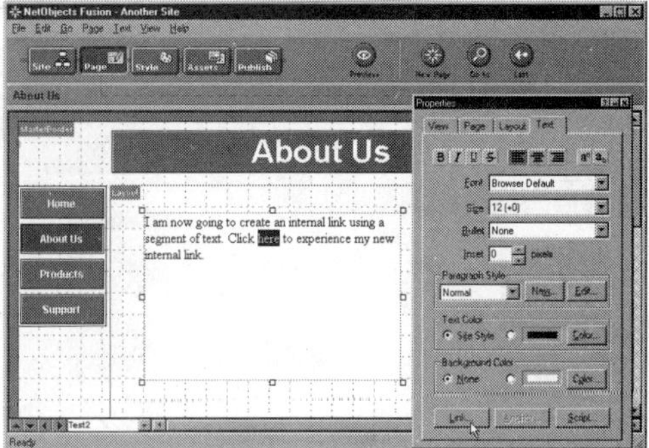


**Figure 9.17**
*Select the desired content element, and click the Link button in the Properties Palette to create a link.*

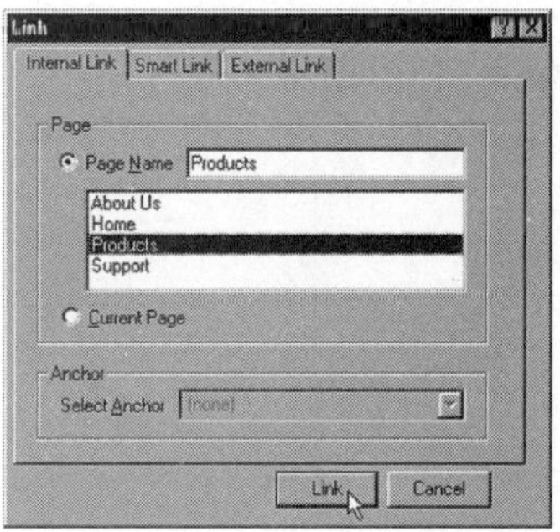


**Figure 9.18**
*Select the desired page in the Link dialog box.*

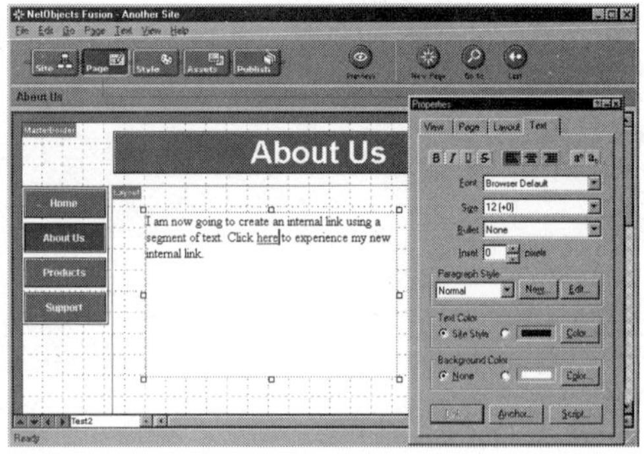


**Figure 9.19**
*Text used as a link is displayed underlined and in the color defined in the selected SiteStyle.*

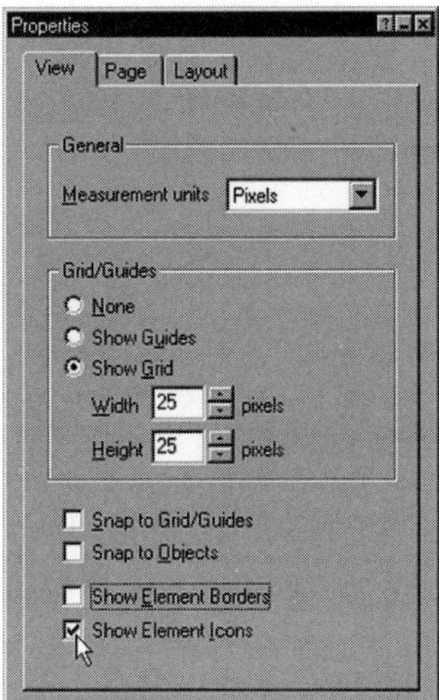


**Figure 9.20**
*To display link icons, select the Show Element Icons option in the View tab of the Properties Palette.*

**Figure 9.21**
*If the Show Element Icons option is selected in the View tab of the Properties Palette, then content elements like this drawn rectangle will appear with a link icon in the upper left corner when defined as a link.*

4. Click the Link button (**Figure 9.18**).

   The selected content element is displayed as a link on your page. If the link is a text segment as in our example, it is displayed as a link—underlined and in the link color defined for the SiteStyle you're using **(Figure 9.19)**.

## ✔ Tips

- Select the Show Element Icons option in the View tab of the Properties Palette **(Figure 9.20)** if you want link icons to appear on graphical content elements defined as links on your pages **(Figure 9.21)**.
- You can "unlink" an element by selecting it, clicking the Link button in the element's properties tab, and then clicking the Unlink button in the Link dialog box.
- See the section on anchors later in this chapter to create a link to another spot on the current page using an anchor.

## Creating a Smart Link

A smart link is a special type of internal link. With a Smart Link, instead of creating a link to a specific page by name, you create a link to a relative position within your site. For example, you can create a Smart Link to the parent of the current page. If you later restructure your site and move or replace the parent page, the Smart Link is automatically updated to point to the new parent page.

With Fusion you can create a Smart Link using virtually any content element from segments of text to images to drawn shapes (see Chapter 11 for using multimedia in Web pages).

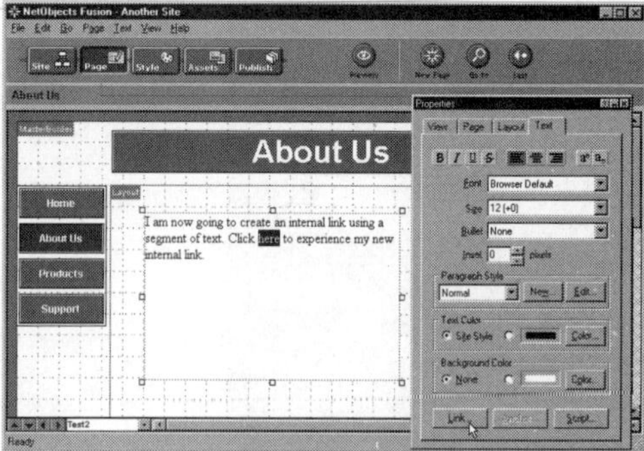


**Figure 9.22**
*Select the desired content element, and click the Link button in the Properties Palette to create a link.*

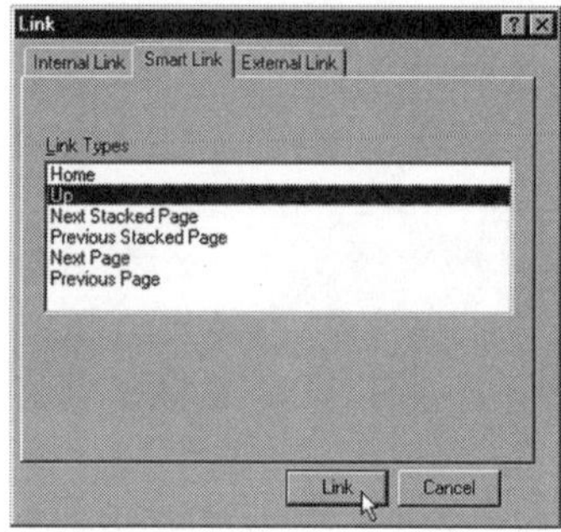


**Figure 9.23**
*Click the Smart Link tab in the Link dialog box, and select the desired Link Type.*

### To create a Smart Link:

1. Select the element you wish to use as the "clickable" link on your Web page. If you want to use text as the link, select the desired segment of text (see Chapter 8 for selecting text).

   The properties tab for the selected element is displayed **(Figure 9.22)**. A Link button is displayed at the bottom of the properties tab for all "linkable" content elements.

2. Click the Link button.

3. In the Link dialog box that is displayed, click the Smart Link tab.

   The Smart Link tab is displayed with a list of Link Types **(Figure 9.23)**:

   **Home** creates a link to the site's home page.

   **Up** links to the parent of the current page.

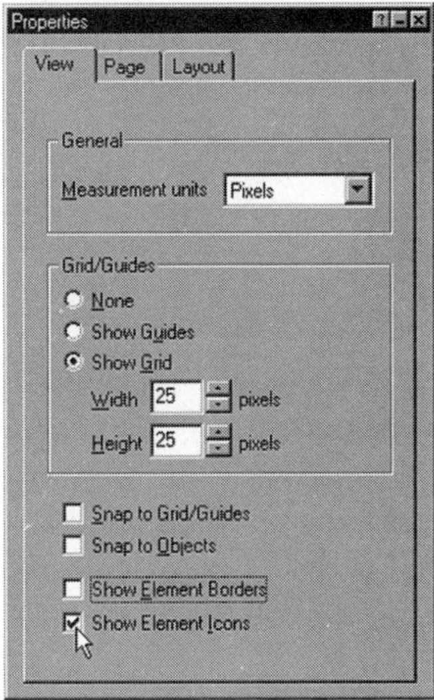


**Figure 9.24**
*To display link icons, select the Show Element Icons option in the View tab of the Properties Palette.*

**Figure 9.25**
*The Show Element Icons option displayed.*

**Next Stacked Page** links to the next page in a stack (see Chapter 14 for stacked pages).

**Previous Stacked Page** links to the previous page in a stack (see Chapter 14 for stacked pages).

**Next Page** links to the right sibling of the current page in the site structure (see Chapter 4).

**Previous Page** links to the left sibling of the current page in the site structure (see Chapter 4).

4. Select the desired link type.
5. Click the Link button to create the link.

## ✔ Tips

- Select the Show Element Icons option in the View tab of the Properties Palette **(Figure 9.24)** if you want link icons to appear on graphical content elements defined as links on your pages.

  If the Show Element Icons option is selected in the View tab of the Properties Palette, then content elements like this drawn rectangle will appear with a link icon in the upper left corner when defined as a link **(Figure 9.25)**.

- You can "unlink" an element by selecting it, clicking the Link button in the element's properties tab, and then clicking the Unlink button on the Link dialog box.

## Creating an External Link

In addition to the automated links created by Fusion in navigation bars, you can create links manually. With external links you can create links between pages within your Web site and Internet documents beyond your site. With Fusion you can create an external link using virtually any content element from segments of text to images to drawn shapes (see Chapter 11 for using multimedia in Web pages).

### To create an external link:

1. Select the element you wish to use as the "clickable" link on your Web page. If you want to use text as the link, select the desired segment of text (see Chapter 8 for selecting text).

   The properties tab for the selected element is displayed **(Figure 9.26)**. A Link button is displayed at the bottom of the properties tab for all "linkable" content elements.

2. Click the Link button.
3. In the Link dialog box that is displayed, click the External Link tab.

   The External Link tab is displayed.

4. Select the appropriate Internet protocol from the list labeled URL **(Figure 9.27)**:

   **http://** to link to a Web page

   **ftp://** to link to an FTP server

   **mailto:** to create an e-mail link

   **news://** to link to a newsgroup

   and so on.

**Figure 9.26**
*Select the desired content element, and click the Link button in the Properties Palette to create a link.*

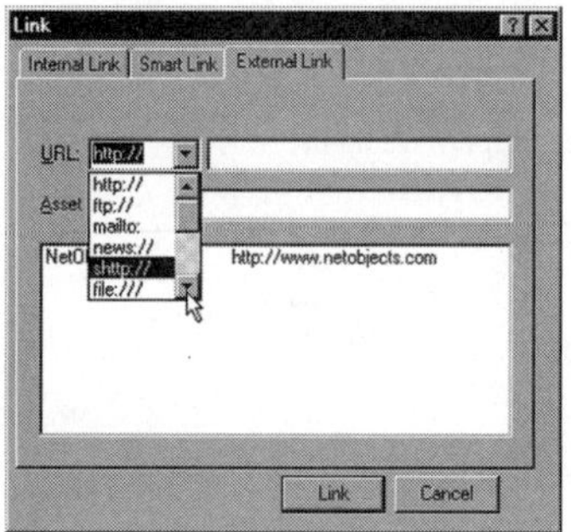


**Figure 9.27**
*Select the desired Internet protocol from the drop-down list..*

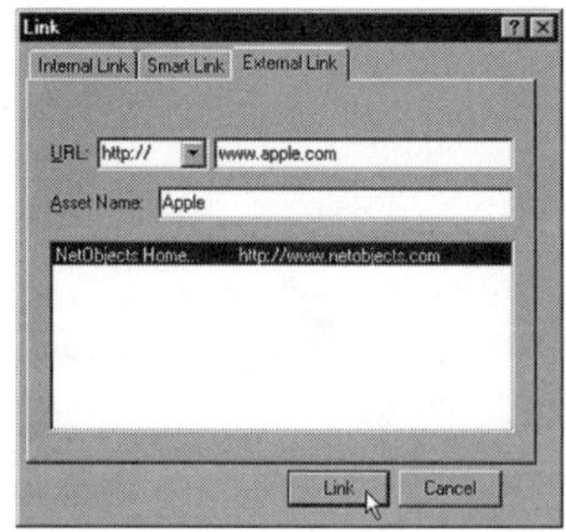


**Figure 9.28**
*Type or select the desired URL in the URL field, and enter a name for the URL in the Asset field.*

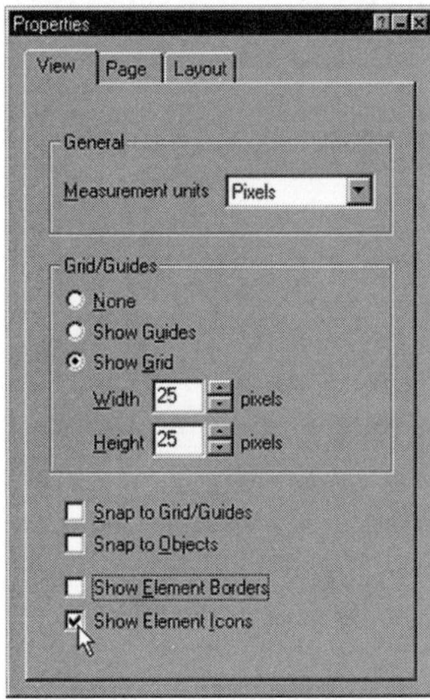


**Figure 9.29**
*To display link icons, select the Show Element Icons option in the View tab of the Properties Palette.*

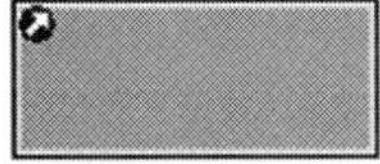

**Figure 9.30**
*Link icon displayed in a drawn rectangle.*

5. Type the desired URL (minus the protocol) in the field opposite the list of Internet protocols **(Figure 9.28)**.

   If you have previously defined an external link for the current site using the same URL, then that URL will be displayed in the list on the External Link tab. Rather than typing the URL again, you can simply select it from the list.

6. Click the Link button.

### ✔ Tips

- Select the Show Element Icons option in the View tab of the Properties Palette **(Figure 9.29)** if you want link icons to appear on graphical content elements defined as links on your pages **(Figure 9.30)**.
- To modify the URL defined for a particular external link, click the Link button in the element's properties tab, then type the desired URL in the URL field. Click the Link button when done, and the link is updated.
- You can "unlink" an element by selecting it, clicking the Link button in the element's properties tab, and then clicking the Unlink button on the Link dialog box.

## Using Anchors

Anchors are place holders on pages within your site. Anchors are commonly used on very long pages to help visitors to your site navigate through lengthy text passages and quickly reach their text destination. Anchors are used as targets for these internal links.

As with the links previously described, Fusion lets you can create an anchor link using virtually any content element from segments of text to images to drawn shapes (see Chapter 11 for using multimedia in Web pages).

### To create an anchor:

1. Select the element you wish to use as the anchor on your Web page. If you want to use a point in text as the anchor, click at the desired location within the text (see Chapter 8 for selecting text).

   The properties tab for the selected element is displayed **(Figure 9.31)**. The Anchor button is displayed at the bottom of the properties tab for all content elements which can be used as anchors.

2. Click the Anchor button.
3. In the Add Anchor dialog box that is displayed **(Figure 9.32)**.
4. Type a name for the anchor (without any spaces).

   Any anchors already defined for the current page are displayed in the Anchors on Page field.

5. Click the OK button to create the anchor.

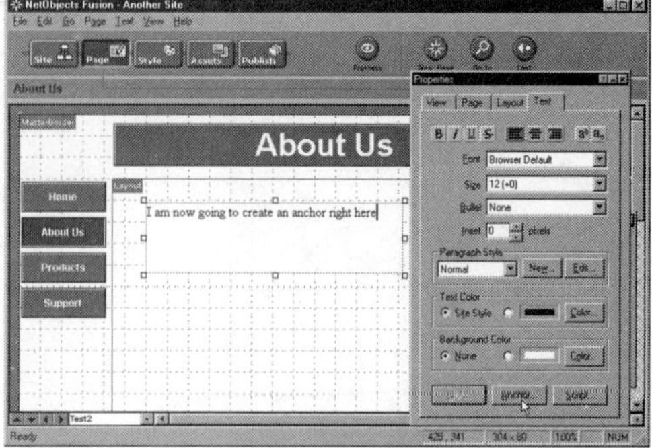


**Figure 9.31**
*Select the desired content element, and click the Anchor button in the Properties Palette to create an anchor.*

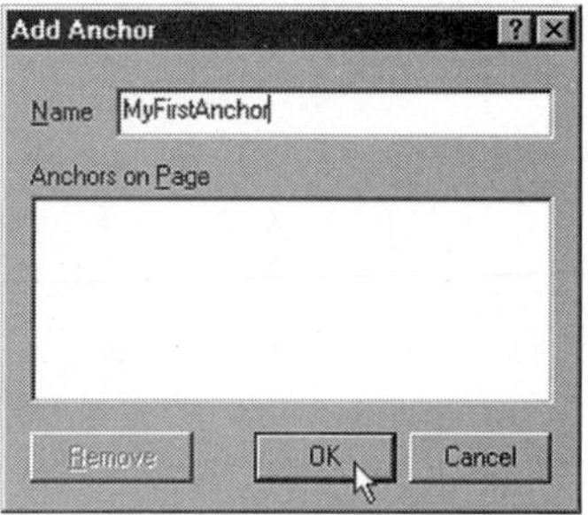


**Figure 9.32**
*Type a name for the new anchor, and click the OK button.*

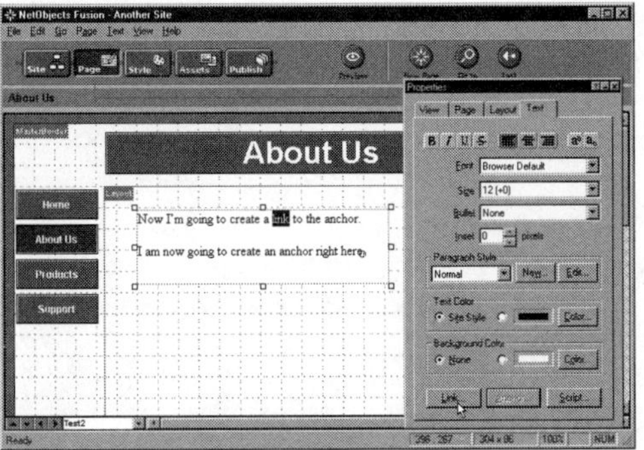

**Figure 9.33**
*Select the desired content element, and click the Anchor button in the Properties Palette to create an anchor.*

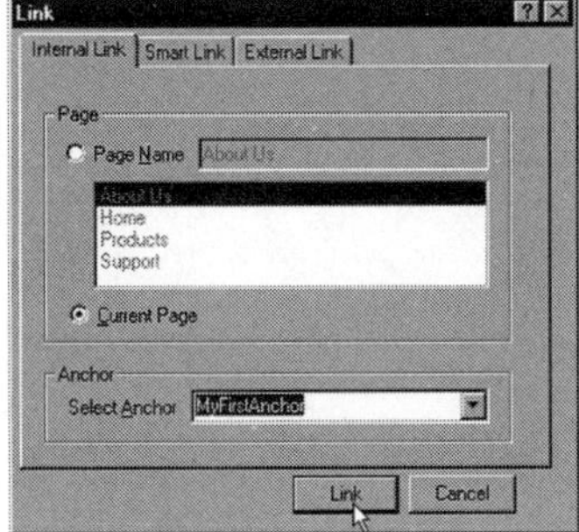

**Figure 9.34**
*Select Current Page and select an anchor from the list.*

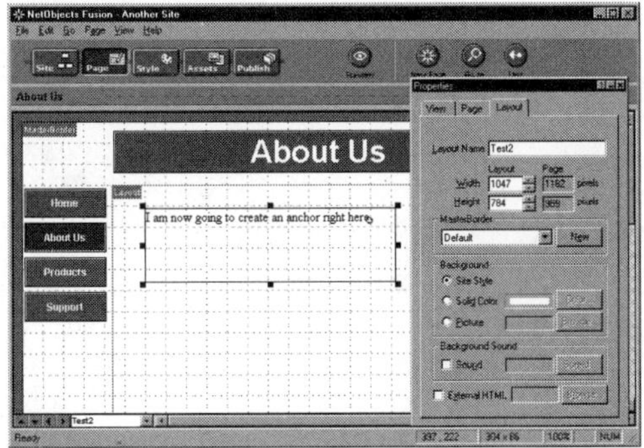

**Figure 9.35**
*Anchors marked with small icon when Show Elements is selected.*

## To link to an anchor:

1. Select the element you wish to use as the link to your anchor. If you want to use text as the link, click select the desired text segment (see Chapter 8 for selecting text).

   The properties tab for the selected element is displayed **(Figure 9.33)**. A Link button is displayed at the bottom of the properties tab for all content elements which can be used as links.
2. Click the Link button.
3. In the Link dialog box, click the Current page option **(Figure 9.34)**.
4. Select an anchor from the Anchor drop-down list.
5. Click the Link button.

### ✔ Tip

- Select the Show Element Icons option in the View tab of the Properties Palette if you want anchor icons to appear on content elements defined as anchors on your pages **(Figure 9.35)**.

## Creating an Imagemap

*picture tool*

Imagemaps are graphic images in which a number of areas or "hotspots" have been defined as links. Imagemaps allow you to use a single graphic image for a number of different links.

### To create an imagemap:

1. Select a picture on a page (see Chapter 11 for using pictures).
2. Select the picture tool in the Tools Palette (If the Tools Palette is not displayed, select Tools Palette from the View menu).

   Secondary picture tools appear in the bottom of the Tools Palette **(Figure 9.36)**. The bottom row of these secondary picture tools are used for creating hotspots on images:

   is used to create a rectangular hotspot.

   is used to create an elliptical hot spot.

   is used to create a polygon hotspot.
3. Select the desired hotspot tool.
4. If you are using the rectangular or elliptical hotspot tools, click and drag on the image to draw the hotspot desired **(Figure 9.36)**.

   To create a polygon hotspot, click to establish each corner of the polygon, then double-click to close the polygon.

   After drawing a hotspot on an image, the Link dialog box appears **(Figure 9.37)**.

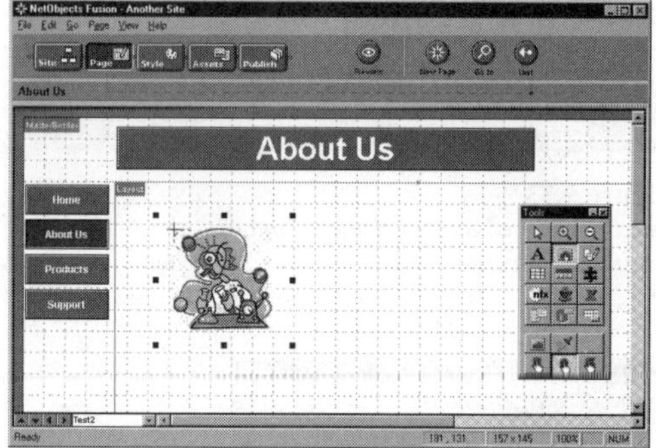


**Figure 9.36**
*Select the picture tool and the secondary picture tools appear at the bottom of the tools palette. Select the desired hotspot tool and draw a hotspot on the image.*

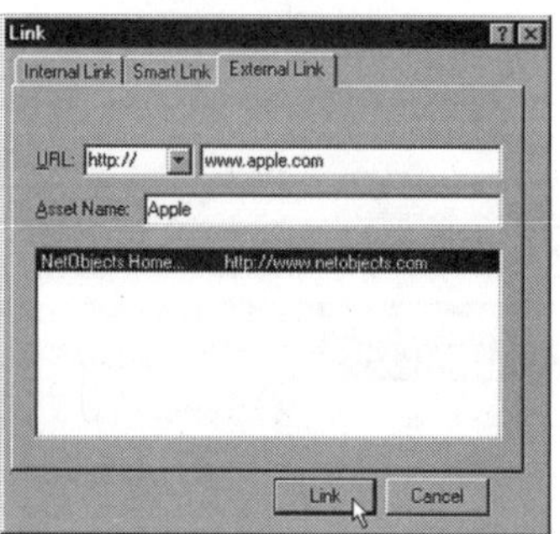


**Figure 9.37**
*The Link dialog appears after a hotspot has been drawn.*

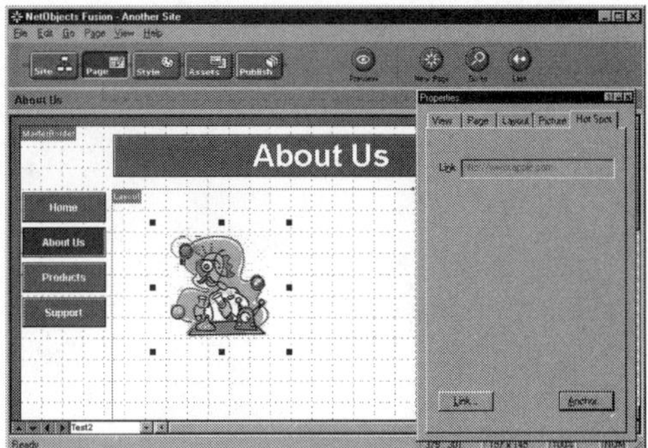

**Figure 9.38**
*Use the Hotspot properties tab to edit a hotspot link.*

5. Use the Link dialog box to define a link for the hotspot (see the previous sections for creating different types of links).

6. Click the Link button in the Link dialog box.

   The hotspot on your image has now been defined as a link. You can place as many hotspots on an image as you like, but hotspots must not overlap or extend beyond the image.

### ✔ Tips

- To make a hotspot an anchor, create the hotspot, click the Cancel button in the Link dialog box, then select Anchor from the Hotspot properties tab, and define the anchor as in the previous section.
- You can edit a hotspot by clicking on it, and then clicking the Link or Anchor button in the Hotspot properties tab **(Figure 9.38)**. The Link dialog box is displayed.
- Delete a hotspot by selecting it, and choosing Delete Element from the Edit menu.
- You can copy and paste an imagemapped picture complete with hotspots (and links) within the current page or to any other page in the site.

# Tables

## Introducing Tables

Tables offer a convenient way to organize both text and images into rows and columns. You can create a table in Fusion much as you create any other content element. When creating a table, however, you must also specify the number of table columns and rows for your table.

### To create a table:

1. In Page View, select the table tool in the tools palette **(Figure 10.1)**.

   The mouse pointer becomes a crosshair.

2. Position the pointer on your page approximately where you want the upper left corner of the new table to be positioned.

3. Click and drag down and to the right.

   A dotted line indicates the table boundary **(Figure 10.2)**.

4. Release the mouse button when the table is the desired size.

   The table dialog box appears **(Figure 10.3)**.

5. Type or select the number of columns for your table.

6. Type or select the number of rows for your table.

7. In the Settings area of the Table dialog box, select the type of object to be displayed in each column of your table.

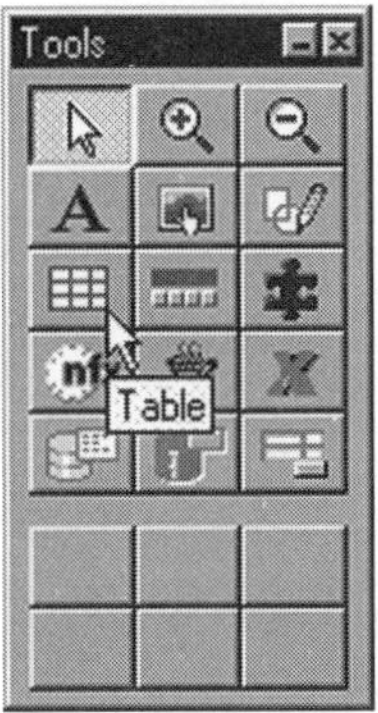


**Figure 10.1**
*Select the table tool in the tools palette..*

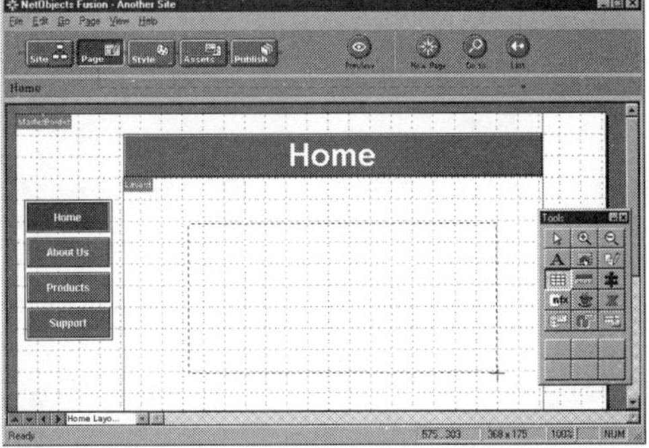


**Figure 10.2**
*Create the table border by clicking and dragging.*

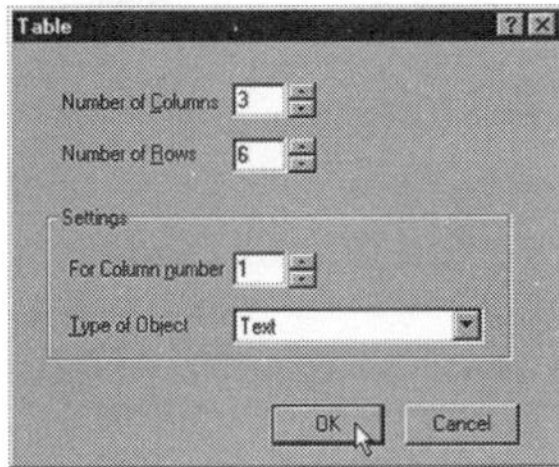


**Figure 10.3**
*The table dialog box appears, allowing you to enter the number of rows, columns, and data type for each column.*

The choices for objects displayed in table columns are **Text** and **Picture**. The default setting is Text, but you can choose Picture for any columns in your table.

**8.** Click OK.

The new table appears as specified on your page **(Figure 10.4)**.

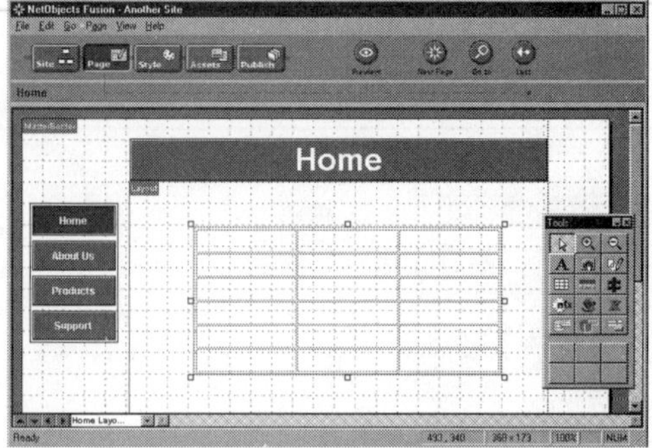

**Figure 10.4**
*The table appears on the page.*

### ✔ Tips

- Once created, a table can be moved **(Figure 10.5)** and resized **(Figure 10.6)** by clicking and dragging, the same way as for text boxes (see Chapter 8).
- When a table is resized, the columns and rows may not be resized as expected. See the next page for manually resizing columns and rows.

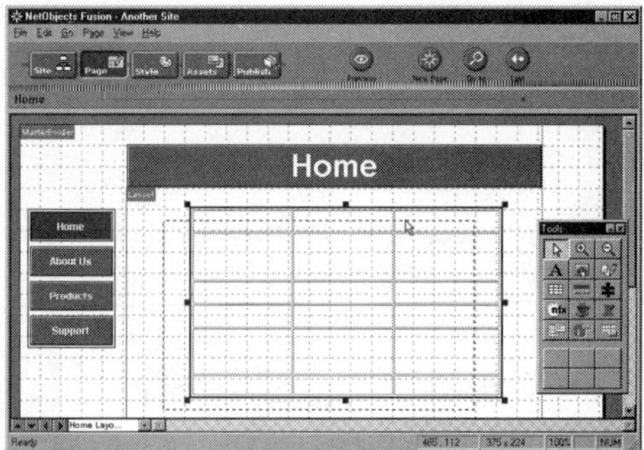

**Figure 10.5**
*Move a table by dragging the border with the arrow pointer.*

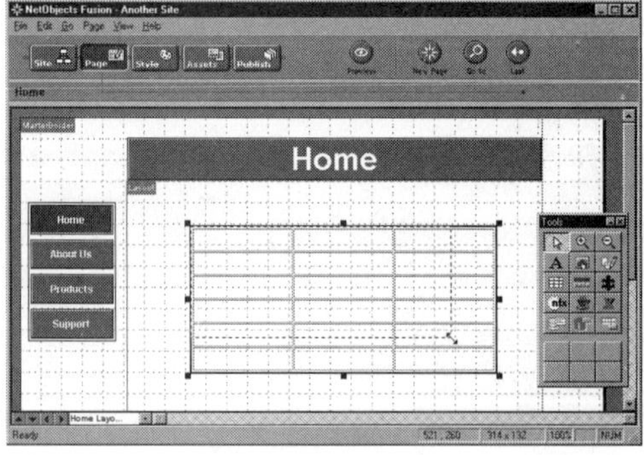

**Figure 10.6**
*Resize a table by dragging a corner handle diagonally.*

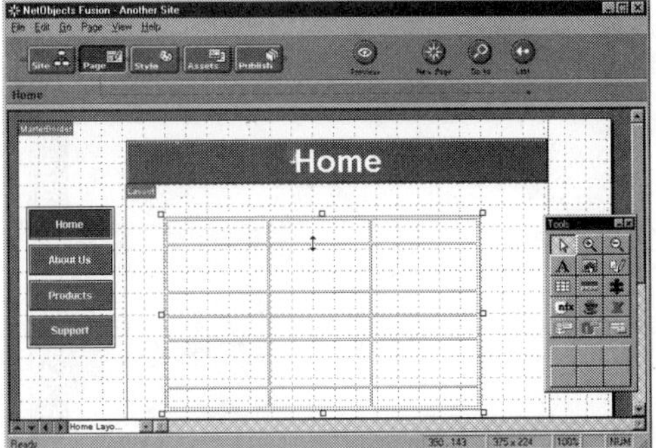


**Figure 10.7**
*Position the pointer over a table grid line.*

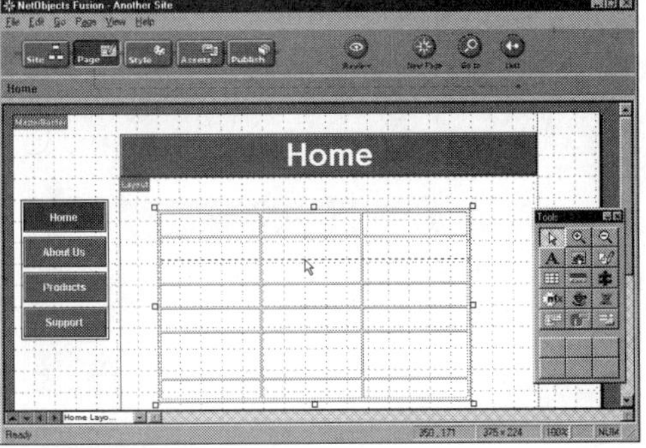


**Figure 10.8**
*Click and drag the grid line to the desired position.*

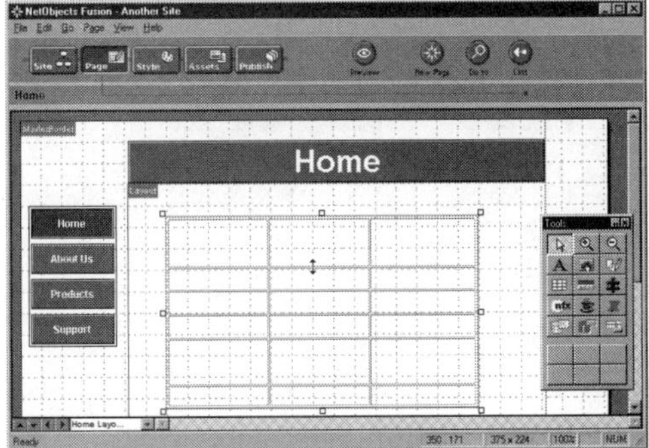


**Figure 10.9**
*The grid line is moved to the new position.*

## Resizing Rows and Columns

When a table is created, by default the rows and columns are all of equal size. When a table is resized, however, both rows and columns may be resized unevenly. You can correct or adjust the sizes of both rows and columns by dragging table grid lines.

### To resize a table column or row:

1. Click on the desired table to select it.
2. Position the mouse over a table grid line **(Figure 10.7)**.

   The mouse pointer becomes a double-ended arrow pointing in the directions in which the grid line can be dragged.
3. Click and drag the grid line to resize the row or column **(Figure 10.8)**.
4. Release the mouse button to stop dragging the grid line.

   The grid line is moved, resizing the column or row **(Figure 10.9)**.

## Adding and Removing Rows and Columns

After creating a table, you may wish to add or remove rows or columns. This is done using the element pop-up menu.

### To add a table column or row:

1. Click on the desired table to select it.
2. Select the table cell *below* which you want to insert a row or *to the right* of which you want to insert a column.
3. Right-click the selected cell to display the element pop-up menu *(Mac users Ctrl + Click to display the element pop-up menu.)* **(Figure 10.10)**.
4. Select the appropriate menu option from the pop-up menu:

   **Add Row...** inserts a new row below the selected cell **(Figure 10.11)**.

   **Add Column...** displays the Cell Type dialog box **(Figure 10.12)** in which you select the type of data (Text or Picture) you wish the new column to contain. A new column is then inserted to the right of the selected cell.

### ✔ Tip

- After a column has been given a content setting (Text or Picture), you can change the content setting for any given cell by selecting that cell, and then selecting **Cell Type** from the pop up menu.

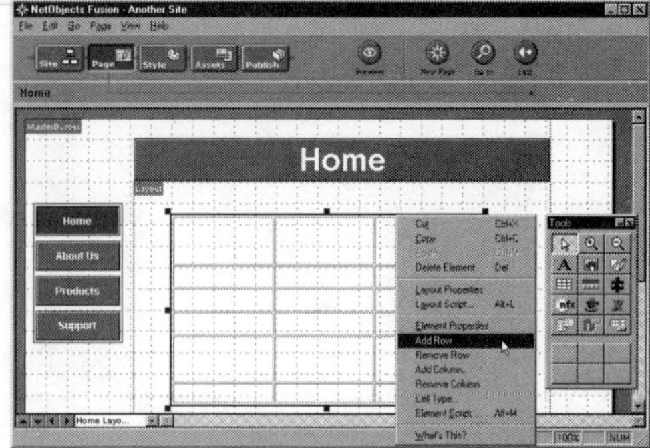


**Figure 10.10**
*Right-click the desired cell to display the element pop-up menu.*

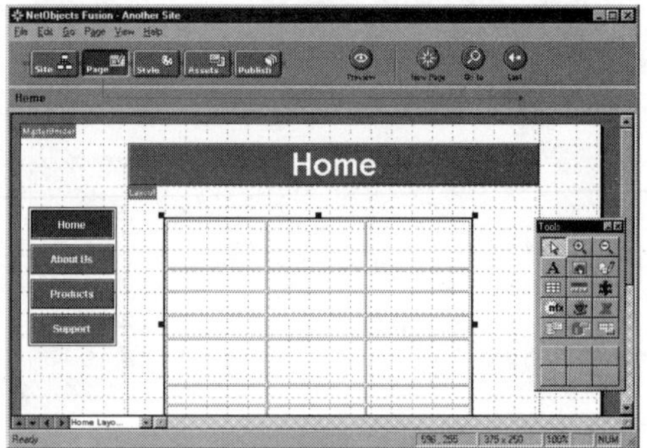


**Figure 10.11**
*Make the desired selection from the pop-up menu.*

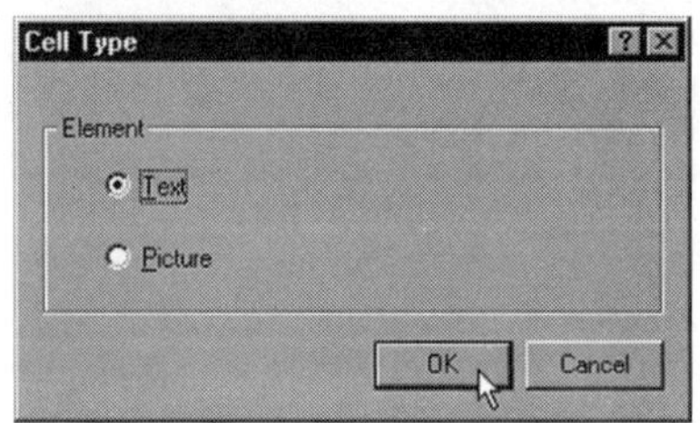


**Figure 10.12**
*When you insert a new column, you must specify its content type.*

Adding and Removing Rows and Columns

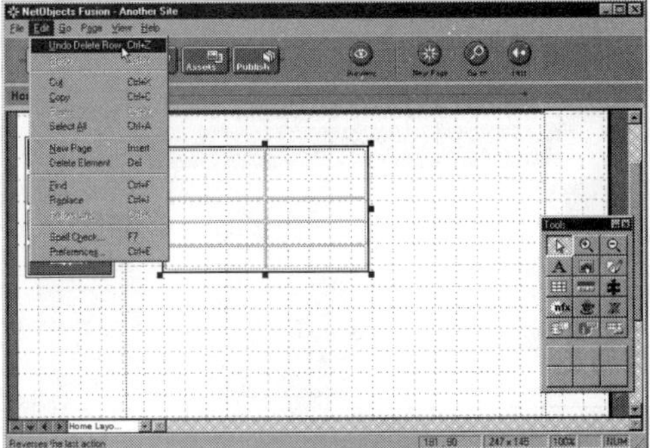

**Figure 10.13**
*Select Undo Delete Row (or Undo Delete Column) from the Edit menu to undo a delete operation.*

## To remove a table column or row:

1. Click on the desired table to select it.
2. Select a table cell in the row or column that you wish to delete.
3. Right-click the selected cell to display the element pop-up menu. *(Mac users Ctrl + Click to display the element pop-up menu.)*
4. Select the appropriate menu option from the pop-up menu:

   **Remove Row** deletes the row containing the selected cell.

   **Remove Column** removes the column containing the selected cell.

   The selected column or row is removed from the table.

### ✔ Tip

- If you remove a table row or column accidentally, or change your mind immediately afterward, you can undo the delete by selecting Undo Delete Row (or Undo Delete Column) from the Edit menu **(Figure 10.13)**. The keyboard shortcut is Ctrl + Z. *Mac users, Command + Z.*

# Changing the Content Setting for Table Cells

After creating a table, you may wish to change the content setting for a given cell from Picture to Text or vise versa. You can do this using the element pop-up menu.

### To change the content setting for a cell:

1. Click on the desired table to select it.
2. Select the cell for which you wish to modify the content setting.
3. Right-click the selected cell to display the element pop-up menu *(Mac users Ctrl + Click to display the element pop-up menu.)*
4. Select the Cell Type option from the pop-up menu **(Figure 10.14)**.

   The Cell Type dialog box appears, offering you the options of Text or Picture **(Figure 10.15)**.
5. Select the desired content option.
6. Click OK.

   The selected cell content setting is modified as specified. If you changed a text cell to a picture cell, the open file dialog box appears allowing you to select an image to display.

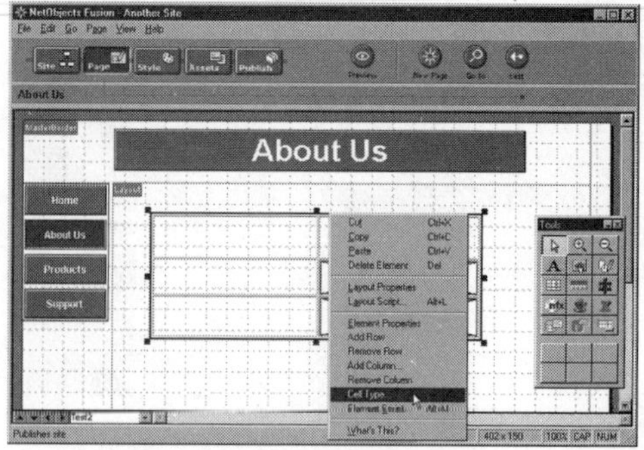


**Figure 10.14**
*An image displayed in a picture table cell.*

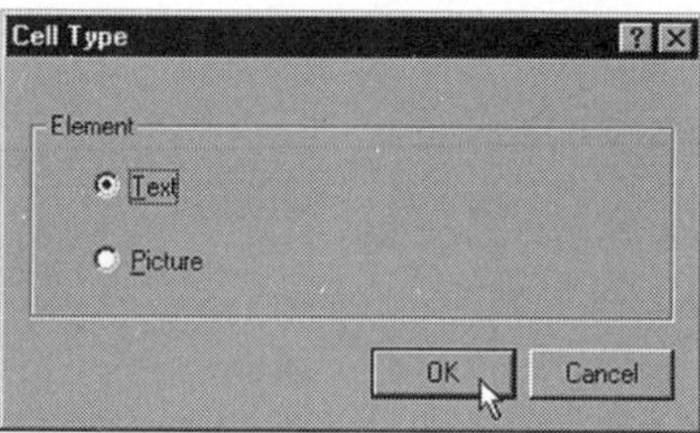


**Figure 10.15**
*Cell Type dialog box*

### ✔ Tip

- When you change a text cell to a picture cell, a dialog box appears. You can use this dialog box to select an image file. Or you can choose not to place an image in the cell by selecting the Cancel button.

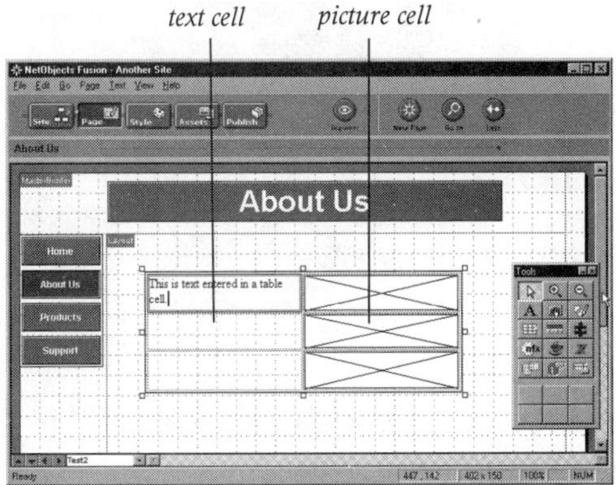


**Figure 10.16**
*Table cells defined to contain text appear empty until text is entered, while empty cells defined to contain pictures are marked by an X.*

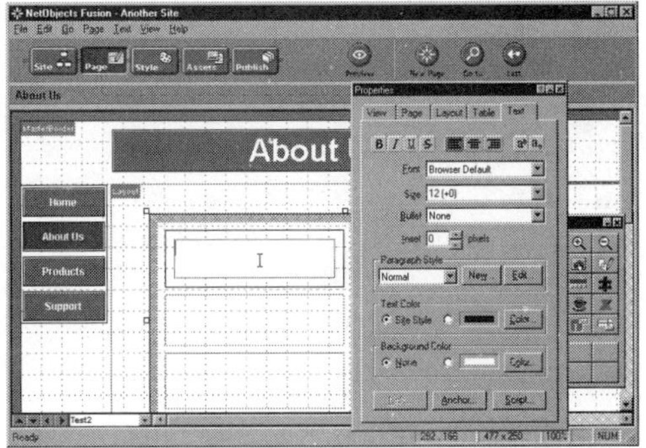


**Figure 10.17**
*When a text cell is selected, the Text tab in the Properties Palette is displayed.*

# Entering, Editing, and Formatting Text in Table Cells

Table cells are defined to hold either text or picture content. Cells defined to contain text appear empty until text is entered, while empty cells defined to contain pictures are marked by an X **(Figure 10.16)**.

## To enter text in a table cell:

1. Click in the desired table cell that is defined to contain text.

   A dotted border appears inside the cell, and a text cursor is displayed.

2. Begin typing or paste text into the cell **(Figure 10.16)**.

## To format text in a table cell:

1. Click in the desired table cell containing text.

   The Text tab of the Properties Palette is displayed **(Figure 10.17)**.

2. Use options in the Text properties tab to format text in table cells (see Chapter 8).

### ✔ Tip

- To edit text in table cells, use the same techniques presented in Chapter 8.

## Placing Pictures in Table Cells

Table cells are defined to hold either text or picture content. Cells defined to contain pictures are marked by an X when empty **(Figure 10.18)**.

### To place a picture in a table cell:

1. Click in the desired table cell that is defined to contain a picture.

   A dialog box will appear **(Figure 10.19)**.

2. Use the dialog box displayed to locate and open the desired image file.

   The selected image is displayed in the selected cell **(Figure 10.18)**.

### ✓ Tip

- If the dialog box does not appear when you click on a picture cell, try this: Select the desired cell. Right-click *(Mac users Ctrl + Click)* to display the element pop-up menu. Select Cell Type, and choose Text in the Cell Type dialog box. Click OK. Now repeat this procedure, but this time change the cell content setting back to Picture. Click OK, and the dialog box appears.

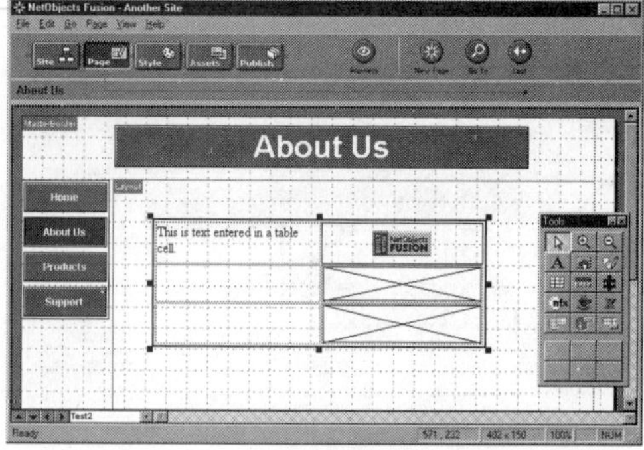


**Figure 10.18**
*An image displayed in a picture table cell.*

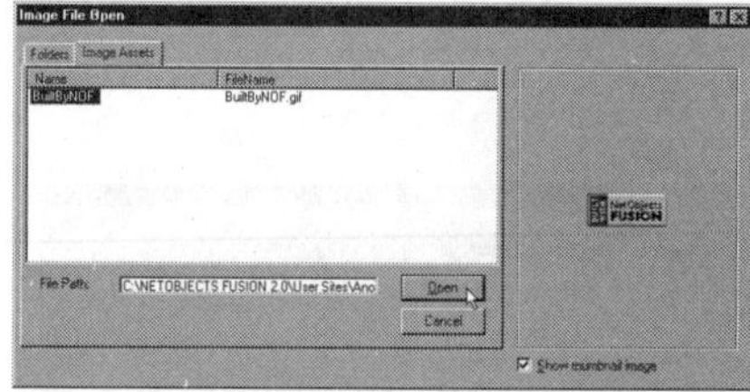


**Figure 10.19**
*The dialog box displayed allows you to select an image to place in a table cell that is defined to contain pictures.*

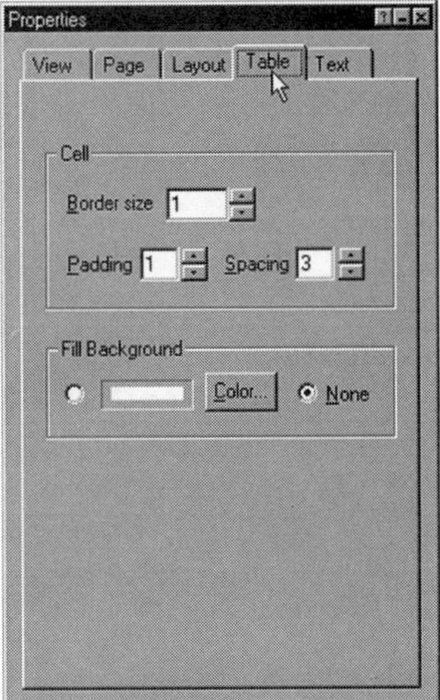


**Figure 10.20**
*Table properties include border size, padding spacing, and fill background.*

**Figure 10.21**
*If in selecting a table, the Text or Picture tabs of the Properties Palette are displayed, you can click the Table tab to display table properties instead.*

# Accessing Table Properties

Once a table has been created, you can modify a number of its properties using the Table tab in the Properties Palette.

### To access Table properties:

1. If the Properties Palette is not already displayed, choose Properties Palette from the View menu.
2. Click on a table to select it.

   When the selected object is a table, the Table tab is displayed in the Properties Palette **(Figure 10.20)**. The Table properties include settings for the table border, for cell padding, and for cell spacing. In addition, you can use Table properties to set a fill background color for the table.

### ✔ Tip

- If you selected a cell containing text or images, the Text or Picture tabs may be displayed **(Figure 10.21)**. If either is the case, you can then simply click on the Table tab in the Properties Palette to display table properties **(Figure 10.20)**.

## Changing the Table Border, Cell Padding, and Spacing

The table border is identical to the border of other content elements like text boxes. It surrounds the table and has a three-dimensional appearance **(Figure 10.22)**. Cell padding is the space between a cell border the cell contents **(Figure 10.23)**. Cell spacing is the amount of space between cell borders **(Figure 10.24)**.

### To change the border size:

1. Select the table whose border you would like to size.
2. Type or select a size (in pixels) for the border using the Border size field in the Table properties tab.

   The table border changes to reflect your selections **(Figure 10.22)**.

### To change cell padding:

1. Select the table whose cell padding you would like to adjust.
2. Type or select a size for the cell padding using the Padding field in the Table properties tab.

   The padding for the cells in the selected table change to reflect your selections **(Figure 10.23)**.

### To change cell spacing:

1. Select the table whose cell spacing you would like to adjust.
2. Type or select a size for the cell spacing using the Spacing field in the Table properties tab.

   The spacing of cells in the selected table change to reflect your selections **(Figure 10.24)**.

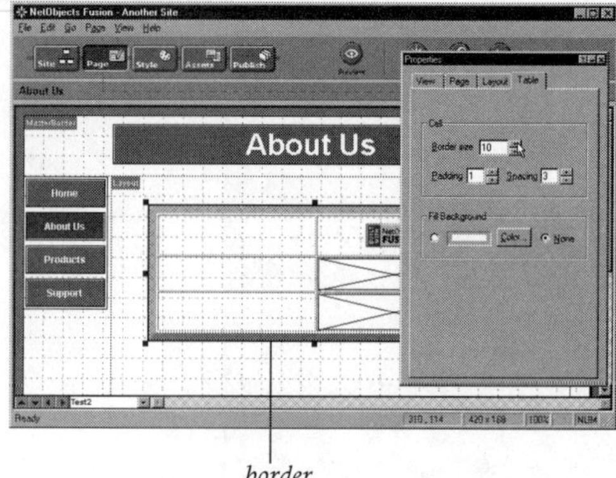


**Figure 10.22**
*Change the border by typing or selecting a value in the Border Size field in Table properties.*

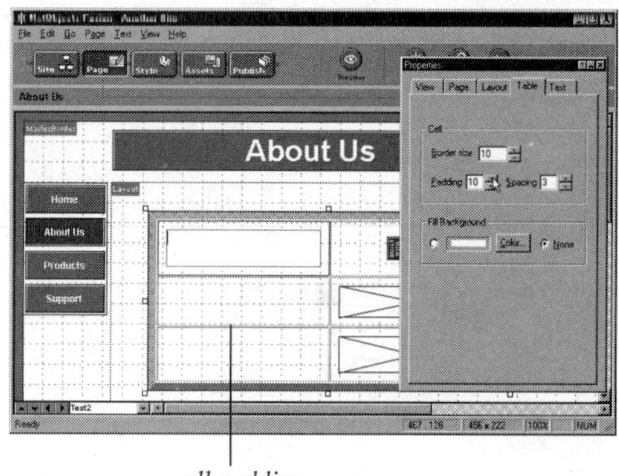


**Figure 10.23**
*Change cell padding by typing or selecting a value in the Padding field in Table properties.*

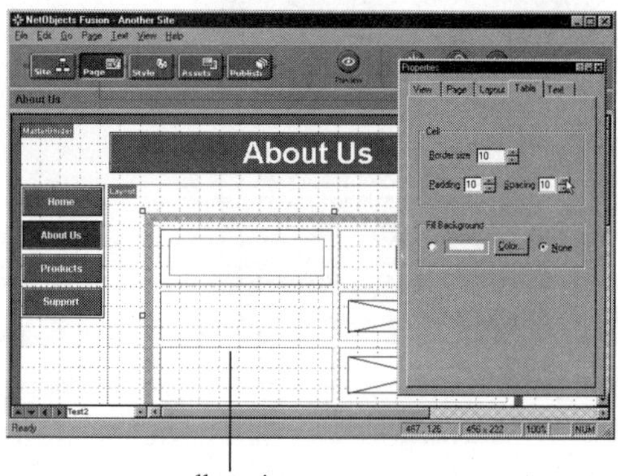


**Figure 10.24**
*Change cell spacing by typing or selecting a value in the Spacing field in Table properties.*

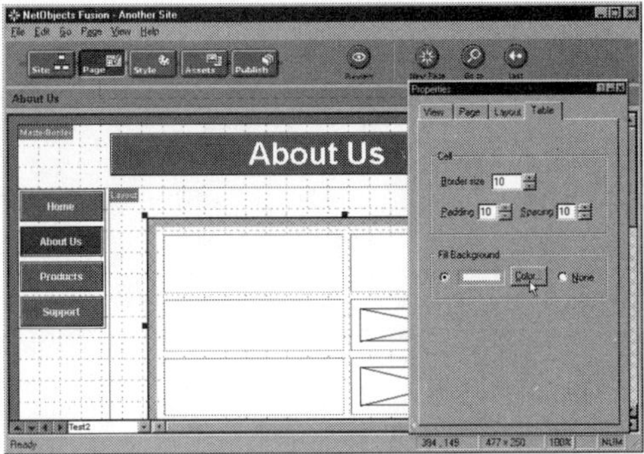

**Figure 10.25**
*Select the color radio button in the Fill Background area of the Table properties tab.*

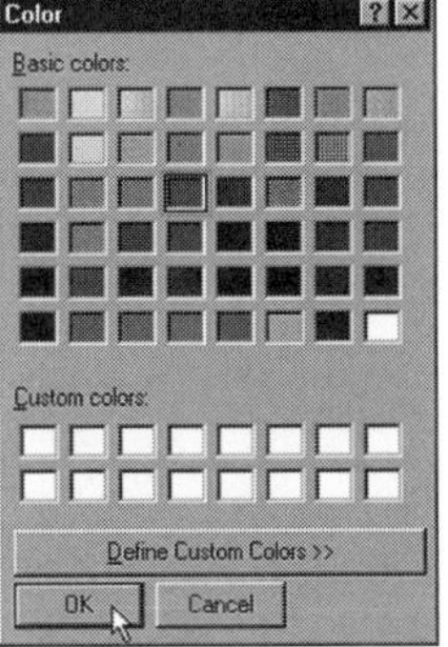

**Figure 10.26**
*Select the desired color from the color palette, and click OK.*

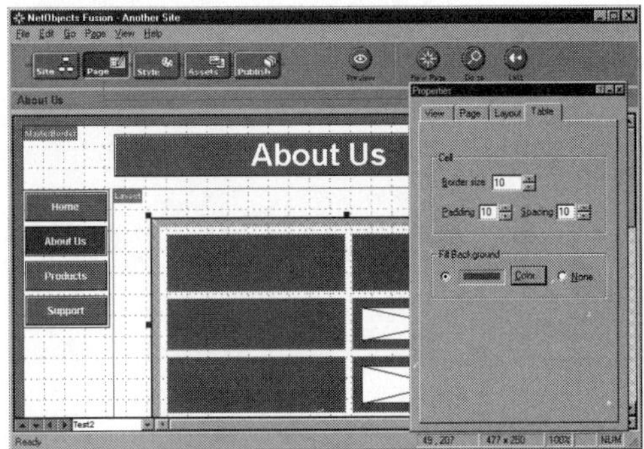

**Figure 10.27**
*The selected color is displayed as the table background.*

# Applying a Table Background

You can use the Table properties tab in the Properties Palette to apply or change a background fill for a table. The background fill is applied to the contents of cells only, and not to cell padding, spacing, or to the table border.

## To apply a background fill:

1. Select the table whose background you would like to set.
2. If the None radio button is selected, click the color radio button in Fill Background area of the Table properties tab **(Figure 10.25)**.
3. Click the Color button to display the color palette **(Figure 10.26)**.
4. Click the desired color in the color palette, or use the Define Custom colors button to define a color not displayed on the palette. *Mac users can define custom colors by clicking a custom color and selecting the Edit... button.*
5. Click OK on the color palette.

   The selected color is displayed as the background of the selected table's cells **(Figure 10.27)**.

# Pictures & Drawings

**Figure 11.1**
*Click the picture tool in the Tools Palette.*

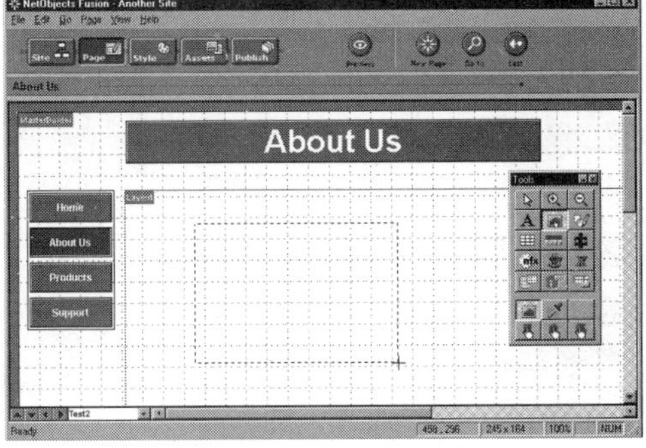


**Figure 11.2**
*Use the picture tool to draw a picture box on your page.*

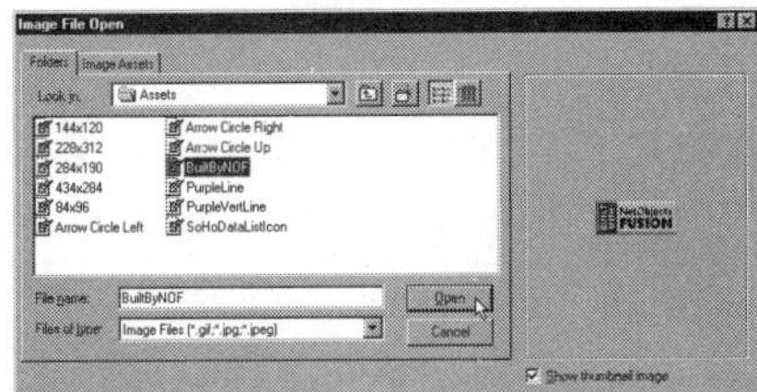

**Figure 11.3**
*Choose the desired image file using the dialog box displayed.*

## Introducing Pictures

Fusion allows you to add image files to both the layout and MasterBorders areas of your Web pages. Each picture you place in your Web pages is an individual image file which is downloaded by the browser when visitors to your site view your pages. There are many graphic file formats, and Fusion supports **BMP**, **PCX**, **PCT**, **GIF**, **JPG**, and Mac pict format files.

### To add an image to a page:

1. In Page View, click the picture tool in the Tools Palette **(Figure 11.1)**.

   Secondary picture tools are displayed at the bottom of the tools palette, and the mouse pointer becomes a crosshair.

2. Position the pointer on your page approximately where you want the upper left corner of the new picture to be positioned.

3. Click and drag down and to the right.

   A dotted outline indicates the picture box outline **(Figure 11.2)**.

4. Release the mouse button when the picture box is the desired size.

   A dialog box appears **(Figure 11.3)**.

5. If you want to use a picture in a supported file format other than **GIF** or **JPG**, make a selection from the **Files of type** drop-down list. *Mac users select All Files from the Show menu in the Open dialog box.*

Since browsers generally support only **GIF** and **JPG** images, Fusion will offer to convert other supported file formats to **GIF** or **JPG** when you attempt to use such files in your pages.

6. Use a dialog box to select an image file from your hard disk, network, or other device.
7. Click Open in the dialog box.

   The selected image appears in the picture box you drew, and the picture box is automatically sized to fit the image **(Figure 11.4)**.

   **or**

   If you want to wait before selecting an image file for display in the picture box, click Cancel in the dialog box displayed.

   An X will appear in the picture box **(Figure 11.5)**, indicating that it is empty. You can then double-click an empty picture box (or select the picture box and click the Browse button (*Mac users click the Select... button*) in the Picture properties tab) at any time to display the dialog box and select an image.

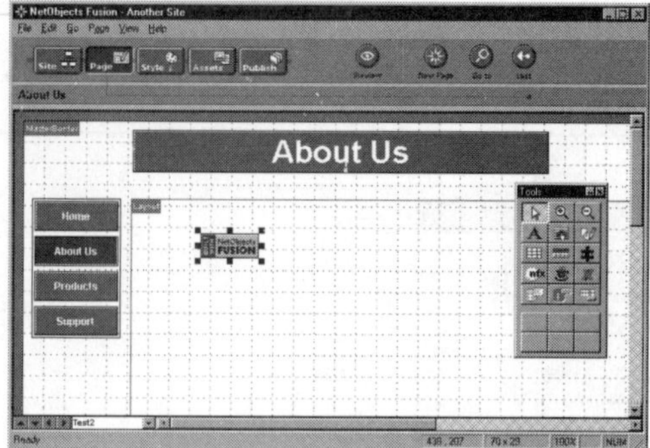


**Figure 11.4**
*The selected image appears in the picture box.*

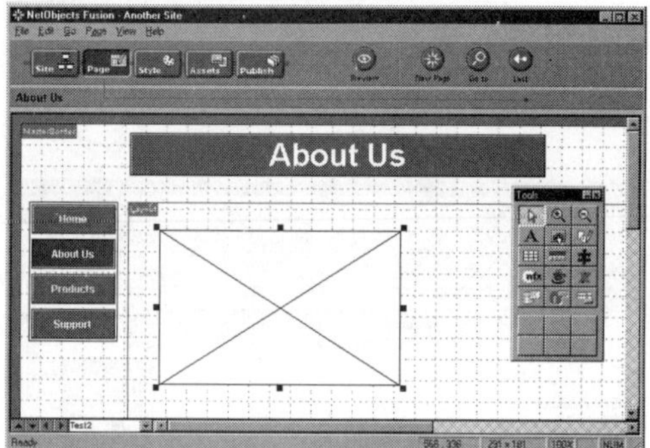


**Figure 11.5**
*An empty picture box.*

### ✓ Tips

- Be careful that images on your pages do not overlap. Most browsers will not display overlapping images, and the way in which the images are "sorted out" may not be what you expected.
- You can use the Cut, Copy, and Paste options in the Edit menu to copy and move picture boxes throughout your site.

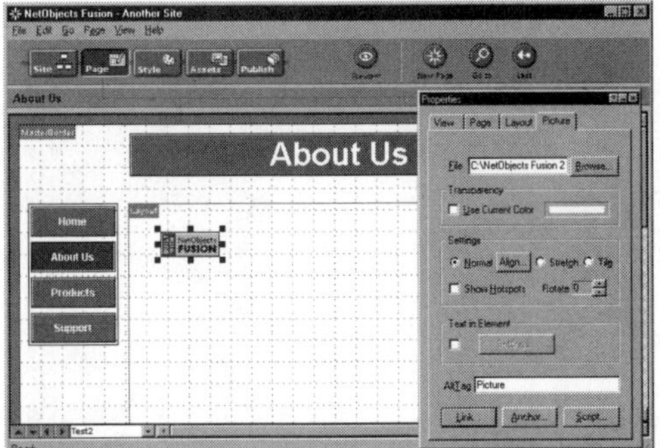


**Figure 11.6**
*Display the Picture tab of the Properties palette by clicking on a picture box.*

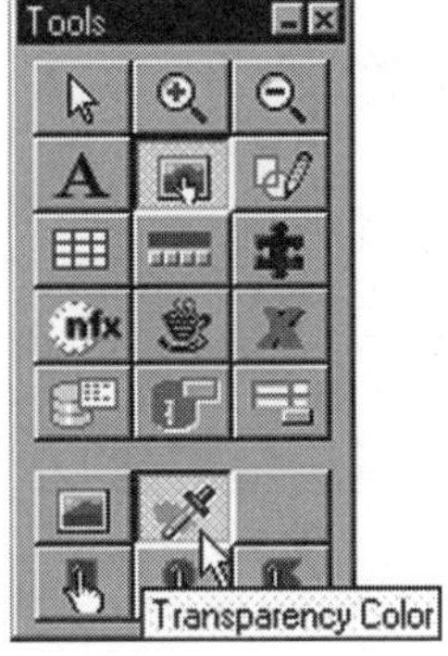


**Figure 11.7**
*Select the Transparency Color tool.*

**Figure 11.8**
*Click to sample a color in a gif image that you wish to make transparent.*

## Using Picture Properties

When you select a picture in the layout or MasterBorders of your Web page, the Picture tab appears in the Properties Palette. Picture properties allow you to specify an image file, make a selected color in **GIF** images transparent, set the alignment and behavior of images within picture boxes, add text to pictures, and assign text to display if the image does not load or is suppressed. Finally, you can use Picture properties to make a picture into a link or an anchor (see Chapter 9).

### To access Picture properties:

1. In Page View, if the Properties Palette is not already displayed, select Properties Palette from the View menu.
2. Click in a picture box on your page to select it.

   The Picture tab of the Properties palette is displayed **(Figure 11.6)**. The properties displayed are for the selected picture box.

### To make an image transparent:

1. Select the Picture tool in the Tools Palette.
2. From the secondary picture tools displayed at the bottom of the Tools Palette, select the Transparency Color tool **(Figure 11.7)**.
3. In any **GIF** image on your page, click a color that you wish to make transparent **(Figure 11.8)**.

   The color appears in the Transparency area of the Picture properties tab.

4. Click the **Use Current Color** checkbox in the Transparency area of the Picture properties tab to make the sampled color transparent.

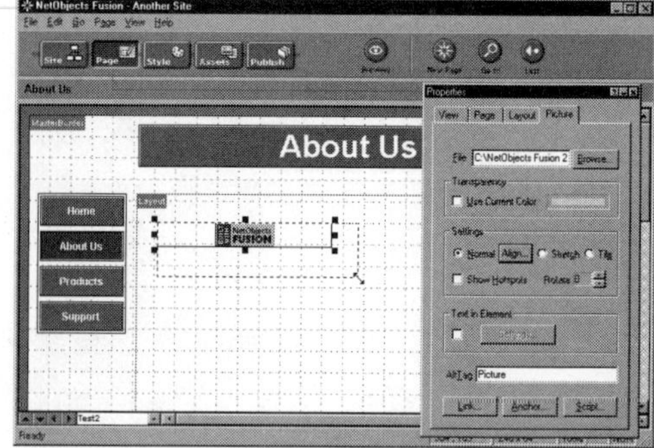

**Figure 11.9**
*With the Normal option selected in Picture properties, click and drag the picture box handles to resize the picture box.*

### To size a picture box:

1. Select the image whose box you wish to resize.
2. Make sure the **Normal** option is selected in the Settings area of the Picture properties tab.
3. Click and drag the desired picture box handle **(Figure 11.9)**.

   The picture box is resized, and the image inside unchanged **(Figure 11.10)**. But the image is positioned within the resized picture box according to selections made in the Alignment dialog box discussed next.

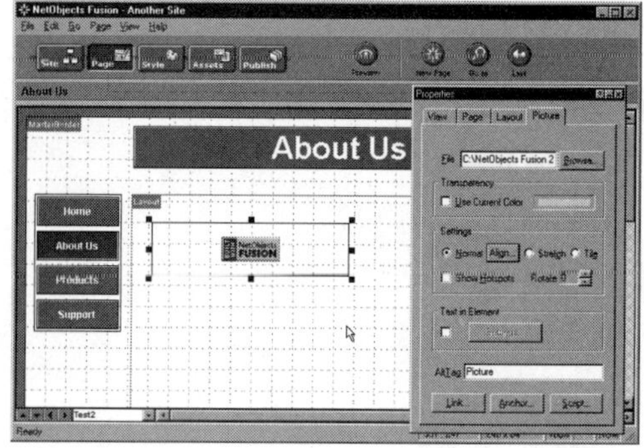

**Figure 11.10**
*The picture box is resized, but the image itself is not.*

✓ **Tip**

- Picture box sizing allows you to effectively "crop" images, by dragging picture box handles until the desired part of the image is visible.

### To set image alignment within a picture box:

1. Select the picture box whose image you wish to reposition within the box.
2. Make sure the **Normal** option is selected in the Settings area of the Picture properties tab.
3. Click the Align button.

   The Alignment dialog box is displayed.
4. Select Horizontal and Vertical alignment options.

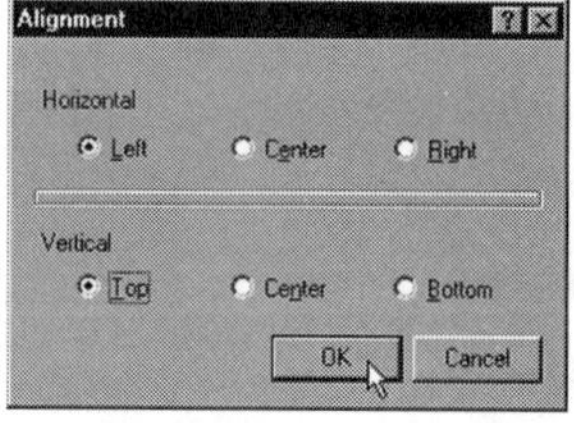


**Figure 11.11**
*Select Horizontal and Vertical alignment options, then click OK.*

Siize a Picture Box

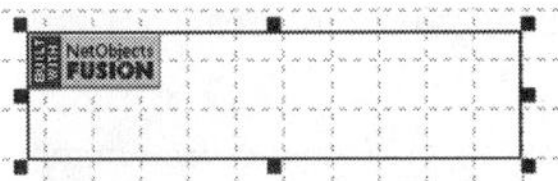


**Figure 11.12**
*The image is positioned within the picture box according to your alignment selections.*

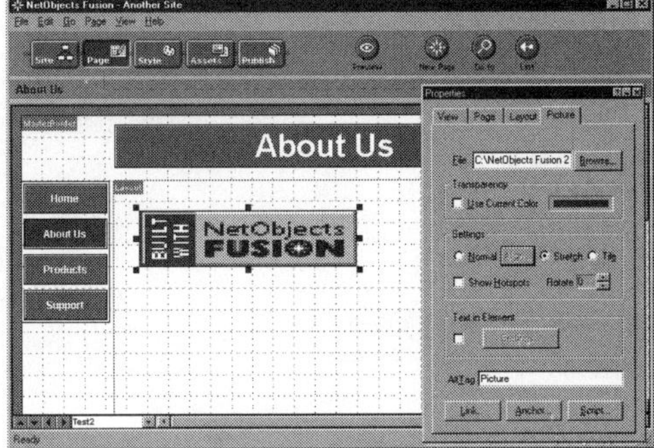


**Figure 11.13**
*Select the Stretch option to size the image to the picture box.*

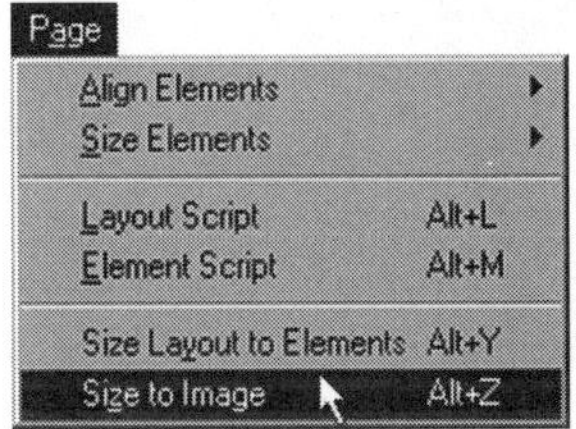


**Figure 11.14**
*To make a picture box exactly fit an image, choose Size to Image from the Page menu.*

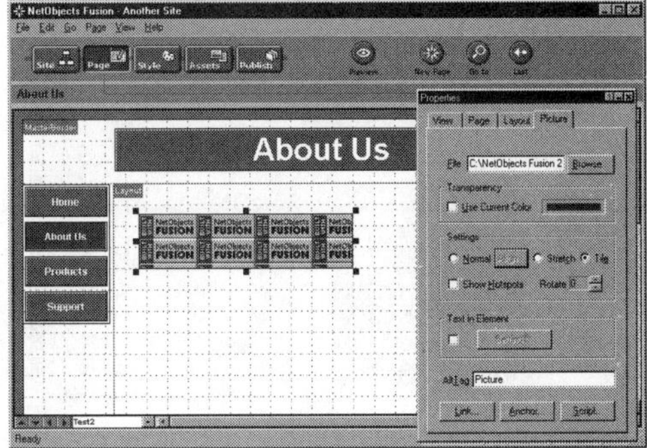


**Figure 11.15**
*Select the Tile option to tile an image within a picture box.*

5. Click OK **(Figure 11.11)**.
6. The image inside the selected picture box is repositioned in accordance with your alignment selections **(Figure 11.12)**.

## To make an image exactly fit a picture box:

1. Select the picture box whose image you wish to size.
2. Select the Stretch option in the Settings area of the Picture properties tab.

   The image is reduced, enlarged, and/or skewed to exactly fit the picture box **(Figure 11.13)**.

### ✔ Tip

■ To size a picture box to exactly the size of the image inside, select the desired picture box and choose Size to Image from the Page menu **(Figure 11.14)**.

## To tile an image to fill a picture box:

1. Select the picture box whose image you wish to size.
2. Select the Tile option in the Settings area of the Picture properties tab.

   The image is tiled to fill the picture box **(Figure 11.15)**.

### To change the orientation of an image inside a picture box:

1. Select the picture box whose image you wish to rotate.
2. Click the up and down arrow buttons next to the **Rotate** field in the Settings area of the Page properties tab.

   The image is rotated in 90° increments **(Figure 11.16)**.

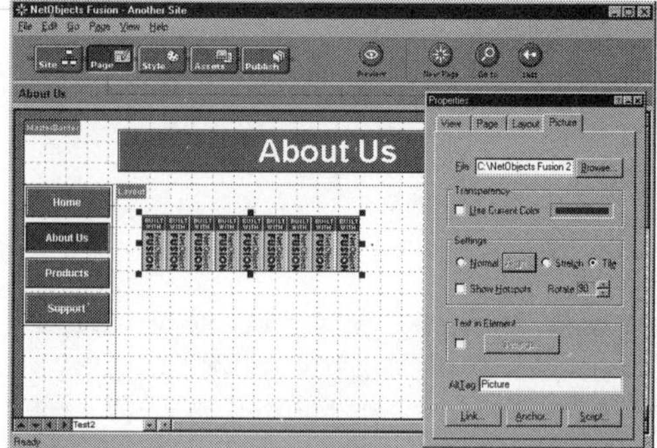


**Figure 11.16**
*The image is rotated as specified. Here the image is both tiled and rotated 90 degrees.*

### To show imagemap hotspots:

If an image is defined as an imagemap (see Chapter 9), then you can display defined hotspots by selecting the **Show Hotspots** checkbox in the Settings area of the Picture properties tab.

### To add text to a picture box:

1. Select the picture box to which you wish to add text.
2. Select the **Text in Element** check box in the Page properties tab.

   The Settings button is enabled.
3. Click the Settings button.

   The **Text in Element Settings** dialog box appears **(Figure 11.17)**.

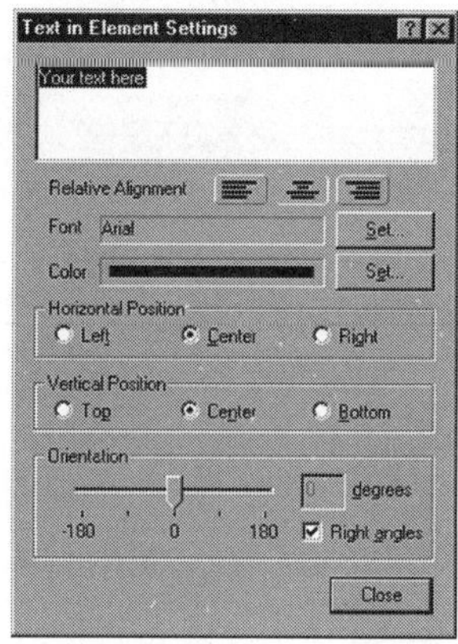


**Figure 11.17**
*The Text in Element Settings dialog box.*

4. Replace the text "Your text here" with the text you wish to appear in the picture box.
5. Select the desired **Relative Alignment** option **(Figure 11.18)**. These options align lines of text with one another.

   left justifies lines of text.

   centers lines of text.

   right justifies lines of text.

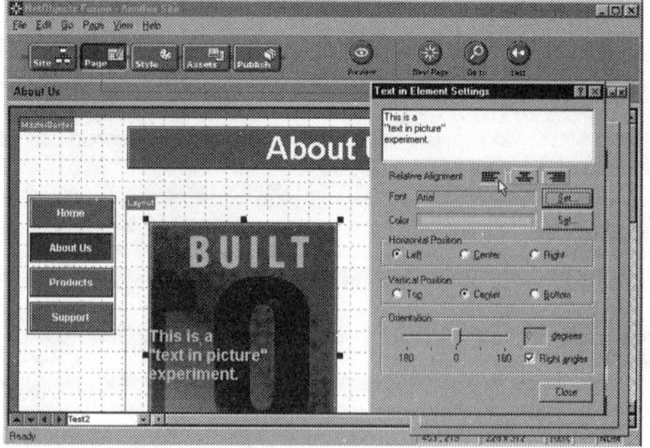


**Figure 11.18**
*Select the desired Relative Alignment option.*

Change image orientation

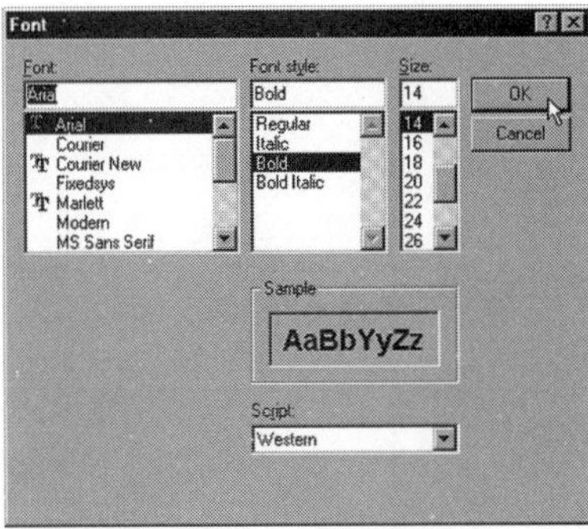


**Figure 11.19**
*Select a font, size, and style.*

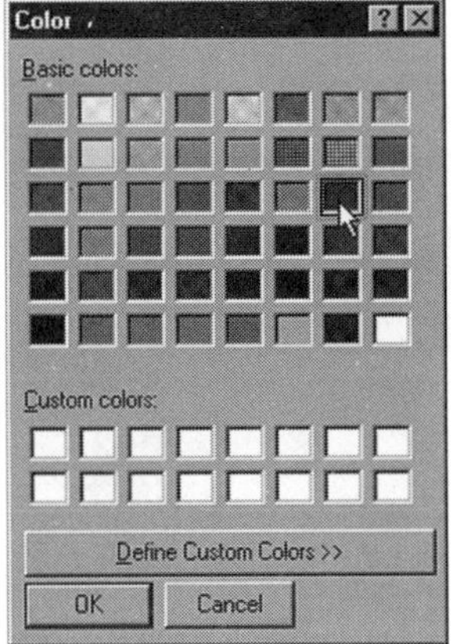


**Figure 11.20**
*Select a text color.*

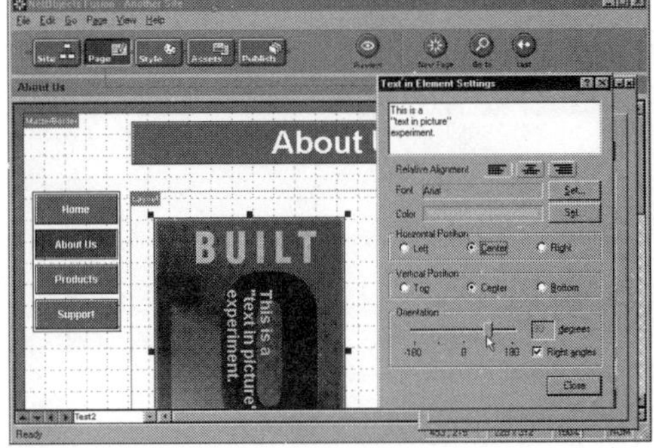


**Figure 11.21**
*Select the desired text Orientation using the slider control.*

6. Click the **Set** button opposite the **Font** field to select the font, size, and style using the **(Figure 11.19)** Font dialog box.
7. Click the **Set** button opposite the **Color** field to choose a text color from the Color Palette **(Figure 11.20)**.
8. Select a **Horizontal Position** option for positioning the text horizontally within the text box.
9. Select a **Vertical Position** option for positioning the text vertically within the text box.
10. Use the slider control in the **Orientation** area to select a rotation angle for your text **(Figure 11.21)**. In Windows 95, you can select **Right angles** to restrict rotation to 90° increments.
11. Click the **Close** button on the Text in Element Settings dialog box, and the specified text becomes a part of the selected image.

✔ **Tip**

- If you define a picture box larger than the image inside, and add text which extends beyond the image but not beyond the picture box boundaries, then when the page is viewed in a Web browser, the text will be cropped at the edges of the image.

## To specify text to display when an image fails to load:

1. Select the picture box for which you wish to specify alternate text.
2. Type desired alternate text in the **Alt Tag** field in the Picture properties tab.

## Using the Draw Tools

Fusion allows you to add shapes and lines to your pages that you draw yourself using the Drawing tools. You can draw rectangles, rounded rectangles, ellipses, polygons, lines, and even HTML rules. You can also control the border and fill of the shapes you draw.

**Figure 11.22**
*With Draw tool, a selection of secondary tools are displaye*

### To draw rectangle, rounded rectangle, or ellipse on a page:

1. In Page View, click the Draw tool in the Tools Palette **(Figure 11.22)**.

   Secondary Draw tools are displayed at the bottom of the tools palette, and the mouse pointer becomes a crosshair.

2. Select one of the following secondary drawing tools:

   to draw a rectangle.

   to draw a rounded rectangle.

   to draw an ellipse.

3. Position the pointer on your page approximately where you want a corner of the new drawn shape to be positioned.

4. Click and drag to draw the desired shape.

   A dotted outline indicates the drawn shape outline **(Figure 11.23)**.

5. Release the mouse button when the drawn shape is the desired size **(Figure 11.24)**.

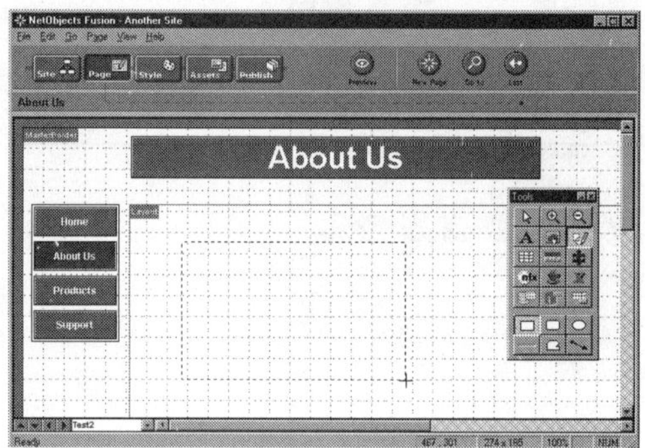


**Figure 11.23**
*Click and drag to draw the new shape on the page.*

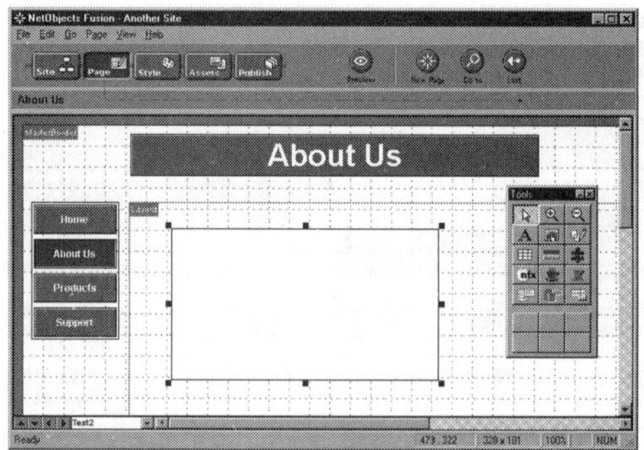


**Figure 11.24**
*A rectangle drawn on a page.*

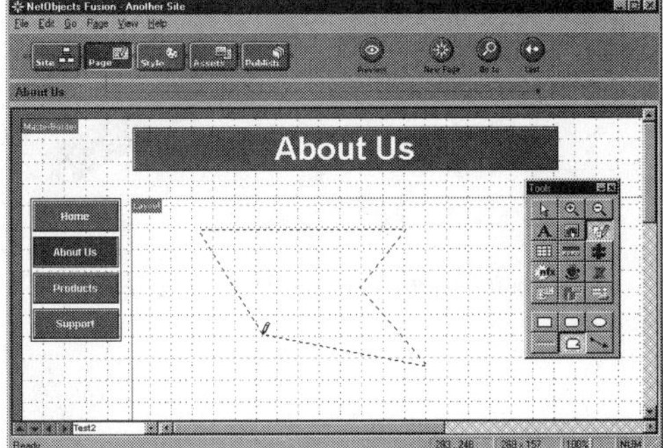


**Figure 11.25**
*Click for each corner of your new polygon.*

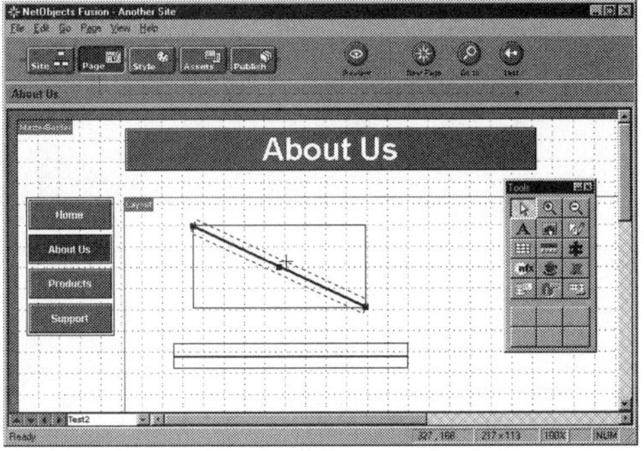


**Figure 11.26**
*A line (top) and an HTML rule (bottom) drawn on a page.*

## To draw a polygon:

1. In Page View, click the Draw tool in the Tools Palette.
2. Select the polygon secondary draw tool: .
3. Click where you wish to place each corner of the polygon **(Figure 11.25)**.
4. Double-click to complete the polygon.

## To draw a line or HTML rule:

1. In Page View, click the Draw tool in the Tools Palette.
2. Select one of the following secondary drawing tools:

   to draw an HTML rule line.

   to draw a line.
3. Position the pointer on your page approximately where you want an end of the new line or rule to be positioned.
4. Click and drag to draw the line or rule as desired.
5. Release the mouse button.

   The line or rule appears in a bounding box with handles **(Figure 11.26)**.

### ✔ Tip

- HTML rules can be drawn only horizontally. Lines can be drawn at any angle.

### To modify a drawn shape:

1. In Page View, click the drawn shape you wish to resize.
2. To resize and reshape any drawn shape, drag one of the handles until the drawn shape is the desired size.

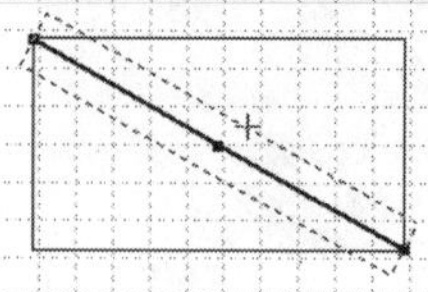

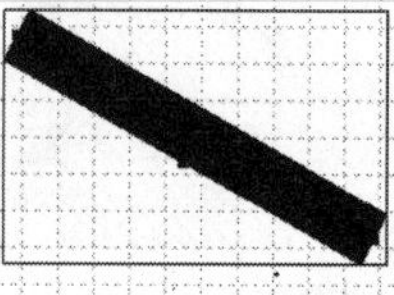

**Figure 11.27**
*You can change the width of a line by dragging the center handle.*

#### ✔ Tips

- Line width **(Figure 11.27)**, length, and angle **(Figure 11.28)** can be changed by dragging the center and end handles respectively.
- Only the length of an HTML rule can be modified by dragging.
- You can change the shape of polygons by dragging handles **(Figure 11.29)**, but sides cannot be added or removed.
- You can drag the extra handle in the lower right corner of a rounded rectangle to adjust the curve and skew of the rectangle corners **(Figure 11.30)**.
- Be careful that drawn shapes on your pages do not overlap. Most browsers will not display overlapping graphics, and the way in which the shapes are "sorted out" may not be what you expected.
- You can use the Cut, Copy, and Paste options in the Edit menu to copy and move drawn shapes throughout your site.

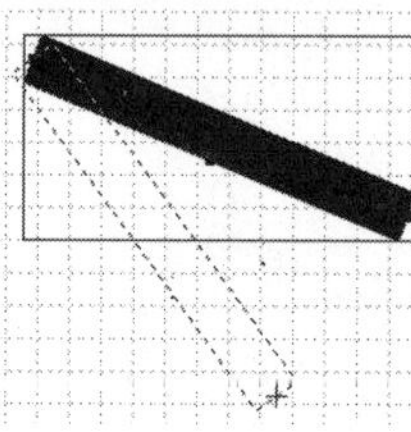

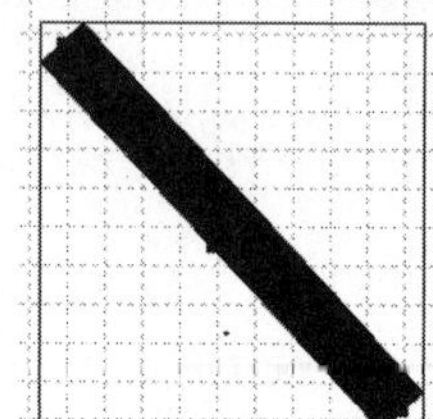

**Figure 11.28**
*You can change the length and angle of a line by dragging the end handles.*

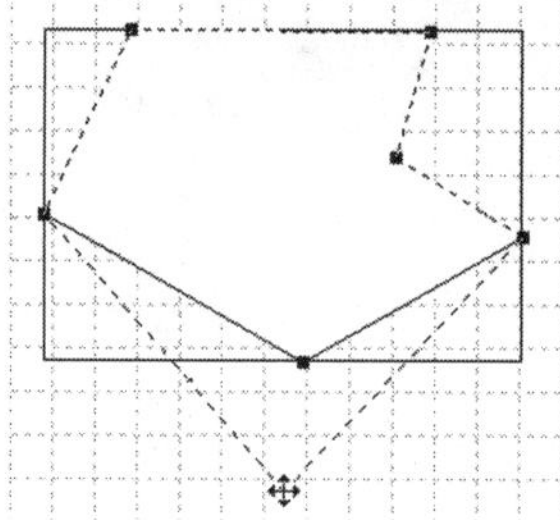

**Figure 11.29**
*Drag polygon handles to reshape the figure.*

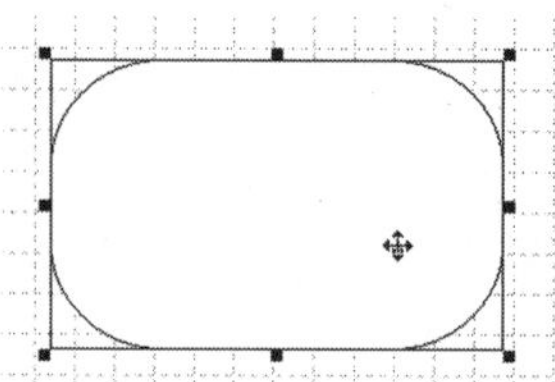

**Figure 11.30**
*Change the degree and skew of the curved corners of a rounded rectangle by dragging the extra handle in the lower right corner.*

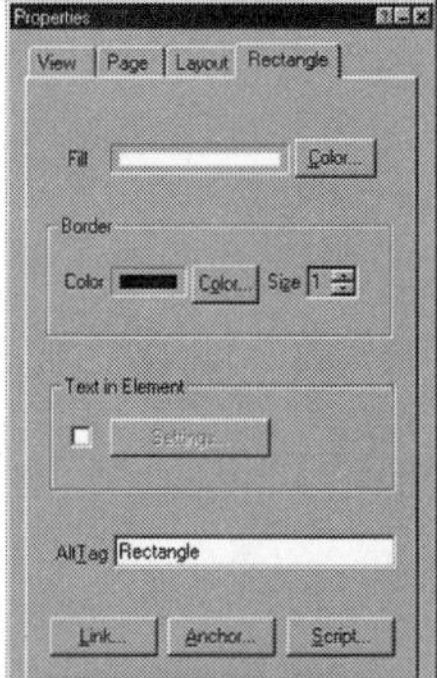
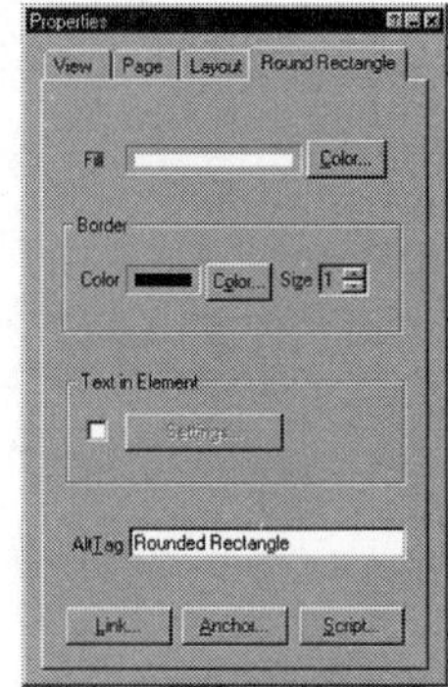
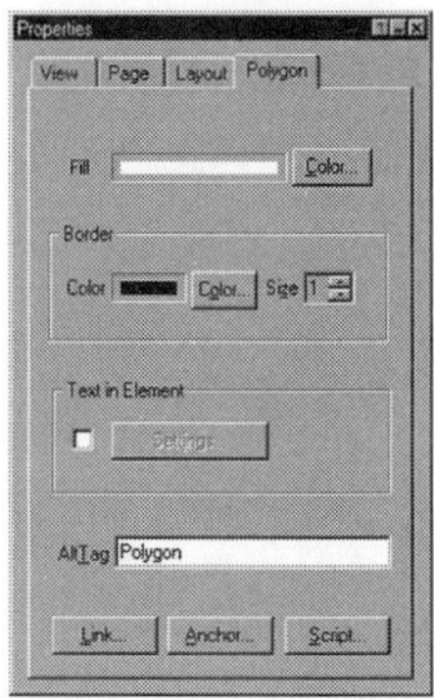
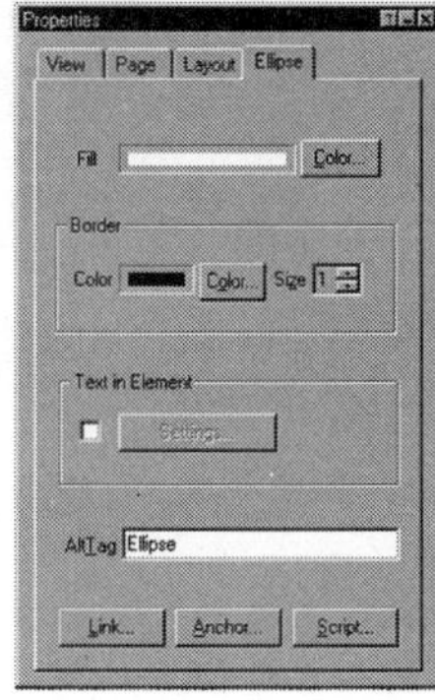

**Figure 11.31**
*Drawn shape properties all offer the same options.*

# Using Drawn Shape Properties

The properties tabs for drawn shapes are all virtually identical **(Figure 11.31)**. Using the Properties Palette tabs for polygons, rectangles, rounded rectangles, and ellipses, you can select the fill color and border size and color for each of these elements. Using the Properties Palette, you can also make these elements into anchors and links (see Chapter 9).

### To access drawn shape properties:

1. In Page View, if the Properties Palette is not already displayed, select Properties Palette from the View menu.
2. Click in a drawn shape on your page to select it.

   The appropriate tab of the Properties palette is displayed **(Figure 11.31)**. The properties displayed are for the selected drawn shape.

### To apply a fill color:

1. Select the drawn shape for which you want to set a fill color.
2. Click the Color button opposite the Fill field in the displayed properties tab.

   The color palette is displayed.
3. Click the desired color in the color palette, or use the Define Custom colors button to define a color not displayed on the palette.

4. Click OK on the color palette.

   The selected color is displayed as the background of the selected drawn shape **(Figure 11.32)**.

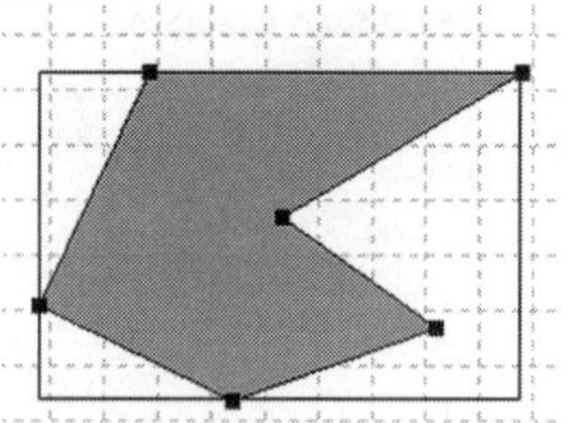

**Figure 11.32**
*A polygon displaying a fill color.*

## To apply a border color:

1. Select the drawn shape for which you want to set a border color.
2. Click the **Color** button opposite the **Color** field in the **Border** area of the displayed properties tab.

   The color palette is displayed.
3. Click the desired color in the color palette, or use the Define Custom colors button to define a color not displayed on the palette.
4. Click OK on the color palette.

   The selected color is displayed as the border color of the selected drawn shape **(Figure 11.33)**.

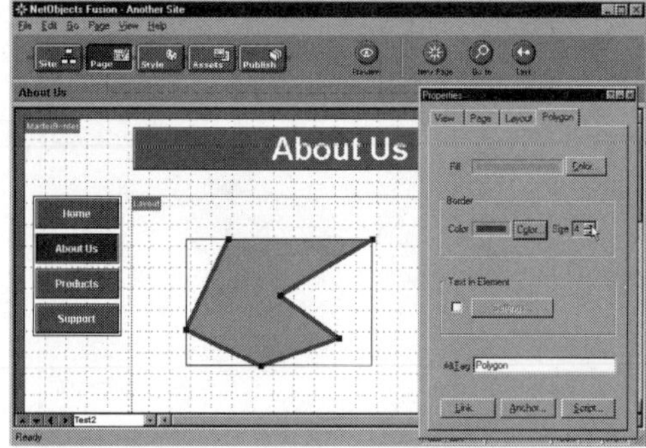


**Figure 11.33**
*A polygon with a fill color, border color, and wider border.*

## To change the border width:

1. Select the drawn shape for which you want to change the border width.
2. Click the up and down arrow buttons opposite the **Size** field in the **Border** area of the displayed properties tab.

   The drawn shape border becomes wider as you increase the Size value **(Figure 11.33)** and narrower as you decrease the Size value.

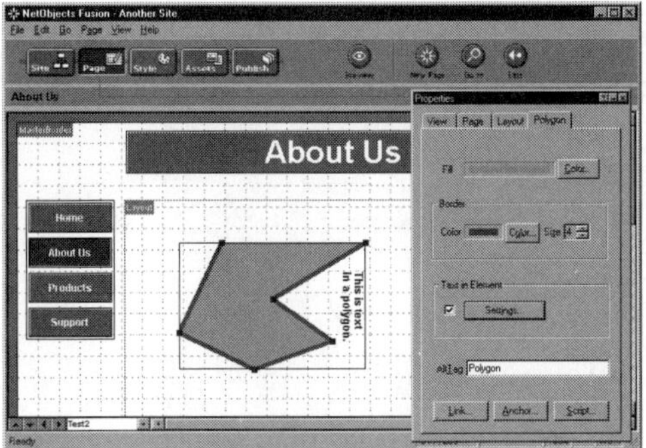


**Figure 11.34**
*Add text to a drawn figure in the same way as you would to a picture.*

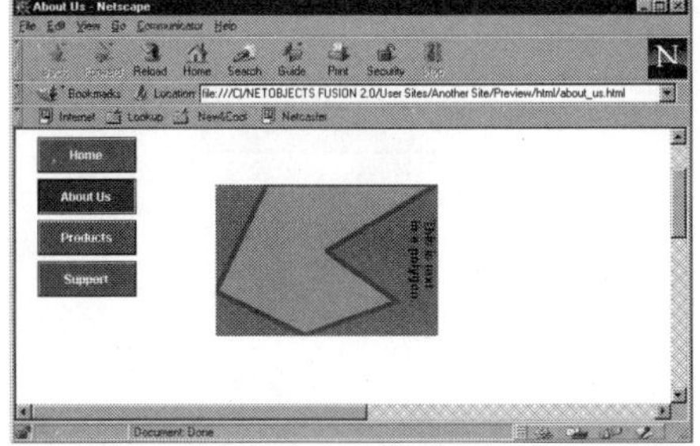


**Figure 11.35**
*Text added to a drawn shape is displayed even if it extends beyond the shape itself (but is contained within the shape's bounding box).*

## To add text to a drawn figure:

See the instructions earlier in this chapter for adding text to images **(Figure 11.34)**. The procedure is the same.

### ✔ Tip

- When you add text to a drawn shape, the text can extend beyond the shape itself and still be displayed by the browser **(Figure 11.35)**. This is in contrast to using text in pictures.

## To specify text to display when an image fails to load:

1. Select the drawn shape for which you wish to specify alternate text.
2. Type the desired alternate text in the **Alt Tag** field in the displayed properties tab.

   When viewed with a browser, if the selected drawn shape is not displayed, the text you entered in the Alt Tag field will be displayed instead.

### ✔ Tip

- Alternative text for images is an important feature for visitors to your site who are using a browser that does not support images and for those visitors who wish to suppress images in order to speed up downloading your pages.

## Using Line Properties

The properties tab for drawn lines allows you to select the line width, the line color, styles, and colors for the line head and tail. Select the fill color and border size and color for each of these elements. Using the Properties Palette, you can also make these elements into anchors and links (see Chapter 9).

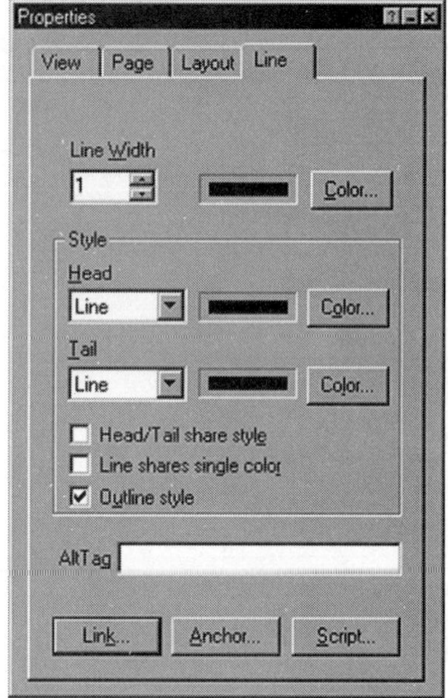


**Figure 11.36**
*Drawn line properties.*

### To access drawn line properties:

1. In Page View, if the Properties Palette is not already displayed, select Properties Palette from the View menu.
2. Click in a drawn line on your page to select it.

   The Line tab of the Properties palette is displayed **(Figure 11.36)**. The properties displayed are for the selected drawn line.

### To change the line width:

1. Select the drawn line you wish to change.
2. Click the up and down arrow buttons opposite the **Line Width** field, or type a point value in the Line Width filed.

   The selected line is displayed in the specified width.

### To apply a line color:

1. Select the drawn line you wish to change.
2. Click the **Color** button opposite the **Line Width** field in Line properties tab.

   The color palette is displayed.

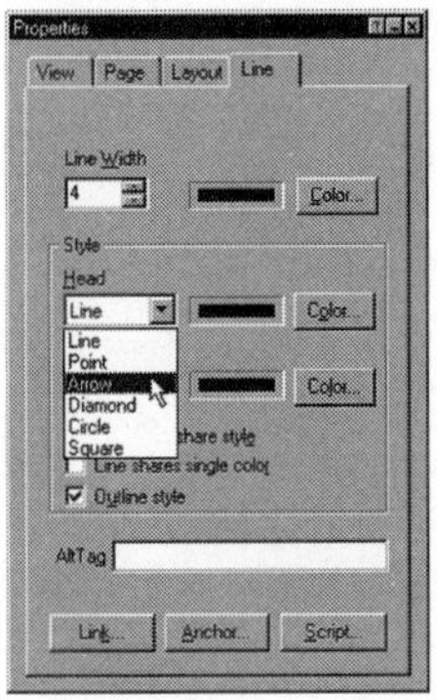


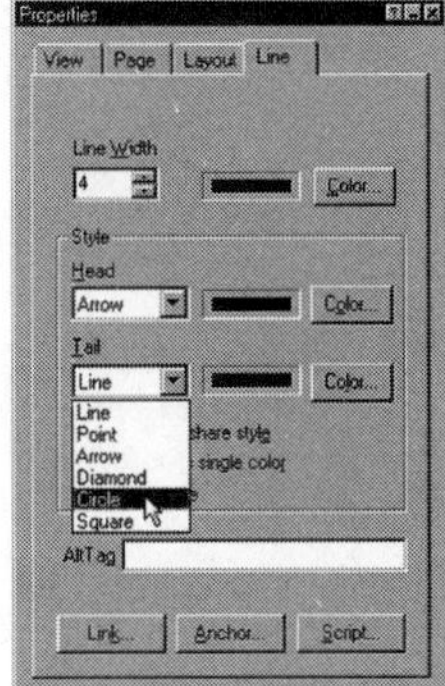


**Figure 11.37**
*Select head and tail styles from the drop-down menus.*

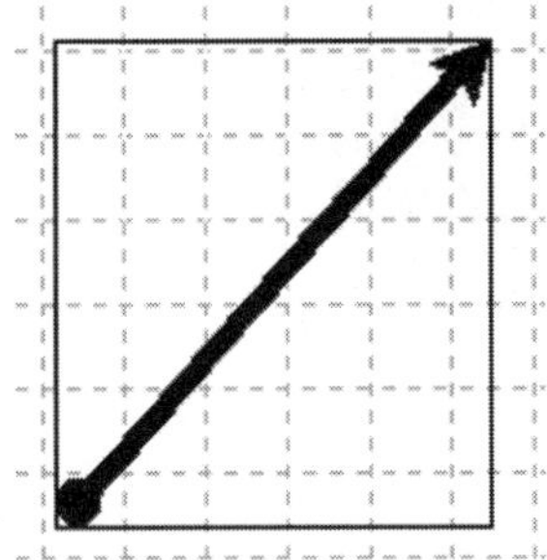

**Figure 11.38**
*The selected line is displayed with the head and tail styles you specify.*

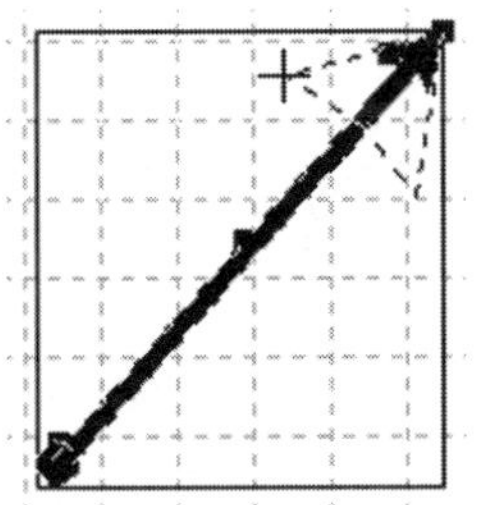

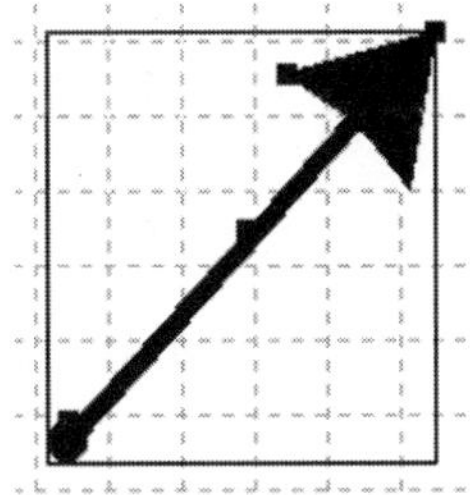

**Figure 11.39**
*You can change the size and shape of head and tail styles by dragging the handles.*

3. Click the desired color in the color palette, or use the Define Custom colors button to define a color not displayed on the palette.
4. Click OK on the color palette.

   The line is displayed using the color selected.

### To add a head and tail style to a drawn line:

1. Select the drawn line you wish to change.
2. Select one of the options from the Head drop-down menu in the Style area of the Line properties tab **(Figure 11.37)**.
3. Select one of the options from the Tail drop-down menu **(Figure 11.37)**.

   The line is displayed with the selected head and tail styles **(Figure 11.38)**.

### ✔ Tip

- You can change the size and shape of head and tail styles by dragging the handles **(Figure 11.39)**.
- You can change the color of head and tail styles by clicking the **Color** buttons opposite the Head and Tail fields.
- To set the tail style to match the head style, select **Head/Tail share style**.
- To use the same color for the head and tail as for the line, select **Line shares single color**.
- To outline the head and tail with the line color, click **Outline style**.

## Using Rule Properties

The properties tab for HTML rules allows you to select the standard HTML rule tag (<HR>), which generates a 3-dimensional appearing horizontal line, or to select the rule image defined for the current SiteStyle.

### To access rule properties:

1. In Page View, if the Properties Palette is not already displayed, select Properties Palette from the View menu.
2. Click a rule on your page to select it.

   The Rule properties tab is displayed **(Figure 11.40)**.

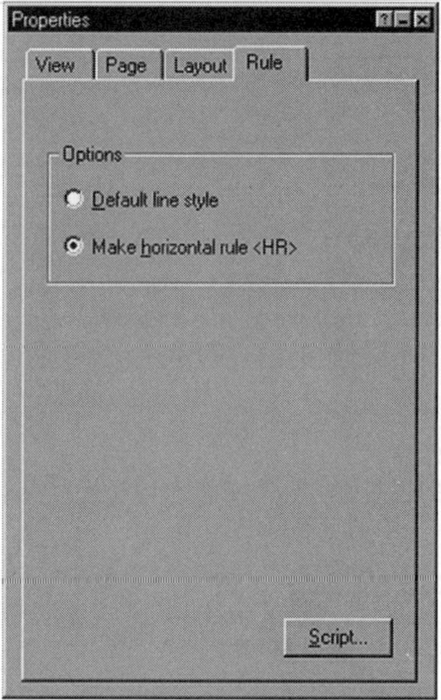


**Figure 11.40**
*Rule properties.*

### To set the rule appearance:

1. Select the rule you wish to change.
2. Click one of the Options displayed in the Rule properties tab.

   **Default line style** will apply the rule image defined for the current SiteStyle to the selected rule.

   **Make horizontal rule <HR>** will make the selected rule appear as a default HTML rule when viewed with a Web browser.

### ✓ Tip

- You can't change the width or other properties of a rule except by changing the rule image defined for the current SiteStyle.

# Rich Media

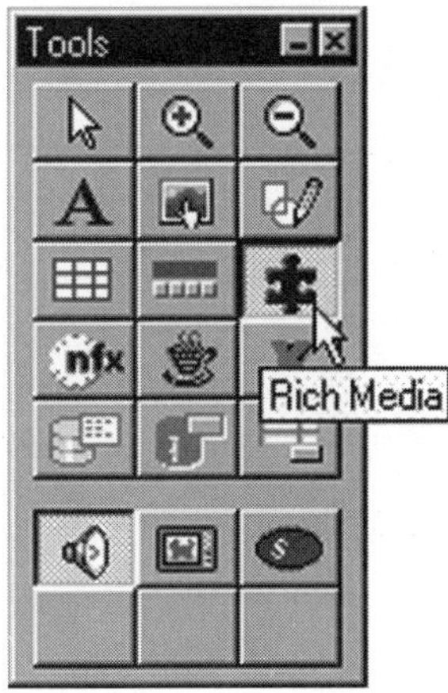


**Figure 12.1**
*Select the Rich Media tool in the Tools Palette.*

## Using the Rich Media Tools

Fusion allows you to easily add rich media to your Web pages such as sound, video, and Shockwave using the Rich Media tools.

### To access the Rich Media tools:

Select the Rich Media tool **(Figure 12.1)** from the Tools Palette.

The three Rich Media tools are displayed in the bottom of the Tools Palette:

- allows you to add a sound file (or other downloadable file).
- allows you to add a motion video file.
- allows you to add a Shockwave file.

### ✔ Tip

- When using Rich Media in your site, don't forget that some visitors will not be using browsers capable of displaying and playing rich media files.
- If media presented in your site requires a plug-in or other "helper" application to be interpreted by browsers, then include links for downloading these tools.

## Adding Sounds

You can add sounds that play when the user clicks a button, and you can add background sounds that play when a page is viewed. Adding a background sound is covered in Chapter 7 on page 103.

Figure 12.2
*Select the Sound tool.*

### To add a sound file to a page:

1. Select the Sound tool **(Figure 12.2)**.
2. Click and drag to create a box on your page.

   An open dialog box appears **(Figure 12.3)**.
3. Select the file types to display using the Files of type drop-down menu.
4. Select the desired sound file.
5. Click the Open button.

   A sound icon appears on the page, and the Sound properties tab is displayed **(Figure 12.4)**.

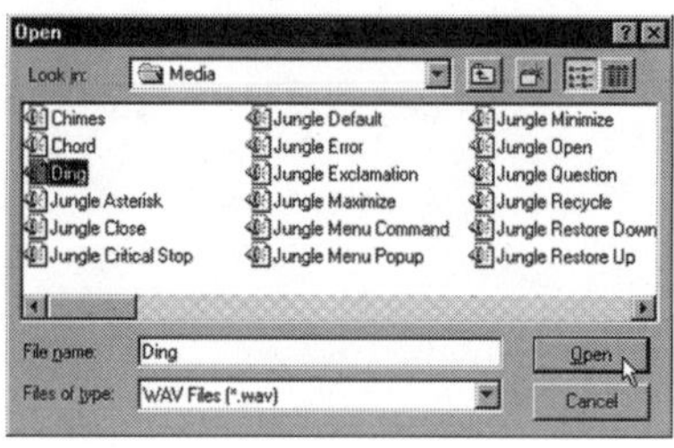


Figure 12.3
*Select the desired sound file using the open dialog box.*

### ✔ Tips

- Sound file formats supported by Fusion are **ra** and **ram** (RealAudio files), **wav** (Windows audio), **aiff**, **midi**, and **au**.
- You can also use the Sound tool to allow visitors to your site to download files of other types. Simply use the open dialog box to select any file you wish to offer for download.

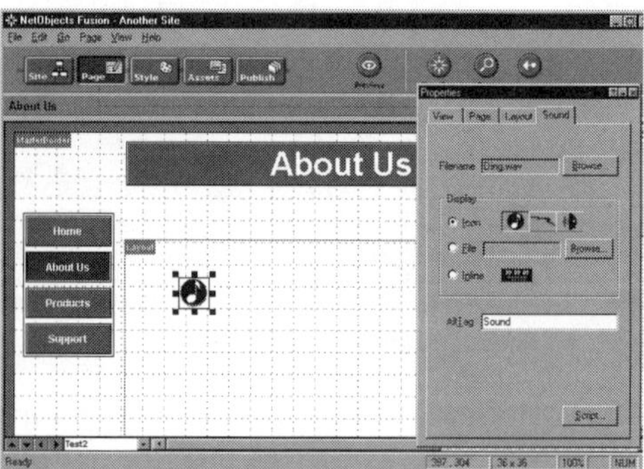


Figure 12.4
*The Sound tab is displayed in the Properties Palette.*

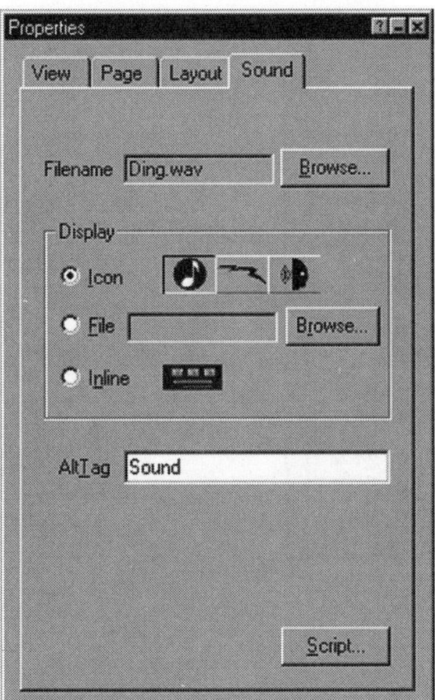


**Figure 12.5**
*Select the Sound tool.*

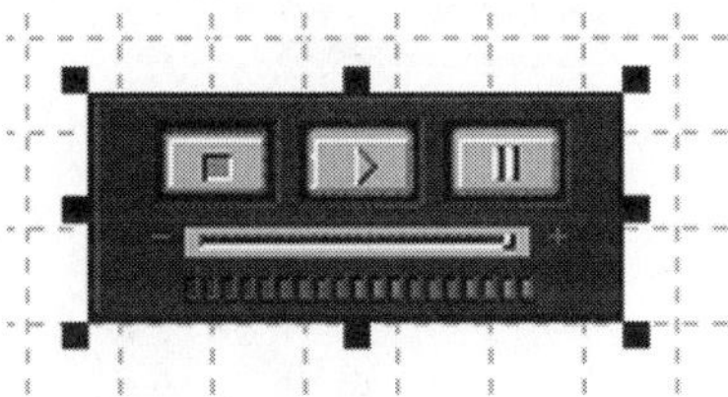

**Figure 12.6**
*The inline player control bar.*

### To set sound properties:

1. Select the desired sound element on a page.

   The Sound properties tab is displayed **(Figure 12.5)**.

2. Click the **Browse** button (*Mac users, click the Select... button*) opposite the **Filename** field to select a different sound file using the open dialog box.

3. Select one of the three **Display** options:

   **Icon** allows you to choose from three standard sound icons for use as the clickable sound button on your page.

   **File** allows you to choose a graphic file for use as the clickable sound button.

   **Inline** displays the standard inline player control bar **(Figure 12.6)** that visitors can use to play the sound.

4. Type any desired text in the **Alt-Tag** field for display if the Display graphics associated with the selected sound file aren't loaded by a visitor's browser.

## Adding Video

You can add digitized movies to your Fusion site that can be played online. You can add video files that open a new browser window and play when the user clicks a button. You can also add inline video files that play inside a frame on your page.

### To add a video file to a page:

1. Select the Video tool **(Figure 12.7)**.
2. Click and drag to create a box on your page.

   An open dialog box appears.
3. Select the desired file type(s) to display using the **Files of type** drop-down menu.
4. Select the desired video file.
5. Click the Open button.

   A video icon appears on the page, and the Video properties tab is displayed **(Figure 12.8)**.

### ✔ Tips

- Video file formats supported by Fusion are **mov** and **qt** (QuickTime), **mpeg** and **mpg**, and **avi**.
- Be sure to include links to download sites for browser plug-ins needed to view video files in your site.

**Figure 12.7**
*Select the Video tool.*

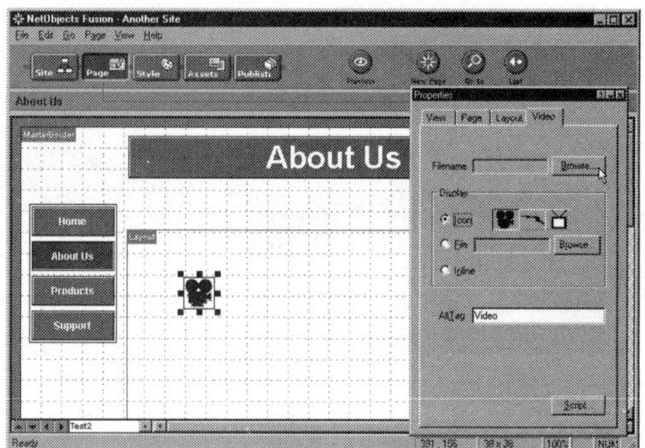


**Figure 12.8**
*The Video tab is displayed in the Properties Palette.*

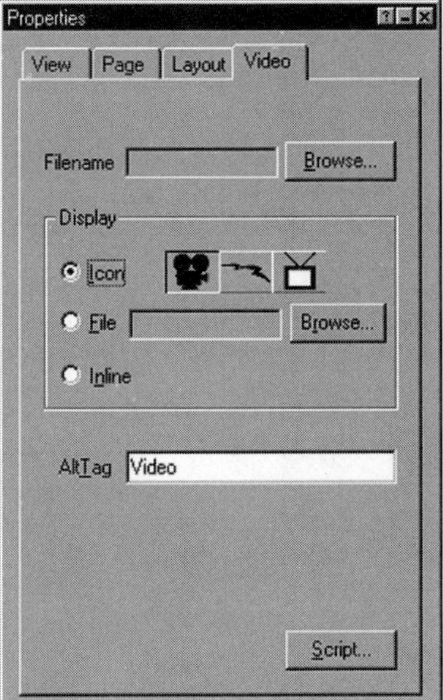


**Figure 12.9**
*The Video Properties tab.*

### To set video properties:

1. Select the desired video element on a page.

   The Video properties tab is displayed **(Figure 12.9)**.

2. Click the **Browse** button *(Mac users, click the Select... button)* opposite the **Filename** field to select a different video file using the open dialog box.

3. Select one of the three **Display** options:

   **Icon** allows you to choose from three standard video icons for use as the clickable button on your page for playing the video file.

   **File** allows you to choose a graphic file for use as the clickable video button.

   **Inline** displays the first frame of the video file inside the box you drew. The video file plays inside that box when the box is clicked.

4. Type any desired text in the **Alt-Tag** field for display if the Display graphics associated with the selected video file aren't loaded by a visitor's browser.

## To Add a Shockwave File to a Page

Shockwave files can be added to your site using the Shockwave tool. These files will be played inline on your Web pages only if visitors have the appropriate Shockwave plug-in installed for their browser.

### To add a video file to a page:

1. Select the Shockwave tool **(Figure 12.10)**.
2. Click and drag to create a box on your page.

   An open dialog box appears.
3. Select the desired file type(s) to display using the **Files of type** drop-down menu.
4. Select the desired Shockwave file **(Figure 12.11)**.
5. Click the Open button.

   A Made with Macromedia icon appears on the page, and the Shockwave properties tab is displayed **(Figure 12.12)**.

### ✔ Tips

- Shockwave file formats supported by Fusion are **dcr** (Shockwave for Director 4.0 and 5.0), **dir** (Director), **dxr** (Protected Director), and **swa** (Shockwave Audio).
- Be sure to include a link to a Shockwave plug-in download site if you include Shockwave files.
- NetObjects includes some Shockwave files you can use in your sites in the Parts\Plugin Parts\Shockwave folder.

**Figure 12.10**
*Select the Shockwave tool.*

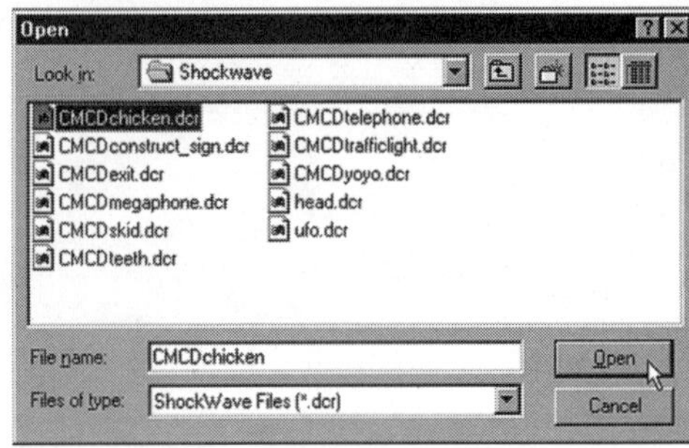


**Figure 12.11**
*Select the desired Shockwave file using the open dialog box.*

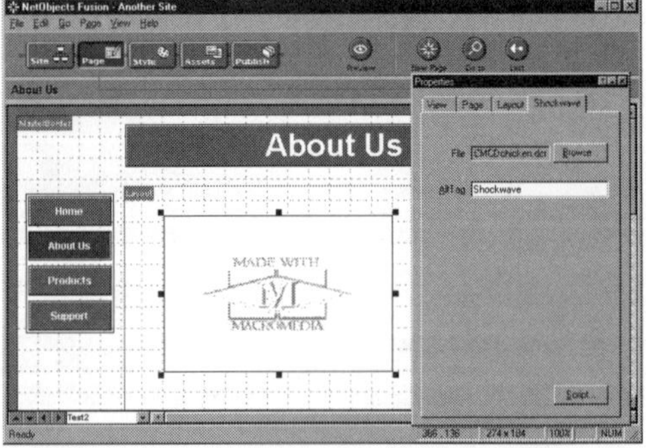


**Figure 12.12**
*The Shockwave tab is displayed in the Properties Palette.*



Adding Shockwave Files

**Figure 12.13**
*Select the Java Applet tool.*

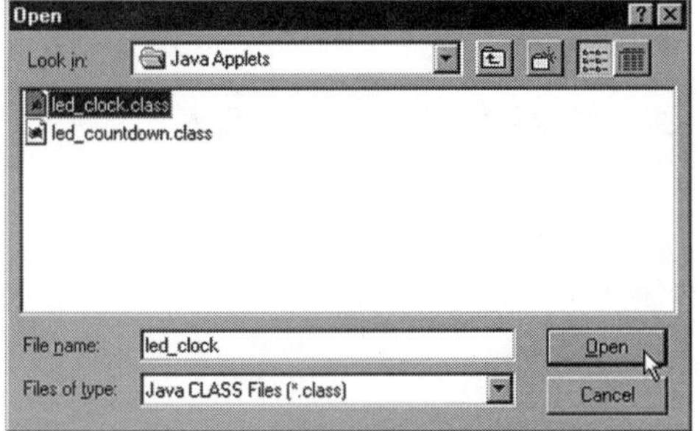


**Figure 12.14**
*Select the desired Java Applet file using the open dialog box.*

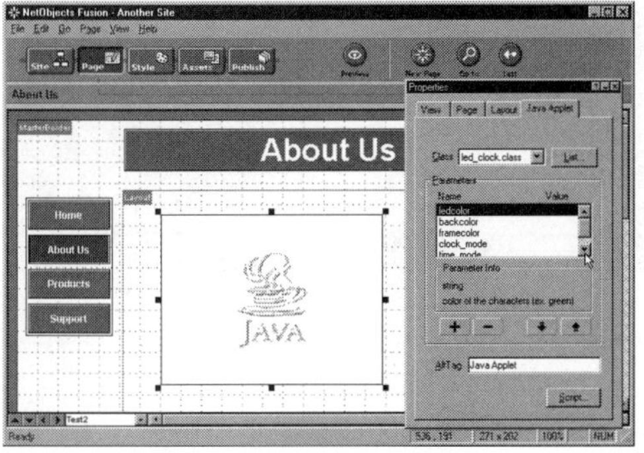


**Figure 12.15**
*The Java Applet is displayed in the Properties Palette.*

# Adding Java Applets

Java applets are small applications embedded in your pages that generally run on the "client side" of an Internet transaction. In other words, rather than running on a host computer, the application actually runs on the computer of the visitor to your site.

Standard Java applets can be added to your site and configured using the Java Applet properties tab.

### To add a Java applet to a page:

1. Select the Java Applet tool **(Figure 12.13)**.
2. Click and drag to create a box on your page.

   An open dialog box appears.
3. Select the desired Java Applet file **(Figure 12.14)**.
4. Click the Open button.

   A Java icon appears on the page, and the Java Applet properties tab is displayed **(Figure 12.15)**.

### To set Java Applet properties:

1. Select the desired Java applet element on a page.

   The Java Applet properties tab is displayed **(Figure 12.15)**.
2. To choose a different Java applet, choose from the **Class** drop-down list.

3. To add or delete applets to/from the Class drop-down list, click the **List** button opposite the Class field.

   The Java Applet Files dialog box is displayed **(Figure 12.16)**. Select an applet and click the **Delete** button to delete an applet. Use the **Add** button to display the Add Java Applet Files dialog box **(Figure 12.17)**.

   Using this dialog box, you can select an applet to add to the Java Applet Files dialog box (and to the Class drop-down list). Select an applet, and click Open.

4. To set applet parameters, double-click a Name in the Parameters list.

   The Enter Value dialog box is displayed with the name of the selected parameter in the Name field **(Figure 12.18)**. Use the information displayed in the Parameter Info area of the Java Applet properties tab for guidelines regarding valid Values for the selected parameter **(Figure 12.18)**.

5. To add or remove an applet parameter, click the + and − buttons in the Parameters area of the Java Applet properties tab respectively.

6. To change the order of parameters listed, click the ↓ and ↑ buttons.

7. To display alternative text for an applet which cannot be displayed by a browser, enter that text in the **Alt Tag** field.

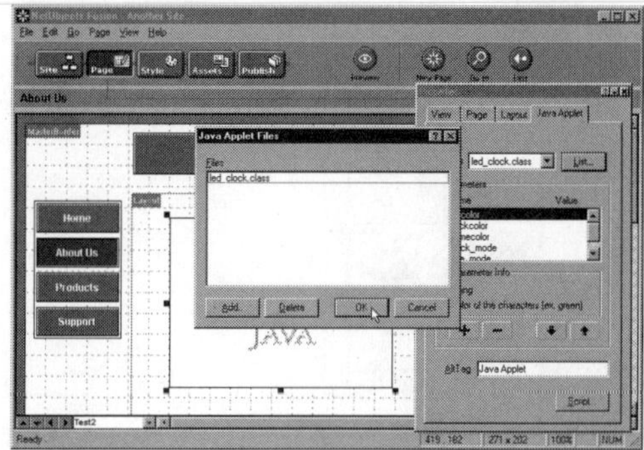

**Figure 12.16**
*Click the List button to display the Java Applet Files dialog box.*

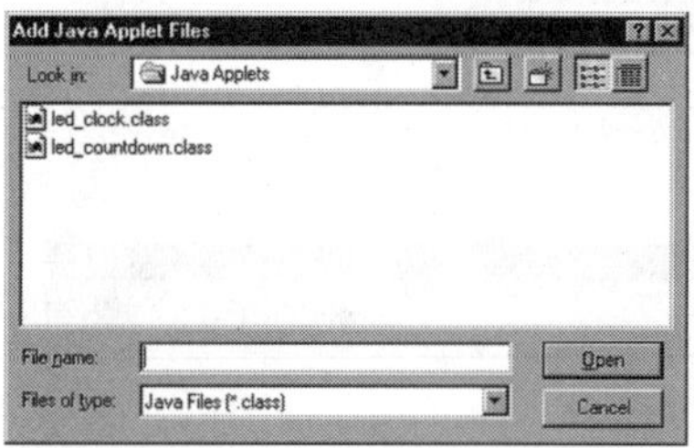


**Figure 12.17**
*Use the Add Java Applet Files dialog box to add an applet to the Class drop-down list.*

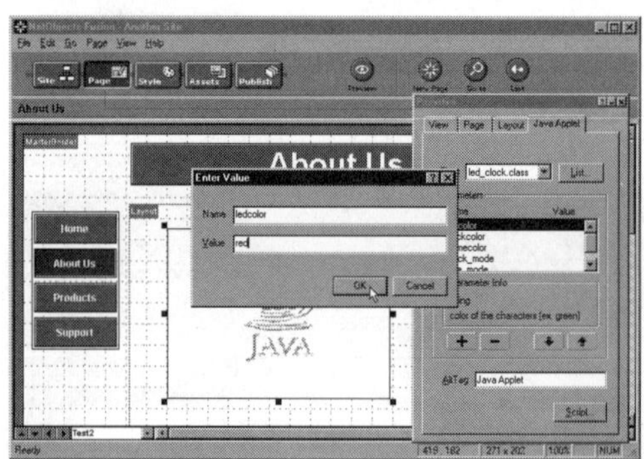

**Figure 12.18**
*Use the Enter Value dialog box to type values for the selected Java Applet parameter.*

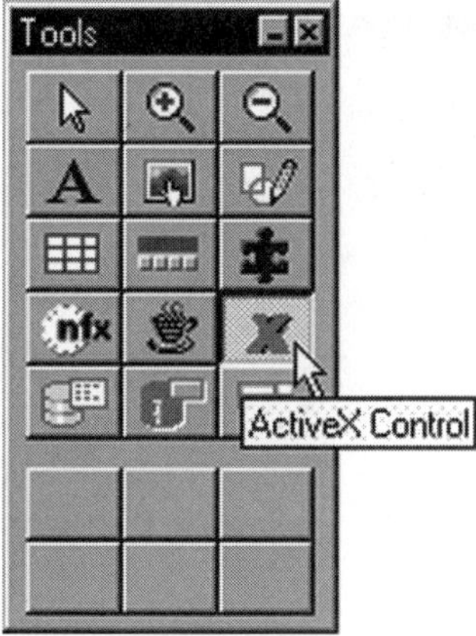


**Figure 12.19**
*Select the ActiveX tool.*

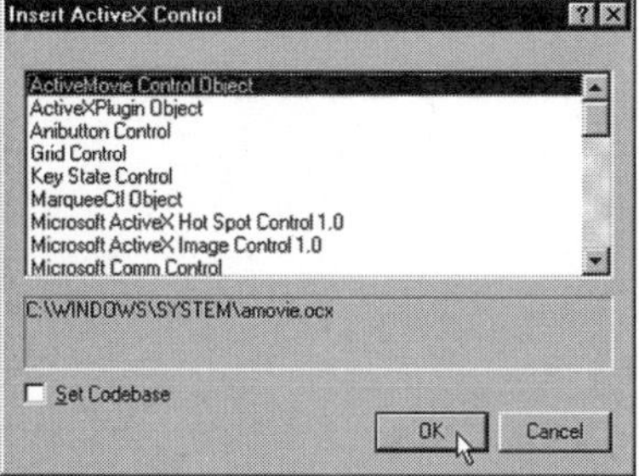


**Figure 12.20**
*Select the desired ActiveX control displayed.*

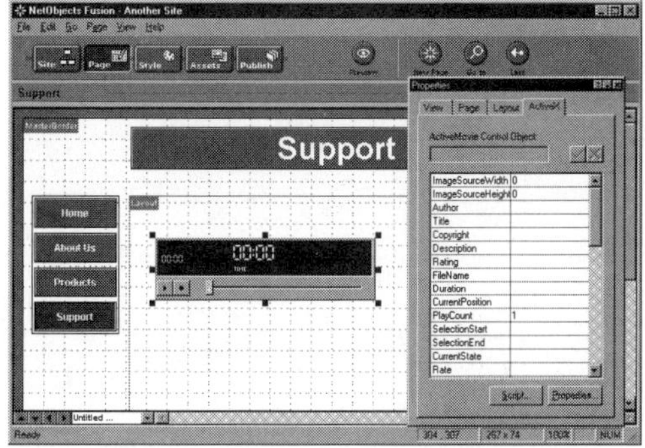


**Figure 12.21**
*The ActiveX control and the ActiveX properties tab are displayed.*

## Adding ActiveX Controls

ActiveX controls are one facility that allow you to add interactive and rich media features to your site. Microsoft Internet Explorer version 3.0 and later has built-in support for ActiveX controls.

### To add an ActiveX control to a page:

1. Select the ActiveX Control tool **(Figure 12.19)**.
2. Click and drag to create a box on your page.

   The Insert ActiveX Control dialog box is displayed **(Figure 12.20)**.This dialog box displays all of the ActiveX files (ocx) currently installed in your system. ActiveX control files can be downloaded from the Microsoft Web site.
3. Select the desired ActiveX control displayed, and click OK.

   The selected ActiveX control is displayed in the box you drew with the ActiveX Control tool, and the ActiveX properties tab is displayed **(Figure 12.21)**.
4. To edit parameters for the selected ActiveX control, select the desired parameter, and type a parameter value in the text field at the top of the properties tab.

   Confirm an edit by clicking the ✓ button. Cancel an edit by clicking the ✕ button.

5. Click the Properties button in the ActiveX properties tab to display the Control Properties dialog box for the selected ActiveX control **(Figure 12.2)**. You can use this dialog box to set additional properties.

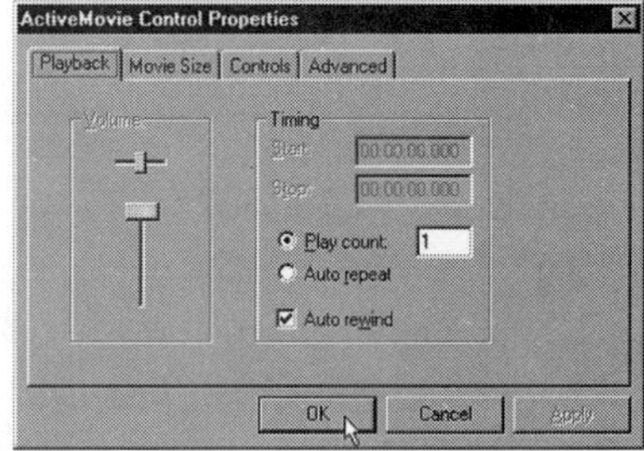


**Figure 12.22**
*Selected ActiveX control.*

## ✓ Tip

- ActiveX controls may become more widely supported by browsers as the technology matures, but it is important when adding ActiveX controls to your site that you remember only visitors using the Microsoft Internet Explorer will be able to enjoy the added capabilities you have provided.

# Forms

**Figure 13.1**
*Select the Forms tool in the Tools Palette.*

## Introducing Forms

Most browser support forms—interactive page elements with which you can request or submit information to a Web site's server. Common form elements include text fields, drop-down lists, checkboxes, and radio boxes. Web pages containing form elements generally also contain special buttons for submitting information and for resetting or clearing form information.

### To access the Forms tools:

Select the Forms tool **(Figure 13.1)** from the Tools Palette.

The six Forms tools are displayed in the bottom of the Tools Palette:

Button tool.

Checkbox tool.

Radio button tool.

Field Edit tool.

Multi Line field tool.

Combo Box tool.

✔ **Tip**

- Common gateway interface (CGI) scripts are used by the Web site server to handle information downloaded from forms. Because CGI support is completely up to the Web server administrator, you should check with your local Webmaster or Internet Service Provider (ISP) before implementing forms with Fusion. CGI scripts are discussed further later in this chapter.

## Adding Radio Buttons

Radio buttons consist of text and a small clickable circle. A selected radio button is displayed with a dot inside the circle. When a group of radio buttons appear on a page, only one can be selected at a time, and one radio button will always be selected. When a radio button is clicked, it is selected, and all other radio buttons in the group are deselected.

### To add radio buttons:

1. In Page View, select the Form Radio Button tool in the Tools Palette **(Figure 13.2)**.
2. Click and drag on the page to specify an area for the radio button.

   The new radio button appears on the page **(Figure 13.3)** with "Text" as its default label . The Radio Button properties tab is displayed in the Properties Palette.
3. Enter a name for the radio button group in the **Group Name** field **(Figure 13.3)**.

   Fusion will use the group name of each radio button to determine its logical grouping with other radio buttons on the page. Make sure the Group Name you enter is compatible with the CGI script you will be using to process the form.
4. In the **Button** field, enter the text you want displayed with the radio button on the page **(Figure 13.3)**.
5. In the **Value Sent** field, enter the value you want sent to the CGI script that processes the form **(Figure 13.3)**.

**Figure 13.2**
*Select the Forms Radio Button tool.*

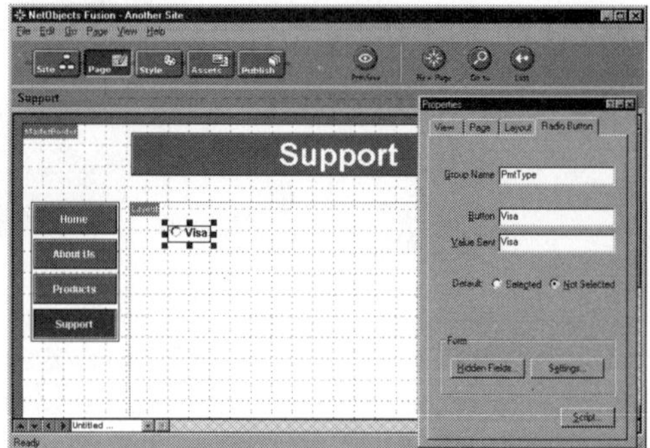


**Figure 13.3**
*Click and drag to draw an area for the radio button, then specify the Radio Button properties.*

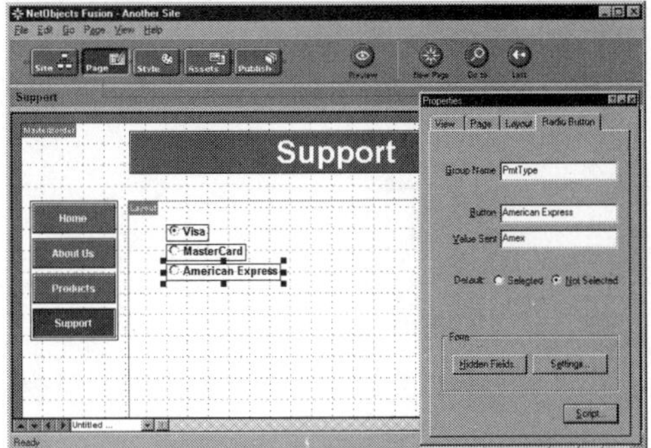

**Figure 13.4**
*Add more radio buttons, then arrange them as desired.*

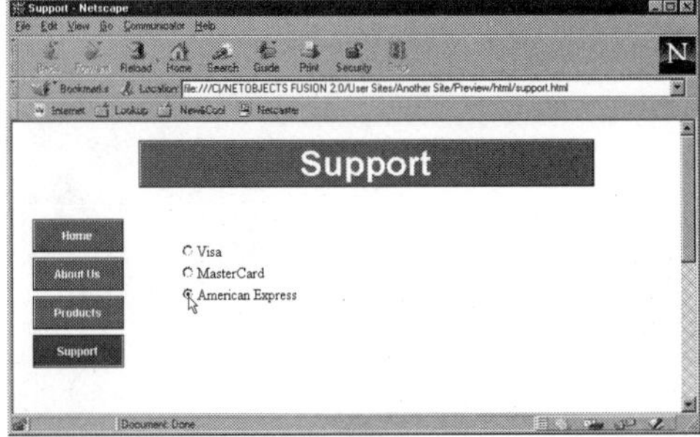

**Figure 13.5**
*Preview radio buttons in a Web browser to make sure they are arranged and appear as expected.*

6. Select one of the **Default** settings, Selected or Not selected.

   These settings affect the way in which the default radio button is displayed (filled or not) when the form is displayed. Visitors to your site can then select and deselect radio buttons as desired.

7. Repeat steps 1–6 to add more radio buttons in the same group.

   Make sure that you use the same Group Name for each radio button in a group **(Figure 13.4)**.

8. Use the Select tool to drag radio buttons into the desired positions on the page.

9. Preview your page in as many different Web browsers as you can **(Figure 13.5)**.

## ✓ Tips

- Your form may be arranged differently than you expect when previewed in a Web browser. In addition, different browsers may display form elements very differently.
- Radio buttons always appear in groups of two or more. If you are tempted to use a single radio button, use a check box instead.

## Adding Checkboxes

Checkboxes consist of text and a small clickable square. A selected checkbox is displayed with an X inside the clickable square. Checkboxes are used to select a number of options from a list or to select and deselect a single option. Unlike radio buttons, check boxes may be used singly as well as in groups.

**Figure 13.6**
*Select the Forms Checkbox tool.*

### To add checkboxes:

1. In Page View, select the Forms Checkbox tool in the Tools Palette **(Figure 13.6)**.
2. Click and drag on the page to specify an area for a checkbox.

   The new checkbox appears on the page with Text as its default label **(Figure 13.7)**. The Checkbox properties tab is displayed in the Properties Palette.
3. Enter a name for the checkbox in the **Name** field **(Figure 13.7)**.

   This is the name your CGI script will use to identify the data downloaded from this form element, so make sure the name you enter is compatible with the CGI script you will be using to process the form.
4. In the **Label Text** field, enter the text you want displayed with the checkbox on the page **(Figure 13.7)**.
5. In the **Value** field, you can enter the value you want to send to the CGI script that processes the form **(Figure 13.7)**.

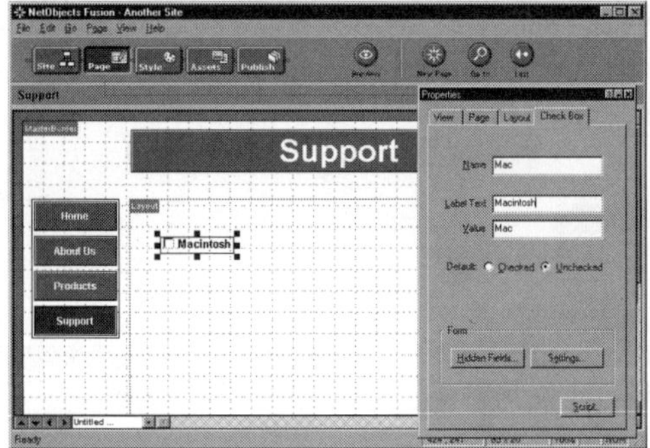


**Figure 13.7**
*Click and drag to draw an area for the checkbox, then specify the Checkbox properties.*

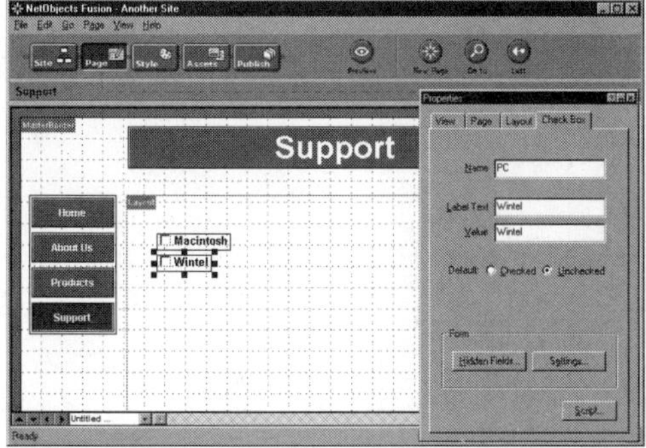


**Figure 13.8**
*If you wish, add more checkboxes, then arrange them as desired.*

6. Select one of the **Default** settings, Selected or Not selected.

   These settings affect the way in which the default checkbox is displayed (checked or unchecked) when the form is displayed. Visitors to your site can then select and deselect checkboxes as desired.

7. To create a list using checkboxes, you can repeat steps 1–6 to add more checkboxes **(Figure 13.8)**.

8. Use the Select tool to drag checkboxes into the desired positions on the page.

9. Preview your page in as many different Web browsers as you can **(Figure 13.9)**.

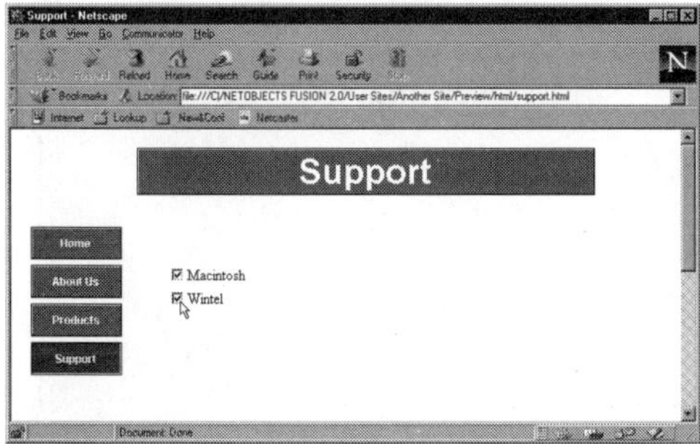


**Figure 13.9**
*Preview checkboxes in a Web browser to make sure they are arranged and appear as expected.*

### ✔ Tip

- Your form may be arranged differently than you expect when previewed in a Web browser. In addition, different browsers may display form elements very differently.

## Adding a Single-Line Field

Text fields are used for submitting data that cannot be easily implemented using checkboxes, radio buttons, or menus. Fusion offers two type of text fields, a single-line field and a multiple-line field. A single-line text field can be of any length. In fact, you can configure a field to allow text entered to extend beyond the visible length of the field.

### To add a single-line field:

1. In Page View, select the Form Edit Field tool in the Tools Palette **(Figure 13.10)**.
2. Click and drag on the page to specify an area for a single-line field.

   The new field appears on the page, and the Single Line properties tab is displayed in the Properties Palette **(Figure 13.11)**.
3. Enter a name for the field in the **Name** field **(Figure 13.11)**.

   This is the name your CGI script will use to identify the data downloaded from this form element, so make sure the name you enter is compatible with the CGI script you will be using to process the form.
4. In the **Text** field, enter any text you want displayed in the field as a default. Users will then be able to change this text.
5. In the **Visible Length** field, specify a character length for the field **(Figure 13.12)**.

   The field will be displayed using the length specified.

**Figure 13.10**
*Select the Forms Edit Field tool.*

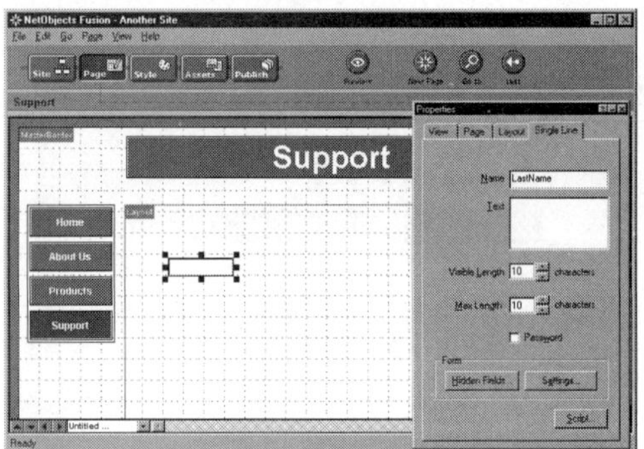


**Figure 13.11**
*Click and drag to draw an area for the text field.*

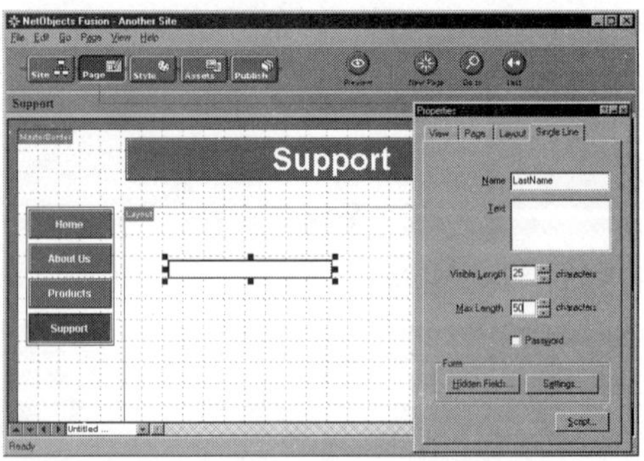


**Figure 13.12**
*Specify the Visible Length in characters for the field.*

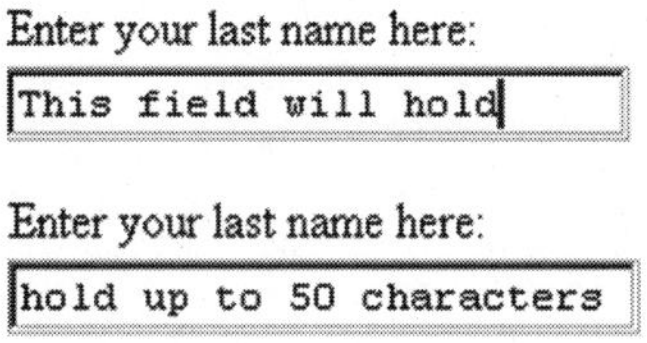

Enter your last name here:

This field will hold

Enter your last name here:

hold up to 50 characters

**Figure 13.13**
*Text scrolls left when the Max Length of a field is longer than its Visible length (onscreen label added separately).*

Sensitive data:

**Figure 13.14**
*Use the Password option to protect user-entered data from prying eyes (onscreen label added separately).*

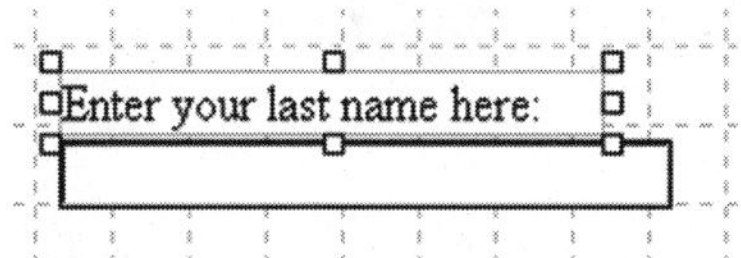


**Figure 13.15**
*If you wish, add a field label using the text tool.*

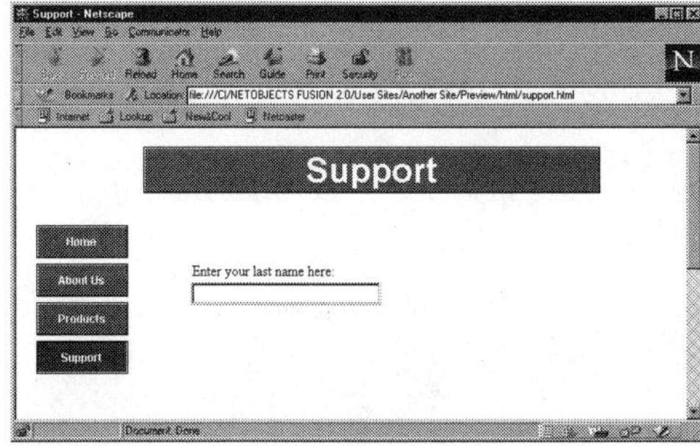


**Figure 13.16**
*Preview text fields in a Web browser to make sure they appear as expected.*

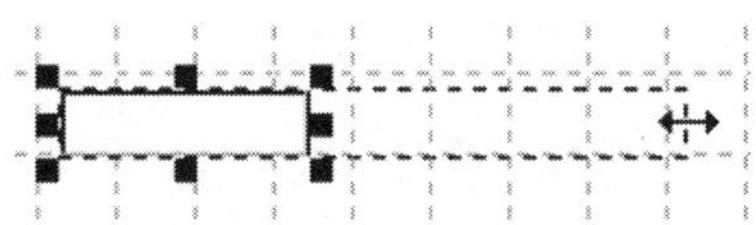

**Figure 13.17**
*Fields cannot be resized by dragging their handles.*

6. In the **Max Length** field, specify the maximum number of characters allowed in the field.

   For good manners sake, visitors to your site should be able to at least "fill" the field with text, so Max Length should not be less than that specified for Visible Length.

   If you set Max Length to a number greater than the Visible Length, most browsers will scroll text entered to the left as data is entered so that the cursor is always visible **(Figure 13.13)**.

7. If you will be using the text field for entering information like credit card numbers or user passwords that visitors may not want displayed, select the **Password** option **(Figure 13.14)**.

   The Password option places a bullet in the field for each character typed by the visitor, thereby keeping the entered data private from onlookers.

8. If you wish to add an onscreen label to a text field, use the text tool to do so (see Chapter 8 for working with the text tool)**(Figure 13.15)**.

9. Preview your page in as many different Web browsers as you can to ensure that your text fields and labels are displayed as expected **(Figure 13.16)**.

### ✔ Tip

- While fields have draggable handles **(Figure 13.17)**, they cannot be resized by dragging.

## Adding a Multiple-Line Field

Multiple-line fields differ from single-line fields in that they can hold more than one line of text.

**Figure 13.18**
*Select the Forms Multi-Line tool.*

### To add a multiple-line field:

1. In Page View, select the Form Multi-Line tool in the Tools Palette **(Figure 13.18)**.
2. Click and drag on the page to specify an area for a multiple-line field.

   The new field appears on the page, and the Multi-Line properties tab is displayed in the Properties Palette **(Figure 13.19)**.
3. Enter a name for the field in the **Name** field **(Figure 13.19)**.

   This is the name your CGI script will use to identify the data downloaded from this form element, so make sure the name you enter is compatible with the CGI script you will be using to process the form.
4. In the **Text** field, enter any text you want displayed in the field as a default.
5. In the **Visible Length** field, specify the width of the field in *characters*.

   The field will be displayed using the length specified **(Figure 13.20)**.
6. In the **Visible Height** field, specify the maximum number of *lines of text* that will be visible in the field.

   The field will be displayed using the height specified **(Figure 13.20)**.

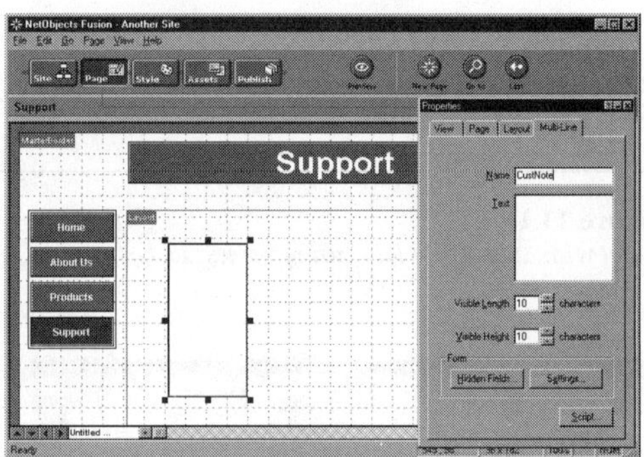


**Figure 13.19**
*Click and drag to draw an area for the multi-line field.*

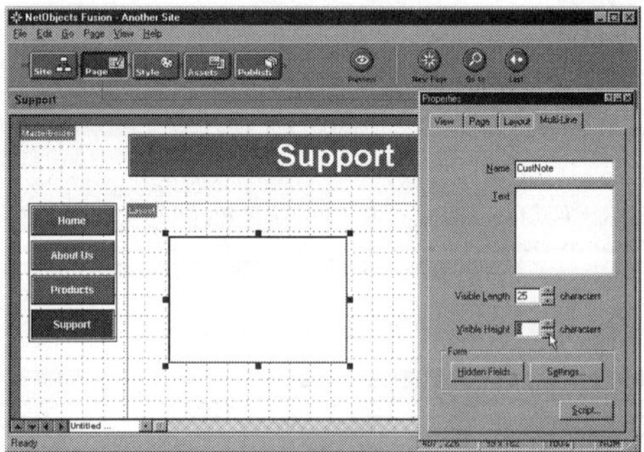


**Figure 13.20**
*Specify the Visible Length and Visible Height in characters.*

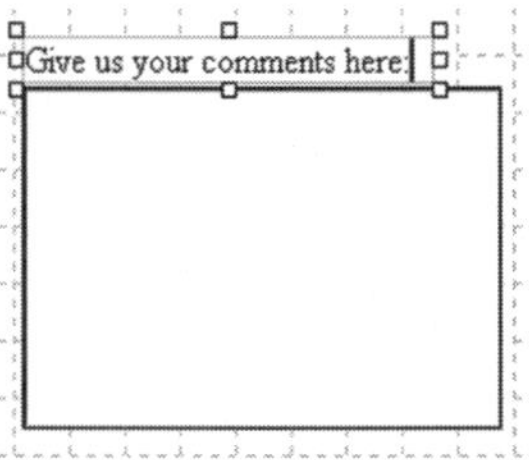


**Figure 13.21**
*If you wish, add a field label using the text tool.*

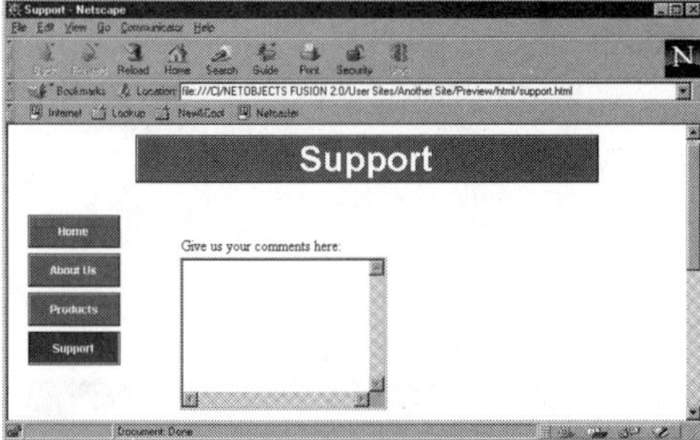


**Figure 13.22**
*Preview text fields in a Web browser to make sure they appear as expected.*

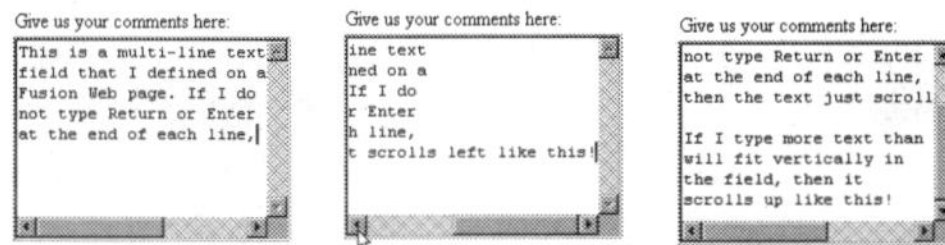


**Figure 13.23**
*Text scrolls left and up when the right and bottom boundaries of the field are encountered.*

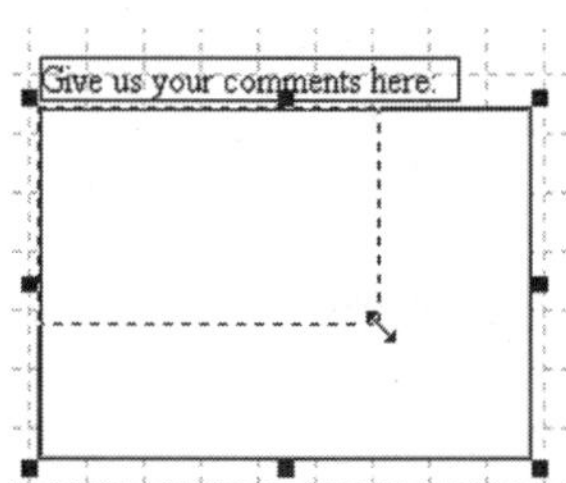


**Figure 13.24**
*Fields cannot be resized by dragging their handles.*

7. If you wish to add an onscreen label to a text field, use the text tool to do so (see Chapter 8 for working with the text tool)**(Figure 13.21)**.

8. Preview your page in as many different Web browsers as you can to ensure that your fields and labels are displayed as expected **(Figure 13.22)**.

## ✓ Tips

- When visitors to your site enter text in a multiple-line field, text will not automatically wrap when the right edge of the field is reached. Instead, entered text appears on the same line until Return or Enter is pressed. Likewise, text scrolls upward when the maximum number of visible lines have been filled **(Figure 13.23)**.
- While fields have draggable handles **(Figure 13.24)**, they cannot be resized by dragging.

## Adding a Combo Box

Fusion's Combo Boxes allow you to create drop-down menus and scrolling list boxes from which visitors to your site can select one or more items.

**Figure 13.25**
*Select the Forms Combo Box tool.*

### To add a Combo Box:

1. In Page View, select the Form Combo Box tool in the Tools Palette **(Figure 13.25)**.
2. Click and drag on the page to specify an area for a Combo Box.

   The new field appears on the page, and the Combo Box properties tab is displayed in the Properties Palette **(Figure 13.26)**.
3. Enter a name for the field in the **Name** field **(Figure 13.26)**.

   This is the name your CGI script will use to identify the data downloaded from this form element, so make sure the name you enter is compatible with the CGI script you will be using to process the form.
4. Select a Combo Box **Type**:

   **drop-down List** displays a menu as previewed in **Figure 13.27**. Only one item at a time can be selected using a drop-down list.

   **List Box** displays a scrollable box as previewed in **Figure 13.28**. Multiple items can be selected in a List Box if the **Allow multiple selections** option is checked.
5. If you've selected List Box as your Combo Box type, then the **Visible Height** field is available. Specify here the maximum number of lines of text that will be visible in the List Box.

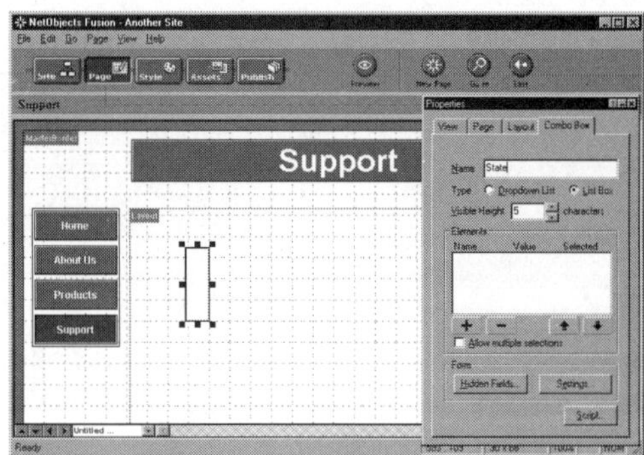


**Figure 13.26**
*Click and drag to draw an area for the Combo Box field.*

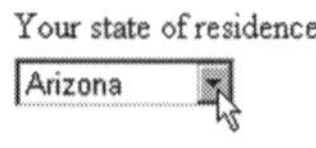


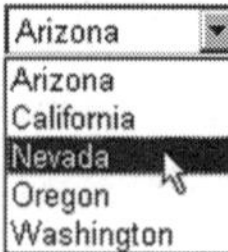


**Figure 13.27**
*drop-down List*

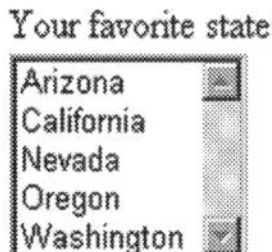


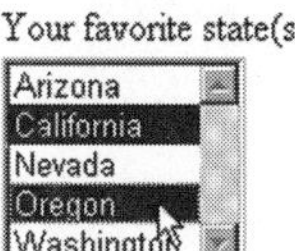


**Figure 13.28**
*List Box*

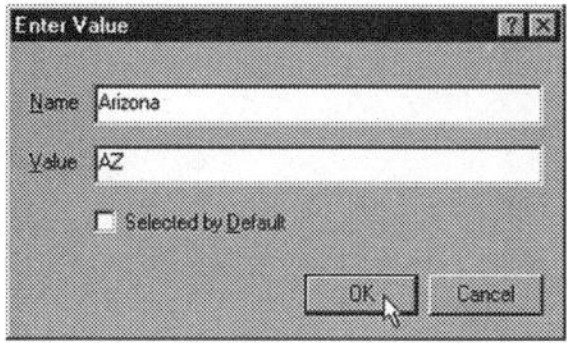


**Figure 13.29**
*Use the Enter Value dialog box to enter list element information.*

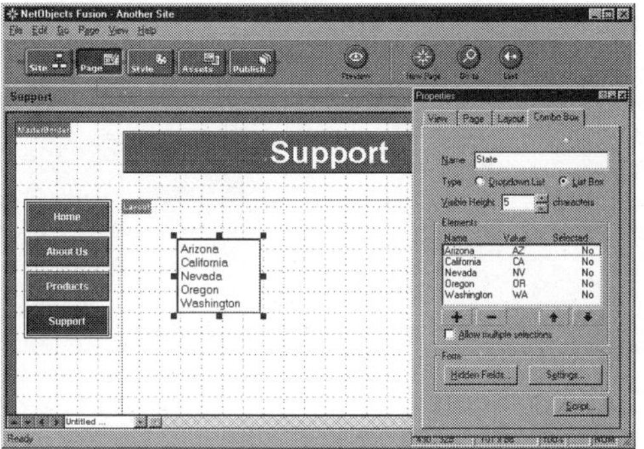


**Figure 13.30**
*A List Box with five elements entered.*

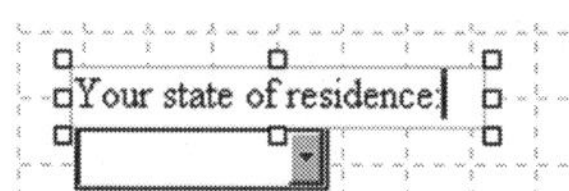


**Figure 13.31**
*Use the text tool to add a label to a drop-down List or List Box.*

6. Click the **+** button to add a list item.

   The Enter Value dialog box is displayed **(Figure 13.29)**.

7. Enter the item name in the **Name** field (make sure the name is consistent with the CGI you'll be using).
8. Type the text you wish displayed as the list item in the **Value** field.
9. Click **Selected by Default** if you want this list item automatically selected when the page containing this Combo Box is displayed.
10. Click OK

    The new item is displayed in the Elements list in the Combo Box properties tab.

11. Repeat steps 6–10 to add other list items **(Figure 13.30)**.
12. Use the ↑ ↓ buttons to reorder items in the elements list.
13. If you wish to add an onscreen label to a Combo Box, use the text tool to do so (see Chapter 8 for working with the text tool) **(Figure 13.31)**.

## ✔ Tips

- While fields have draggable handles **(Figure 13.21)**, they cannot be resized by dragging.
- To remove an element from the list, select it and click the **–** button.

## Adding Reset and Submit Buttons

Two typical buttons you will find on most Web pages containing form elements are reset and submit buttons. The reset button is used for clearing visitor-entered information from the form, and for "resetting" the form to its default values. The submit button is used for submitting a completed form to the Web site's server for processing.

To create a reset button, you will use the Button tool on the Tools Palette. To create a submit button, you can can either use the Button tool, or you can use the NetObjects Component, AutoForm (see Chapter 14 for other NetObjects Components).

If you will be using your own CGI script to handle the form (or a CGI script from a third party), then use the Button tool to create your submit button. Otherwise, you can use the AutoForm component which automatically uses the Forms-Handler CGI script that comes with Fusion.

### To add a reset or submit button using the Button tool:

1. In Page View display the page containing your form, and select the Form Button tool in the Tools Palette **(Figure 13.32)**.
2. Click and drag on the page to specify an area for the button.

   The new button appears on the page, and the Button properties tab is displayed in the Properties Palette.

**Figure 13.32**
*Select the Forms Button tool.*

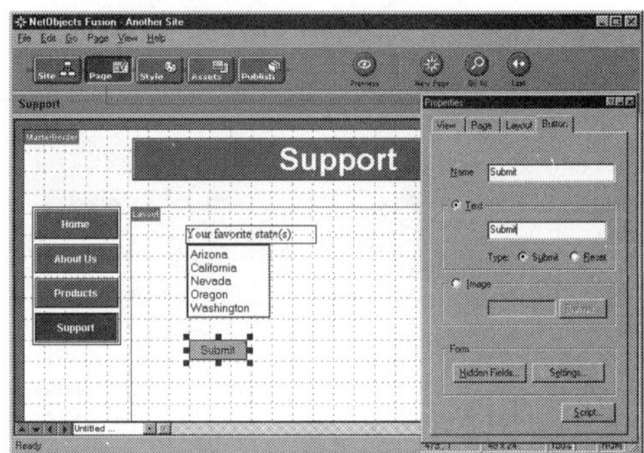


**Figure 13.33**
*Enter a name for the button and text it will display (if desired).*

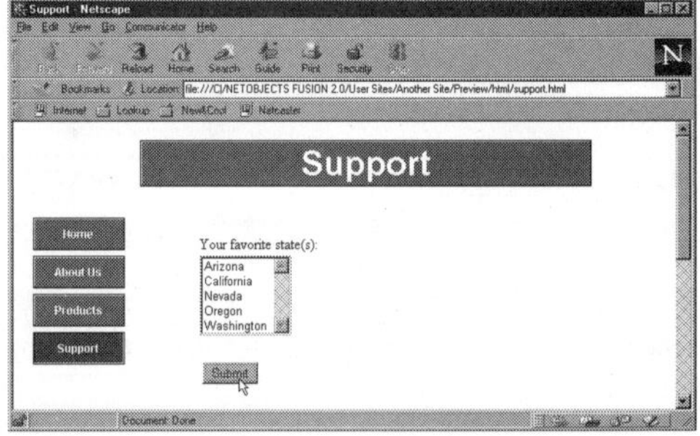


**Figure 13.34**
*Submit button previewed in Netscape Navigator.*

**Figure 13.35**
*Select the AutoForm tool.*

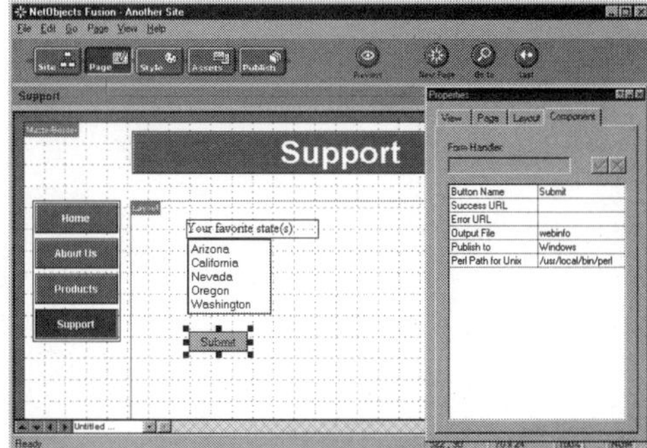


**Figure 13.36**
*The new AutoForm button appears on the page, and the Component properties tab is displayed.*

3. Enter a name for the button in the **Name** field **(Figure 13.33)**.

   Use the name called for by the CGI script you will use.

4. Select a either the **Text** or **Image** option.

5. If you've selected the Text option, enter the text you want displayed in the button in the field provided.

   If you've selected the Image option, click the Browse button (*Mac users click the Select... button)* to display the dialog box, and select an image to use for the button.

6. In the Text area of the Button properties tab, select a button **Type**, either Submit or Reset.

7. If the CGI script you will be using requires hidden fields, click the Hidden Fields button on the Button properties tab.

   See the last section in this chapter for more on hidden fields.

### To add a submit button using the AutoForm component:

1. In Page View display the page containing your form,

2. Select the NetObjects Components button, then select the AutoForm tool in the Tools Palette **(Figure 13.35)**.

3. Click and drag on the page to specify an area for the submit button.

   The new button appears on the page, and the Component properties tab is displayed in the Properties Palette with the name Form Handler at the top **(Figure 13.36)**.

**4.** Set each of the following Auto-Form properties by clicking the property and setting its value in the field provided near the top of the properties tab **(Figure 13.37)**:

**Button Name** is the name you want displayed on the button. The button will automatically adjust its length to fit the name you specify.

**Output File** is the name of the file on the Web site server to which the Forms-Handler.cgi will write information submitted using your form. This file will be created by the CGI script in the following folders on the Web server:

***c:\webdata*** on Windows based servers.

***.../your_site_folder/assets/webdata*** on Mac and Unix Web servers.

**Perl Path for Unix** is required for the Forms-Handler.cgi. You will need to get this information from your local Webmaster or Internet Service Provider.

Click the ✕ button to cancel a change to a property. *Mac users select Cancel.*

Click the ✓ button to confirm a change. *Mac users select OK*

**5.** Set each of the following Auto-Form properties by double-clicking the property.

**Success URL** is the page you want to display when the form is successfully submitted. You must create this page in your Web site.

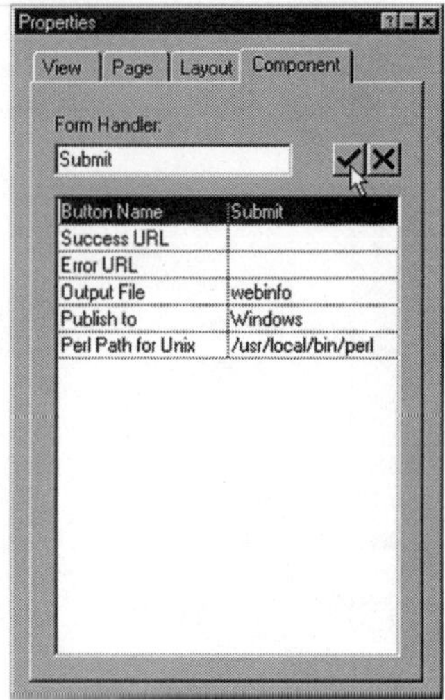


**Figure 13.37**
*Click a property and change its value in the field provided.*

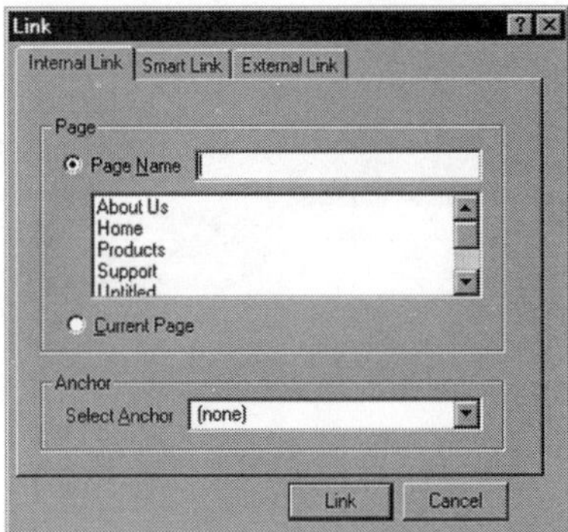


**Figure 13.38**
*Use the Link dialog box to set the success and error pages.*

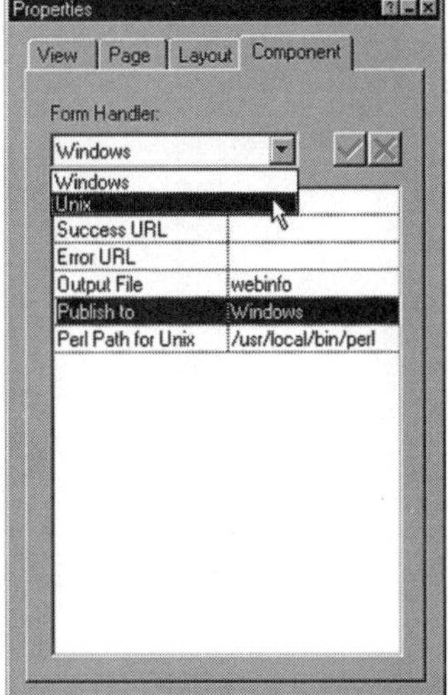


**Figure 13.39**
*Select Windows or Unix from the drop-down menu for the Publish to property.*

**Error URL** is the page you want displayed when the form submission fails for some reason. You must create this page in your site.

The Link dialog box is displayed **(Figure 13.38)**. Use the Link dialog box to select links to desired success and error pages (see Chapter 9 for more on links).

6. Set the **Publish to** property by clicking it and selecting Windows or Unix from the drop-down menu at the top of the properties tab **(Figure 13.39)**.

   Check with your local Webmaster or Internet Service Provider if you're not sure what type of server your site is being published to.

## ✓ Tip

- Check the AutoForm usage note available on NetObjects Web site (**www.netobjects.com/support**) for up-to-date information on configuring your Web server for use with Forms-Handler.cgi.

## Adding Hidden Fields

If you are not using the AutoForm component for your submit button, and are therefore not using the Forms-Handler.cgi provided with NetObjects Fusion, then you will need to define the hidden fields required by your chosen CGI.

Hidden fields typically include the URLs of pages to which to you send visitors when a form is successfully submitted or when a form fails to submit correctly. Other typical hidden fields include a subject for an e-mail message and a recipient e-mail address (for forms that send an e-mail message).

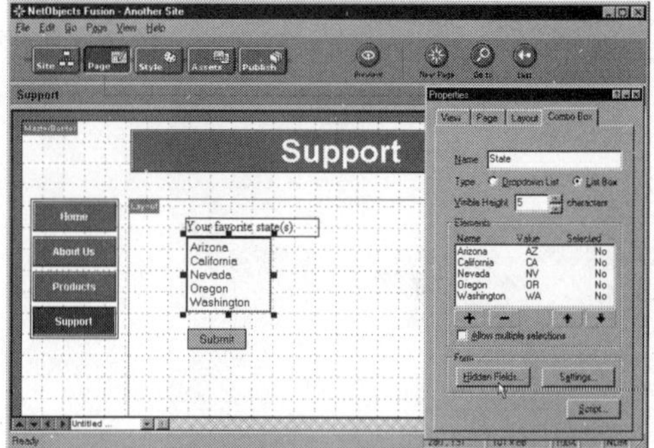


**Figure 13.40**
*Select a form element, and click the Hidden Fields button in the displayed properties tab.*

### To add hidden fields:

1. In Page View, select any form element on the page.
2. In the properties tab displayed, click the Hidden Fields button **(Figure 13.40)**.

   The Hidden Fields dialog box is displayed **(Figure 13.41)**. All of the hidden fields currently defined for the form are listed.
3. Click the + button to add a new hidden field to the form.

   The Enter Value dialog box is displayed.
4. Enter a name for the hidden field in the **Name** field **(Figure 13.42)**.

   Make sure the name you use is the one (exactly) called for by your CGI script.
5. Enter the value for the field in the **Value** field.
6. Click OK.

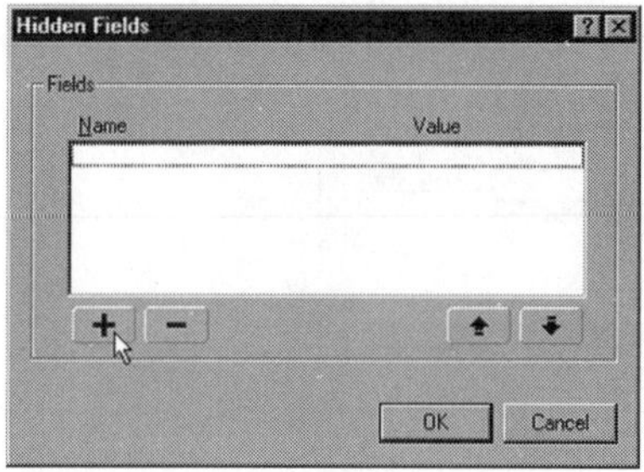


**Figure 13.41**
*The Hidden Fields dialog box is displayed.*

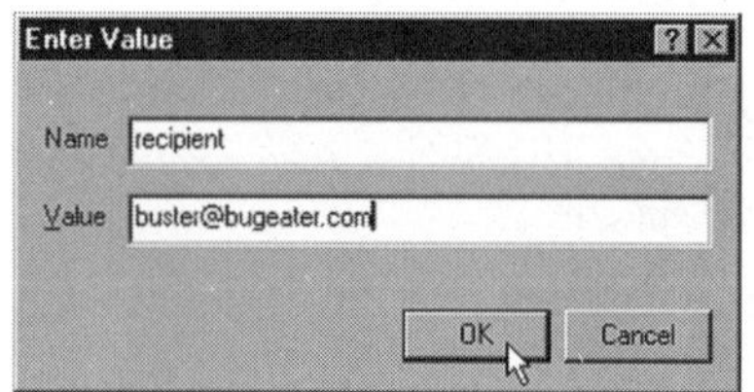


**Figure 13.42**
*Type a name and value for the new hidden field, then click OK.*

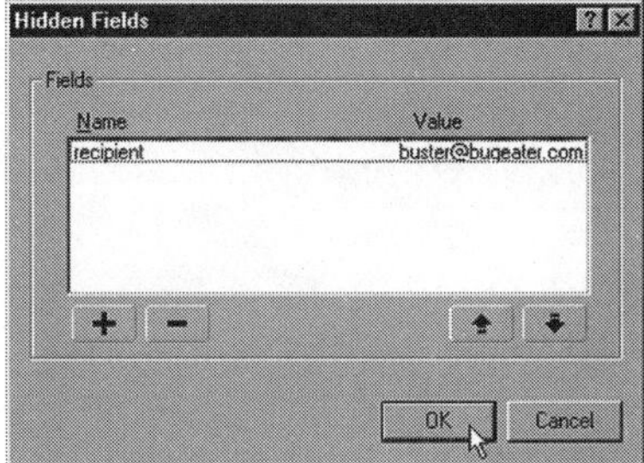


**Figure 13.43**
*The new hidden field is listed in the Hidden Fields dialog box.*

The new hidden field is displayed in the Hidden Fields dialog box **(Figure 13.43)**.

7. Repeat steps 3–6 to add all of the hidden fields required by your CGI.

8. Click OK in the Hidden Fields dialog box when all of the needed hidden fields have been entered.

✔ **Tip**

- You need only add hidden fields using one form element, as all form elements share the same Hidden Fields and Settings information.

## Applying a CGI Script

If you are not using the AutoForm component for your submit button, and are therefore not using the Forms-Handler.cgi provided with NetObjects Fusion, then you will need to specify which CGI script you will be using to process your form. You need only apply a CGI script to one form element.

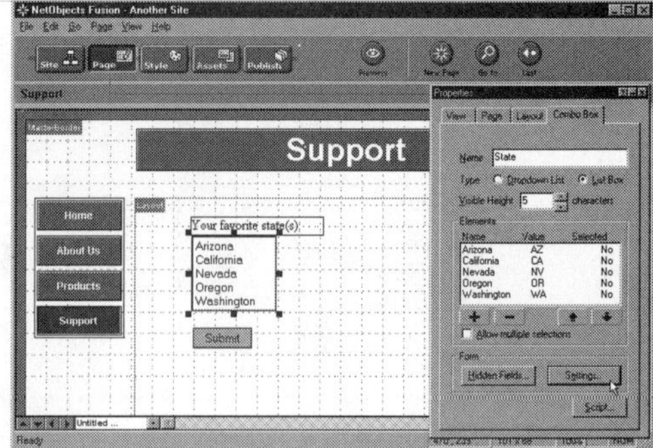


**Figure 13.44**
*Select a form element, and click the Settings button in the displayed properties tab.*

### To apply a CGI script:

1. In Page View, select any form element on the page.
2. In the properties tab displayed, click the Settings button **(Figure 13.44)**.

   The Form Settings dialog box is displayed **(Figure 13.45)**.
3. Enter a name for the form in the **Form Name** field **(Figure 13.45)**.
4. Click the Browse button (*Mac users click the Select... button*) to select the desired CGI script.

   The open dialog box is displayed **(Figure 13.46)**.
5. Use the open dialog box to select the desired CGI script, then click Open.

   When you publish your site, the path shown in the File field in the Form Settings dialog box will be used by Fusion to copy the CGI script to the server.
6. In the **Action** field, enter the URL where the selected CGI will be located once your site is published.

   When the submit button on your form is selected, the CGI script located at the address specified in the Action field will be executed.
7. Click OK.

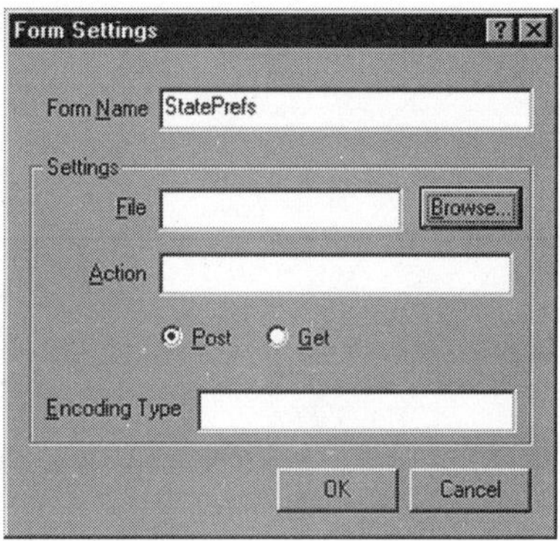


**Figure 13.45**
*The Hidden Fields dialog box is displayed.*

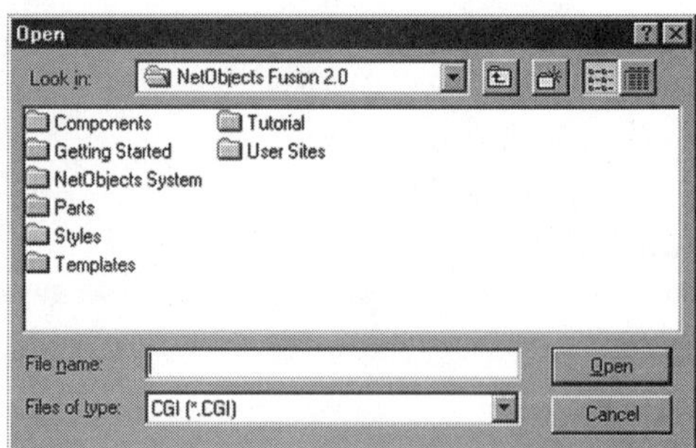


**Figure 13.46**
*Select the desired CGI script using the open dialog box.*

# NetObjects Components

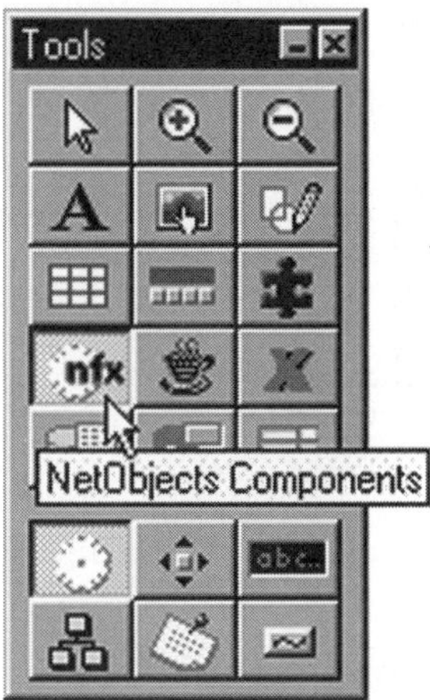


**Figure 14.1**
*Select the NetObjects Components tool in the Tools Palette.*

## Using the NetObjects Components Tools

Fusion provides a number of small applications you can embed in Web pages by clicking and dragging. These applications, called NetObjects Components, add advanced functionality to your Web pages which would otherwise be more difficult to achieve through custom scripting and/or programming.

### To access the NetObjects Components tools:

Select the NetObjects Components tool **(Figure 14.1)** from the Tools Palette.

The six NetObjects Components tools are displayed in the bottom of the Tools Palette:

- Additional NetObjects Components (Rotating Picture, Picture Loader, and Time Based Picture)
- DynaButtons
- Ticker Tape
- SiteMapper
- Message Board
- AutoForm (covered in Chapter 13)

### ✔ Tip

- When you use rich and interactive media such as NetObjects Components in your site, don't forget that some visitors will not be using browsers capable of displaying such information.

## Adding a Rotating Picture

You can create the illusion of a rotating image by displaying different pictures in succession to create an animation effect. The Rotating Picture component allows you to easily place and set up a rotating picture on your Web pages.

### To add a rotating picture:

1. Select the secondary NetObjects Components tool **(Figure 14.2)**.
2. Click on the page where you wish to place the rotating picture.

   The Installed Components dialog box appears **(Figure 14.3)**.
3. Select Rotating Picture, and click OK.

   The Component properties tab is displayed, and an element appears on the page **(Figure 14.4)**. This element displays the first image defined for the rotating picture.

   The name of the selected NetObjects Component, Rotating Picture, is displayed at the top of the properties tab.
4. Set the first two properties of the the Rotating Picture by clicking each property and setting its value in the field provided near the top of the properties tab.

   **Pause Time (Seconds)** is the amount of time each image is displayed.

   **Number of Images** is the total number of images to be displayed.

   Confirm a change made to a property by clicking the ✓ button. *Mac users click OK.*

**Figure 14.2**
*Select the NetObjects Components tool.*

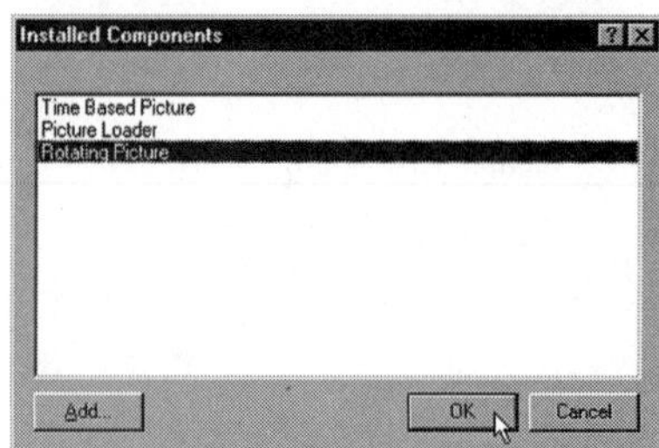


**Figure 14.3**
*Select the Rotating Picture, and click OK.*

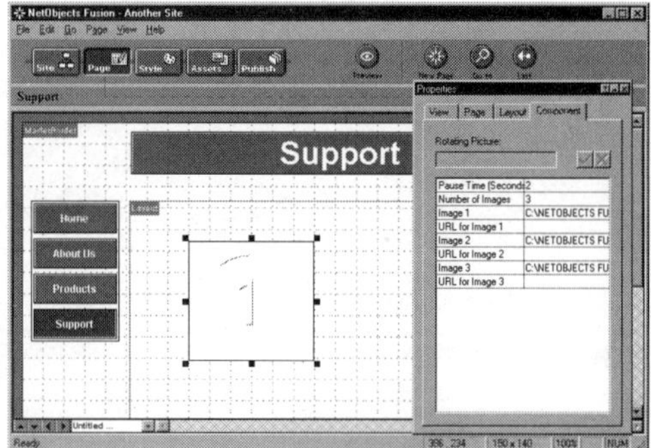


**Figure 14.4**
*The Component tab appears in the Properties Palette.*

**Figure 14.5**
*Rotating Picture (with the default images and properties) previewed in Netscape Navigator.*

Cancel a change by clicking the ✖ button. *Mac users click Cancel.*

5. Set the remaining properties of the Rotating Picture:

   **Image 1, 2, & 3** are the paths and file names of the first, second, and third images to be displayed.

   **URL for Image 1, 2, & 3** are the URLs of links for each image (if desired) to be displayed.

   Use the [...] button to display the dialog box when one of the Image or URL properties is selected.

   **or**

   Double-click Image and URL properties to display the dialog box.

6. Test your new rotating picture **(Figure 14.5)** by previewing, staging, or publishing your site (see Chapter 17 and page 84).

   Notice when you preview, stage, or publish your site that Java is initialized by your browser (assuming you are using a Java compatible browser) and that the NetObjects Component is an applet running on the page.

## ✔ Tip

- See Chapter 9 for more on using the Links dialog box.

## Adding Time Based Pictures

You can add a place holder to your site in which different pictures are displayed at different times of the day. You can even associate different links with each picture to change the look and functionality of your site for different times of day.

### To add time based pictures:

1. Select the secondary NetObjects Components tool **(Figure 14.6)**.
2. Click on the page where you wish to place the time based pictures.

   The Installed Components dialog box appears **(Figure 14.7)**.
3. Select Time Based Picture, and click OK.

   The Component properties tab is displayed, and an element appears on the page **(Figure 14.8)**.

   The name of the selected NetObjects Component, Time Based Picture, is displayed at the top of the properties tab.
4. Set the following properties by clicking each property and setting its value in the field provided near the top of the properties tab.

   **Number of Images** is the total number of images to be displayed.

   **Start Time for Image 1, 2, & 3** are the times of day at which you wish each image displayed.

   Confirm a change made to a property by clicking the ✓ button. *Mac users click OK.*

   Cancel a change by clicking the ✗ button. *Mac users click Cancel.*

**Figure 14.6**
*Select the NetObjects Components tool.*

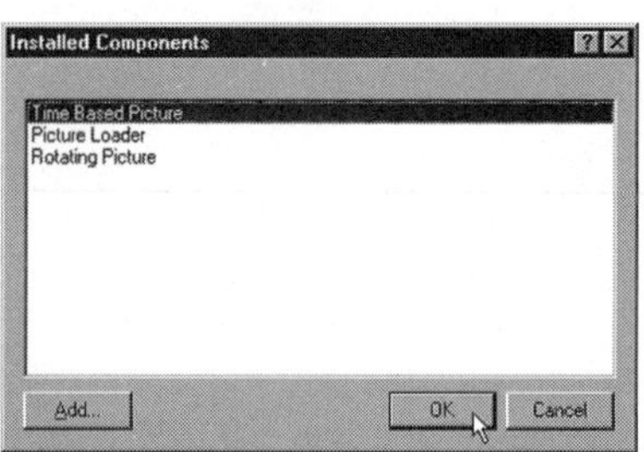


**Figure 14.7**
*Select Time Based Picture, and click OK.*

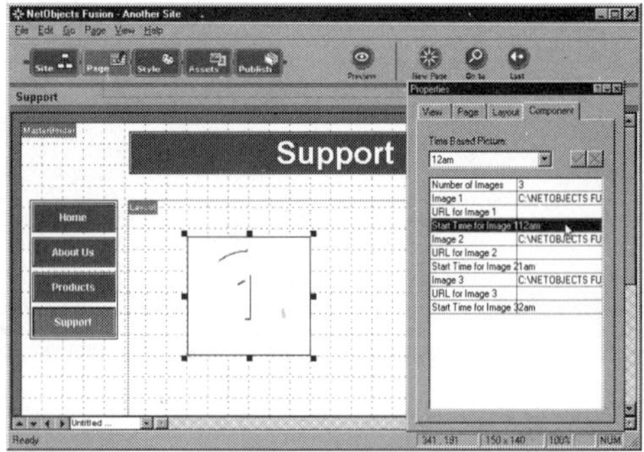


**Figure 14.8**
*The Component tab appears in the Properties Palette.*

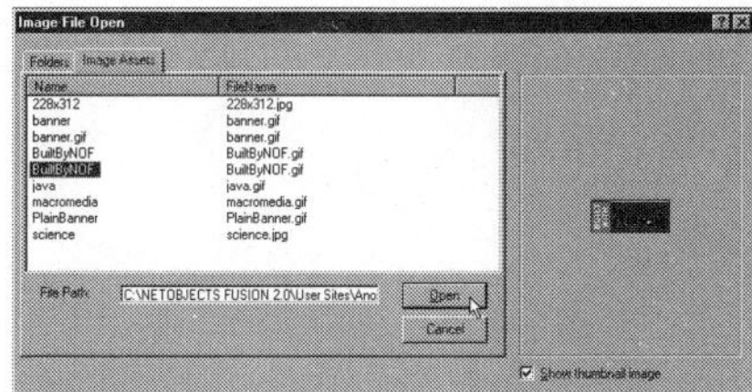

**Figure 14.9**
*Choose images to display using the dialog box displayed.*

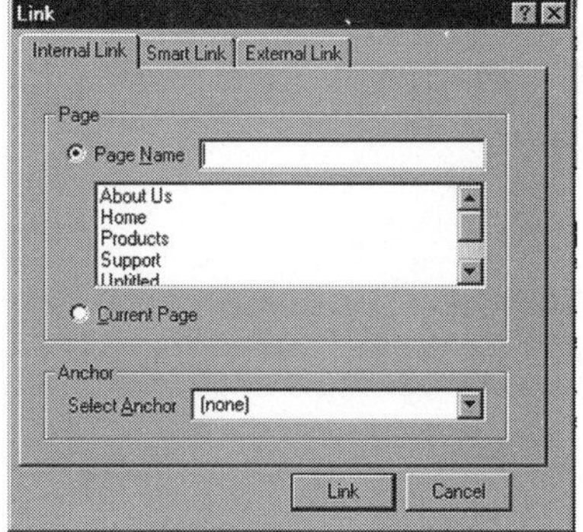


**Figure 14.10**
*Specify links using the Links dialog box.*

**5.** Set the remaining properties:

**Image 1, 2, & 3** are the paths and file names of the first, second, and third image to be displayed.

**URL for Image 1, 2, & 3** are the URLs of links for each image (if desired) to be displayed.

Use the ... button to display the open dialog box **(Figure 14.9)** or Link dialog box **(Figure 14.10)** when one of the Image or URL properties is selected.

**or**

Double-click Image and URL properties to display the dialog box.

### ✔ Tip

■ See Chapter 9 for more on using the Links dialog box.

## Using a Picture Loader

The Picture Loader component allows you to specify a picture to download from an external source and display inline in your pages. The picture to be displayed is specified by its URL.

### To add a rotating picture:

1. Select the secondary NetObjects Components tool **(Figure 14.11)**.
2. Click and drag to draw a box for displaying the desired image.

   The Installed Components dialog box appears **(Figure 14.12)**.
3. Select Picture Loader and Click OK.

   The Component properties tab is displayed, and a place holder appears on the page **(Figure 14.13)**. This element will display the downloaded image.

   The name of the selected NetObjects Component, Picture Loader, is displayed at the top of the properties tab.
4. Set the **Image URL** property by clicking it and setting its value in the field provided near the top of the properties tab.

   Enter a complete URL for an image file, as in this example: **http://www.bugeater.com/gifs/apple.gif**

   Confirm a change made to a property by clicking the ✓ button. *Mac users click OK.*

   Cancel a change by clicking the ✗ button. *Mac users click Cancel*

   The image will appear when you preview your site.

**Figure 14.11**
*Select the NetObjects Components tool*

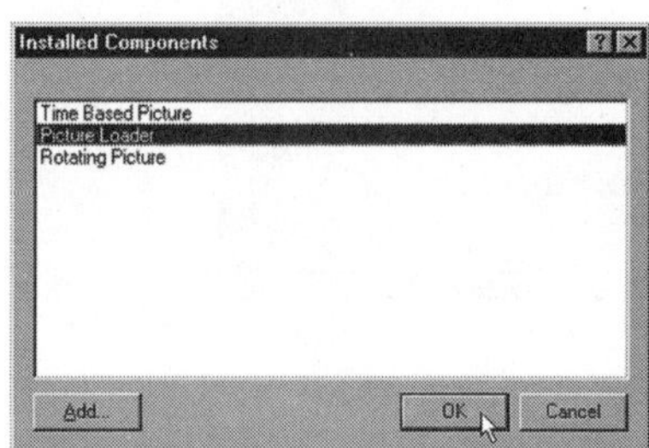


**Figure 14.12**
*Select Picture Loader, and click OK.*

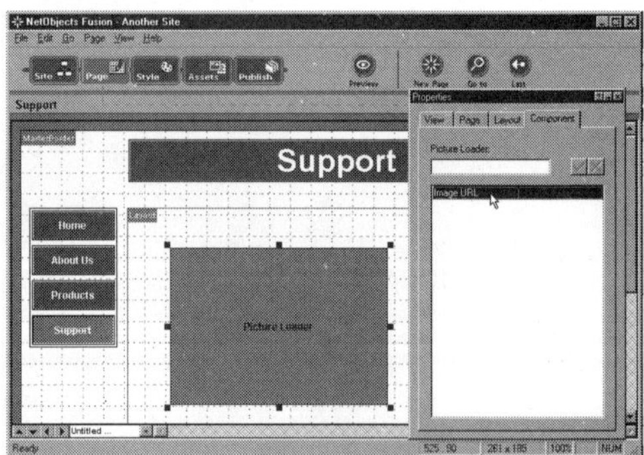


**Figure 14.13**
*The Component tab appears in the Properties Palette.*

**Figure 14.14**
*Select the Dynabuttons tool.*

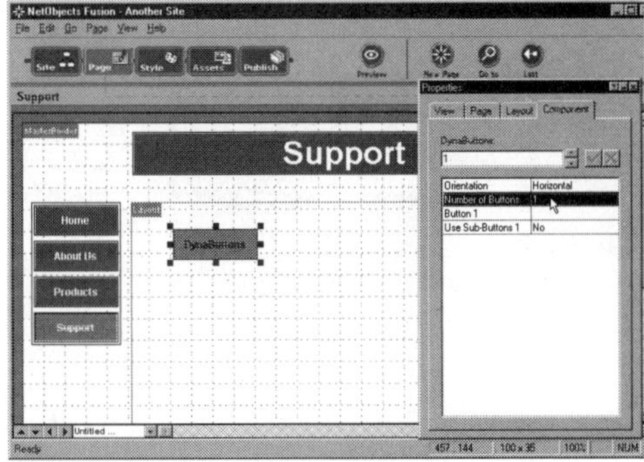


**Figure 14.15**
*The DynaButton placeholder appears on the page, and the Component property tab is displayed.*

## Using DynaButtons

DynaButtons are link buttons you can place anywhere on your page layouts or in the MasterBorders. You can create bars of DynaButtons (up to 20 buttons) and even define sub-buttons for DynaButtons. DynaButtons are displayed using the button style defined for the current SiteStyle, or you can define your own graphic images for each button. DynaButtons are special becaure they appear to be depressed with the mouse pointer is passed over them.

### To add DynaButtons:

1. Select the DynaButtons tool **(Figure 14.14)**.
2. Click and drag to draw a box for the DynaButtons.

   The Component properties tab is displayed, and a place holder appears on the page **(Figure 14.15)**.

   The name of the selected NetObjects Component, DynaButtons, is displayed near the top of the properties tab.
3. Set the following DynaButtons properties by clicking each property and setting its value in the field provided near the top of the properties tab.

   **Orientation** is the orientation of the DynaButton bar (horizontal or vertical).

   **Number of Buttons** is the number of buttons to be displayed in the DynaButton bar.

**Use Sub-Buttons 1, 2, 3,...** allow you to specify that any buttons will have sub-buttons **(Figure 14.16)**.

**Number Sub-Buttons** allow you to set the number of sub-buttons for any given button.

Confirm a change made to a property by clicking the ✓ button. *Mac users click OK.*

Cancel a change by clicking the ✗ button. *Mac users click Cancel*

4. Set the **Button 1, 2, 3...** and **Sub-Button...** properties that allow you to specify links for each button.

   Use the ... button to display the Link dialog box **(Figure 14.17)** when one of the Button or Sub-Button properties is selected.

   **or**

   Double-click Button and Sub-Button properties to display the Link dialog box.

6. Use the Link dialog box to specify each link, then click the Link button.

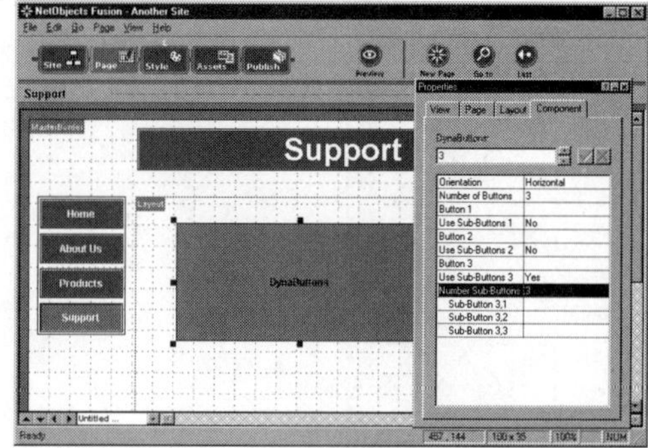


**Figure 14.16**
*The Component tab for a DynaButton bar with multiple buttons and sub-buttons.*

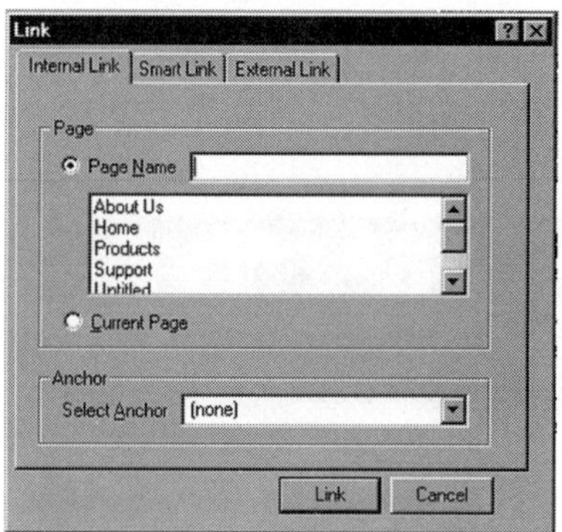


**Figure 14.17**
*Specify links using the Links dialog box.*

### ✓ Tips

- See Chapter 9 for more on using the Links dialog box.
- Since DynaButtons are displayed just using a place holder in Fusion, you should check pages with DynaButtons by previewing, staging, or publishing your site (see Chapter 17 and page 84).

**Figure 14.18**
*Select the Ticker Tape tool.*

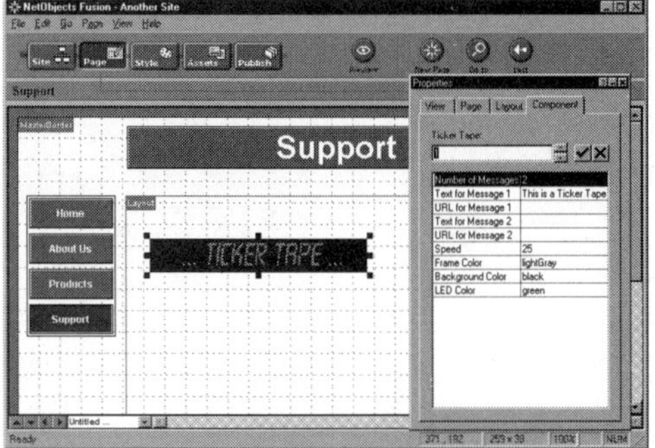


**Figure 14.19**
*The Ticker Tape place holder appears, and the Component property tab is displayed.*

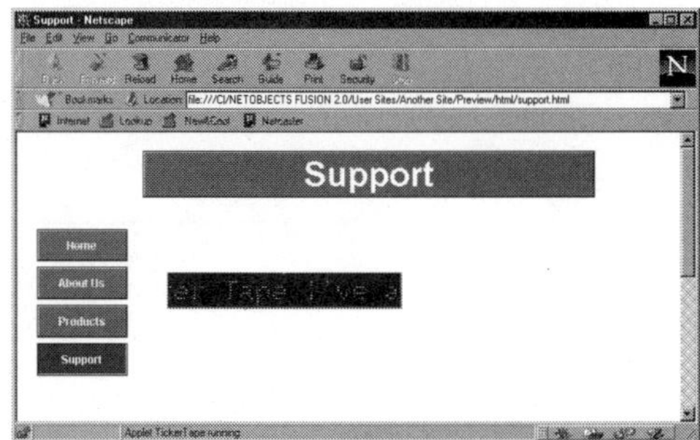


**Figure 14.20**
*A Ticker Tape being previewed in Netscape Navigator.*

## Adding a Ticker Tape

A Ticker Tape is a scrolling message you can define and place on your pages.

### To add a Ticker Tape:

1. Select the Ticker Tape tool **(Figure 14.18)**.
2. Click and drag to draw a box for the Ticker Tape on your page.

   The Component properties tab is displayed, and a Ticker Tape place holder appears on the page **(Figure 14.19)**.

   The name of the selected NetObjects Component, Ticker Tape, is displayed near the top of the properties tab.
3. Set all of the Ticker Tape properties except URL for Message... by clicking the property and setting its value in the field provided near the top of the properties tab.

   **Number of Messages** is the number of messages to be displayed in the Ticker Tape element.

   **Text for Message...** is the text of each message.

   **Speed** is how fast you want the message to move. Raising the number increases the speed.

   **Frame Color** is the color for the border around the Ticker Tape. The default is gray.

   **Background Color** is the color of the Ticker Tape display. The default is black.

   **LED Color** is the color of the text displayed on the Ticker Tape background. The default is green.

Confirm a change made to a property by clicking the ✔ button. *Mac users click OK.*

Cancel a change by clicking the ✖ button. *Mac users click Cancel*

**4.** Set the **URL for Message...** properties. These allow you to specify links for each Ticker Tape message (if you want to).

You can use the ... button to display the Link dialog box **(Figure 14.21)** when one of the URL for Message... properties is selected.

**or**

Double-click URL for Message... properties to display the Link dialog box.

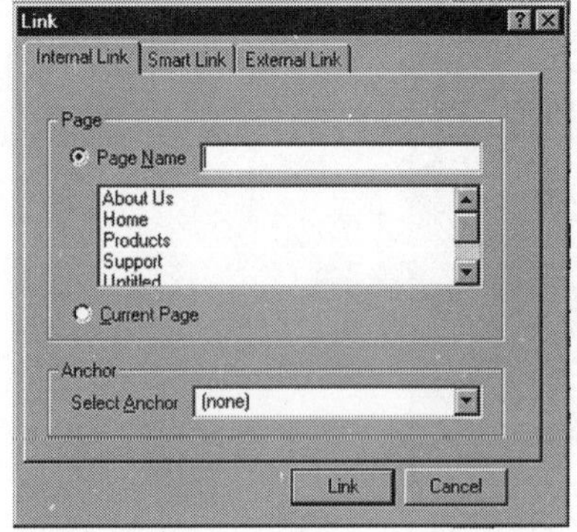


**Figure 14.21**
*Specify links using the Links dialog box.*

### ✔ Tips

- See Chapter 9 for more on using the Links dialog box.
- Since a Ticker Tape is displayed in Fusion with just a place holder, you should check pages containing Ticker Tapes by previewing, staging, or publishing your site (see Chapter 17 and page 84).

Figure 14.22
*Select the SiteMapper tool.*

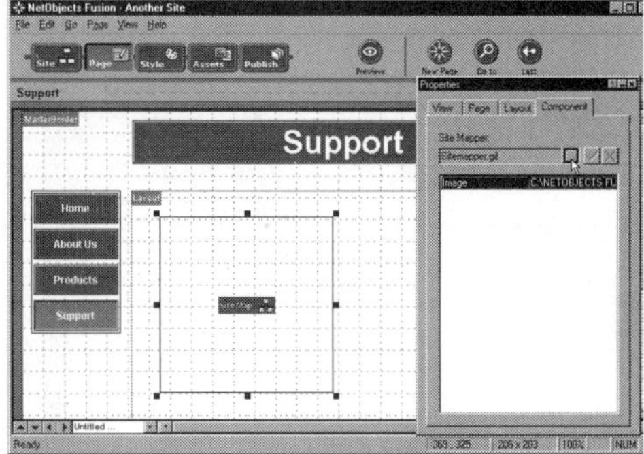


Figure 14.23
*The Site Map button appears on the page, and the Component property tab is displayed.*

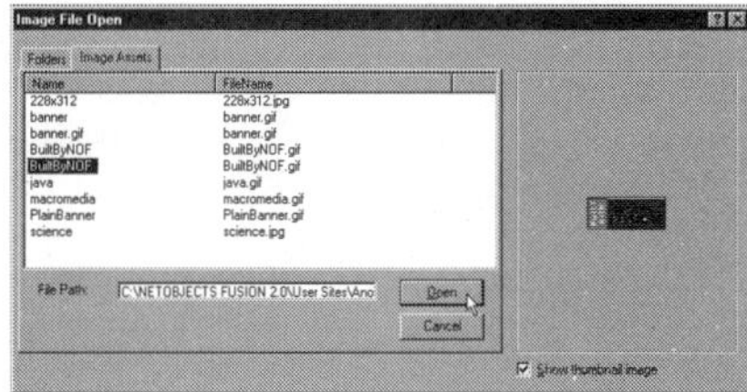

Figure 14.24
*Choose the image file to use for the Site Map button.*

## Creating a Site Map

SiteMapper is a facility that allows you to create an interactive map of your site. A site map can be a very useful navigation tool for visitors to your site. It can also help visitors become familiar with the structure of your site.

When a visitor to your site clicks a Site Map button, a new browser window opens displaying a map of your site similar to the one you see in Site View.

### To add a site map:

1. Select the SiteMapper tool **(Figure 14.22)**.
2. Click and drag to draw a box for the Site Map button.

   The Component properties tab is displayed, and a Site Map button appears on the page **(Figure 14.23)**.

   The name of the selected NetObjects Component, Site Mapper, is displayed near the top of the properties tab.
3. You can select a different image to be displayed as the Site Map button by selecting the Image property and clicking the [...] button to display the open dialog box **(Figure 14.24)**.

   **or**

   Double-click the Image property to display the open dialog box.

### ✓ Tip

- Preview or stage your site to check your Site Map.

## Adding a Message Board

The Message Board facility allows you to build a message board right into your site. When a visitor to your site clicks a Message Board button, a new browser window opens displaying the message board. Visitors to your site can view messages by thread, subject, author, and time. Visitors can also reply to messages and post new messages.

### To add a message board:

1. Select the Message Board tool **(Figure 14.25)**.
2. Click and drag to draw a box for the Message Board button.

   The Component properties tab is displayed, and a Message Board button appears on the page **(Figure 14.26)**.

   The name of the selected NetObjects Component, BBS, is displayed near the top of the properties tab.
3. Set the parameters for the Message Board (BBS):

   **Subdirectory** is the name of the directory on the server where you want to keep the Message Board (bbs is the default).

   **Page Title** is the name that appears in the title bar of the browser's Message Board window.

   **Publish to** allows you to select your Web server platform (Macintosh, Windows, or Unix).

   **Perl Path for Unix** is used only if you are publishing your site to a Unix server. This is the path to the Perl 5 interpreter on the Unix

**Figure 14.25**
*Select the Message Board tool.*

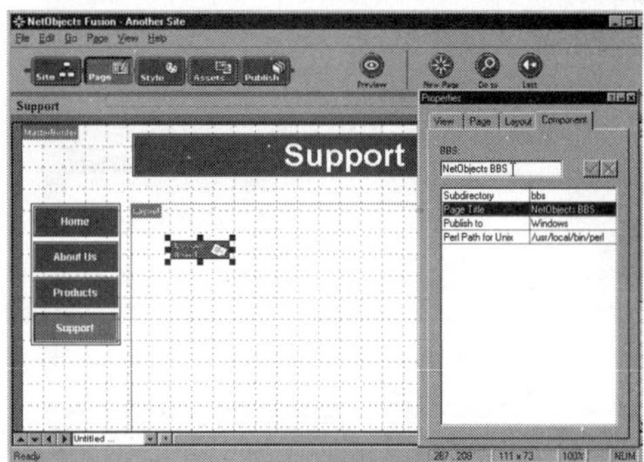


**Figure 14.26**
*The Message Board button appears on the page, and the Component property tab is displayed.*

server. Get this information from your local Webmaster or your Internet Service Provider.

### ✔ Tips

- Only one Message Board is allowed per site.
- You cannot change the image file used for the Message Board button.
- Visitors to your site will only be able to access your Message Board if they are using a browser, such as Netscape Navigator 3.0 and higher, which supports the Netscape Javascript standard.
- Your Message Board will work only if your Web site's server is able to run CGI scripts. Check with your Webmaster or Internet Service Provider regarding publishing a site with a Message Board.
- Check the NetObjects web site at **www. netobjects.com/support** for more information on setting up your server for a site with a Message Board.

## Adding New NetObjects Components

As NetObjects and others develop additional components, you can add them to your NetObjects Components list **(Figure 14.28)**.

### To add new NetObjects Components:

1. Select the secondary NetObjects Components tool **(Figure 14.27)**.
2. Click on the page.

   The Installed Components dialog box appears **(Figure 14.28)**.
3. Click the Add button.

   The Install Components dialog box is displayed **(Figure 14.29)**. Use this dialog box to select new NetObjects components you have downloaded from the NetObjects Web site or that you have obtained from other sources.
4. Click Open.

   The new component is displayed in the listed Installed Components.
5. To add the new component to a Web page, select it in the Installed Components dialog box, and click OK.

   The new component appears on your page where you clicked in Step 2.

✔ **Tip**

- NetObjects Components must have **nfx** or **class** file extensions. *Mac NetObjects Components do not need file extensions*

**Figure 14.27**
*Select the NetObjects Components tool.*

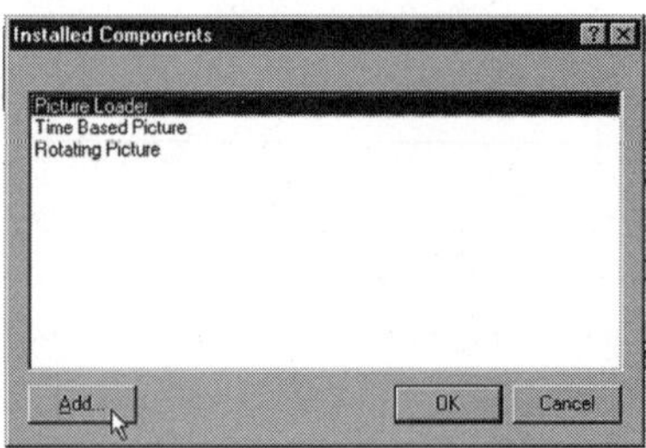


**Figure 14.28**
*Select the Add button to add a new component to the list.*

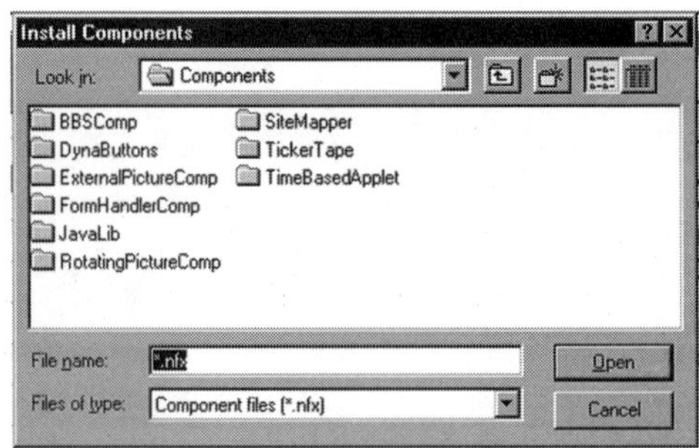


**Figure 14.29**
*Select a new component, then click Open.*

# Data Publishing 15

## Understanding Database Publishing

NetObjects Fusion lets you publish the contents of internal and external data sources to your Web site. Database publishing with Fusion is a three-step process. First, the creation of a **data object**; a collection of data fields within a record or row from your data source. Second, a **data list** can be configured on your Web page that acts as an index for your data when you publish your site.

Fusion creates a set of stacked **data pages** as you make a data list. Each page in the stack displays the data from a single record or row from your data source. The data displayed on your Web page is only updated when you republish your Web site.

You may publish external data sources such as Microsoft Access, Lotus 123, Microsoft Excel, or any other SQL-compliant product that supports either ODBC or ISAM connectivity. Or you can use internal data sources within Fusion itself as your data source.

### ✔ Tip

- Using database-to-Web products such as EveryWare's Tango, Allaire's Cold Fusion, and Netscape's LiveWire, you can create dynamic links between databases and your Web pages. Just create empty Form Edit fields on a page, then add appropriate scripts to the fields by clicking Script in the Field properties tab and entering the script in the Inside Element Tag field of the Element Script dialog box.

See **www.netobjects.com** for more information on data publishing.

**Figure 15.1**
*Select the Data List tool in the Tools Palette.*

## Using the Data List Tool

The Data List tool on the Tools palette **(Figure 15.1)** is the starting point for Data Publishing. You use this tool to draw and define a Data List on your pages.

The first step in defining a Data List is to select or create a data object—a description of the data you'll be using in your data list.

### To create a new Data Object:

1. Select the Data List tool from the Tools Palette **(Figure 15.1)**.
2. Click and drag to draw a Data List object on your page **(Figure 15.2)**.

   The Data Publishing dialog box will appear **(Figure 15.3)**.

   In the Data Publishing dialog box, the Data Object field is a drop-down list that contains the names of the data objects already defined. If you have not already defined any data objects, then the default will be Sample.

   The fields defined for the selected data object are listed in the Sort By drop-down list and in the Data List section of the dialog box.
3. Click the New button next to the Data Object list.

   The Data Object dialog box appears **(Figure 15.4)**. You will use this dialog box to define either a new external or internal data object.

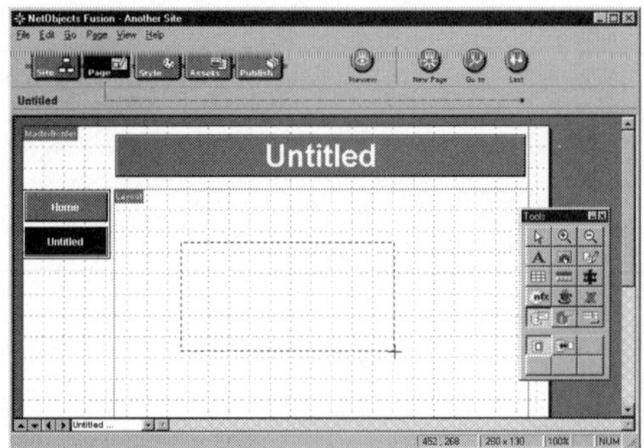


**Figure 15.2**
*Draw a Data Object on your page.*

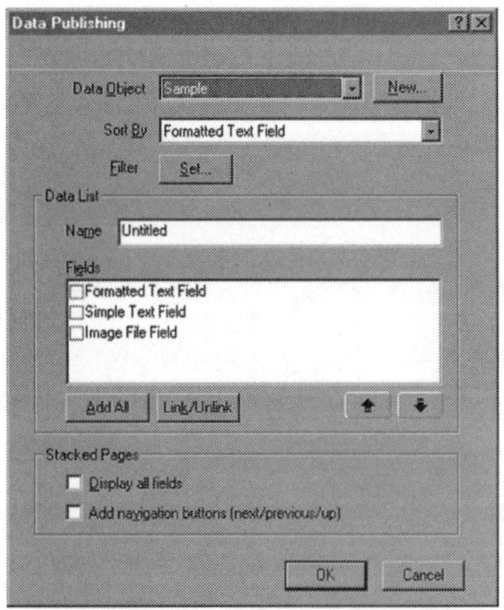


**Figure 15.3**
*The Data Publishing dialog box.*

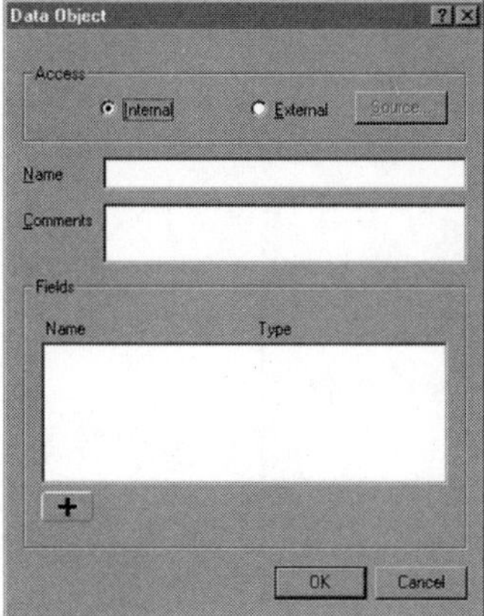


**Figure 15.4**
*Define your data object using the Data Object dialog box.*

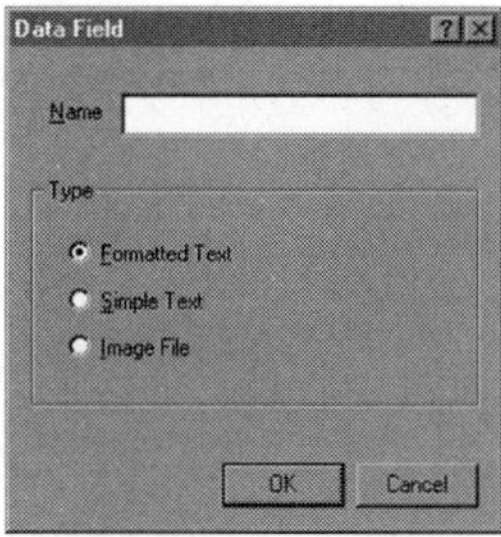


**Figure 15.5**
*Add fields to your Data Object description using the Data Field dialog box.*

## Defining Data Objects

Data Objects may access internal or external data sources. An internal data source is created within NetObjects Fusion. Fields are defined and populated by the site developer. An external data source exists outside of Fusion and is accessed using one of the pre-installed database drivers in Fusion, or through an ODBC driver installed in your own system.

### To define an Internal Data Object:

1. Use the Data List tool to draw a Data List object on your Web page. (See previous page.)
2. With the Data Object dialog box open **(Figure 15.4)**, select the Internal option from the Access section. *Mac users skip this step, you can only create internal data objects.*
3. Type a name for your new data object in the Name field.
4. You may type a description or other note in the Comments field.
5. In the Fields section of the Data Objects dialog box, click the large plus sign.

   The Data Field dialog box appears **(Figure 15.5)**.
6. Type a name of a field for your new internal data object in the Name field.
7. Select the appropriate field Type.

   **Formatted Text** allows paragraph formatting and font attributes within the field.

   **Simple Text** fields contain no special formatting

   **Image** fields will contain pictures.

8. Click OK.

   The field you just defined appears in the Data Object dialog box Fields area.

9. Repeat Steps 5–8 to create additional data fields as needed **(Figure 15.6)**.

10. Click OK.

   Your new internal data object is displayed as the selected Data Object in the Data Publishing dialog box. Notice that the fields you defined for the new data object are displayed in the Sort By drop-down list and in the Fields box in the Data List area of the Data Publishing dialog box.

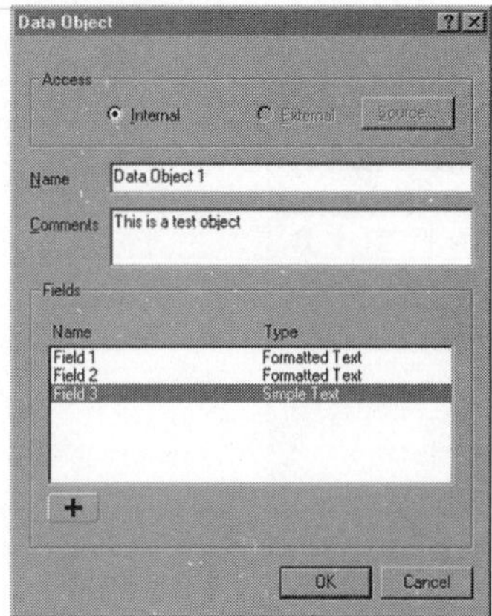


**Figure 15.6**
*Create data fields as needed.*



## To define an external Data Object in Windows:

*Mac users cannot create external data objects and can skip these numbered steps.*

1. Use the Data List tool to draw a Data List object on your Web page.

2. With the Data Object dialog box open, select the External option.

3. Click the Source button **(Figure 15.7)**.

   The Data Source Type dialog box is displayed **(Figure 15.8)**.

4. From the Type drop-down list, select the file type that you wish to use as a data source.

   The drop-down list contains the pre-defined data types that Fusion will recognize. The ODBC option allows you to use other drivers that you may have installed.

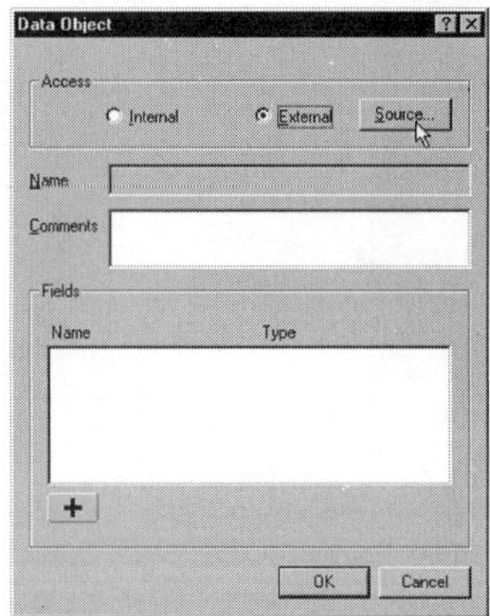


**Figure 15.7**
*Select the External option in the Data Object dialog box, and then click the Source button.*

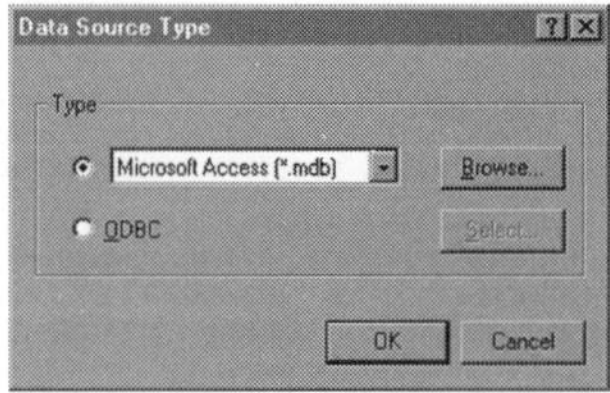


**Figure 15.8**
*Select the type and source for your external data object using the Data Source Type dialog box.*

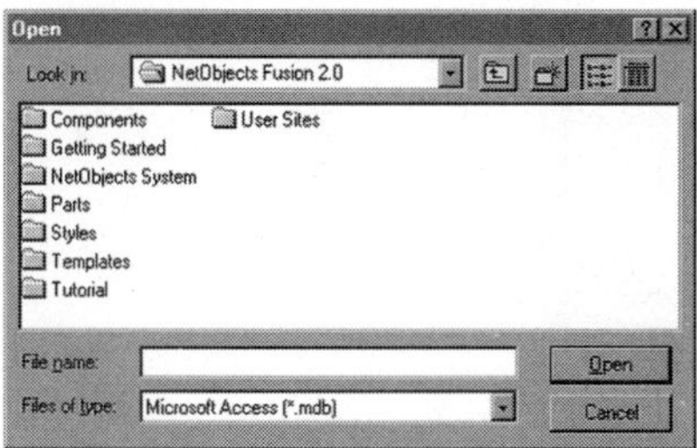


**Figure 15.9**
*Select a specific file to use as a data source.*

**Figure 15.10**
*Use the Select dialog box to select from multiple tables or worksheets.*

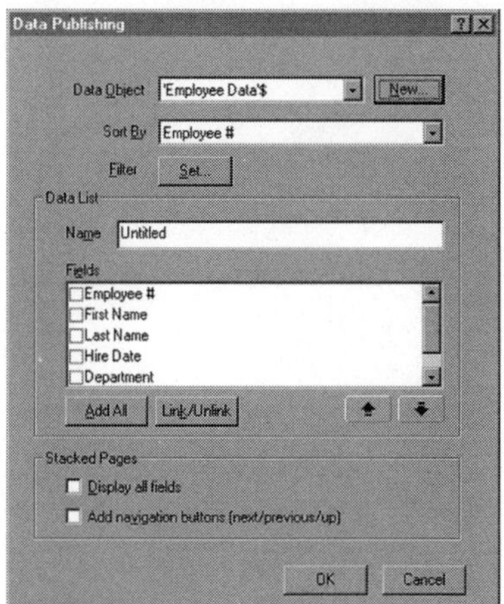


**Figure 15.11**
*An external data object displayed in the Data Publishing dialog box.*

5. Click on the Browse button to display the open dialog box. *Mac users click the Select....button.*
6. Use the open dialog box to select a specific file to use as a data source **(Figure 15.9)**.
7. Click the Open button.

   If the data source you selected has multiple tables (as can be the case in MS Access), or multiple worksheets (as can be the case in MS Excel) the Select dialog box will appear **(Figure 15.10)**.
8. If the Select dialog box is displayed, choose the table or worksheet containing the data to publish, then click OK.

   Your new data object will appear in the Data Publishing dialog box as shown in the example in **Figure 15.11**.

### ✔ Tips

- Both Microsoft Access and Excel are commonly used as data sources for Fusion Web sites. You can use either product to create a small table or spreadsheet to explore the functionality described in this section of the book.
- NetObjects Fusion 2.0 will not recognize Office 97 file formats. If you are using Office 97 make sure you save your file as an Excel 5-95 file, or use an earlier version of Access.

## Defining a Data List

**Figure 15.12**
*Select the Data List tool in the Tools Palette.*

Once a Data Object has been defined, you can create a Data List. A Data List acts as an index of sorts for the data you will be publishing on your Web site. In its simplest form a Data List would consist of one or two fields from your data source acting as pointers to the data contained on stacked data pages. Users of your Web site would select the data that they want to view from a key entry in your Data List and the appropriate data page would then be displayed.

### To define a data list:

1. Select the Data List tool from the Tools Palette **(Figure 15.12)**.
2. Click and drag to draw a Data List object on your page.

   The Data Publishing dialog box appears.
3. Choose the data object you wish to use from the Data Object drop-down list **(Figure 15.13)** (You can also create a new Data Object by clicking the New button. See the previous sections for details).
4. If you want the data list (and data pages) sorted on one of the data object's fields, select the desired field from the Sort By drop-down list. All of the fields defined for the selected data object appear in this list.
5. Type a name for your new data list in the Data List Name field.
6. From the list of available fields displayed, select those fields that you want to appear in the data list by

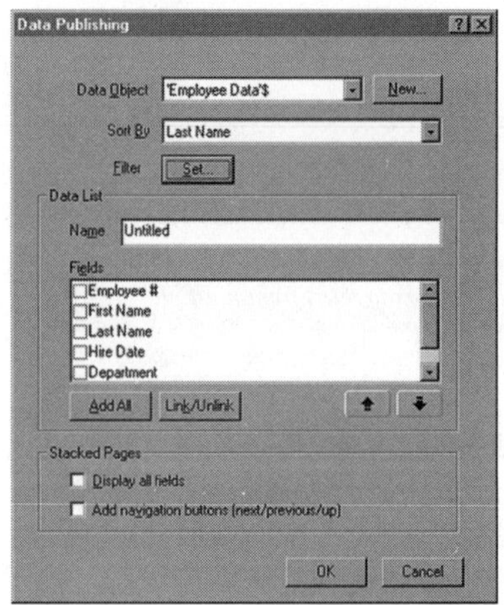


**Figure 15.13**
*Choose the data object you wish to use from the drop-down list.*

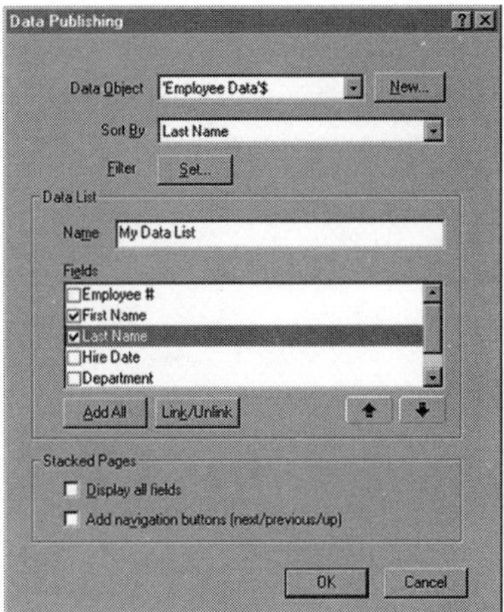


**Figure 15.14**
*Select the fields you wish to use by clicking the check boxes.*

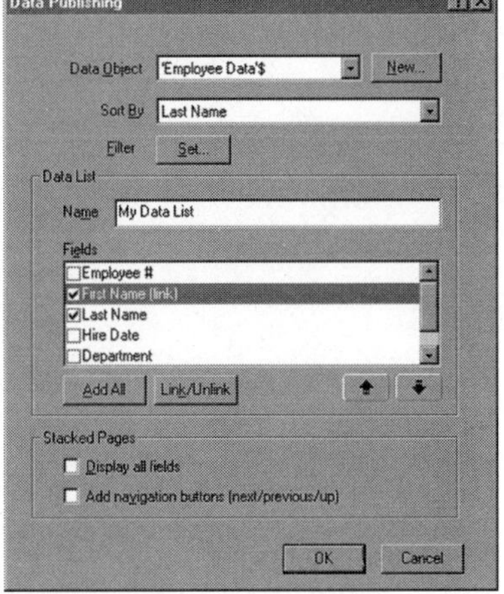


**Figure 15.15**
*When a data list field is linked, the word link appears next to the field name.*

clicking the small box in front of each field name **(Figure 15.14)**.

7. Use the buttons at the bottom of the Data List area as follows:

   **Add All** adds all of the available data fields to your Data List.

   **Link/Unlink** lets you link (or unlink) specific fields in your data list to the corresponding data page. Fusion automatically provides a button next to each record in your data list. This button is linked to the corresponding data page. When you link a specific field, visitors to your site will be able to click either the data list button *or* the linked field to go to the corresponding data page. You can only link fields you have selected to appear in the data list, and when a field is linked, the word *link* appears next to its name in the Data Publishing dialog box **(Figure 15.15)**.

   The ↑ ↓ buttons allow you to change the order in which the fields are displayed.

8. Select the desired options from the Stacked Pages section of the Data Publishing dialog box.

   These options allow you to tell Fusion what will appear on the stacked data pages that are generated when you leave the Data Publishing dialog box.

   **Display all fields** causes all the data fields defined for the selected data object to appear on the data pages.

   **Add navigation buttons** places a set of small navigation buttons on each of your stacked Data Pages. These buttons allow you to navigate within the stack of data pages without having to constantly return to the page displaying the data list.

It's a good idea to choose both of these options when creating your new pages. You will see in the next section how to remove or add data fields if you wish, but since the navigation buttons are added when the pages are created, you can't add them easily after the pages are created.

9. Click OK.

When you leave the Data Publishing dialog box, Fusion does two things:

First, Fusion places the data list you just defined on the displayed page. Column headers are displayed bearing the names of the fields you selected. A button linking each record to its corresponding data page appears at the left of the first (and only) row **(Figure 15.16)**.

Second, Fusion generates a set of stacked data pages that are children of the page on which your data list was placed.

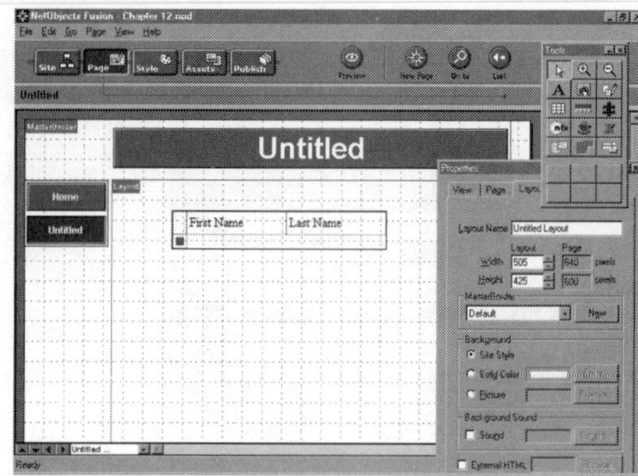


**Figure 15.16**
*Data list defined.*

### ✔ Tip

- You will probably notice at this point that your data list is empty. Don't panic. Fusion only displays data in a data list when the page is previewed or published.

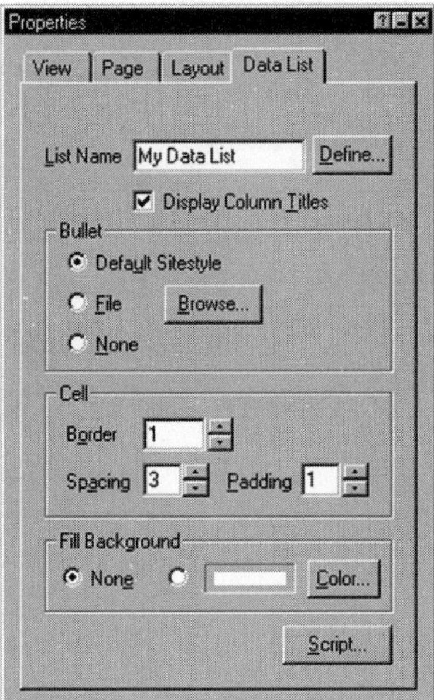


**Figure 15.17**
*Use the Data List Properties Tab to modify an existing data list.*

## Modifying a Data List

You may change the fields displayed, data list name, column header display, data list button, cell properties, and fill background of an existing data list using the Data List tab in the Properties Palette.

### To modify data list properties:

1. Click a data list in Page View to select it.

   When a data list is selected in Page View, the Data List tab in the Properties Palette is displayed **(Figure 15.17)**.

2. To change the name of the selected data list, type a new name in the **List Name** field.

3. To change the definition of the data list, including the fields displayed, the sort order, data filtering, the order of fields, and field linking, click the **Define** button.

   The Data Publishing dialog box is displayed, which you can use as described in steps 4–9 in the previous section.

4. To hide column headers in the data list (recall that selected field names are used as data list column headers), click the **Display Column Titles** box to deselect it **(Figure 15.18)**.

5. To change the appearance of the data list button (that's the button preceding each row in the data list), select one of the options in the **Bullet** area of the Data List tab.

**Default Sitestyle** uses the data list icon defined for the currently applied SiteStyle.

**File** allows you to specify a graphic file to use as the data list button by clicking the Browse button, and selecting a file using the displayed dialog box. *Mac users click the Select....button.*

**None** eliminates the data list button from the selected data list **(Figure 15.18)**. If you select this option, you must use the **Link/Unlink** button in the Data Publishing dialog box to allow users to navigate from the data list to associated data pages.

6. To change cell properties in the data list, use the **Border**, **Spacing**, and **Padding** fields in the **Cell** section of the Data List tab (see changing cell properties in table cells, Chapter 10).
7. To modify the fill background of the data list, use the options provided in the **Fill Background** section of the Data List (see changing table backgrounds, Chapter 10).

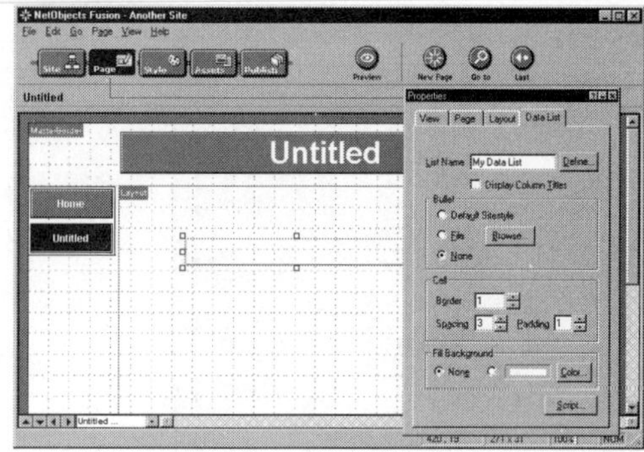


**Figure 15.18**
*A data list object with column titles hidden and no data list button.*

## ✔ Tips

- In addition to the Define button on the Data List properties tab, you can also access the Data Publishing dialog box for an existing data list by double-clicking the data list object in Page View.
- Once a data list is defined, you cannot change the data object used by that data list, nor can you change the Stacked Pages options on the Data Publishing dialog box.

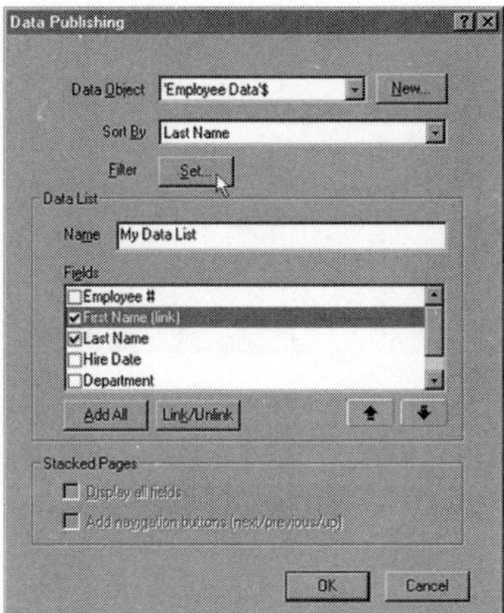


**Figure 15.19**
*Filter data by using the Set... button.*

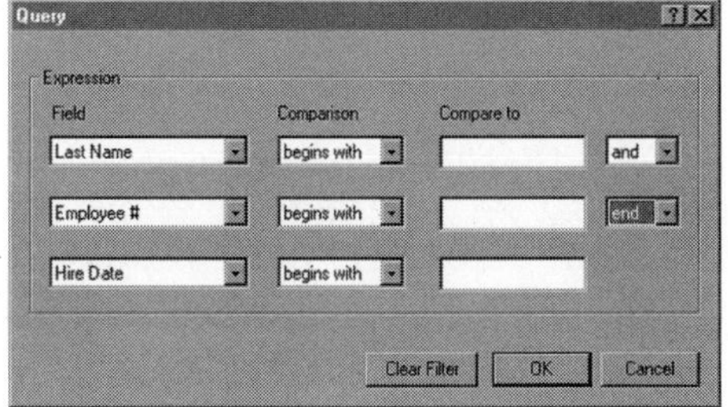


**Figure 15.20**
*Use the Query dialog box to define data filtering parameters.*

# Filtering Data

Once a Data Object has been created, you can define how your Data Pages will be organized. Remember that when you publish data using Fusion, a series of Data Pages is created, one page for each record.

You saw the Sort By option in the Data Publishing dialog box when defining a new data list. You can also filter data using the **Set** button in the Data Publishing dialog box. The Set button allows you to set parameters that will determine which rows from your data source will be included when your site is published. In effect, you define a query on your data.

### To use the query dialog box:

1. Display the Data Publishing dialog box. (Select an existing Data List, and click the Define button in the Data List properties tab; or double-click an existing data list object.)
2. Next to **Filter** on the Data Publishing dialog box, click the **Set** button **(Figure 15.19)**.

   The **Query** dialog box appears **(Figure 15.20)**.

   Each of the data fields defined for the data object used in your data list is displayed in the **Field** drop-down lists.
3. Select a field from the first Field drop-down list that you wish to use as the basis for filtering your data. For example, if you want to display records only if the value of a particular field matches some value, then select that field.

4. Select a comparison method from the corresponding **Comparison** drop-down list **(Figure 15.21)**.

   The comparison choices allow you to specify the way in which you wish to compare values in the selected field with the value specified in the Compare to field.

5. In the **Compare to** field, enter a value with which the data in the selected field will be compared.

   In the example shown in **Figure 15.22**, to display only employees hired in 1990, then you could enter 90 in the Compare to field for Hire Date.

6. If you wish to filter data based on values in more than one field, use the and/or operators to create compound statements for up to three fields. Use the end operator to indicate the end of a compound statement **(Figure 15.22)**. Fusion will ignore filter parameters following an end operator.

7. To apply filter parameters defined in the Query dialog box, click OK. To instead cancel changes made or clear all filter parameters, click the Cancel or Clear Filter button.

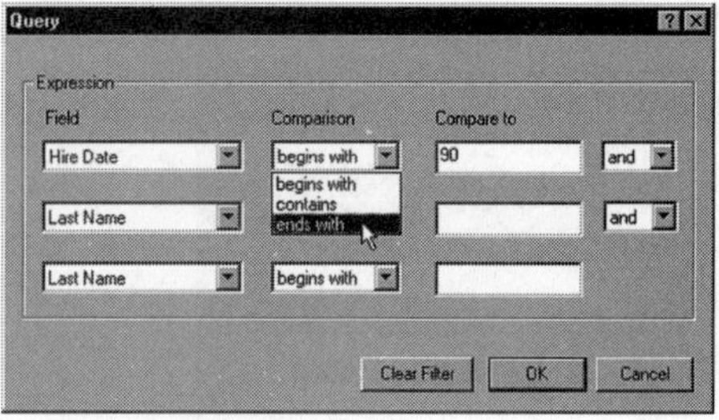


**Figure 15.21**
*Select a comparison method from the Comparison drop-down list.*

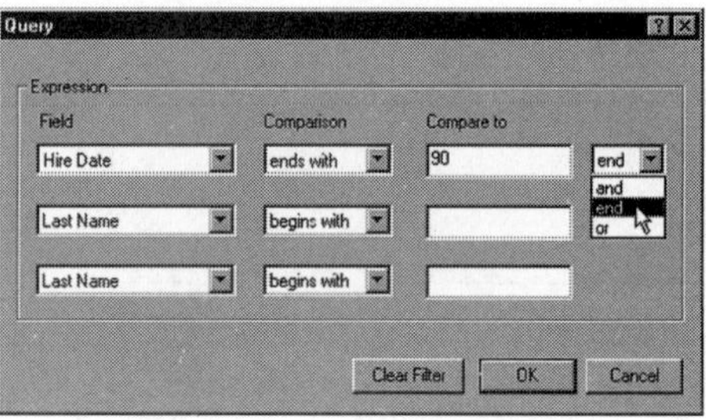


**Figure 15.22**
*Use the end operator to end a query statement.*

✔ **Tip**

■ We found that if you use anything but a simple text field as the first data field in the Query dialog box, the Comparison options appear to be blank. Even a simple text field containing numeric data will cause this glitch. Perhaps upcoming patches from Fusion will remedy the situation.

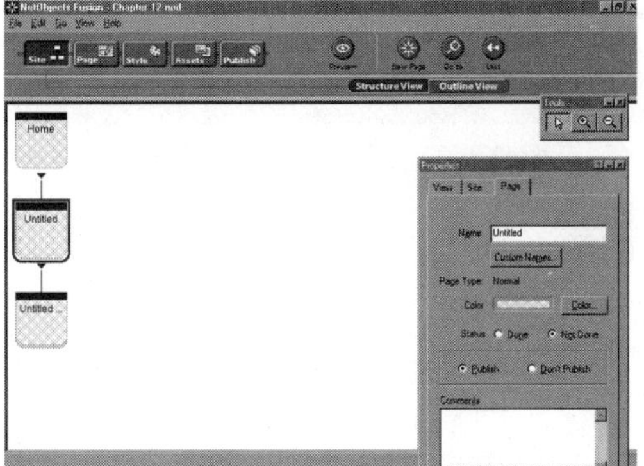

**Figure 15.23**
*You can view the stacked data pages created for a data list in Site View.*

**Figure 15.24**
*Use the down-arrow page navigation button to go to the Page View for the child of the current page.*

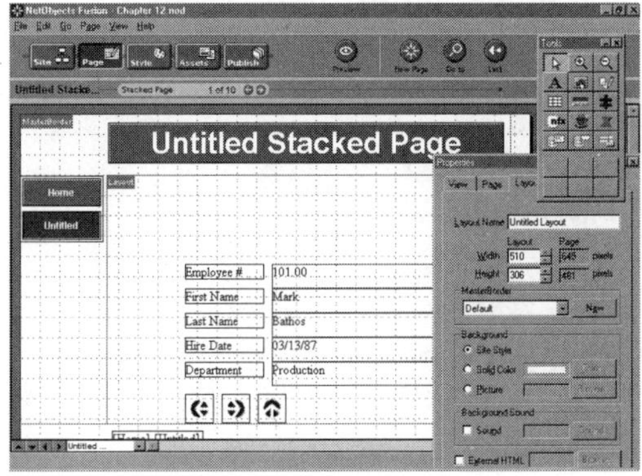


**Figure 15.25**
*One of the stacked data pages for a data list.*

## Working with Data Pages

When a data list is created, Fusion creates the first in a stack of data pages that will be populated with data from your data source. When you publish or preview your site, one stacked data page is created for each row or record in your data source. These pages are the children of the page on which you defined the data list.

### To view data pages for a data list:

You can display a data page for a particular data list in one of two ways: Go to Site View **(Figure 15.23)**, and double-click the desired stacked pages. Alternatively, while viewing the page on which the data list resides, you can click the down page navigation button **(Figure 15.24)** in the bottom left of the Page View screen.

Using either method, the first data page for the data list will be displayed in Page View, as in the example in **Figure 15.25**. Notice the navigation buttons at the bottom of the page in the example. These buttons were created because **Add navigation buttons** was selected in the Stacked Pages section of the Data Publishing dialog box at the time the data list was defined.

Notice also that a yellow navigation tool appears in the Control bar of stacked data pages. It displays which page of the stack you are currently viewing, allows you to move forward and backwards through the stack, and allows you to add and delete pages from the stack using the plus and minus sign buttons.

## To edit data pages:

1. Display a data page for the desired data list in Page View (see previous page).
2. Edit the data pages for a data list in any way you'd like. Refer to related chapters for information on adding text, multimedia, tables, frames, customizing the MasterBorders, layout, navigation bar, and so on.

   When you edit data pages, however, remember that each data page in a stack is identical except for the data presented on it. Any design changes made to one page will be reflected on all the pages in the stack.

## To preview data pages:

1. Click the Preview button in the Control bar.

   **Figure 15.26** displays an example of a data page being previewed. Notice that the data fields contain values from the data source.
2. Use the navigation buttons provided at the bottom of the data page to view each data page in the stack or to view the data list page.

### ✔ Tip

- If the Preview button previews only the current page, then choose Preferences from the Edit menu to make sure that the Entire Site option is selected in the Preview section **(Figure 15.27)**. Then try the Preview button in the Control bar once again.

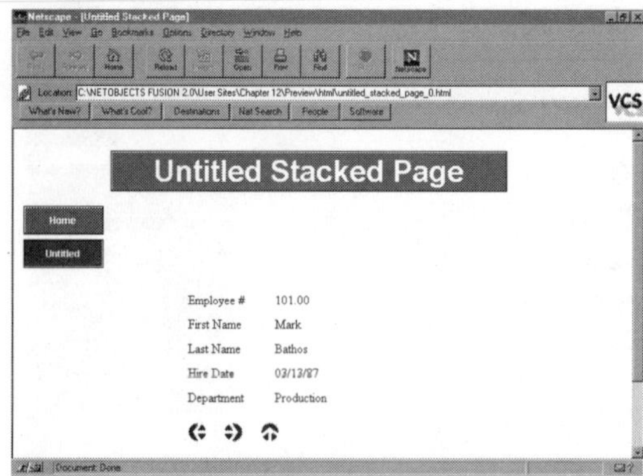


**Figure 15.26**
*Previewing a stacked data page.*

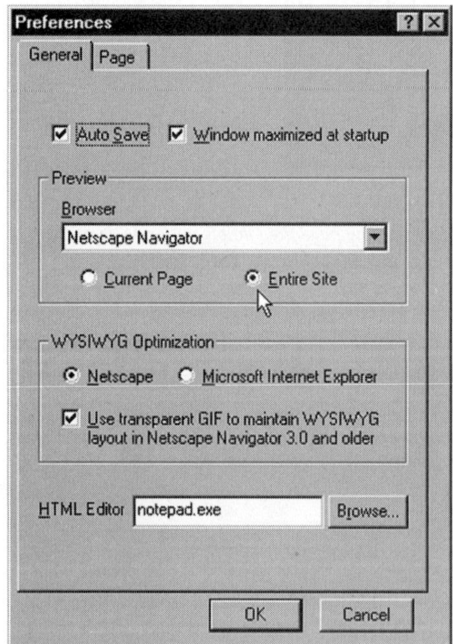


**Figure 15.27**
*Make sure Entire Site is selected in the Preview section of the Preferences dialog box.*

Edit data pages

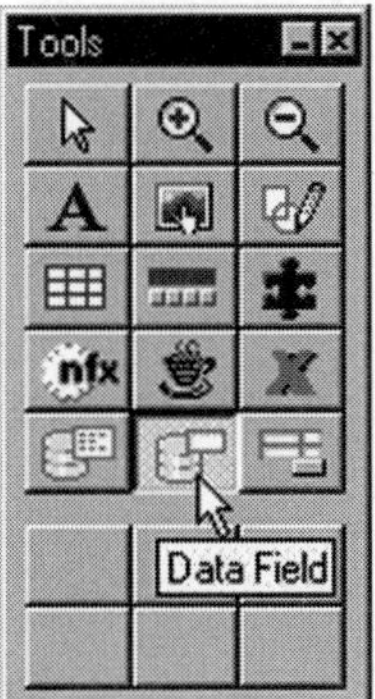


**Figure 15.28**
*The Data Field tool becomes available when a data page is displayed.*

**Figure 15.29**
*Choose a data field from the Name drop-down list.*

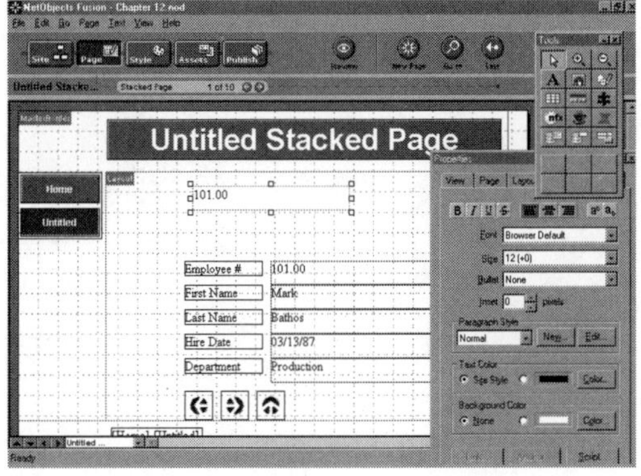


**Figure 15.30**
*The new data field is displayed.*

# Using the Data Field Tool

The Data Field tool is only available in the Page View Tools Palette when a stacked data page is displayed. The Data Field tool is used for adding data fields to data pages.

### To add a data field to a data page:

1. With a stacked data page displayed in Page View, select the Data Field tool from the Tools Palette **(Figure 15.28)**.
2. Click and drag to draw a Data Field object on the page.

   The Data Field dialog box is displayed **(Figure 15.29)**.
3. Click the arrow to select the desired data field from the Name drop-down list.
4. Click OK.

   The name of the new field is displayed within the field object you just defined **(Figure 15.30)**.

### ✔ Tip

- Remove, resize, and move a data field in the same way as for any other element. Use the mouse to move and resize a data field. To remove a data field, select it and choose Delete Element from the Edit menu, or press the Delete key.

## Working with Data Field Properties

When a data field is selected, the Data Field properties tab is displayed **(Figure 15.31)**. Using Data Field properties, you can only change the data object field that is displayed. No other display options are provided.

For text fields, however, you can use Text properties **(Figure 15.32)** to format the look of the text within the data field. To display the Text properties tab, either select text within a text field, or click on the Text tab in the Properties Palette. See page 108 for more on formatting text.

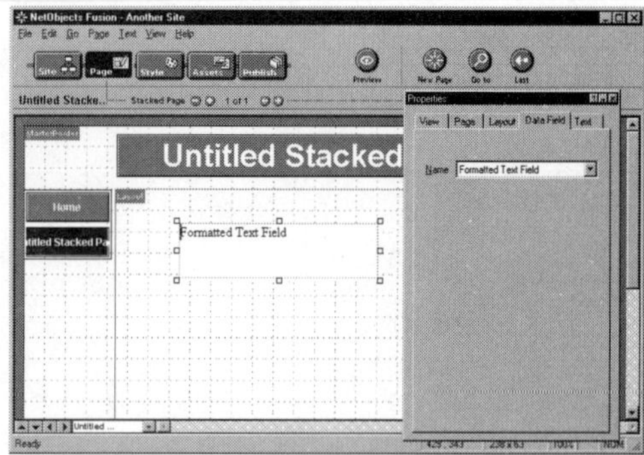


**Figure 15.31**
*The Data Field properties tab is displayed when a data field is selected on a data page.*

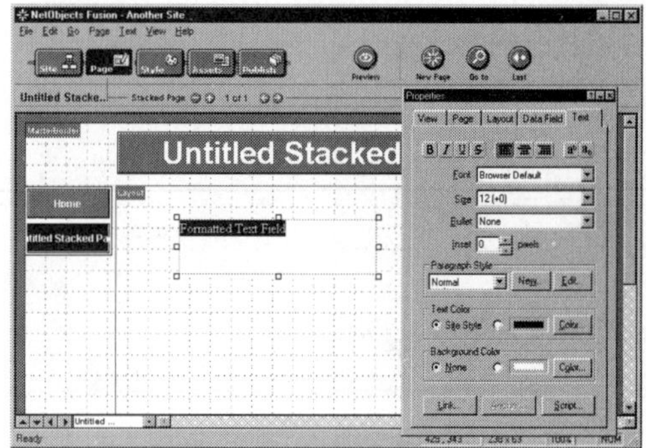


**Figure 15.32**
*The Text properties tab is displayed when the text in a data field is selected on a data page.*

# Site Management

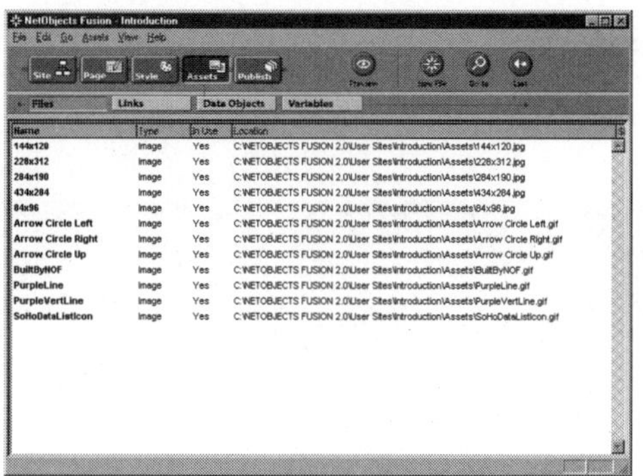

**Figure 16.1**
*Manage Web site assets with Asset View.*

## Understanding Web Site Management

Managing all of the files that together constitute a complete Web site can be a frustrating and challenging activity. If you've created Web sites in the past, then you can probably testify to the time that you had to devote to testing every link, ensuring that all of your graphics were located in the referencing directories, and in general just making sure that everything your pages needed was available. These files are known as assets.

NetObjects Fusion provides a tool set designed to simplify Web site management. Asset View **(Figure 16.1)** provides a single view of all Files, Data Objects, Variables, and Links used in your Web pages. Asset View provides critical data for each of these asset categories regarding how each asset is being used and where it is located. Asset View not only allows you to keep track of assets used in your site, it also allows you to add, modify, or delete assets.

## Getting to Asset View

When Fusion is launched, its default is Site View. It's easy to determine which view you are in by looking at the Control Bar: the view navigation button for the currently displayed view is selected.

### To get to Asset View:

If the navigation buttons in the Control Bar indicate you are not in Asset View, select the Assets button **(Figure 16.2)**.

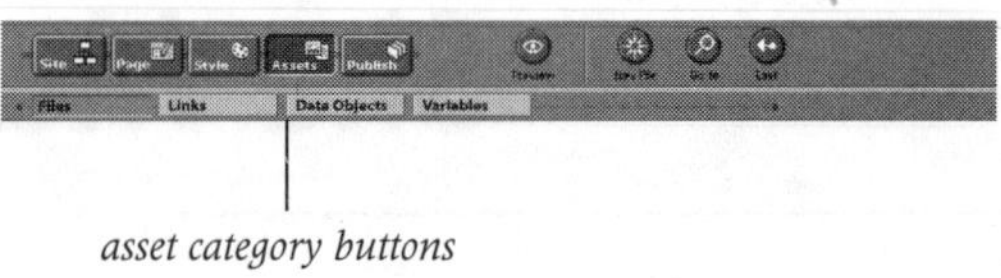


**Figure 16.2**
*The Control Bar with the Asset View navigation button selected and the asset category buttons displayed.*

## Working in Asset View

Asset View allows you to choose the asset category you wish to examine. The category buttons are located on the Control Bar **(Figure 16.2)**.

### To view an asset category:

In Asset View, click the desired asset category button.

The selected category of assets is displayed. File assets are displayed in the example in **Figure 16.3**.

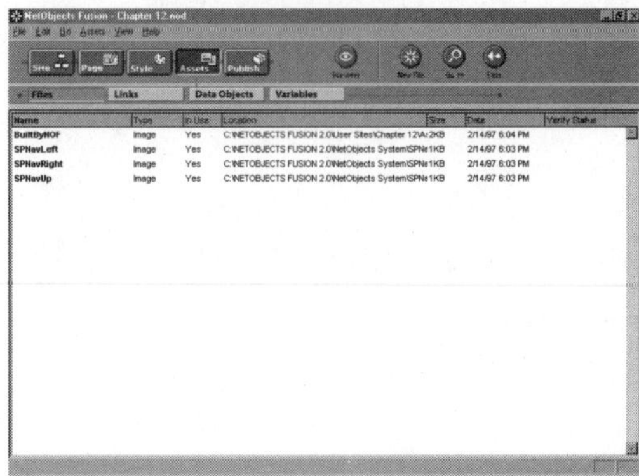

**Figure 16.3**
*Click the desired asset category button to display your site assets within that category.*

Each category provides information about the objects it contains. This information is arranged in columns with headers **(Figure 16.4)** at the top of each column.

### To sort assets:

Click a column header to sort the listed elements using values in that column.

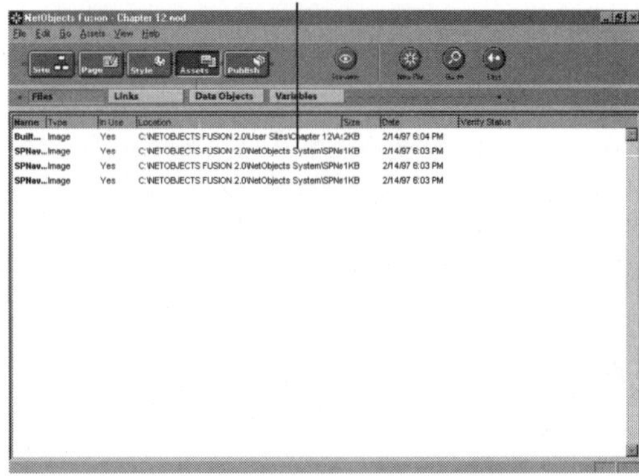


**Figure 16.4**
*Change column widths by dragging the separator between column headers left or right.*

### To change column widths:

Drag the separator between column headers left or right to modify column widths.

**Figure 16.4** shows the column of Name data for Files narrowed.

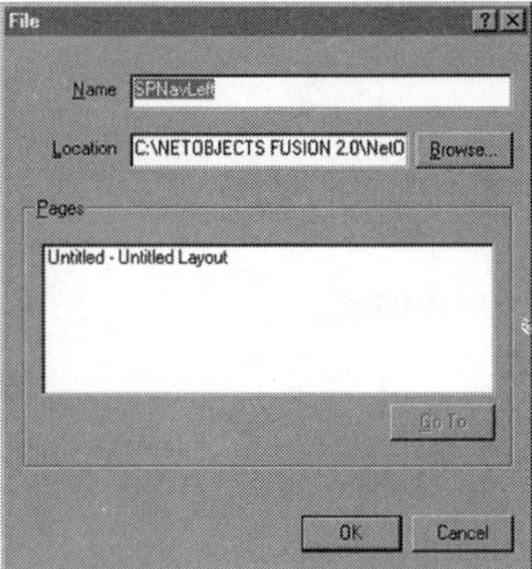


**Figure 16.5**
*Double-click an asset to view its dialog box.*

## Working with File Assets

File assets are the components that we use to give our Web sites character and functionality. Pictures, sounds, video clips, and applets are all examples of file assets. In Asset View, you can quickly edit, delete, add, and even verify file assets. Changes you make to file assets in Asset View are reflected on all the pages in your site that use the asset(s) you change.

### To edit a file asset:

1. In Asset View, click the Files category button.
2. Double-click the desired file asset listed.

   The File dialog box for the selected file asset is displayed **(Figure 16.5)**. Using this dialog box, you can change the name Fusion uses for the asset by editing the Name field. You can also associate a different source file with the asset by typing a path and file name in the Location field, or by using the Browse button. *Mac users use the Select button.*
3. Make any desired changes using the File dialog box.
4. Click OK.

### ✔ Tips

- Fusion's default file asset name is the name of the file itself (less the file extension), but you can change the asset name without affecting its association with a particular file.
- If you change the file referenced by a file asset, that change is reflected on every page the asset is used.

## To view a page where a file asset is used:

1. In Asset View, double-click the desired file asset.

   The File dialog box for the selected file asset is displayed **(Figure 16.6)**.

   In the Pages section of the File dialog box, the pages are listed on which the selected file asset is used.
2. Select one of the pages displayed.
3. Click the Go To button.

   Fusion displays the selected page in Page View.

   You can return to Asset View by clicking the Assets button in the Control Bar.

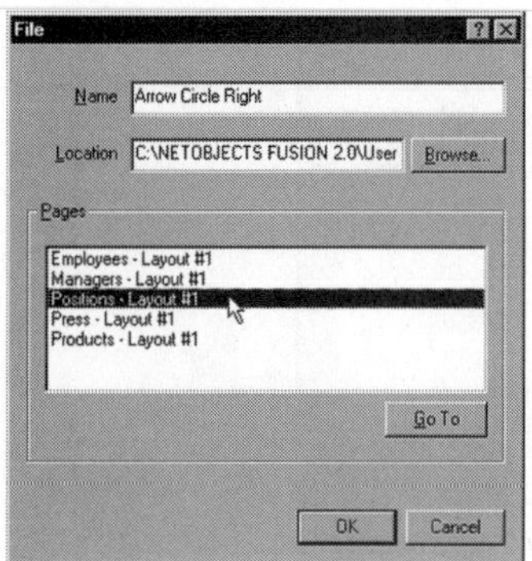


**Figure 16.6**
*Select a page name listed in the Pages section of the File dialog box, and click Go To to display that page.*

## To delete a file asset:

1. Select the file asset you wish to delete from those listed in Asset View.
2. Choose Delete File Asset from the Edit menu **(Figure 16.7)**.

   Fusion will warn you that your action cannot be undone **(Figure 16.8)**.
3. Click Yes in the warning dialog box to continue.

   If the file asset you are deleting is currently in use on one or more pages in your site, Fusion will warn you that the file is in use **(Figure 16.9)**.
4. Click Yes in the warning dialog box (if displayed).

   The asset is deleted from your site.

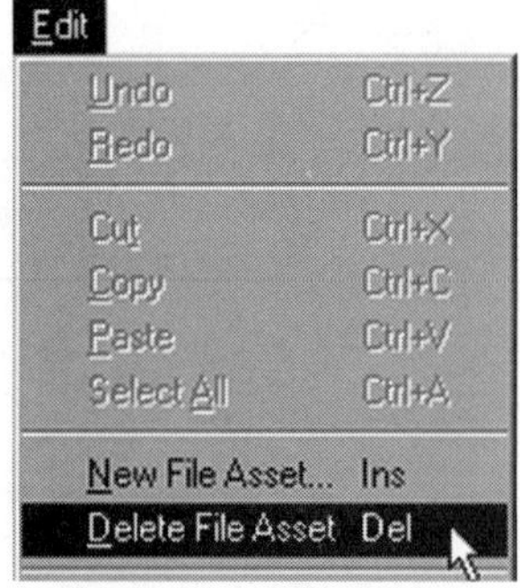


**Figure 16.7**
*Select Delete File Asset from the Edit menu.*

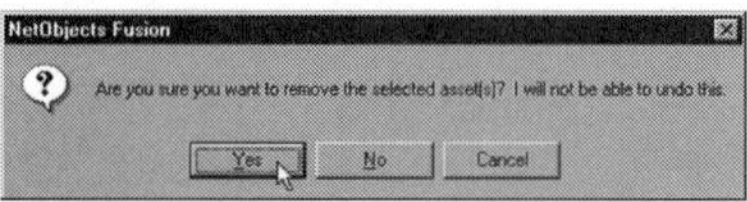


**Figure 16.8**
*Fusion warns you that deleting a file asset cannot be undone.*

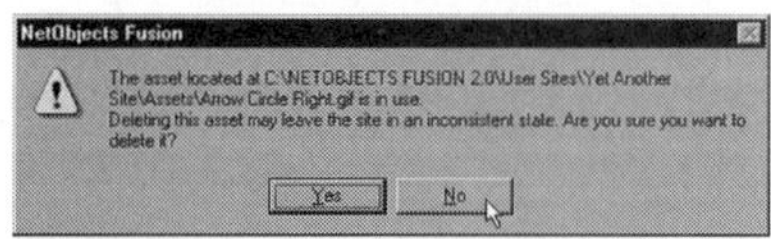


**Figure 16.9**
*Fusion warns you if you attempt to delete a file asset that is in use.*

Working with File Assets

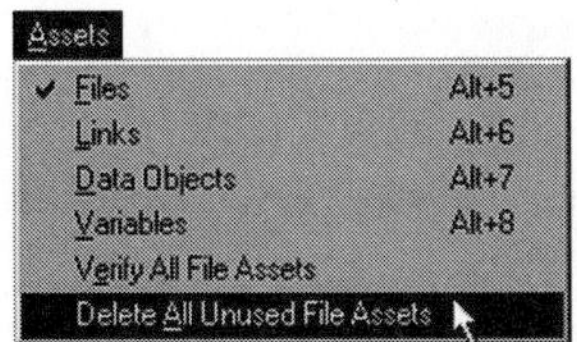


**Figure 16.10**
*Choose Delete All Unused File Assets from the Assets menu to delete all unused assets as a group.*

**Figure 16.11**
*Click the New File button to add a new file asset.*

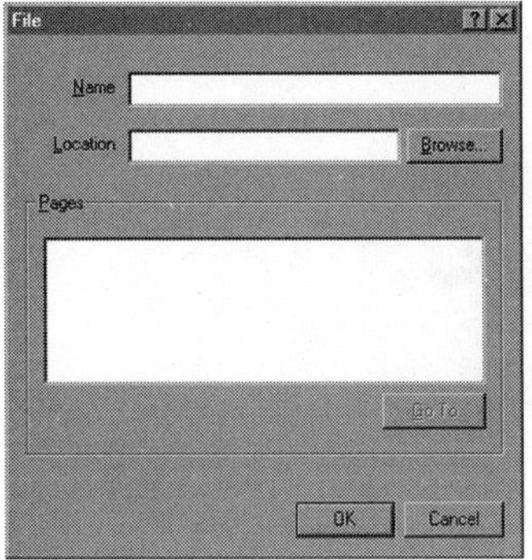


**Figure 16.12**
*Type a name for your new file asset in the Name field, then click the Browse button to choose a file.* Mac users choose the Select... button.

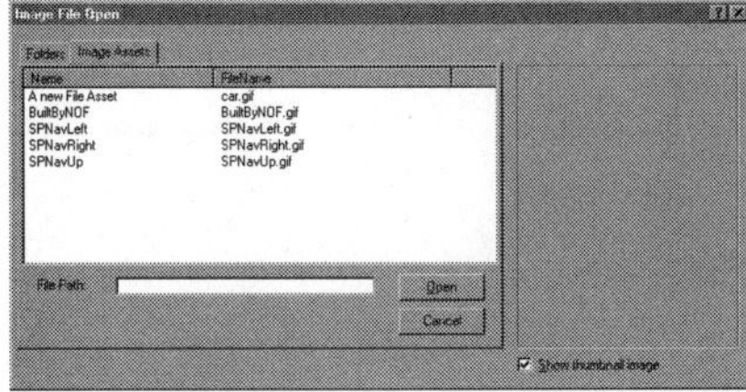

**Figure 16.13**
*To add a file asset to a page, select it from the Asset tab of the dialog box displayed.*

## ✔ Tips

- You can also delete a file asset by selecting it in Asset View and pressing the Delete key.
- The only way you can restore a deleted asset is by manually adding it to a layout.
- Choosing the Delete All Unused File Assets option from the Assets menu will allow you to clear all unused file assets as a group **(Figure 16.10)**.

## To add a file asset

1. Click the New File button the Control Bar **(Figure 16.11)**.

   **or**

   Select New File Asset from the Edit menu.

   In either case the File dialog box is displayed **(Figure 16.12)**.
2. Type a name for your new file asset in the Name field.
3. Click the Browse button. *Mac users click the Select... button.*

   The open dialog box is displayed.
4. Use the open dialog box to locate and open the file you wish to use for the new file asset.
5. Click OK in the File dialog box.

   The new file asset appears in the Files category in Asset View.

## ✔ Tip

- You can now use this new file asset on any page(s) in your site by selecting it from the Assets tab in the dialog box that appears when adding any type of file asset to a page **(Figure 16.13)**.

## To verify file assets:

1. From the Assets menu select the Verify All File Assets option **(Figure 16.14)**.

   The verification process checks to ensure that the path information for each of your file assets is correct.

   If the verification process reveals a missing file, then a dialog box is presented **(Figure 16.15)** with which you can update the file's location.

2. If you are asked to locate any missing file assets, update the location information as requested and click OK, or select Skip to ignore the missing asset file.

   After the file verification process is completed successfully, a dialog box appears notifying you of a successful completion of the process **(Figure 16.16)**.

3. Click OK.

   The verification status for each file asset is displayed in the Verify Status column in Assets View **(Figure 16.17)**.

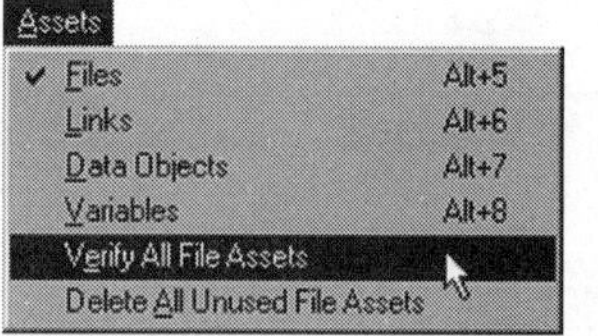


**Figure 16.14**
*Choose Verify All File Assets from the Assets menu.*

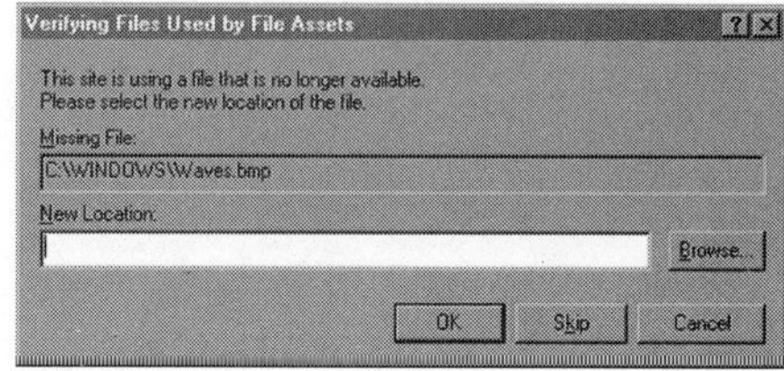


**Figure 16.15**
*If a file is not found successfully, Fusion presents a dialog box with which you can update the file location information.*

**Figure 16.16**
*Fusion confirms that is has successfully completed the verification process.*

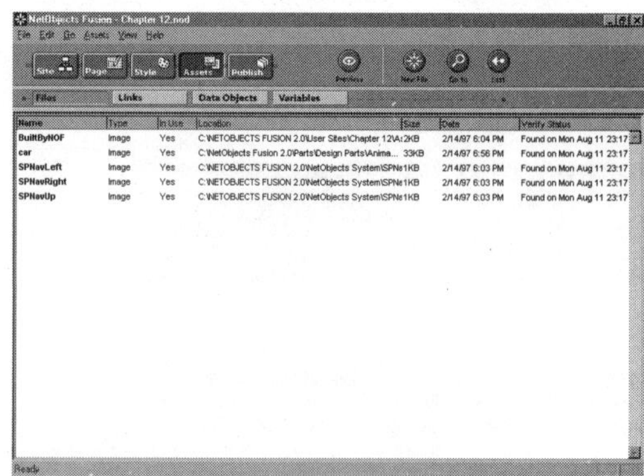

**Figure 16.17**
*File verification status is displayed in the Verify Status column.*

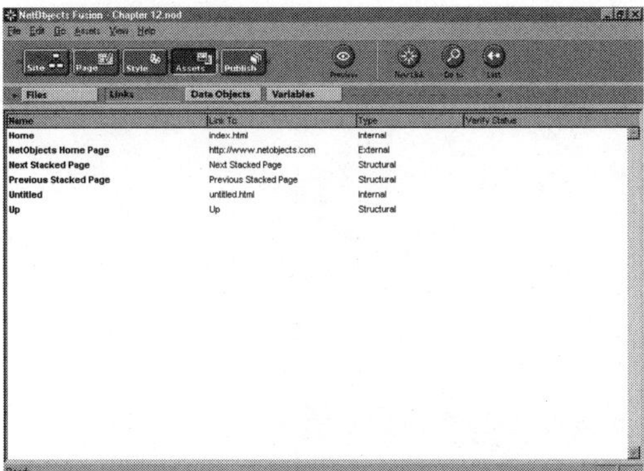


**Figure 16.18**
*Click the Links category button to display link assets in Asset View.*

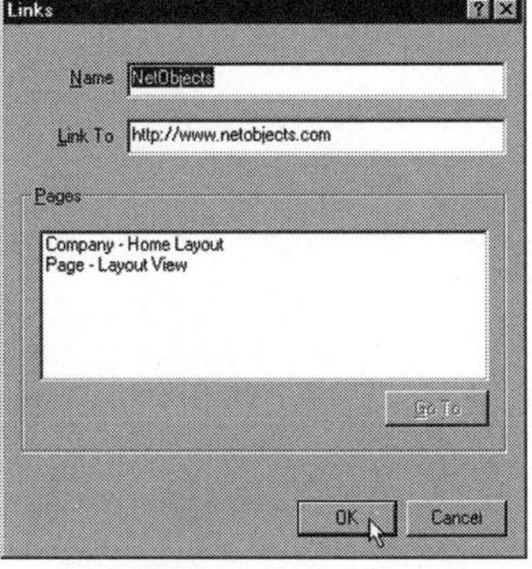


**Figure 16.19**
*You can edit external link names and URLs.*

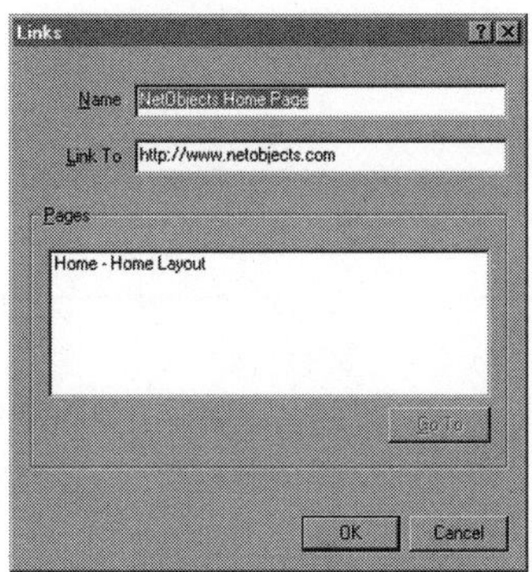


**Figure 16.20**
*Internal links cannot be modified in Asset View.*

# Working with Links

In Chapter 9 we introduced several different kinds of links. External Links provide access to other Web sites, pages within the site are linked with Internal Links, and Smart Links link pages within your site by their relative position rather than their name. Chapter 9 provides a detailed description of how links are created and managed in Page View.

While links can be added to your site and modified in Page View, you can also use Asset View to modify and add external links, to delete unused links, and to verify all link assets used throughout your site.

## To edit an external link asset:

1. In Asset View, click the Links category button **(Figure 16.18)**.
2. Double-click one of the links displayed in the list.

   A Links dialog box is displayed **(Figure 16.19)**. Using this dialog box, you can change the name or URL of the selected external link.

### ✔ Tips

- Smart Links are listed as Structural links under Type in Assets View.
- Internal links (including SmartLinks) cannot be edited in Asset View **(Figure 16.20)**.

### To view a page where a link asset is used:

1. In Asset View, double-click the desired link.

   The Link dialog box for the selected link asset is displayed.

   In the Pages section of the Link dialog box, pages are listed on which the selected link asset is used.
2. Select one of the pages displayed.
3. Click the Go To button.

   Fusion displays the selected page in Page View.

   You can return to Asset View by clicking the Assets button in the Control Bar.

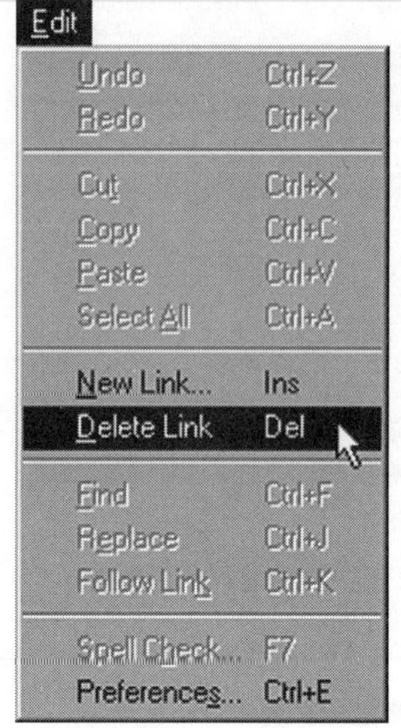


**Figure 16.21**
*Select Delete link from the Edit menu to delete an unused link.*

### To delete a Link

1. In Asset View, select an unused link.
2. Select the Delete Link option from the Edit menu **(Figure 16.21)**.

   If the selected link is in use, Fusion displays the dialog box shown in **Figure 16.22**.
3. Click Yes.

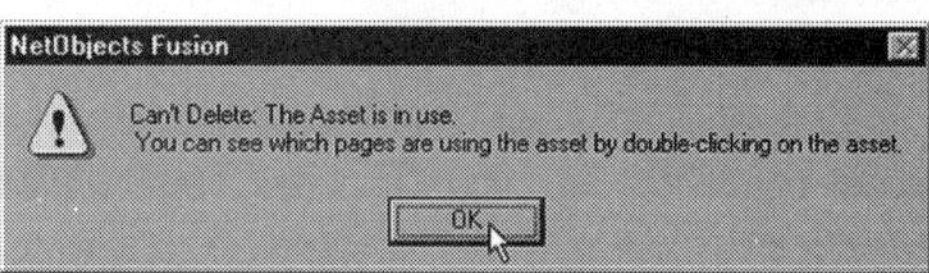


**Figure 16.22**
*You cannot delete links that are in use from Assets View.*

### ✔ Tips

- Double-click a link displayed in Assets View to determine if it is in use. If no pages are listed in the Pages area of the Links dialog box, then the link is not in use and can be deleted.
- Deleted Links cannot be recovered once they are removed. They must be recreated.

Working with Links

**Figure 16.23**
*Click the New Link button to add a new external link.*

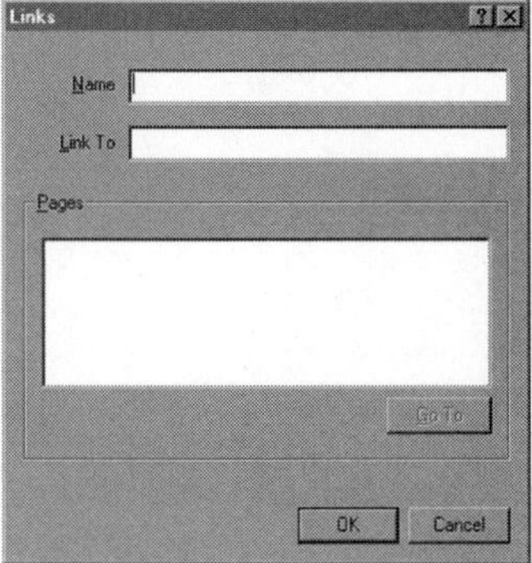


**Figure 16.24**
*Enter the name and URL for the new external link in the Link dialog box.*

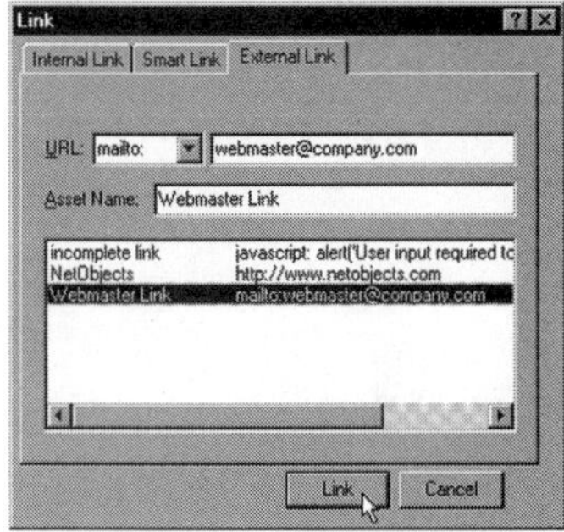


**Figure 16.25**
*To use a link created in Assets View on a page, select it from the External Link tab in Page View's Link dialog box.*

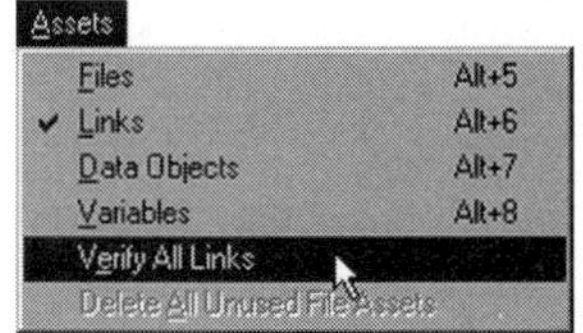


**Figure 16.26**
*Choose Verify All Links from the Assets menu.*

## To add an external link:

1. Select the New Link button from the Control Bar **(Figure 16.23)**.

   **or**

   Select the New Link option from the Edit menu.

   In either case an external Link dialog box is displayed **(Figure 16.24)**.
2. Type a name for your new external link in the Name field.
3. Type the URL for your new external link in the Link To field.

### ✔ Tip

- You can now use this new link on any page(s) in your site by selecting it from the External Link tab in the Link dialog box that appears when creating a link in Page View **(Figure 16.25)**.

## To verify link assets:

From the Assets menu select the Verify All Links option **(Figure 16.26)**.

The verification process checks to ensure that the destinations referenced by all links in your site are valid.

The verification status for each link asset is displayed in the Verify Status column in Assets View. If verification fails, the Verify Status column will contain an explanation.

### ✔ Tip

- You can specify a new destination for a Link by following the steps for editing an external link.

## Working with Data Objects

Data objects are used to publish data on your Web site from either internal or external data sources. The process for creating and editing data objects in Page View was discussed in Chapter 15. In Asset View you can also create new data objects, edit existing data objects, and delete those that are unused.

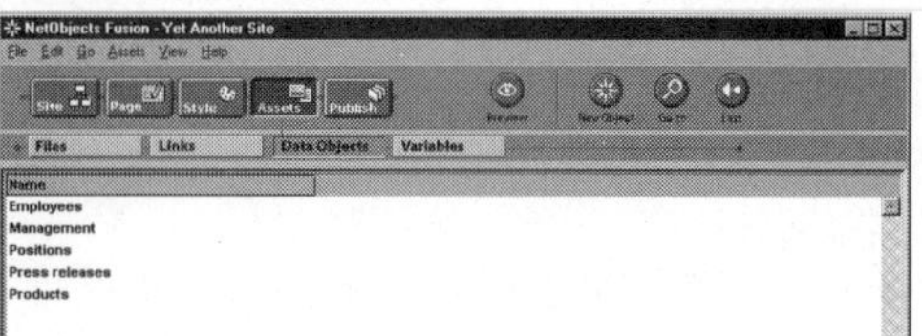

**Figure 16.27**
*Click the Data Objects category button to display data object assets.*

### To edit a data object:

1. In Asset View, click the Data Objects category button **(Figure 16.27)**.
2. Double-click the desired data object in the list displayed.

   The Data Object dialog box is displayed **(Figure 16.28)**. Using this dialog box, you can change the name of the data object and add comments and fields to the data object definition.
3. Make desired changes in the Data Object dialog box.
4. Click OK.

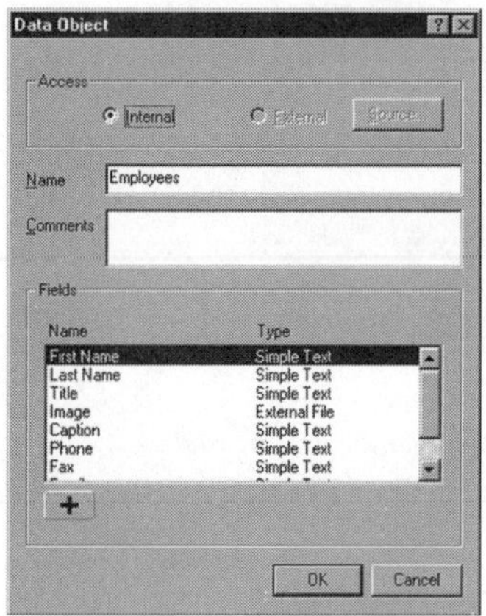


**Figure 16.28**
*Use the Data Object dialog box to edit a data object in Asset View.*

### To delete a data object:

1. Select a data object.
2. Select Delete Data Object from the Edit menu.

   If the selected link is in use, the Delete Data Object menu option is disabled **(Figure 16.29)**. Only unused data objects can be deleted.

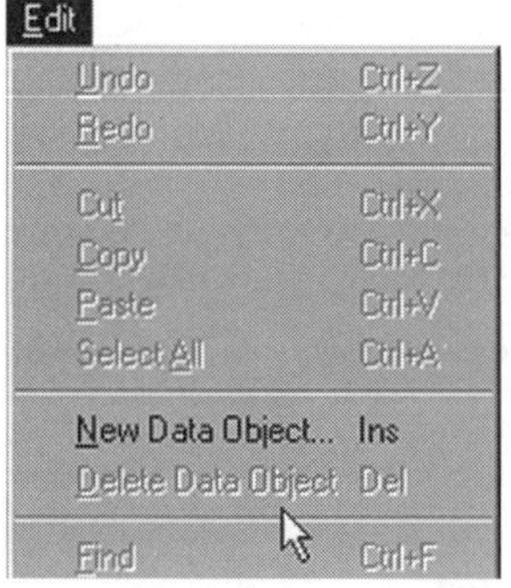


**Figure 16.29**
*Only unused data objects can be deleted.*

### ✓ Tip

- Deleted data objects cannot be recovered once they are removed. They must be recreated.

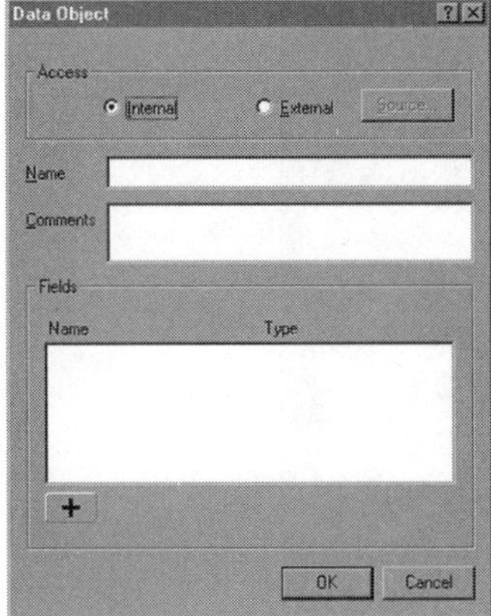


**Figure 16.30**
*Click the New Object button in the Control Bar and a new Data Object dialog box appears.*

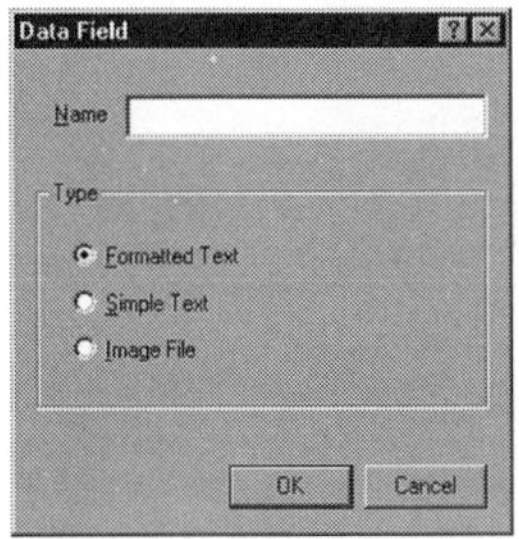


**Figure 16.31**
*Type a data field name, select a data type, and click OK.*

## To add an internal data object:

1. Select the New Object button from the Control Bar.

   **or**

   Select the New Data Object option from the Edit menu.

   In either case the Data Object dialog box will appear **(Figure 16.30)**.

   In either case the Data Object dialog box will appear with the Internal Access option selected as the default. *Mac users can only create internal data objects.*
2. Type a name for your new data object in the Name field.
3. Type any comments desired in the Comments field.
4. Click on the large plus symbol button to add a field.

   The Data Field dialog box is displayed **(Figure 16.31)**.
5. Type a field name in the Name field.
6. Select a data type.
7. Click OK.
8. Repeat steps 4–8 until all of the fields you want have been created, then click OK in the Data Object dialog box.

### ✔ Tips

- Chapter 15 describes the process of creating new data objects in detail.
- To add an external data objects in Windows, follow step 1 above, then refer to Chapter 15 for detailed instructions.

## Verifying Data Objects

Asset View doesn't have a facility for verifying data objects like the one used for verifying file assets and links. However, Fusion does check to ensure that the location information provided for each of your data objects can be verified.

When opening your site in Fusion, and when you choose to either Preview or Publish your site, Fusion connects to the data source(s) defined for the site's data objects. If the process establishes that the data source files are not where they are expected to be, then an error message is displayed.

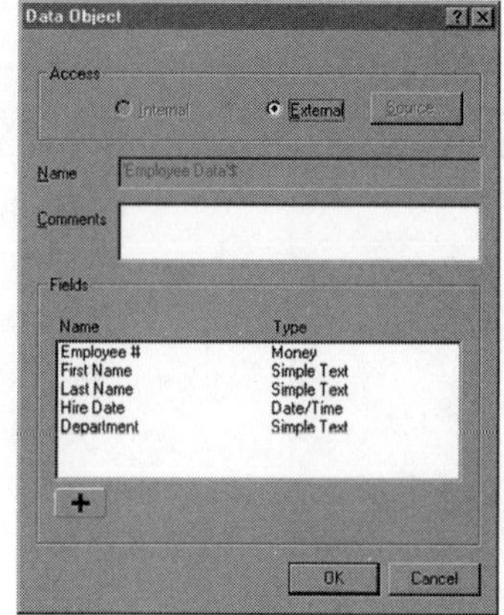


**Figure 16.32**
*To redefine the data source for a data object, the data object must be recreated.*

### ✔ Tips

- When the physical location of a data source for an existing data object changes, the data object must be recreated using the new location data. **Figure 16.32** displays the Data Object dialog box for an existing data object. Notice that you cannot redefine the data source.
- Make sure when you create your Data Object using external data sources that they are fairly static. If they're comprised of files that are moved around often, you will create a considerable amount of work for yourself.

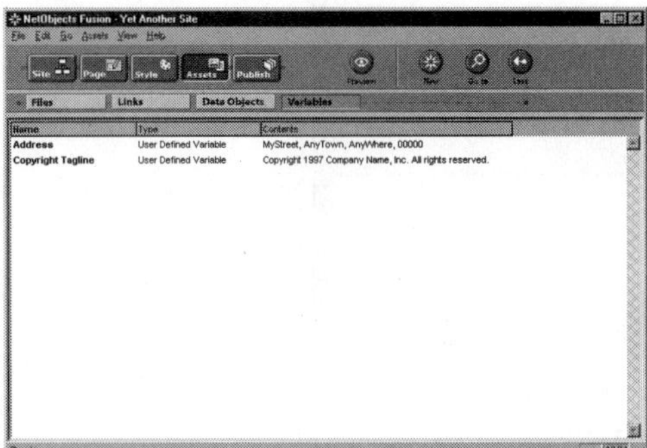

**Figure 16.33**
*Click the Variables category button to display variables defined for your site.*

**Figure 16.34**
*Edit the name and value of user-defined variables using the Edit Variable dialog box.*

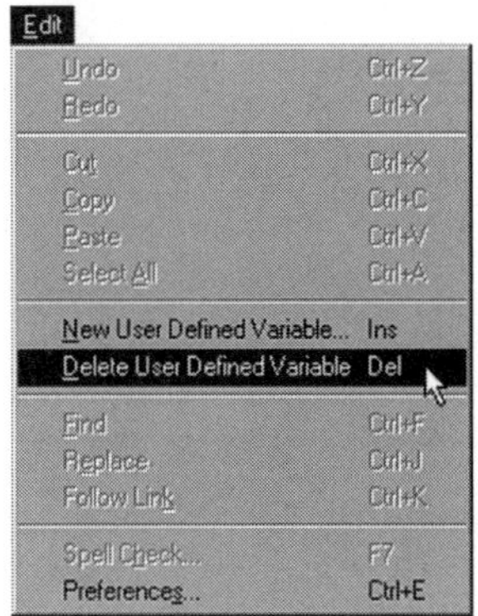


**Figure 16.35**
*Select Delete User Defined Variable from the Edit menu.*

# Working with Variables

Text variables were introduced in Chapter 8. Variables are used to globally modify selected text within your site. Only user-defined variables can be edited, added, or deleted from within Asset View. However, Asset View provides the name, type, and value of all types of variables defined in your site.

## To edit a user-defined variable:

1. In Asset View, click the Variables category button **(Figure 16.33)**.
2. Double-click the desired variable in the displayed list.

   The Edit Variable dialog box is displayed **(Figure 16.34)**. Using this dialog box, you can change the selected variable's name and value.
3. Make desired changes in the Edit Variable dialog box.
4. Click OK.

## To delete a user-defined variable:

1. Select a variable listed in Asset View.
2. Select Delete User Defined Variable from the Edit menu **(Figure 16.35)**.

### ✓ Tip

- Deleted variables cannot be recovered once they are removed. They must be recreated.

### To add a variable

1. With the Variables category displayed in Asset View, click the New button in the Control Bar.

   **or**

   Select New User Defined Variable from the Edit menu.

2. In either case the New Variable dialog box is displayed **(Figure 16.36)**.
3. Type a name in the Variable name field.
4. Type the new variable's value in the Value field.
5. Click OK.

   The new variable will now be listed as an available user-defined variable in the Insert Variable dialog box in Page View. See Chapter 8 for detailed information on inserting variables in Page View.

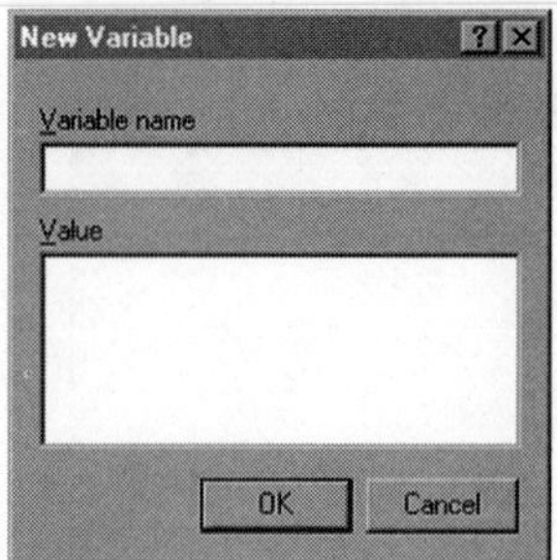


**Figure 16.36**
*Use the New Variable dialog box to define a new variable.*

# Publish a Web Site

17

## Understanding Web Site Publishing

Publishing a Web site refers to the process of generating the HTML files that comprise your Web pages, and together with all of the assets used in your pages, placing those files in specific locations on Internet-connected servers. With NetObjects Fusion, publishing your Web site to the Internet, or to your local Intranet, is a very simple process. Even seasoned pros will appreciate the embedded FTP application within Fusion that allows single button publishing of an entire site. Fusion does a good job of taking the stress out of the Web site publishing equation. You will find that Fusion's publishing tools need very little to work well in almost any environment, from a large organization to a home-based business.

Once Fusion is properly configured for publishing your site, you won't have to worry about your publishing settings again unless something changes. And since Web server configurations are usually fairly static, you shouldn't be required to make changes often. If you are working with an ISP (Internet Service Provider) to gain access to the Internet, you will most likely find them eager and willing to help you successfully launch your new site.

In any case, don't let unfamiliar techno-garble that inevitably creeps into any discussion of Web site publishing hold you up. Prepare for success!

## Getting to Publish View

If you are not in Publish View, select the Publish button **(Figure 17.1)**.

Publish View has three primary tools: Settings, Stage, and Publish **(Figure 17.2)**. **Settings** is used to prepare for staging or publishing your site. **Stage** and **Publish** generate and move your site's files to either a local or remote server.

**Figure 17.1**
*Control Bar with Publish View navigation button selected.*

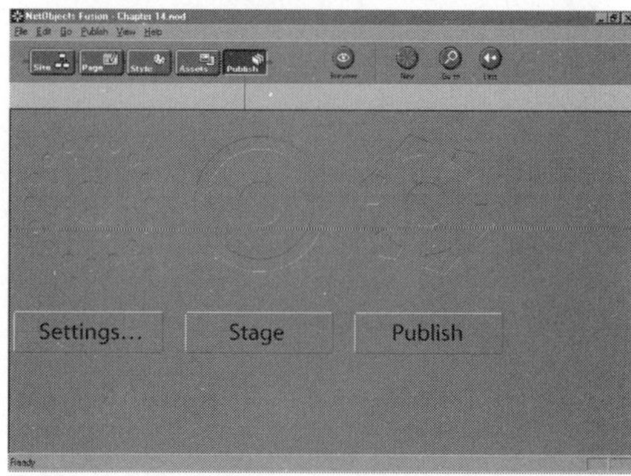


**Figure 17.2**
*Web site in Publish View.*

## Configuring a Site For Staging or Publishing

You use the Settings tool to configure your site for staging or publishing It is also used for creating modified sites (covered later).

You'll only have to do the configuration activity once. After configuring your site for publishing or staging, you just change your settings if the destination data for your Web site files changes. If you have configured your site for staging, you must still configure it for publishing before publishing the site.

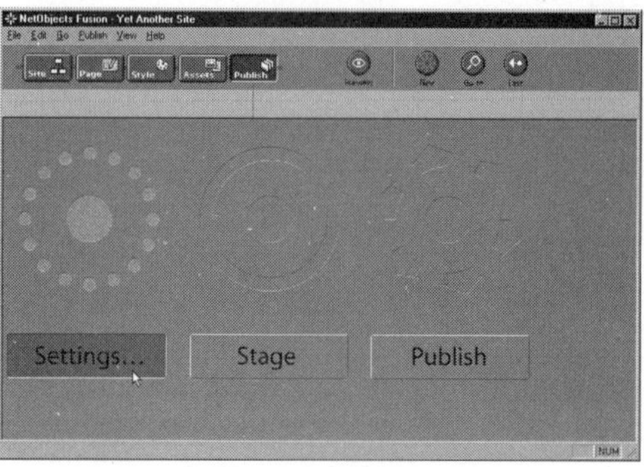


**Figure 17.3**
*Click the Settings button to begin configuring site for publishing.*

### To begin configuring a site for staging or publishing:

1. Click the Settings button **(Figure 17.3)**, or choose Settings from the Publish menu.

   The Configure Publish dialog box appears **(Figure 17.4)**.

2. If you are configuring your site for publishing, click the Publish tab.

   Using the Configure Publish dialog box, you can define where you want to stage or publish your site, set parameters for your home page, and choose what files to re-stage or re-publish following modifications.

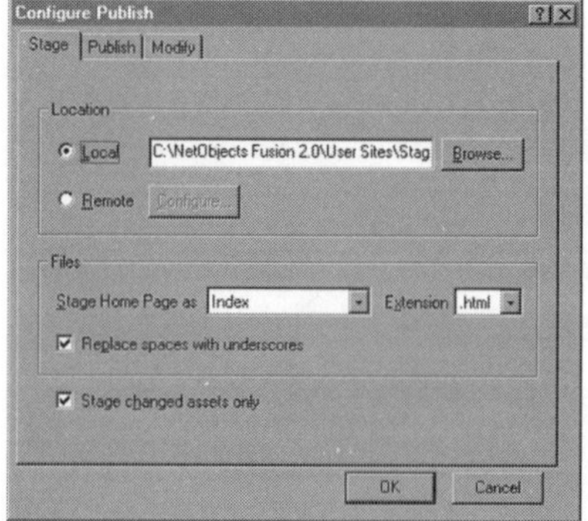


**Figure 17.4**
*Configure Publish dialog box*

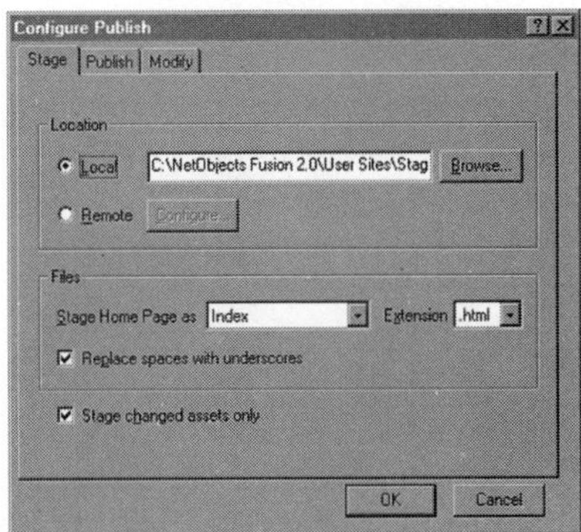


**Figure 17.5**
*Select Local in the Configure Publish dialog box.*

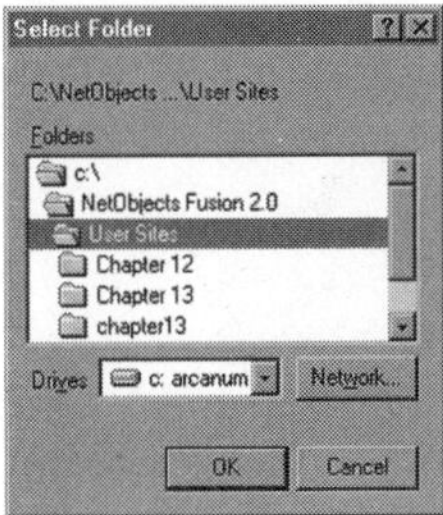


**Figure 17.6**
*Choose a destination location using the Select Folder dialog box.*

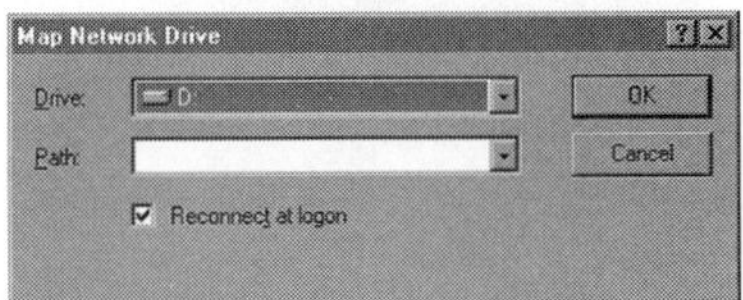


**Figure 17.7**
*Map Network Drive dialog box.*

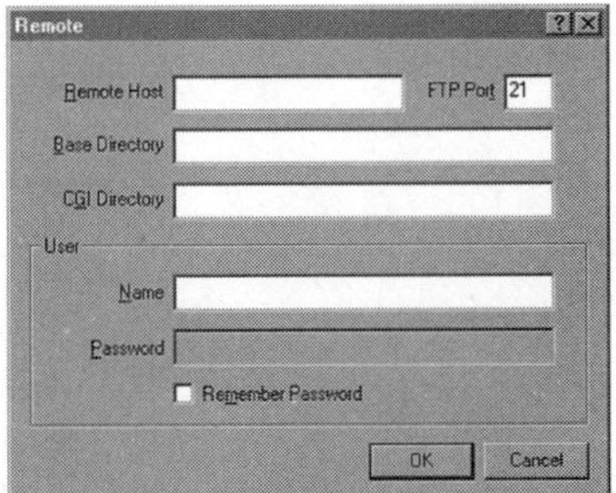


**Figure 17.8**
*Use the Remote dialog box to specify a remote location.*

### To configure your site for local staging or publishing:

1. Choose Local option in the Location area of the Configure Publish dialog box **(Figure 17.5)**.
2. Click the Browse button.. *Mac users click the Select... button.*

   The Select Folder dialog box is displayed **(Figure 17.6,)**.
3. Use the Select Folder dialog box to select the location where you want to stage or publish your site. The Network button can be used to add a network drive to the Drives drop-down list **(Figure 17.7)**.
4. Click OK in the Select Folder dialog box when location is selected.

### To configure your site for remote staging or publishing:

1. Choose Remote in the Location area of the Configure Publish dialog box.
2. Click the Configure button.

   The Remote dialog box is displayed **(Figure 17.8)**. To complete the fields in this dialog box, gather the following information from your local Webmaster or Internet Service Provider (ISP). A Webmaster is the person who has responsibility for your local Inter- or Intranet infrastructure.

   **Remote Host**—The name of the Sever that will host your Web site.

   **FTP Port**—File Transfer Protocol (FTP) used to transfer files from one computer system to another, and is a built-in function of Fusion. The default value, 21, is a standard FTP port setting for many systems. Check with your ISP or Webmaster to see if this value will work for you.

**Base Directory**—This is the full path name of the directory where your HTML files will reside. You must use the complete pathname.

**CGI Directory**—The full pathname of the directory where your Common Gateway Interface (CGI) scripts reside. CGI scripts are required, for example, if you define any forms in your site (see Chapter 12). You must use the complete pathname.

**User Name**—Login name by which the host system recognizes you.

**Password**—Your password associated with the user name entered.

3. Once you have the information above, enter it into the appropriate fields in the Remote dialog box, as in the example in **Figure 17.9**.
4. Click OK in the Remote dialog box.

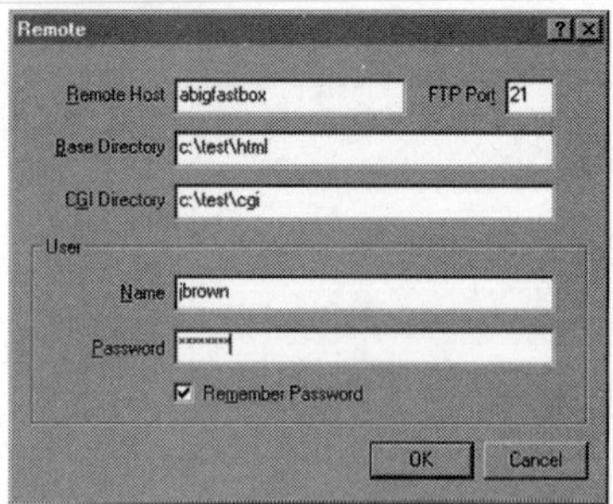


**Figure 17.9**
*Remote dialog box configured to Stage a site.*

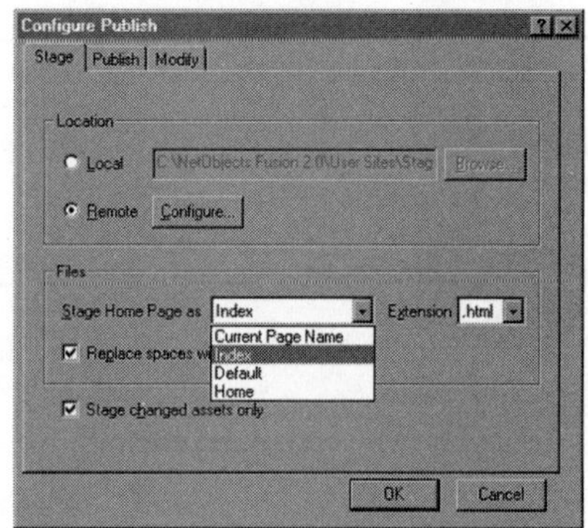


**Figure 17.10**
*"Stage Home Page as" drop down list.*

✔ **Tip**

■ You must select the Remember Password option to enter a password into the Password field. To be prompted for a password each time you stage your Web site, leave the password blank.

### To set other configuration options:

1. Choose an option from the **Stage Home Page as** drop-down list **(Figure 17.10)**.

These tell Fusion the name of your home page HTML document. Check with your ISP or Webmaster before making your selection. Some systems require home pages named Index. Others require that a home page is named Home.

2. Choose an option from the **Extension** drop-down list.

   Your selection will determine whether all of your HTML files contain the file extension .htm or .html. As a rule, Macintosh and Unix servers will use a file extension .html, and Windows servers use the .htm option. Again, get this information from your ISP or local Webmaster.

3. If desired,, click to deselect the **Replace spaces with underscores** option.

   This option refers to the file names throughout your Web site. Don't deselect this option unless you have been advised to do so. Netscape Navigator, for instance, requires these underscores to interpret your file names.

4. If desired, click to select the **Stage (or Publish) changed assets only** option.

   This means Staging or publishing just those files that have been modified since the last time the site was staged or published speeds up the process.

## Staging a Web Site

Images that don't load correctly, links that are broken, and pages that don't display as expected will all conspire to irritate visitors to your site, and probably send them packing. By Staging your work for testing before publishing, you can ensure that your site is bug free when you publish it.

Staging differs from previewing (see Chapter 6) in that when you stage your site, the files which comprise your site are organized in exactly the same way they will be when your site is published. Staging differs from publishing in that sites are generally staged to a local disk rather than to the Web server where they will later be published.

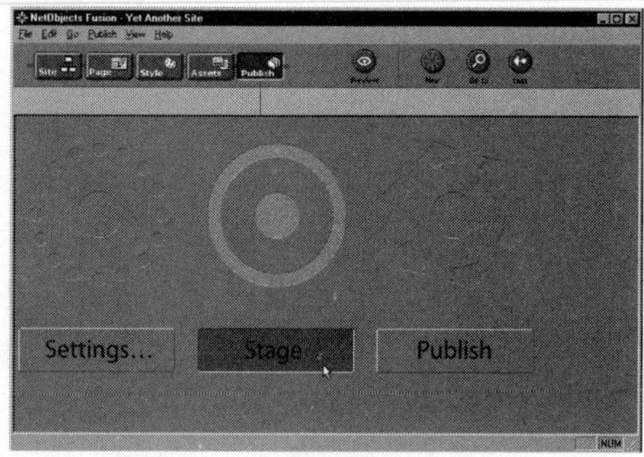


**Figure 17.11**
*Click the Stage button in Stage View.*

#### To stage a Web site:

1. After you have configured your site for staging (see previous section), click the Stage button in Stage View **(Figure 17.11)**.

   Fusion will generate HTML documents for each page in your site **(Figure 17.12)**, and then transfer all of your site's assets to the location specified. When staging is complete, **Figure 17.13** appears.
2. Click OK **(Figure 17.13)**.
3. Begin testing your staged site by opening the home page in your Web browser.

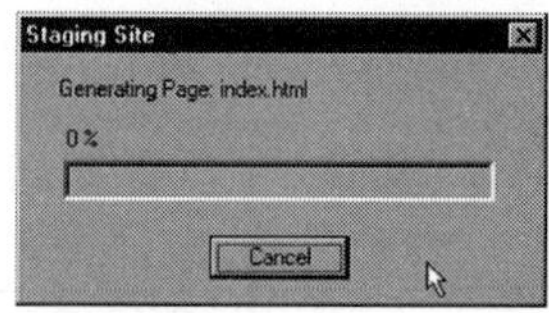


**Figure 17.12**
*Fusion will begin the process of staging your site.*

**Figure 17.13**
*When staging is complete, Fusion lets you know*

✔ **Tip**

- Before publishing, test, make changes in Fusion, restage, and test some more until you are completely satisfied with the operation of your site.

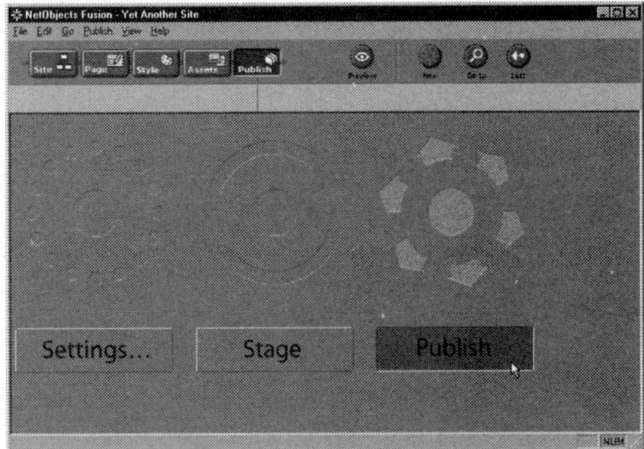


**Figure 17.14**
*Click the Publish button in Publish View.*

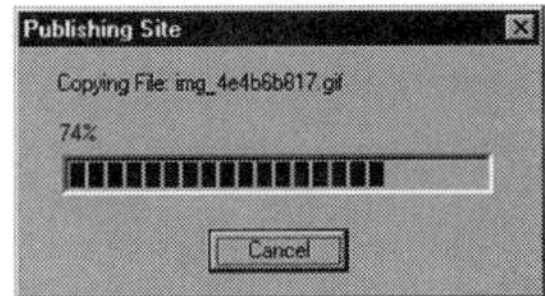


**Figure 17.15**
*Fusion will begin the process of publishing your site.*

**Figure 17.16**
*When publishing is complete, Fusion lets you know.*

# To Publish a Web Site

Publishing a Web site entails placing all of the files for that site on either a local or remote server to be accessed from the Internet, or as a part of an Intranet.

Once you have staged and thoroughly tested your Web site, you are ready to take the plunge.

## To publish a Web site:

1. After you have configured your site for publishing (see earlier section), click the Publish button in Stage View **(Figure 17.14)**.

   Fusion will generate HTML documents for each page in your site, and then transfer all of your site's assets to the location specified **(Figure 17.15)**. Fusion notifies you when publishing is complete **Figure 17.16** appears.
2. Click OK **(Figure 17.16)**.
3. You (and the rest of the Internet community) can now access your Web site using a Web browser like Netscape Navigator.

✔ **Tip**

■ You will need to check with your ISP or Webmaster to determine your site's URL.

## Accommodating Visitors

Fusion provides a set of configuration options that allows you to create multiple versions of your published Web site to accommodate visitors to your site who may not wish to wait for large graphics to download.

### To modify the graphics intensity of your site:

1. In Publish View, click the settings button.
2. Click the Modify tab **(Figure 17.17)**.
3. Make selections from the Modifiers area of the Modify tab.

   **Text Only** suppresses all of your site's image files when it is published.

   **Grayscale** creates a 256-shades of gray copy of your site when published.

   **Low Bandwidth (4-color GIF's and half-resolution JPEG's)** degrades definition of the images in your site so they are one half their original size.
4. Click OK.

   When you publish your site, Fusion creates a folder with a unique name for each version, including the site you originally designed.

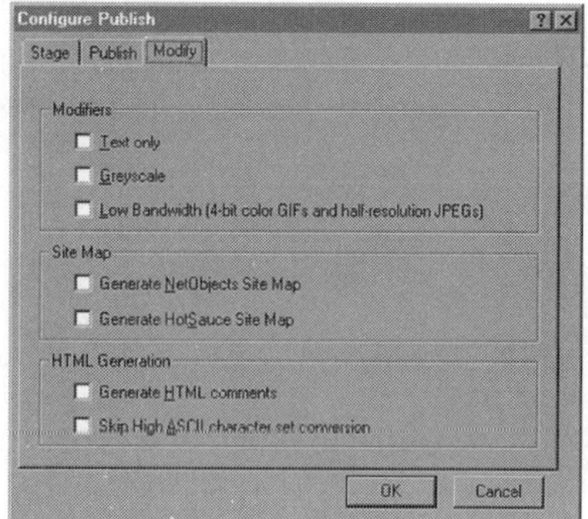


**Figure 17.17**
*Configure Publish dialog box showing Modify tab.*

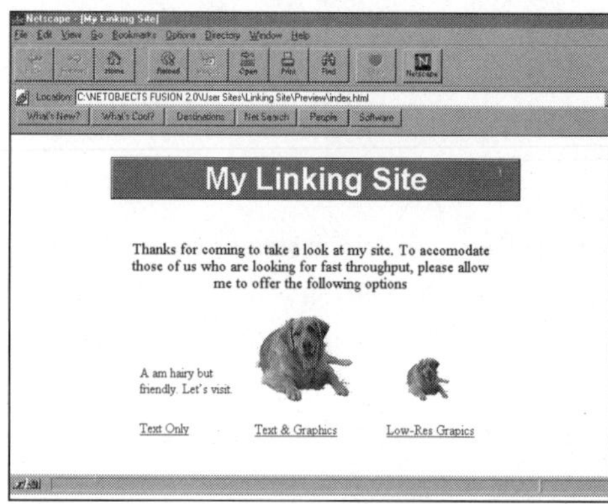


**Figure 17.18**
*Sample Web page showing multiple version links.*

✔ **Tip**

- If you publish multiple versions of your site, you might want to create and publish a single home page containing manual links to the home pages of each version **(Figure 17.18)**.

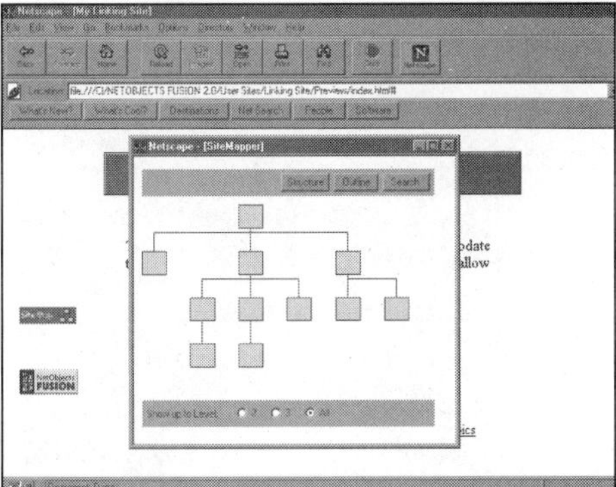

**Figure 17.19**
*NetObjects site map.*

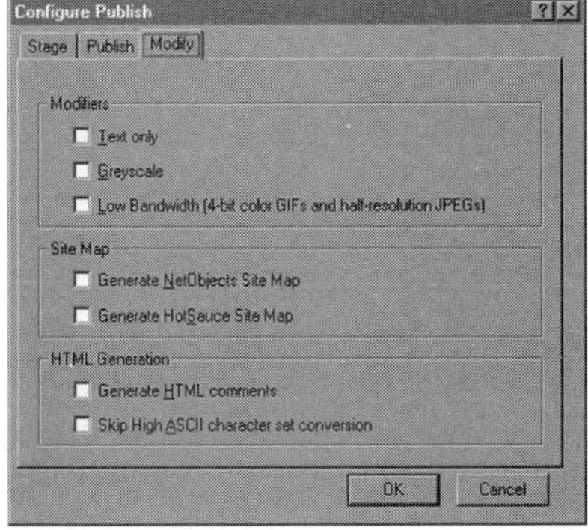


**Figure 17.20**
*Configure Publish dialog box showing Modify tab.*

# Including a Site Map

NetObjects Fusion has embedded Java-based applications, known as components, that provide useful functionality to your Web site. The SiteMapper component adds a visual map for visitors to your site. (See Chapter 11.)

When activated by a visitor to your site, SiteMapper opens another browser window and allows users to get a detailed look at your entire site structure as either a graphic, or as an outline. **Figure 17.19** shows an example of a site map generated by SiteMapper.

### To generate a site map:

1. In Publish View, click the settings button.
2. Click the Modify tab **(Figure 17.20)**.
3. Make selections from the Site Map area of the Modify tab.

   **Generate a NetObjects Site Map** places a button on your site's home page for users using Fusion's format.

   **Generate HotSauce Site Map** places a button on your site's home page for users using Apple's HotSauce format.
4. Click OK.

### ✔ Tip

- See Chapter 11 for details on using site maps in your site.

## Setting HTML Generation Options

Fusion offers two options for modifying the way in which HTML is generated for the pages in your site. With these options, you can have Fusion add comments to Web page files. You can also select the way Fusion will handle special ASCII characters.

### To set HTML generation options:

1. In Publish View, click the settings button.
2. Click the Modify tab **(Figure 17.20)**.
3. Make selections from the HTML Generation area of the Modify tab.

   **Generate HTML comments** causes Fusion to add comments at the beginning and end of each page **(Figure 17.21)**.

   **Skip High ASCII character set conversion** should not be selected unless you are an experienced developer and are using special characters in your site.
4. Click OK.

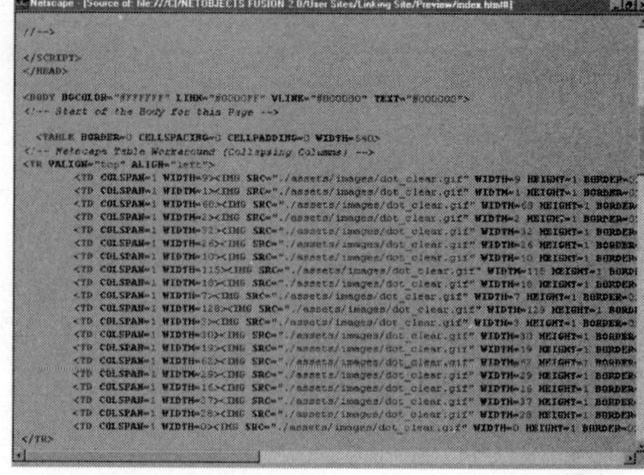

**Figure 17.21**
*HTML page generated with comment.*

# Index

## Q



## R



## S

## V



## W



## Z